I0006389

IIS
Security

IIS
Security

Marty Jost
and Michael Cobb

McGraw-Hill/Osborne
New York Chicago San Francisco
Lisbon London Madrid Mexico City Milan
New Delhi San Juan Seoul Singapore Sydney Toronto

McGraw-Hill/Osborne
2600 Tenth Street
Berkeley, California 94710
U.S.A.

To arrange bulk purchase discounts for sales promotions, premiums, or fund-raisers, please contact **McGraw-Hill**/Osborne at the above address. For information on translations or book distributors outside the U.S.A., please see the International Contact Information page immediately following the index of this book.

IIS Security

1234567890 CUS CUS 0198765432

ISBN 0-07-222439-8

Publisher
  Brandon A. Nordin
Vice President & Associate Publisher
  Scott Rogers
Senior Acquisitions Editor
  Jane Brownlow
Project Editor
  Jenn Tust
Acquisitions Coordinator
  Emma Acker
Technical Editor
  Matthew Berry
Copy Editor
  Lisa Theobald

Proofreaders
  Linda Medoff, Paul Medoff,
  Marian Selig
Indexer
  Marjorie Jost
Computer Designers
  Tara A. Davis, Tabitha M. Cagan
Illustrators
  Michael Mueller, Lyssa Wald
Series Design
  Lyssa Wald, Peter F. Hancik
Cover Series Design
  Jeff Weeks

This book was composed with Corel VENTURA™ Publisher.

ABOUT THE AUTHORS

Marty Jost is an experienced security professional and consultant who specializes in Windows NT/2000, IIS, firewalls, PKI, and authentication. He frequently speaks at industry security conferences and has published several books and articles on computer networking and security.

Michael Cobb, MCDBA, CISSP, is a recognized expert in information security with a strong background in financial systems, specializing in network, database, and Internet security. As a contributing editor for *E-Business* and *Internet Security Advisor Magazines*, Mike regularly reports on the latest security technologies and threats.

AT A GLANCE

CONTENTS

ACKNOWLEDGMENTS

I would like to express my thanks to my collaborator, Mike Cobb, for his hard work and contributions, to my good friend Stephen Cobb, who provided a great deal of material on Web privacy for Chapter 12, to Matt Berry for his flexibility and attention to detail, to Marjorie Jost for providing the finishing touches, and to the fine folks at Osborne for keeping the project on track.

Marty Jost

To my wife and best friend, Jane, for her support and understanding, and my brother Stephen for all his help and enthusiasm.

Michael Cobb

INTRODUCTION

The news media are constantly highlighting new occurrences of viruses, intrusions, and thefts perpetrated against some hapless institution or company who didn't have appropriate security at their Web site. It's scary sounding stuff, and those are only the ones you hear about. Who knows how many sites lose valuable digital assets or intellectual property because of flawed authentication or directory security, possibly even from acts by employees on their intranet, without their knowledge.

So what do you do about it? Stay off the Internet? Take down your Web site? Of course not. How long could you stay competitive in business that way? No, the solution is to understand the threats and vulnerabilities and then take appropriate measures to mitigate the risks.

IIS Security is a guide that will help you to understand the requirements, methods, practices, and procedures to protect your Microsoft IIS Web site from being the next unfortunate victim of a security breach. Along the way, step-by-step procedures will explain how to use Microsoft provided security features. However, we believe in taking a more comprehensive approach to security, so Web security measures will be discussed in a broader context to help you plan and implement security that will protect all of the systems and applications that interact with their Microsoft IIS Web environment.

Protecting a Web environment requires more than the configuration of a few "out of the box" features on your Web server. It requires planning, implementing, testing, maintaining, and monitoring a set of systems and safeguards that work together and complement each other. Our intention with this book is to give you the background and insight that will help you to conceive and implement a practical and viable security framework and a proven approach for guarding your site. Therefore, among other things, we will spend time explaining the dangers to sites, the best practices of security professionals to protect against those dangers, the many tools that security professionals use, the configuration of those tools, and the ongoing processes that help an organization remain vigilant over time.

We have divided this book into three sections that address all of the above issues, plus we've included appendixes and a list of references that may help you continue your research about security after you finish this guide.

PART I: EXPOSURE, RISK, AND PREVENTION

Part I provides the background that will help you understand some of the common vulnerabilities of Web sites, explains how hackers work, and dissects attacks to show how an intrusion on the site may happen. This information will provide a foundation for a related discussion of strategies for defense.

As Part I progresses, the discussion will move to the setup and hardening of your server. We will make recommendations for hardware and software configurations. You will be shown how to remove known vulnerabilities and advised on do's and don'ts for Internet versus intranet deployments.

Chapter 1, "Web Security Threats," will discuss and categorize various threats your Web site faces from both external and internal sources. Various types of security incidents common to the Internet will be defined and explained. You will get a peek into the world of the hacker and gain a perspective on the way they work. The discussion will list the methods, tools, and resources that hackers use.

Chapter 2, "Defacing, Damage, and Denial," examines some of the most common Web site vulnerabilities that are exploited by hackers. The discussion will take a look at malicious code attacks such as viruses, worms, and Trojan horses. Examples and case studies will dig into some well-known attack methods, such as buffer overflows and distributed Denial of Service attacks. Where relevant, it will explain why some of the attack methods are able to defeat some protection mechanisms, and it will also provide some of the tools and procedures that can help prevent future incidents from succeeding.

Chapter 3, "Preparing and Hardening Your Web Server," explains how to eliminate common administrative oversights, vulnerable default settings, configuration errors that open the door for unauthorized entry, information theft, data modification, and introduction of malicious code or programs. Step-by-step procedures will be given to show you how to eliminate the holes by initially disabling all but the minimally required services, then adding services only as required by applications. In the process, the purpose of each service will be discussed to help the Web administrator fully understand the consequences of the configuration. Chapter 3 will also explain how to use Microsoft utilities and checklists to set a secure baseline and provide best practice recommendations to improve on that foundation.

Chapter 4, "Accounts, Authorization, and Security Policy," will discuss the issues of physical access restrictions, multi-level administration, directory security, and rights and permissions for role players on the site. You will be walked through the configuration of anonymous user accounts and authentication mechanisms. Much attention is given to account management, authorization, and access control in both Windows 2000 and IIS.

Chapter 5, "Security Auditing and Logging," will discuss the configuration of logging and auditing features for monitoring your Web site to detect signs of attacks or intrusions. You will learn how to set up and configure secure log files and be advised on maintenance procedures. Step-by-step procedures are included for audit settings so that you can create a legally enforceable audit trail of user activity on your site.

PART II: ADMINISTRATION

Part II discusses the implementation of the plans, policies, and procedures not covered in Part I. This section of the book covers additional details of configuring a secure network and Web environment with Microsoft IIS and gives advice on numerous security issues.

Chapter 6, "Deployment Issues," covers final preparations that should be implemented before putting your site into production. The chapter will discuss final check, backup, and recovery measures required to confidently finalize your Web server configuration. The discussion will include domain security, traffic filtering, and masking of Internet addresses. It will also discuss the appropriate use of perimeter defense and DMZs to augment the security measures you have learned about in Chapters 1–5. Finally, it will discuss remote management if you host your site at an ISP or hosting service.

Chapter 7, "The Security Management Lifecycle," covers the post-deployment management lifecycle of your site and discusses the methods and tools used to monitor Web site conditions, as well as how to react to possible attacks. It will discuss the parameters of normal Web site usage and behavior and make recommendations for using system alerts and other features and tools to help you stay on top of things. It includes recommendations and best practices to respond to security incidents. It also discusses site auditing to trace and identify the precise cause and damage your site may experience.

Chapter 8, "Using Encryption," will discuss the encryption features of Windows 2000 and IIS that can be used to protect your site and its content. The basics of encryption systems, public-key cryptography, digital certificates, and public-key infrastructure will be explained. You will learn how to acquire and install Microsoft and third-party digital certificates. Finally, you will be shown how to configure SSL and/or TLS encrypted sessions on your IIS server.

Chapter 9, "Third-Party Security Enhancements," focuses on mostly non-Microsoft hardware and software products that can enhance the physical security, software security, and logging and auditing capabilities of IIS including firewalls, VPNS, log analyzers, encryption accelerators, and more.

PART III: ADVANCED TOPICS

After you have successfully installed and configured the basic IIS Web Services there is a wealth of other services, media, and features you may add to your Web site that also must be deployed securely. This section covers those advanced services and capabilities and the measures you can take to protect them.

Chapter 10, "Securing FTP, NNTP, and Other IIS Services," outlines the procedures for securely using IIS FTP, NNTP, and SMTP services, Windows Media Services, and even the FrontPage server extensions.

Chapter 11, "Active Content Security," discusses the methods and tools used to secure the interactive scripts, server pages, and applications that can be added to a Web site to give the site a more up-to-date and dynamic image. The security techniques you learn in this chapter will help you ensure your deployment of active content without compromising the security of your IIS server.

Chapter 12, "Web Privacy." Privacy is a security-related topic that has far-reaching ramifications for Web sites. Many Web sites keep detailed information on customers and clients, and there is a business and legal expectation that you will provide and maintain confidentiality and appropriate care of that information. This chapter will cover this issue and provide practical advice on how to handle privacy management.

PART IV: APPENDIXES

Part IV provides several aids and resources that should help you maximize the benefits you get from reading this book. Installing and configuring your Web environment in a secure manner is only part of the process of security management. You are the guardian of your Web environment, and you need to be diligent and proactive in managing it.

Appendix A, "Security Resources." No individual can guard an installation alone. This Appendix will point you to other security resources, professional organizations, training, and public domain information that will help keep you abreast of the latest security threats, tips, research, products, training, and other useful information.

Appendix B, "Glossary," provides a summary of the many security terms not necessarily defined in this book but that are commonly encountered in security literature. The Glossary also includes their acronyms to help if you need to lookup the definition of a term that you come across in our chapters or in the other security information you find.

Appendix C, "Reference Tables," is exactly what it says—access control, auditing, and other miscellaneous security settings for Windows 2000 and IIS—organized in tables in one place for you convenience.

Appendix D, "Microsoft IIS Authentication Methods." In Chapter 4, we touched upon Web site authentication settings besides anonymous authentication but deferred the in-depth discussion to this Appendix because those methods are specific to Windows-only environments. This Appendix completes that discussion.

SUMMARY

One of the better quotes we have heard, though we do not remember the source, is that "security is a journey, not a destination." Put another way, security is an ongoing process where you apply your knowledge and experience to deploy the best protection you can, and then watch and adjust to conditions as they change. In this book, we have attempted to help you build the necessary foundation of knowledge to plan, deploy, and manage a practical and reasonable set of security measures for your Web site so that you can begin your journey.

PART I

Exposure, Risk, and Prevention

CHAPTER 1

Web Security Threats

Your Web site is your organization's face to the world. For customers, your Web site presents brand and product information. It's a marketing, selling, and support tool that you use to communicate with your customers. For your employees, it's a place where they can find news and information on benefits and training materials. Your partners might use it for any number of information-gathering purposes. In short, your site is a hub of information that customers, employees, and important third parties depend on to carry out business. So naturally it's important that you protect the Web site, not only the Web pages, but everything your site is connected to; all the information you present, distribute, and collect through your site; and the image you leave with your customers.

The goal of this book is to show you how to protect your Microsoft Internet Information Server (IIS) Web site and its services to ensure that it performs its critical functions correctly and to avoid negative customer experiences or business losses due to security breaches. Ultimately, we hope to help you devise a security framework for your organization that will protect your Web site against the threats, both known and unknown, that it faces in the interconnected world of the Internet. The best way to begin is to look at the security threats in greater detail to gain some insight that will help you in planning eventual defenses.

SECURITY INCIDENTS

You may remember the rapid spread of a malicious worm program called Code Red. This particular worm's *modus operandi* was to infect one server and from there automatically launch attacks on other nearby servers, eventually spreading to thousands and thousands of Microsoft operating systems. Code Red was designed to flood Web servers with data, which it did so successfully that it caused the virtual shutdown of large portions of the Internet, as sites became overloaded with more data than they could handle.

A worm such as Code Red is just one of dozens of known methods used to hamper, damage, or steal from Web sites. Because these threats are a fact of life, Web managers must prepare themselves to guard their sites against them or suffer the consequences.

Sources

The Code Red incident revealed how vulnerable Web servers can be to Internet assaults. You've probably also read about corporate espionage, information warfare, cyber-terrorism and organized crime on the Internet. To be sure, a lot of threats and bad guys are out there on the Internet.

 SECURITY ALERT   Threats can exist as much on the inside of an organization as they do on the outside. Don't spend a lot of energy and resources making sure you are well protected against external threats only to leave yourself unprotected and vulnerable to malicious insiders.

According to the FBI, a fact that is often overlooked by security administrators is that most computer crime is perpetrated by members and employees within an organization. Insufficient internal protection can be a costly oversight. Think about the consequences should someone gain access to confidential salary information from the internal HR Web site, even if the breach is enabled by an honest mistake, such as inadequate access restrictions on a file directory. Need we discuss the damage a disgruntled or dishonest employee can cause through snooping, theft, or sabotage? Clearly, the threats to your business and the need for security are a serious issue on your intranet.

Incident Categories

Security threats to your Web site fall into several incident categories. Some incidents affect the accessibility and reliability of your site, which are most commonly manifested as *Denial of Service* (DoS) incidents. The Code Red incident was a good example of a DoS incident. Other incidents work against the content and data of a site, as people try to damage, snoop, steal, modify, delete, or deposit something on the site. Such incidents are most commonly called *cracking* incidents.

Hacking is the term that describes the perpetration of both DoS and cracking incidents. For your reference, the definitions of these acts and incident categories, per the National Security Administration's glossary of terms (included in an abridged form in Appendix A), are as follows:

- **Denial of Service**   Action(s) that prevent any part of an automated information system from functioning in accordance with its intended purpose.
- **Hacking**   Unauthorized use or attempts to circumvent or bypass the security mechanisms of a computer information system or network.
- **Cracking**   The act of breaking into a computer system or network.

The word *attack* is commonly used to describe the procedures of a hacking incident. Many different attack techniques can be employed within DoS and cracking incident categories.

TIP   Some people in the Information Technology (IT) industry and academia maintain that hacking is distinctly different from cracking because the motives of hackers (as opposed to crackers) are *not* malicious. They believe hacking helps victims by exposing weaknesses, which allows victims to tighten their security before they suffer any real harm. We certainly agree that the practice of security has improved as organizations have become more aware of the flaws in their IT products. We have tried to choose a generic definition of hacking that we think is nonjudgmental.

Social and Physical Attacks

One of the most effective methods hackers and crackers use to gain access to password-secured systems is to gain the confidence of an unsuspecting individual by posing as a technical support person who needs the user's password. *Social engineering* is the term used to describe this kind of attack technique, which is based on exploitation or manipulation of human behavior to gain the objective.

Some attacks are pretty unsophisticated. One of the most effective DoS attack methods involves knocking out the system's power source or communication lines, either by cutting them off from the outside or shutting them down on the inside. This type of attack is called a *physical attack* since it involves an assault on the organization's physical assets.

Some attacks combine physical access with technical tricks. For example, if an attacker has physical access to a computer, he or she can sometimes reboot it into a different operating system from a removable disk to get to the computer's data. Sometimes attackers need only proximity and don't need physical access. For example, with the advent of wireless networking technologies, attackers can sometimes use radio receivers to eavesdrop on computer communications.

The defenses against social and physical attacks are straightforward. Putting machines in secure locations and using video security cameras are solutions already widely used by organizations to protect against physical attacks. User education and security policies can help defend against behavior-based attacks. All of these defenses are common-sense measures, and you don't need to read this book to learn how to implement them. However, we think it's worth emphasizing the importance of a formal set of security procedures and processes for your organization that will minimize the likelihood that mistakes, carelessness, or ignorance will be the cause of a preventable incident. The issue of policy within your security framework will be a recurring theme throughout all of our topic discussions.

Network Attacks

It seems the threats and attacks we hear about most often are manifested through the Internet with technical strategies and machinations. Indeed, they are probably the most dangerous types of attacks because they can be launched by anybody from anywhere in the world. For example, the Code Red worm was thought to have originated in China, the theft of several hundred-thousand credit card numbers from CD Universe was accomplished by a hacker in Russia, the Melissa virus was spread from the apartment of a hacker in New Jersey, and nobody seems to know (or probably just won't say) where the defacement of the CIA Web site originated from. These were all successful, highly publicized network-based attacks that caused great damage and concern. But, remember, they can happen over your intranet network, too.

Network attacks fit into the same DoS and cracking categories as the physical and social engineering attacks described previously. Some network attacks work by taking advantage of bugs and flaws in software that can be exploited to block access or gain entry into a system. Other attacks take advantage of opportunities created by misconfiguration or administrator oversights that leave doors open to entry. Still other attacks try to intercept and take control of connections or data transfers occurring between two systems. Hackers have used a lot of documented methods to accomplish their goals, and many of these are outlined in Chapter 2. Furthermore, what can make security management a frustrating task is that new methods are being devised constantly.

Many attack methods use tools readily available on the Internet that simplify and automate attack procedures, so hacking has become an activity in which even amateurs can participate. In fact, some security pundits have speculated that most hacking is done by amateurs out of curiosity or a sense of mischief. Perhaps this is true. Nonetheless, the incidents are still costly if they damage or shut down a Web site that performs critical business functions. Our own observation about hacker motives is that personal publicity, exposure of a political cause, avoiding financial responsibility, and greed are also common motivations. Now, in the aftermath of the terrorist attacks of September 11, 2001, we also are concerned about terrorism as well.

DEFENSIVE OBJECTIVES

In a technical environment as new, rapidly changing, and widely exposed as the Internet, it is impossible to achieve perfect security. But it is still possible to provide adequate protections and safeguards to reduce the likelihood of serious loss or catastrophe. If your organization responds appropriately, it can recover from the incidents it may experience. Potential losses can be minimized if your organization has made contingency plans to address problems.

Therefore, security management is driven by three primary objectives:

- **Prevention**   Create safe procedures and a safely configured Web environment that attempts to prevent intrusion of harmful agents and minimizes the likelihood of compromise or loss.
- **Detection**   Maintain and monitor Web activity so that you stay on top of changing security conditions and events.
- **Response**   Take appropriate action when an attack or intrusion is detected so that the incident can be controlled and potentially prosecuted.

An organization should also make sure it has a disaster recovery plan, in addition to security measures, that includes redundancy of systems and offsite backups in case the worst does happen.

HACKER STRATEGIES

Studying hacking methods, and how they exploit system vulnerabilities, can give you knowledge and insight that helps you make good security decisions. Most hacking attacks are designed to zero-in on specific weaknesses in hardware, firmware, operating systems, network services, and applications. At one time or another, nearly every type of component related to the Internet has experienced a security breach.

Table 1-1 provides a short list of hacking targets and the types of attacks used to exploit them. As you can see, each target category may be exploited for either DoS or cracking security breaches, impacting Web site availability, confidentiality, content, or data. Although this list is not complete, it gives you a feel for the magnitude of the vulnerabilities.

TIP   A good reference for known vulnerabilities in Internet software and hardware products is *Hacking Exposed: Network Security Secrets and Solutions,* by Stuart McClure, Joel Scambray, and George Kurtz (McGraw-Hill/Osborne).

Target	Type of Attack	How It Works
Attacks on network infrastructure	Hacking router tables	Looking at router files that will reveal information about the network so as to facilitate other attacks, or changing router entries to disrupt network operation
	Flooding hosts, routers, or firewalls	Overloading router firewalls or servers so that they become bogged down or crash attempting to process excessive amounts of information
	Sniffing	Using software to listen to the client network interface, server network interface, or network wire for packets that interest the user
	Spoofing	Pretending to be someone else (generally used in the context of an IP address)
Attacks on servers	Hacking operating system accounts and passwords	Using accounts on the Web server's operating system host left open to the Internet and/or trying to guess the account password to gain access to host network resources
	Overflowing buffers	Causing the system memory to overflow and allowing a hacker to give the system instructions to run another program that will allow system access
	URL decoding	Discovering information about a Web server configuration from a bug that causes a malformed URL, and using that bug to identify and penetrate file directories
	Masquerading	A form of spoofing pertaining to impersonating the identity of a user
	Hijacking	"Stealing" the connection of a user after the user has legitimately authenticated to a system
Attacks on content and information	Defacing Web sites with graffiti	Gaining access to Web content and images that are then modified and defaced
	Violating confidentiality	Gaining access to proprietary or confidential information, which could include classified government information, trade secrets, or personal information

Table 1-1.   Common Targets and Attack Methods

Target	Type of Attack	How It Works
	Deleting files	Breaching file system security and removing and wiping out information from storage
Attacks on financial assets	Fraudulent transfers	Using the illicit authentication of an account to move funds into another account
	Repudiation	Gaining unauthorized access to a system and removing the record of liability for a commercial transaction

Table 1-1.   Common Targets and Attack Methods *(continued)*

The wide variety of attack methods is worth noting, as is the variety of targets. Another difficulty you face in your quest for security is that of the many different technologies and products that support a network and Web site—each has its own potential weaknesses.

SECURITY IS INTERDEPENDENT

Many attacks can be mounted against network routers and operating systems and not just the Web server application itself. Because Microsoft Internet Information Server 5 is fully integrated into Windows 2000, when you are talking about securing Microsoft IIS, you are also talking about securing Windows 2000. Likewise, attacks on other network devices and network infrastructure, such as firewalls, routers, and other servers and clients, can also occur. Any weakness in those devices can leave a hole in the perimeter defense, exposing your site where you might have considered it protected and possibly revealing important information about the site that can be used to launch an attack.

 SECURITY ALERT   Security systems are only as strong as their weakest links. Your Web content is not the only resource or asset at risk if your site security is inadequate. Therefore, it's a best practice to implement multiple types of security across the network. Chapter 6 will discuss the practice of using perimeter security to augment server security.

Security Breach Examples

To some degree, all your systems depend on each other to ensure total network security. A bug, mistake, or oversight in your IIS Web server configuration could make your entire network vulnerable if the problem is serious enough. Figure 1-1 shows a hypothetical network configuration that can be used to explain several scenarios for how this could happen.

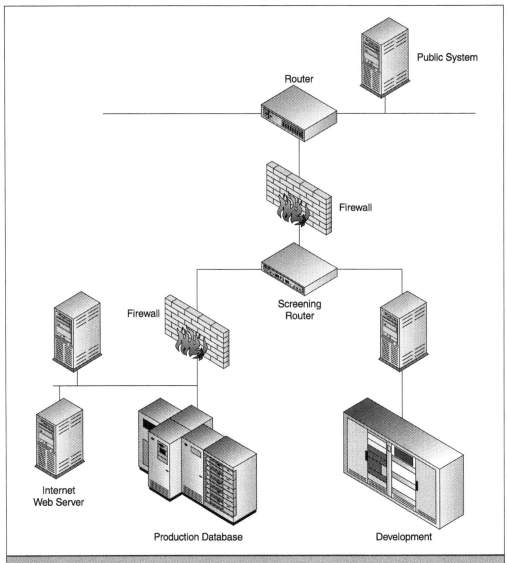

Figure 1-1. A typical network configuration with a database-backed Web site

An Open Port Can Be Like an Open Door

Firewalls are generally configured to protect internal assets by masking the real IP addresses of the systems behind them and to block network access attempts that are initiated from the outside, unless the user on the outside is a valid and authenticated member of the organization. However, your Web server may be exempted from this policy if you want it to be on the Internet. So the firewall may be configured to open a path to let traffic through to the Web server—and only to the Web server. Unfortunately, once this port is opened, if your Windows operating system or Web server is improperly configured a skillful hacker can find out information about its network addresses, users, and directories that will allow him to attack other systems on the network.

CHALLENGE

Web Applications Can Compromise Your Database

Notice back in Figure 1-1 that the Web site is connected to one of the organization's databases, a common occurrence on Web sites that allows customers to look up products in a catalog or to submit personal data for the company's use. Consequently, your Web site will put the database at risk if your configuration is not secure. Microsoft IIS Web sites often provide interactivity between a database and a customer by running an Active Server Page (ASP) that contains a little program on the server built with Microsoft's ActiveX toolkit. The ActiveX program shows the customer a search box or a form they fill out, and then it translates what is input into the form into Structured Query Language (SQL), which it uses when it sends messages or requests information from the database. Should a hacker gain access to this program, they could build SQL messages to see or modify the data in the database.

TIP   You *have* to be thorough. Don't leave holes in your site that can be exploited to attack other systems. Learn as much as you can about the threats you face so that you can build a solid defense.

Written Security Policy

Assuming you have more systems in your network than a single Web server, you must realize that security will require close collaboration and cooperation with other people in your organization who will manage other systems and will trust that you have done your job properly.

It's fair to say that no organization with any sophisticated IT resources is going to maintain a secure network environment successfully without some form of written policy, procedures, and checklists. As guardian of Web security for your organization, you need to make sure that your part of the organizational security policy is going to be adequate, so that it will guide the personnel who will work with you, who will follow you, or who will be end users of your Web platform.

HACKING METHODOLOGY

The first thing to realize about hackers is that they are often well armed. Many of them do extensive research, studying, and experimenting with known flaws in popular computing products or trying to discover new ones.

Serious hackers are part of a community that shares information with fellow hackers, spreading and publishing knowledge through word of mouth or on the Internet, in magazines, newsletters, technical forums, and conferences. Much of the information is legitimate security research intended for benevolent use. But who can say whether everyone who takes advantage of the information has good intentions?

Figure 1-2 shows a page from a hacking-related Web site called Antionline.com. It lists some of the many categories of available hacking resources.

Through the hacking community, hackers also have access to a large body of hacking tools and scripts that makes their task relatively easy. Products as popular as Microsoft IIS, Windows 2000, and Windows XP provide attractive hacking targets, so a lot of these tools target Microsoft platforms. These tools can automatically find available computers, crack passwords, monitor or sniff network packets, and perform exploits on known bugs.

Broadcast Attack Methods

With tools, hackers can mount attacks that are *broadcast* in nature, meaning they are not originally aimed at a specific organization but rather at a broad group of potential victims.

Viruses and worms fall into the category of a broadcast attack. They attack in a broad and random manner, using mechanisms such as e-mail to spread themselves, and causing significant damage. Viruses and worms will be covered in detail in Chapter 2, which includes some case studies that explain how some well-known examples worked.

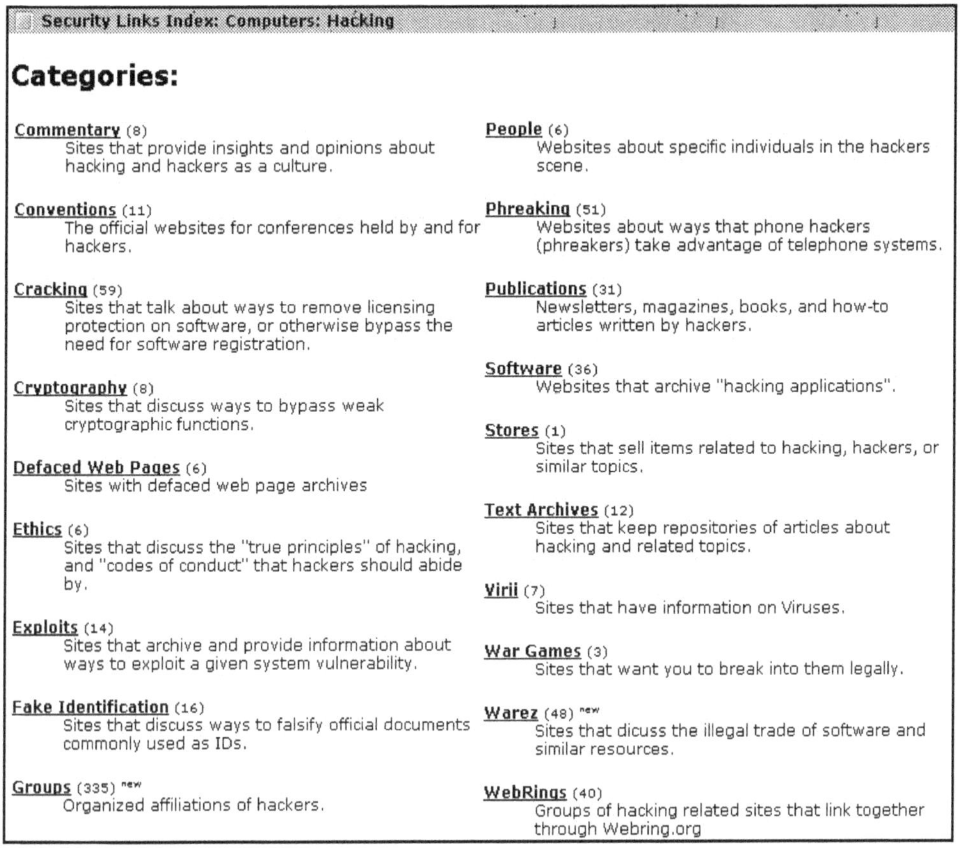

Security Links Index: Computers: Hacking

Categories:

Commentary (8)
Sites that provide insights and opinions about hacking and hackers as a culture.

Conventions (11)
The official websites for conferences held by and for hackers.

Cracking (59)
Sites that talk about ways to remove licensing protection on software, or otherwise bypass the need for software registration.

Cryptography (8)
Sites that discuss ways to bypass weak cryptographic functions.

Defaced Web Pages (6)
Sites with defaced web page archives

Ethics (6)
Sites that discuss the "true principles" of hacking, and "codes of conduct" that hackers should abide by.

Exploits (14)
Sites that archive and provide information about ways to exploit a given system vulnerability.

Fake Identification (16)
Sites that discuss ways to falsify official documents commonly used as IDs.

Groups (335) new
Organized affiliations of hackers.

People (6)
Websites about specific individuals in the hackers scene.

Phreaking (51)
Websites about ways that phone hackers (phreakers) take advantage of telephone systems.

Publications (31)
Newsletters, magazines, books, and how-to articles written by hackers.

Software (36)
Websites that archive "hacking applications".

Stores (1)
Sites that sell items related to hacking, hackers, or similar topics.

Text Archives (12)
Sites that keep repositories of articles about hacking and related topics.

Virii (7)
Sites that have information on Viruses.

War Games (3)
Sites that want you to break into them legally.

Warez (48) new
Sites that dicuss the illegal trade of software and similar resources.

WebRings (40)
Groups of hacking related sites that link together through Webring.org

Figure 1-2. A sample page from the Antionline Web site

Hacking can also be accomplished using broadcast techniques. At least initially, a hacker can aim at a broad group or even a random group and then focus on any that reveal vulnerabilities. Of course, if the attack is coming from inside your intranet, it wouldn't be so random.

Preliminary Reconnaissance

A hacker using broadcast techniques might begin an attack by doing a *ping sweep,* a process in which the hacker uses an automated program to ping a large range of IP addresses to see if something responds. This is the point at which your Web site might become a target if it is not adequately protected and it responds to those pings. When a hacker gets a ping response, they next might run one of the tools that identifies the operating system of the respondent. Once the hacker knows the operating system, they know some of the weaknesses, because such information will be easy to find in the hacker literature.

Scanning

After finding a potential victim, the hacker may perform a process called *scanning* to see what services are available, which in this context means he uses a tool based on the Internet Transaction Control Protocol (TCP) and User Datagram Protocol (UDP) to determine whether services like Hypertext Transfer Protocol (HTTP—the Web), Simple Network Management Protocol (SNMP), Post Office Protocol (POP—e-mail), or File Transfer Protocol (FTP) services are being run on the system.

Having discovered any or all of the information sought by pinging and scanning, the hacker might be in a position to run a set of vulnerability-specific exploit tools to mount a DoS attack. Alternatively, if the hacker were lucky enough to discover the address and name of one of your servers, they may use cracking tools to gain entry into that system. For example, they may now start checking for log-in accounts and use tools such as automated password dictionaries to try to guess passwords. Or they may try to exploit well-known buffer overflow holes by sending large amounts of data that includes a Trojan Horse program that they are trying to introduce into your environment.

Tools

These reconnaissance and scanning methods illustrate how you may become a victim of even a hacker who has done little preparation in advance of an attack. The tools do most of the hacker's work.

TIP   Experienced hackers are contemptuous of the amateurs who use these tools and call them "script kiddies," because they feel such amateurs haven't paid their dues.

Table 1-2 contains a short list of some of the broadcast and scanning tools that hackers use. Many of them are worth your time to investigate because they can also be defensive tools if you use them to assess your system's vulnerabilities. Some are UNIX based, which is fine with many hackers. In Chapter 7, we'll discuss how you can use Windows tools to perform an assessment to find your own weaknesses before a hacker finds them.

Targeted Attack Methods

In contrast to broadcast attacks, a *targeted attack* specifically identifies an organization as the attacker's next victim. In this type of attack, the hacker may undertake a significant amount of investigation and planning in advance of a primary assault. A hacker who has targeted your network may use a lot of the same tools used in a broadcast attack, but they

Name	Purpose	URL
fping (Unix) Grim's Ping (Win2000)	Sending out single ping requests or mass ping requests in a parallel, round-robin fashion	http://www.fping.com http://www.networkingfiles.com/PingFinger/Grimsping.htm
Nmap	Network Mapper will scan networks to determine which systems are available, what services each host is running, and the operating system used.	http://www.insecure.org/nmap/
Winscan	Scanning TCP and UDP ports and detect and monitor services on Windows NT 4.0 and Windows 2000 systems	http://www.prosolve.com/software/
LC3 (LOphtcrack)	Obtaining passwords from standalone Windows NT and 2000 workstations, networked servers, primary domain controllers, or Active Directory	http://www.@stake.com
Nessus	Auditing a given network and determining any weaknesses; launching predefined exploits, and reporting on the degree of success of each exploit	http://www.nessus.org
Ethereal	This Ethernet sniffer is easy to use and to read what it captures; you can interactively browse the capture data, viewing summary, and detail information for each packet.	http://www.ethereal.com/
Whois	Utility that will indicate the Web address and server address for domain's registrar of record, where full contact information can be found; this tool is Web based.	http://www.internic.net/whois.html

Table 1-2.   Common Hacking Tools

will usually plan and execute the attack in multiple stages and take great care to avoid detection as they perform reconnaissance to learn information that will help mount the main attack.

Footprinting

Hackers call their information gathering process for the target network *footprinting*. The process may begin with procedures as crude as dumpster diving, or they may turn to social engineering for hints about the organization's network architecture. Anything will do if it reveals a fact that gives the attacker a good place to start. If the hacker is an insider, they may already possess the information needed.

If an outside hacker follows a structured approach, they will systematically attempt to compile the information that helps them find what they are looking for. The technique is asymptotic. They will use a combination of tests and tools to collect information from a variety of vulnerable sources and narrow down unknown variables, such as network addresses, to a range that's close enough to allow them to move to the next stage of the attack.

Enumeration

The network mapping phase in the footprinting process is called *enumeration*, a process in which the hacker discovers domain information and network addresses controlled by a target organization by querying the Internet Whois or Domain Name Service (DNS) top-level domain databases. These are the databases on the Internet that allow the target's servers to be found by Web browsers and e-mail users. So the hacker will have references to any public IP address the company uses for Web or mail servers. By using freeware or commercial Whois and host tools, the hacker can learn those addresses and the IP address ranges allocated to the target by the Internet's oversight organizations and make pretty accurate determinations of the other host addresses on the target's network.

Probes

With a specific set of IP addresses in hand, the hacker can now initiate *probes* through a series of scans to discover more information. The hacker would probably use a *pinging* tool to probe for the systems that are alive, a *fingerprinting* tool to find out what operating systems are being used, and a *port scanning* tool that would tell him what services the host is running. Alternatively, the hacker might use an automated tool like Nmap to perform the probes in a batch, but a cautious hacker might worry about being detected and therefore try to stay under the radar with less disruptive tactics.

Exploits

Having successfully probed the target hosts, the hacker can now use exploit specific tools to initiate the attack. If DoS is the goal of the attack, it may soon be accomplished. Otherwise, the hacker will probably initiate the cracking or buffer overflow program that will allow them to penetrate the system.

In some cases, the hacker may use the Web site as a starting point to leapfrog to another system. A Web-based attack that is ultimately targeting the database would be such a case.

You have probably observed that a well-planned targeted attack is much more sophisticated than the average broadcast attack. Frequently, a hacker's initial penetration of a system is just a stage in a complex plan to insert himself into the target system for an extended period of time. So it's common for a hacker to plant a Trojan Horse program or a *back door* on the target system that allows him to capture data or easily re-enter the system.

Stealth Measures

Serious hackers, especially those who hack for financial gain, always try to make sure they hide their presence and cover their tracks. They perform their scans in ways that can evade a network administrator's vigilance and the rules that intrusion detection systems (IDSs) use to scan system network activity. Then, after they successfully invade a system, they remove log entries and doctor the audit trail. Needless to say, it's difficult to defend yourself when you don't even know you are under attack.

CHECKLIST OF THREATS

Can you keep from being targeted? Probably not. If you are a successful organization and you have a presence on the Internet, hackers may consider you fair game. But you can make it harder for hackers to succeed. You will learn how as you continue through this text.

Following is a checklist that summarizes the threats discussed in this chapter:

- ☐ Incident Categories
  - ☐ Denial of Service
  - ☐ Hacking
  - ☐ Cracking
- ☐ Attack Objectives
  - ☐ Disable or penetrate network infrastructure
  - ☐ Take control of servers
  - ☐ Access confidential information or destroy content
  - ☐ Steal assets or repudiate transactions
- ☐ Hacking Methodology
  - ☐ Random search or reconnaissance to research targets
  - ☐ Footprint
  - ☐ Enumerate
  - ☐ Probe
  - ☐ Exploit
  - ☐ Conceal

CHAPTER 2

*Defacing, Damage,
and Denial*

Chapter 1 provided an overview of the security threats to a Microsoft IIS Web site. Poorly protected sites and systems are vulnerable to any number of attacks—from inside the network or from the outside via the Internet.

A hacker's persuasiveness, command of code, knowledge, and experience can give him or her the upper hand when an organization has not taken appropriate security measures on its Web site. With the appropriate technical tools, even an amateur attacker can target system vulnerabilities with a high probability of success.

Sometimes, vulnerabilities result from server misconfiguration or lack of security knowledge on the part of Web site administrators. These are relatively easy problems to correct. Other vulnerabilities result from lack of planning, software design flaws, software bugs, and the nature of Internet protocols. Fixing these types of problems requires a deeper understanding of the issues. This chapter will discuss known IIS vulnerabilities and analyze how they are exploited to attack Microsoft IIS Web servers to help you better defend yourself and stop the attacks.

THE SOURCE OF THE PROBLEM

Your Web site is vulnerable to many forms of hacking attacks for a number of reasons. One reason is that the commercial software products on which Web sites are built are sophisticated and complicated platforms. Like any software, Web site software sometimes contains bugs that can be exploited. However, just as often, security problems exist because of the underlying technology (Internet protocols) on which the Web is based. Internet protocols were not originally designed with a secure environment in mind. Instead, these protocols came from a series of innovations, incremental improvements, and collaborative development projects in academic institutions, industry standards groups, and private enterprises that made their work public. The goal was to connect people together, not keep people out.

Because of this goal, many of the Internet's most frequently used protocols did not originally include security in their design. Although some security has been retroactively added, by and large these protocols remain architecturally flawed from a security point of view, and the cost of adding security implementations has often discouraged adoption of a new architecture.

The open and inclusive nature of Internet protocol development has been a significant factor in the Internet's rampant success. These protocols have become true standards. Consequently, products from many different vendors are able to interoperate fairly well. Unfortunately, because the protocol designers did not always anticipate the security requirements that we need today, the industry has been required to add security to software products on a case-by-case basis. But the vendors can't think of everything. A market has emerged for security products to fill in the gaps. Organizations that use the software and security products struggle to deploy and manage the results.

AN INTERNET PROTOCOL PRIMER

Before you learn about different vulnerabilities, you'll benefit by a brief description of the Internet protocols. The Internet works because the software that runs on it uses a suite of specialized communications protocols. Table 2-1 lists some of these protocols and provides background on terms that will be referenced throughout the next several chapters. If you are already familiar with TCP/IP networking and World Wide Web technologies, you can jump ahead to the next topic.

Protocol	Function
Internet Protocol (IP)	Used to manage network infrastructure and assign addresses to computers that uniquely identify each host by a number combining a network and node ID. An IP address might look like this: 192.168.222.101.
Internet Control Message Protocol (ICMP)	Provides a mechanism for reporting errors within IP to the host that originated an IP packet so that hosts can report problems with the integrity of the data transmissions they send.
Dynamic Host Control Protocol (DHCP)	Enables network administrators to allow a server to dynamically assign IP addresses to hosts on a subnet that they manage, to remove the requirement to assign and maintain a fixed IP address for each host.
Transmission Control Protocol (TCP)	Used to manage communications between processes that run on interconnected hosts that run independent of the network infrastructure managed by IP.
User Datagram Protocol (UDP)	Alternative to TCP for data transmissions between processes that do not require the protocol to provide reliable delivery, perhaps because the processes do their own error correction.
File Transfer Protocol (FTP)	A simple and reliable protocol for the transfer of files between two hosts.
Point to Point Protocol (PPP)	Provides reliable communication and a number of options that automate log-in and configuration of remote hosts.
Simple Mail Transfer Protocol (SMTP)	Used to transfer *outbound* e-mail messages from one host to another.
Post Office Protocol (POP)	Used to transfer *inbound* e-mail messages from one host to another.
Simple Network Management Protocol (SNMP)	Used in network management for the collection of data that helps analyze and report about the performance of networks.
Hypertext Transfer Protocol (HTTP)	The protocol for the Web, used by Web browsers and Web servers to request and send content. The content is usually formatted in HTML.

Table 2-1.   Common Protocols in the TCP/IP Suite

These TCP/IP protocols define a set of standards that software programmers use to make one computer able to exchange information with another computer. This allows software applications to ensure the proper delivery of data. Each protocol plays a different role in the interactions between two computers that are exchanging information.

The Internet Protocols

IP stands for *Internet Protocol,* one of several dozen protocols in the TCP/IP suite, whose role it is to identify computers (called *hosts* in the TCP/IP vernacular) that want to exchange data.

The *Internet Control Message Protocol (ICMP)* operates along with IP, enabling routers to send messages to other routers, so that two computers can find an efficient and reliable path to each other over what is a complicated worldwide network. Figure 2-1 shows a representation of how Internet infrastructure and the IP addressing scheme work.

Transmission Control Protocol (TCP), and to a lesser degree *User Datagram Protocol (UDP),* are used to manage the tasks of transporting the data between two computers. These protocols are used to open connections, deliver the data, verify data, and close connections as part of the information exchange.

The Domain Name System

The Internet is so large and the IP address scheme is so unnatural for humans (although it's quite natural for computers) that it requires some kind of centralized service to help Internet users efficiently find the specific computer they are looking for. A centralized naming service, the Internet *Domain Name System (DNS),* allows humans to search for Web information and to send their e-mails in a natural, human-readable language. Because we have DNS, you can browse for the Web site of your local library by typing the *Universal Resource Locator (URL)* into your browser, such as **www.mylibrary.com**, instead of typing in a cryptic network address like 196.221.68.124. Similarly, you can send an e-mail to santa@northpole.org instead of to 64.230.64.121@232.110.98.101.

TIP The Domain Name Directory is maintained in the United States by a nonprofit corporation called ICANN (Internet Corporation for Assigned Names and Numbers), which used to be a quasi-governmental organization called InterNIC. Europe and Asia have their own management bodies.

The Domain Name Service keeps track of the detailed information needed to locate an entity, so that each individual computer doesn't have to do this. DNS is organized into a hierarchy that makes address searches efficient and fast. Figure 2-2 shows the hierarchy. At the top of the hierarchy is a *Top Level Domain (TLD).* All of the other domains (those familiar .com, .net, and .org designations) branch from the Top Level Domain.

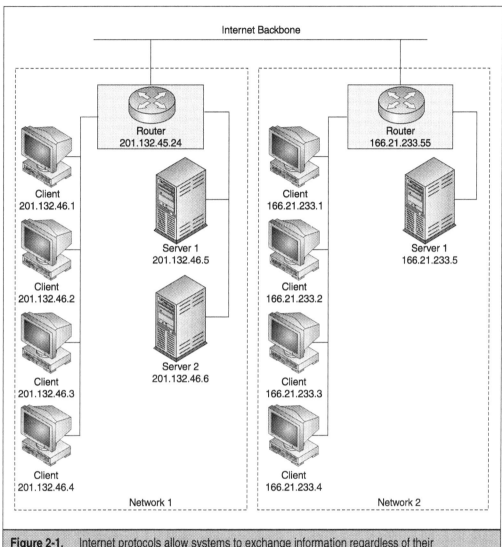

Figure 2-1. Internet protocols allow systems to exchange information regardless of their physical locations.

Applications and Services

The various kinds of information exchanges require different protocols for their transmission and reception of data. For example, Web information is exchanged using *HTTP (Hypertext Transfer Protocol)*, e-mail clients use *SMTP (Simple Mail Transfer Protocol)*,

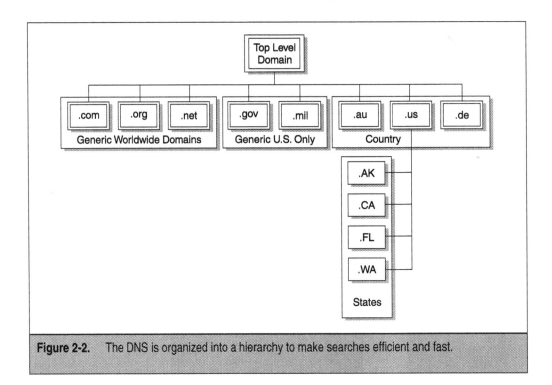

Figure 2-2. The DNS is organized into a hierarchy to make searches efficient and fast.

and files can be exchanged via *FTP (File Transfer Protocol).* Application programs such as a Web browser, an e-mail client, or an FTP client are written to format their data according to the protocol rules of the information they are exchanging.

While each individual computer on the Internet could theoretically communicate directly with every other computer to exchange information, they usually don't, because most information (and the Internet itself) is not managed that way. Instead, most individual computers running a Web browser or e-mail client interact with some kind of server that is running the appropriate *application service,* such as an HTTP Web server and an SMTP e-mail server or a *network service,* such as FTP (file sharing) or Telnet (remote terminals). Many servers run more than one application service at a time. To accommodate such configurations, Internet computer software uses a set of *ports,* identified by number from a range of 1 to 65,535. The port numbers allow the server's operating system to manage multiple applications or network services and multiple client connections on each service. HTTP services are typically configured to use port 80, SMTP services usually are set to port 25, and FTP services are on ports 20 and 21. A more expansive list, though far from complete, is shown in Table 2-2.

The Internet protocol suite contains about 100 protocols. This information focuses on the background material required for the coming discussion of how Microsoft IIS Web server vulnerabilities are exploited by hackers for their mischievous or malicious

Service	Port Used	Transport	Function
FTP	21	TCP	File transfers
Telnet	23	TCP	Remote terminals
SMTP	25	TCP	Outbound mail
Naming services (DNS)	53	UDP	Internet name listings
HTTP	80	TCP	Web
POP	109, 110	TCP	Inbound mail
Remote Control Program (RCP)	111	TCP and UDP	Remote program execution
Network News Transfer Protocol (NNTP)	119	TCP	Internet news lists
Network Time Protocol (NTP)	123	UDP	Time synchronization
NetBIOS (Win NT)	135, 139 137, 138	TCP UDP	Windows networking (non-TCP/IP)
NetBIOS (Win2000)	135, 139, 137, 138, 445	TCP UDP	Windows networking (non-TCP/IP)
Internet Message Access Protocol (IMAP)	143	UDP	Another mail protocol
SNMP	161, 162	TCP and UDP	Network management
Border Gateway Protocol (BGP)	179	TCP	Border gateway management
Lightweight Directory Access Protocol (LDAP)	389	TCP and UDP	Directory services
Secure Sockets Layer (SSL)	443	TCP	Secure, encrypted Web
Syslog	514	UDP	Network logging
Line Printer Deamon (LPD)	515	TCP	Print server (UNIX)
SOCKS	1080	TCP	Network proxy

Table 2-2. Common Application Ports

antics. These concepts will be particularly important to the review of scanning techniques in forthcoming discussions.

KNOWN VULNERABILITIES

The System Administration, Networking, and Security Institute (SANS) is a cooperative research and education organization of more than 90,000 system administrators, security professionals, and network administrators—making it one of the most visible security organizations for the Internet. The members of SANS publish and share security research, information, education, and news with each other and the public.

Each year, SANS compiles a list of the most critical known security vulnerabilities that affect computer and networking systems. This list is called "The Twenty Most Critical Internet Security Vulnerabilities" and is also referred to as "The SANS/FBI Top 20." The list is developed by consensus among the organization members, drawing upon their collective observations, experience, and knowledge. It is frequently updated and can be found at www.sans.org/top20.htm. The list contains general vulnerabilities that affect all systems as well as vulnerabilities that affect only Microsoft systems. Most of the Microsoft IIS-specific vulnerabilities can be fixed by installing the latest Microsoft service packs or security patches. The more general vulnerabilities need to be addressed within the overall framework of your security procedures.

The following section contains a condensed version of the SANS known vulnerability list, with several enhanced descriptions of the problems and a number of additional observations. The section "Buffer Overflows" also contains information pulled from the Symantec Web site (www.Symantec.com).

Top Vulnerabilities That Affect All Systems

Some security vulnerabilities are universal among all information systems. For example, any system that uses passwords is vulnerable to attacks when passwords are used insecurely. So regardless of whether you're running on Windows or UNIX, the following vulnerabilities apply to your Web server.

Default Installs of Operating Systems and Applications

Most software, including operating systems (OS) and applications, comes with an easy-to-use installation program that automatically copies and configures the software onto a computer. However, these install programs often install more components than most organizations need. Many administrators fail to realize how much extra software is actually installed, leaving vulnerable holes in software that catch the administrator off guard.

Application installs often include unneeded sample programs or scripts. For example, OS installs nearly always include extraneous services and corresponding open ports. Attackers break into systems via these ports.

One of the most serious vulnerabilities with Web servers is sample scripts; attackers use these scripts to compromise the system or gain information about it. Sample scripts are a problem because they usually do not go through the same quality control process as other software. Error checking is often forgotten, and the sample scripts offer a fertile ground for *buffer overflow attacks* that cause a script to overwhelm its allocated memory space, allowing the hacker to insert a program of his own into the computer memory and have it executed.

The solution, which involves closing ports, removing sample scripts, and performing other protective measures, is part of a process called *hardening*. This process will be discussed in detail in Chapter 3.

Accounts with Weak or Nonexistent Passwords

Most systems are configured to use passwords as the first, and only, line of defense. Therefore, if an attacker can determine an account name and password, he can logon to the network.

Many systems have built-in or default accounts with default passwords. These accounts usually have the same password out-of-the-box, across installations of the software. Attackers commonly look for these accounts as they are well known to the attacker community; a surprising number of system administrators do not change or remove the defaults.

Easy-to-guess passwords are also a big problem, because attackers can use a *brute force attack* (an attack in which the hacker attempts to guess the password) or mount a *dictionary attack* using tools such as a password dictionary program, trying words and combinations of letters until they find a successful password. If the passwords are short and contain nothing but letters of the alphabet, it's not difficult for a hacker to crack them.

To prevent against brute force and dictionary password attacks, administrators and users should avoid using passwords that are found in the dictionary, people's names, pet's names, or place names. Also, the more characters you use in your password, the more difficult it is to guess. An industry best practice for passwords is to use *strong passwords*, which are passwords of at least eight characters in length that are a combination of numbers, special punctuation characters, and letters of the alphabet with uppercase and lowercase letters (if the system is case sensitive on passwords).

Nonexistent or Incomplete Backups

When a security incident occurs, recovery requires up-to-date backups and proven methods of restoring the data. Some organizations make daily backups but never verify that the backups are actually working. Others construct backup policies and procedures but do not create restoration policies and procedures. Such errors are often discovered after a hacker has entered systems and destroyed or otherwise ruined data. You should make sure you have written backup and restore policies that are practiced and enforced.

Large Number of Open Ports

Both legitimate users and attackers connect to systems via open ports. The more ports that are open, the more ways someone can connect to your system. You have to have some ports open—certainly port 80 for HTTP on your Web server, and possibly ports 25 and 110 for SMTP and POP in your firewall. It's those ports that you don't know are open that can hurt you. If you leave an open port unprotected, all an attacker has to do is use a *scanning attack* to find it, and then he can run an exploit for that port from a hacker toolkit.

The best way to ensure that you don't have unnecessary ports open is to close them all and then open the necessary ports one by one as you install and harden your system.

Not Filtering Packets for Correct Incoming and Outgoing Addresses

Hackers often disguise their IP address to make it appear as though they are a node inside the target's internal network, because they can typically operate more freely and without special notice when they appear as an internal network user. Internal users usually have privileged access to information and systems that are not meant for outsiders. So the outsider posing as an insider can use those privileges to harm the organization. This type of attack is called *spoofing*. This particular type of spoofing attack can be prevented by IP filtering, which is discussed in Chapter 6.

Nonexistent or Incomplete Logging

One of the maxims of security is, "Prevention is ideal, but detection is a must." In a case where you are attacked, without logs, you have little chance of discovering what the attackers did to your system. Without that knowledge, your organization must choose between completely reloading the OS from original media and then hoping the data backups were OK, or taking the risk that you are running a system that a hacker still controls. You cannot detect an attack if you do not know what is occurring on your network. Logs provide the details of what is occurring, what systems are being attacked, and what systems have been compromised. Logs are discussed in Chapter 5.

Vulnerable CGI Program

Most Web servers, including Microsoft IIS, support Common Gateway Interface (CGI) programs to provide Web pages that supply such functions as data lookup and collection. Unfortunately, if these programs are compromised, they can provide a path directly to the OS of the computer running the Web server, which allows an attacker to operate a program with the privileges and power of the Web server software itself. Rogue CGI program attacks are known to have exploited CGI holes to vandalize Web pages, steal credit card information, and set up back doors to enable future intrusions.

Depending on how you use scripts and/or CGI, you can take a number of measures to protect against exploitation. Microsoft security patches are available that fix some of the vulnerabilities of IIS that can be exploited through scripts. Chapter 11 discusses the measures you can take to secure your code if you are developing your own CGI or Active Server Pages (ASPs).

Malicious or Hostile Code

Web sites can be vulnerable to a variety of attacks that plant viruses, worms, or Trojan Horses on their systems. The difficult aspect of malicious code vulnerabilities is that they can come from so many different sources, such as e-mail, file downloads, malformed URLs, and more. While the problem is common to all systems, the implementation will usually, but not always, be specific to a platform. For example, many viruses will affect only the Windows platform. Malicious code will be closely examined later in this chapter.

Platform-Dependent Vulnerabilities

In addition to the universal vulnerabilities outlined, each information system's computing platform will have a set of unique vulnerabilities. Because Windows 2000 and IIS are so widely used, it's not surprising that they are frequently attacked, and their vulnerabilities tend to get a lot of exposure.

The sections that follow list the top known vulnerabilities at the time of this writing. All the vulnerabilities on this list can be mitigated by installing Microsoft Service Pack 2 for Windows 2000, but it's potentially a moving target, so you need to keep yourself up to date with the list on the SANS Web site http://www.sans.org/top20.htm.

Unicode Vulnerability (Web Server Folder Traversal)

Unicode is an industry software standard that makes it easier for organizations to adapt software products for different OSs or to translate Web site content and programs into different languages. It provides a unique number for every character, no matter the platform, program, or language. The Unicode Standard has been adopted by most vendors, including Microsoft, and Unicode source code is part of Windows 2000 and IIS.

Microsoft's use of Unicode has created a vulnerability. By sending an IIS server a carefully constructed URL containing an invalid Unicode UTF-8 sequence, an attacker can force the server to "walk up and out" of a directory and execute arbitrary scripts. This type of attack is also known as the *directory traversal attack*. If the hacker makes his way into the Microsoft IIS directory marked as "executable," the attacker can cause a program he has inserted to be executed on the server.

Buffer Overflows

Multiple buffer overflow vulnerabilities have been noted in Windows 2000 and IIS. These vulnerabilities potentially allow attacks that can either crash the IIS Web server or allow an attacker to run arbitrary code, to perform DoS attacks, or even to use a targeted Web server as a launch platform to attack a third-party system. The following is a synopsis of the identified vulnerabilities.

- When IIS is installed, several extensions for Internet Services Application Programming Interface (ISAPI) are also installed, which allows developers to extend the capabilities of an IIS server using dynamic-link libraries (DLLs). In the past, several of the DLLs, such as idq.dll, were found to contain programming errors that allowed attackers to mount a buffer overflow attack and take full control of an IIS Web server. In Windows 2000, a file called idq.dll was identified as an overflow hole in Microsoft Index Server 2.0 and Indexing Service in Windows 2000. The buffer overflow impacts Windows 2000 Server, Advanced Server, and Server Data Center Edition with IIS 5.0 installed. The vulnerable DLL also ships with Windows 2000 Professional, but it is not mapped by default.

- There is a remote buffer overflow in the way chunked encoding memory is handled by the ASP ISAPI extension installed by default with IIS 5.0. By exploiting this, a remote attacker can either cause the Web server to crash or, if properly implemented, to run arbitrary code of the attacker's choosing. On default installations of IIS 5.0, the code would run with privileges of the IWAM_*machinename*, which is the local unprivileged user access (also called the Internet Guest account, which is covered in Chapter 4).

- A second, similar buffer overflow condition was also discovered in another portion of the data transfer mechanism of the ASP ISAPI extension. This second issue results in the same impact as the initial issue but additionally affects the IIS Web Server application.

- A third buffer overflow condition exists in the manner in which IIS 5.0 and 5.1 provide delimiter safety checks prior to parsing HTTP header fields. It is possible for an attacker to spoof the check, fooling IIS into believing the appropriate delimiters are present when, in fact, they are not. By exploiting this issue, a remote attacker can submit a carefully crafted HTTP request to the server that would overflow the available buffers. Successful exploitation would either cause the Web server to crash or, if properly implemented, to run arbitrary code of the attacker's choosing. On default installations of IIS 5.0 and 5.1, the code would run with privileges of the IWAM_*machinename*.

- A buffer overflow vulnerability exists in the checking of file name validity and size during server-side includes. By carefully crafting a user request, a remote attacker could submit an oversized file name, bypass the security check, and overrun the static buffer, resulting in either a DoS or being able to run arbitrary code with IWAM_*machinename* privileges on the targeted server.

- Another buffer overflow vulnerability exists in the IIS 5.0 Web server component that handles incoming .htr requests. The HTR ISAPI extension, which is a scripting API, is enabled by default during IIS installation. HTR ISAPI functionality is to provide Web-based user password management. By carefully crafting a number of .htr file requests, a remote attacker can cause a buffer overflow allowing arbitrary code to run on the targeted system. This attack can result either in a DoS or, in limited instances, allow the attacker to gain IWAM_*machinename* privileges on the targeted server.

- A DoS condition can be created by the way some ISAPI filters handle error generation. By sending a URL request that exceeds the fixed buffer length set in the ISAPI filter, the attacker can cause an access violation in IIS services.

- A DoS vulnerability in IIS exists when FTP services are enabled. A specific error condition can be created by a particular status request that will result in an access violation in FTP service as well as in Web services. Again, this issue occurs only if FTP services are enabled on the Web server.

- Three separate Cross-Site Scripting (CSS) vulnerabilities affect IIS Web servers. CSS is a passive, social engineering type of attack that can be exploited only if the attacker can get a user to either visit a malicious Web page and execute a hostile link or open a malicious HTML e-mail. CSS allows the attacker to place malicious code inside a Web request from the user's system that is then sent to a third-party Web site. The malicious code executes and runs with the security settings and in the security zone that the user applies to the third-party Web site. This could potentially allow the attacker to obtain data from the third-party Web site that they would not normally be able to obtain.

NetBIOS: Unprotected Windows Networking Shares

The Microsoft File Sharing feature in Windows enables file sharing over networks. A Microsoft OS using File Sharing that is not protected from the Internet exposes critical system files or gives full file-system access to any hostile party connected to the Internet.

Microsoft Files Sharing uses a protocol called Server Message Block (SMB) that enables Windows File Sharing also to be used by attackers to obtain sensitive system information—user and group information (user names, last logon dates, password policy, RAS information), system information, and certain Registry keys may all be accessed via a "null session" connection to the NetBIOS Session Service. This information is useful to hackers because it helps them mount password guessing or brute force password attacks against the Windows target.

Information Leakage via Null Session Connections

On Windows NT and Windows 2000 systems, many local services run under the SYSTEM account, known as LocalSystem on Windows 2000. The SYSTEM account is used for various critical system operations. When one machine needs to retrieve system data from another, the SYSTEM account will open a null session to the other machine.

The SYSTEM account has virtually unlimited privileges and it has no password requirement for access, so you can't logon as SYSTEM. SYSTEM sometimes needs to access information on other machines such as SMB shares, user names, and so on—Network Neighborhood type functionality. Because it cannot log into the other systems using a user ID and password, it uses a null session to get access. Unfortunately, attackers can also log-in as the null session. This affects both Windows 2000 and Windows NT.

Weak Hashing in Security Accounts Manager (SAM)

Although most Windows users have no need for LAN Manager support, Microsoft stores LAN Manager password hashes, by default, on Windows NT and 2000 systems in the SAM along with other passwords. Since LAN Manager uses a much weaker encryption scheme than do the more current Microsoft approaches, LAN Manager passwords can be broken in a short period of time. Even strong password hashes can be cracked in under a month.

The major weaknesses of LAN Manager hashes is that they are always padded or truncated to 14 characters and broken into two, 7-character pieces—a pattern that makes them easier to crack. A password cracking program has to crack only two, 7-character passwords without even testing lowercase letters. In addition, LAN Manager is vulnerable to eavesdropping of the password hashes. This affects both Microsoft Windows NT and Windows 2000 computers.

 SECURITY ALERT   Don't delay in applying the Microsoft Service Packs and Security Updates that fix these problems if you are currently running a vulnerable Web site. Because the vulnerability list is public, you can bet hackers have studied it, along with a lot of other information they can access via the hacker community. You don't want them to get there before you do.

OPPORTUNISTIC SCANNING

Hackers are aware of the weaknesses inherent in the systems they attack. Most of the time, when planning and mounting an attack, they are going to run through a list of systematic procedures that will help them find those vulnerabilities as easily as possible. So the first thing they are likely to check is whether the target has left unsecured NetBIOS ports open. Then they may look for default accounts and passwords that haven't been changed. Therefore, if you are not effective at eliminating the vulnerabilities and closing the holes, a hacker will find them through reconnaissance.

Assume You Are Being Watched

As briefly discussed in Chapter 1, some hackers find random targets while others focus on specific targets, using pings as one of their weapons. Typically, if they are attacking randomly, hackers do ping sweeps to find out what computers are responding. The respondents then go into a small pool of promising targets. If a hacker has already identified and targeted your Web server, he will use a ping, like that shown in Figure 2-3, to make sure it's alive before investigating further or actually attacking.

Scanning is the next stage of information gathering and is used from either the inside or the outside of your network. Scanning is an effective reconnaissance method, because virtually all applications and services that communicate via the Internet listen for and send data via the same basic set of standard communication protocols. Scanning helps a hacker determine what ports on the target are open and what applications and services are in use.

```
C:\WINDOWS>ping 192.168.222.222

Pinging 192.168.222.222 with 32 bytes of data:

Reply from 192.168.222.222: bytes=32 time<10ms TTL=128
Reply from 192.168.222.222: bytes=32 time=1ms TTL=128
Reply from 192.168.222.222: bytes=32 time=1ms TTL=128
Reply from 192.168.222.222: bytes=32 time=1ms TTL=128

Ping statistics for 192.168.222.222:
    Packets: Sent = 4, Received = 4, Lost = 0 (0% loss),
Approximate round trip times in milli-seconds:
    Minimum = 0ms, Maximum = 1ms, Average =  0ms

C:\WINDOWS>
```

Figure 2-3.   A hacker will ping a target before launching an attack.

How Pinging and Scanning Work

Pinging, individually or as a sweep, works by utilizing the attributes of Internet protocols to get information. Virtually all computer OSs have a ping utility built into them. A ping utility sends an ICMP ECHO request packet to a targeted system and waits for an ICMP ECHO reply. If a reply is received, the ping utility indicates that the target is alive. If no response is received, the utility indicates that fact. Ping sweeps require a tool that can broadcast the ping to a range of addresses.

Several ping tools, and URLs to download them, were listed in Table 2 Chapter 1. All the systems that reply are listed as live addresses as in Figure 2-4, a screen shot from the Grims Ping for Windows 2000.

Ping scans can be detected. Therefore, careful hackers are unlikely to use much random ping sweeping. They ping judiciously when the opportunity is there, hoping a single ping won't be noticed, and they use multiple forms of reconnaissance to help them map targets.

An easy defense against external pinging, ping scans can be blocked by the use of ICMP filtering at firewalls and routers. The generally accepted practice among security-minded administrators is to configure those devices to drop all ping requests originating outside the network. That works unless and until the firewall gets penetrated.

Port scanning, like pinging, also uses the attributes of TCP, UDP, and ICMP but employs a different technique. A port scan is accomplished by using a tool that will collect information about the state of the target's TCP or UDP ports. The scanner works by sending a data packet (or probe) to a port and then listening for a response. The response that is returned indicates whether the port is open, in use, or is closed, and it

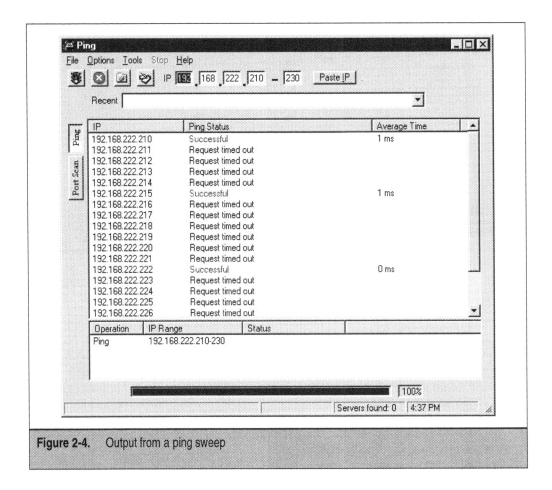

Figure 2-4. Output from a ping sweep

gives clues as to what application is running on that port. Here is example output from a scan directed at a single computer using Nmap:

```
Interesting ports on (xxx.xxx.x.xx):
Port        State       Protocol    Service
21          open        tcp         ftp
80          open        tcp         http
```

Scans can be directed at a single port on a single machine, or they can be sweeps, depending on the tool that performs the scan. Numerous automated scanning tools are available for free on the Internet. Nmap, the most popular tool, is available for both Microsoft Windows and UNIX. Nessus is often used. Both tools contain a large variety of features for scanning that can be used to probe networks large and small.

A port scan makes it possible, with reasonable confidence, to discover what applications and services the target is running. For example, if ports 21 and 80 are open a hacker can assume that the machine is running services for FTP and HTTP, respectively. This is valuable information, because each listening port represents a potential communication channel with the target and each known application or service represents a point of attack to a hacker who is knowledgeable about the system's weaknesses—or even one who isn't, but has the right hacking toolkit.

Some Port Scanning Techniques

Many port scanning techniques can be used, but the combination of the environment and the objective will determine which scanning technique is best. A hacker makes a tradeoff between time and secrecy. Depending on the circumstances, the hacker may operate with impunity and not worry about being detected, or he may operate with stealth. Scans take advantage of Internet protocol features in a variety of different ways.

TIP   The Web sites for both *The Art of Port Scanning* (http://www.insecure.org/nmap/nmap_doc.html) and *Remote OS Detection via TCP/IP Stack FingerPrinting* (http://www.insecure.org/nmap/nmap-fingerprinting-article.html) by Fyodor were used to compile the following section. Refer to these Web sites for more information.

Following are some descriptions of a few TCP scanning techniques that will give you a feel for how and why they are used. Some of these techniques will avoid detection and work from outside the network if the perimeter defense is limited to packet-filtering technology. The Challenge sidebar entitled "TCP Connections" will help you understand the terms if you are not familiar with TCP/IP.

- The TCP ACK scan is used to identify active Web sites that may not respond to standard ICMP pings. The scanning tool will send ACK packets, and if the port is open, the target will send an RST in reply. If the scan gets no response, the port is closed. This scan is direct but will be detected and blocked by packet filtering, which is discussed in Chapter 6.

- The TCP Connect scan uses the *connect* system call of an OS to open a connection to every port that is listening to the network. This technique is fast but will be detected unless the targeted system does not keep a log, as the activity will be recorded in the system logs.

- The TCP SYN scan will send a SYN packet to the target. If the port is open, the target will send a SYN | ACK. In a legitimate connection request, the next step is that the machine that sent the ACK sends a request to open the connection. But in a scan, the scanner now knows the port is open so it breaks the connection. This type of scan is often not detected because the scan does not complete the connection, and many systems do not log uncompleted TCP connections. Some perimeter defense products block these packets and some do not.

- The TCP FIN scan sends FIN packets to the targeted system. On a UNIX machine, the closed ports will respond with an RST. The open ports will ignore the packets, so if a system does not respond, its port is probably open. However, Microsoft ports will send an RST even if they're open. So a FIN scan is not useful to scan ports, but it may be useful to reveal that the target uses Windows. Some OS scanners use this as one of their probes.

- The FTP Bounce scan uses FTP to make proxy FTP connections. When the service that this scan utilizes is open, the attacker can use the host machine as a proxy to scan another target without its address being detected and revealed.

CHALLENGE

TCP Connections

Knowing how TCP connections are established helps you understand how protocol attacks work. To use reliable transport services, TCP hosts must establish a connection-oriented session with one another. Connection establishment is performed by using a "three-way handshake" mechanism.

The handshake mechanism makes use of control bits that are embedded in the packets sent between the two machines. The control bits and their purposes are as follows:

- **ACK**   Acknowledges a successful request for connection
- **RST**   Forces a reset of the connection
- **SYN**   Synchronizes sequencing counters for the connection
- **FIN**   Indicates that there is no more data and closes the connection

A three-way handshake synchronizes both ends of a connection by allowing both sides to agree upon initial sequence numbers. This mechanism also guarantees that both sides are ready to transmit data and that each side knows that the other side is ready to transmit. This is necessary so that packets are not transmitted or retransmitted during session establishment or after session termination.

Each host randomly chooses a sequence number used to track bytes within the stream it is sending and receiving. Then, the three-way handshake proceeds in the following manner:

1. The first host (Host A) initiates a connection by sending a packet with the initial sequence number (X) and SYN bit set to indicate a connection request.

CHALLENGE (continued)

2.   The second host (Host B) receives the SYN, records the sequence number X, and replies by acknowledging the SYN (with an ACK = X + 1). Host B includes its own initial sequence number (SEQ = Y). An ACK = 20 means the host has received bytes 0 through 19 and expects byte 20 next. This technique is called *forward acknowledgment*.

3.   Host A then acknowledges all bytes Host B sent with a forward acknowledgment indicating the next byte Host A expects to receive (ACK = Y + 1).

4.   Data transfer then can begin.

UDP scans are less effective than TCP because the attributes and features of the protocol are different. There is little handshaking and communication during a UDP transmission, so there is not much a scan can do to gather information. However, UDP scans are still usually worth a hacker's while because many Trojan Horse programs like Back Orifice use UDP, as UDP traffic is harder to detect and stop. As a result, occasionally a UDP scan may find a back door through an existing Trojan Horse.

UDP scans usually work by sending empty packets to a port to see what happens. If the port is closed, the OS will send back a message saying the port is unreachable. If the port is open, the empty packet will probably be ignored. Therefore, no response usually means the port is open, unless the port is protected by a perimeter security device that blocks all UDP traffic.

Identifying the Web Server or Operating System

As you saw from the SANS/FBI list, most known vulnerabilities are platform specific. So scanning for a target's operating system, or the vendor and version of the application or service found in the scan, is the next logical move. The information the hacker acquires in the scan for that information will help him choose an exploit.

Sometimes a hacker can get the computer software itself to reveal its Web server software version or OS version. A simple and often used method is to get a client for a service called Telnet and try to log-in. On a Web server, this would be done by Telnetting to the server's port 80 (the HTTP Web services port). On vulnerable systems, when the log-in attempt is made, the server will return a banner identifying its vendor and version information (regardless of whether or not the log-in was successful).

OS scans can be performed by using a scanning tool such as Nmap or Nessus. They work through a fingerprinting utility in the tool that examines the implementation of the target's TCP/IP stack through probes that it sends, and compares the information it learns to a database to match the target to the vendor and version. Usually more than one probe is required to accomplish the identification, but the tools are automated, so it's a relatively fast and easy process. Some of the probes are similar to the scanning techniques for ports.

A Web server security trick sometimes used by administrators to try to fool hackers is changing the Web server banner to name the wrong vendor and software version. However, it's doubtful this would fool anyone for long with Microsoft IIS, since a successful OS scan would quickly narrow the possibilities to a few versions of IIS.

Scanning Techniques to Avoid Detection

One detection avoidance technique, the FTP Bounce scan, has already been discussed. This technique uses a spoof tactic that takes advantage of a proxy to shield the true network address of the scanner. Another detection avoidance technique involves slowing down the rate of the scan so that it avoids notice by IDSs. A slow enough scan rate can fall under the monitoring threshold of activity defined in the IDS rules. To avoid the threat, the IDS threshold rate can be lowered, but if it gets too low the IDS is overwhelmed by reports of false positives from other network activity, and the scanning activity gets lost in the storm of data.

Some scanning techniques will allow scans to pass through perimeter defenses. Packet filtering firewalls can sometimes be bypassed by scans that fragment the IP datagrams in TCP headers, which means the filter does not see a complete TCP header that matches its filter rules, and the scan is allowed to pass.

VULNERABILITY EXPLOITS

Exploits take many forms. Some well known methods are the following:

- **Configuration error exploits**   Methods that take advantage of poor privilege management and/or weak or compromised IDs and passwords that enable a direct attack, entry, and advance. Once a hacker learns the right information via reconnaissance, he can mount a systematic exploit from a list of tricks that may eventually allow him to break in.

- **Malicious Code Exploits**   Methods that introduce foreign code into a Web server, which allows a hacker to steal, modify, or damage a targeted resource or take control of a system through any of the following methods:

    - **Contagion**   A malicious code attack in the form of a virus or worm that enters the victim's network with the aid of internal users (through an executable file on a disk, attached to e-mail, or introduced in the browser) and rapidly and indiscriminately spreads to a large number of systems.

    - **Bugs**   Flaws in the target software, sample scripts, or CGI/Java applets such as buffer overflow holes that will allow the hacker to run an unauthorized, malicious program with sufficient privilege to compromise or damage the system.

- **Trojan Horse**   Software that penetrates the perimeter and Web server security, often through e-mail but possibly introduced by an individual, which establishes a security hole that can be exploited for entry at the moment or anytime in the future.

- **Distributed exploits**   Exploits involving one or more remote computers that hackers utilize to mount an attack on yet another target. The exploits generally make it hard to identify the attack's source.

The configuration error exploits in this list require that the hacker spend enough time and energy to find the errors and break into the system. The other categories take a little more hacking acumen to pull off. Unless the hacker just reuses an existing exploit program, he actually has to write a little code and devise a delivery scheme. But again, using a hacker's toolkit, it's relatively easy for a programmer to compile an attack program and begin the exploit. Distributed exploits are another matter. They require a great deal of planning and preparation, but they are also the hardest to defend against.

Configuration Exploits

Based on what is learned through pings and port scans, a hacker may have amassed enough information to try a targeted attack. Knowing the open ports on a target, the application, or service on the port, the vendor and the version number of the software on the target system is most of the information the hacker needs to begin an attack. With that information in hand, the attacker can consult his resources (which certainly will include the SANS/FBI vulnerability list among the information) and determine whether he has found a combination of variables that can be exploited.

Once in a while, an attacker finds an unsecured port just by trying to connect with a Telnet application. If the target hasn't made it that easy, he will have to try something else, such as logging in to a user account, trying to find a home directory that will list the files and subdirectories, and so on. The attack can also try to exploit other IIS services such as FTP or NNTP.

Malicious or Hostile Code

One of the most dangerous vulnerabilities your Web site must overcome in the new millennium is the exposure it has to newly devised *malicious* or *hostile* code attacks. Viruses, worms, Trojan Horses, intentionally planted syntax violations in interactive Web pages, and custom attack programs written by a hacker are all examples of malicious code. Over the last couple of years, the Internet has experienced increasingly sophisticated attacks using malicious code with greater and greater frequency.

Malicious code attacks can be both untargeted and targeted. Face it, your Web site is on the Internet, so even if you have no enemies and are not singled out, your site is a potential target to broadcast attacks of malicious code. Malicious code attacks can have any number of objectives, including DoS, Web site graffiti, file deletion, and interception of data. When used to deny service, one of the ways the malicious code can exploit a Web server vulnerability such as a buffer overflow bug is by sending the Web server a URL or a program to process that is known to make it crash. Sometimes, a malicious code attack is just a precursor to another form of attack. For example, a hacker may plant a Trojan Horse on an organization's Web server that helps the hacker crack in to another system that is on the target's internal network.

Malicious code in Web pages is a relatively new vulnerability that will be discussed shortly in the "Scripts and Java Applets" section of this chapter. For now, this discussion will focus on viruses, worms, and Trojan Horses, which have been around for some time.

Viruses, Worms, and Trojan Horses

The differences between viruses, worms, and Trojan Horses can be subtle. They are distinguished by their form and the way that they work. A formal definition of each, from the venerable National Security Agency (NSA) Glossary of Terms, is as follows.

- **Virus**   A program that can "infect" other programs, often hiding in them, by modifying them to include a (possibly evolved) copy of itself. A virus is often used for a variety of malicious actions. A virus requires a host program to spread.

- **Worm**   An independent, self-sufficient program or algorithm that replicates itself from machine to machine across network connections, usually performing malicious actions such as using up the computers resources, clogging networks and information systems as it spreads.

- **Trojan Horse**   An apparently useful and innocent program containing additional hidden code that allows the unauthorized collection, exploitation, falsification, or destruction of data. Unlike a virus or worm, Trojan Horses do not replicate themselves, but their exploits can be just as destructive as that of viruses and worms.

In practice, some malicious code attacks combine the characteristics of each of the categories into a hybrid. So the lines between the types can be blurred and the classic distinctions break down. Nevertheless, for the most part the definitions provide a reasonable method of classification. What makes your system most vulnerable to malicious code is the fact that it can attack in many different ways in varying degrees of disguise and stealth. You won't see it coming. But you must assume it will come.

When malicious code attacks, it will do at least the first, and possibly all, of the following three things.

- *It executes its payload*. Malicious code, in any of its forms, is executable program instructions. Whether a virus, worm, or Trojan Horse, once the program instructions load into system memory they can take command of a computer's resources, to the full capability of the current user's security level for the operating system. Malicious code has been known to include instructions as limited as displaying messages on the screen and as consequential as deleting all the files on the computer's hard disk.

- *It covers its tracks.* In an effort to go undetected, malicious code may perform procedures that remove the signs of its existence. For example, if the code is a virus that infected a disk boot sector, it will be loaded as the OS is booting and may then mask its appearance in listings. Other types of code use a wide variety of stealth techniques.

- *It spreads itself.* Once loaded into a computer's memory, malicious code is able to employ a variety of techniques to infect or penetrate other files, programs, and computers with which it interacts. If the malicious code was originally carried and interjected by e-mail, it may try to use the host computer's e-mail to reach other computers. If the code is a macro virus, it loads as its host document is loaded and can infect all other documents that you create with the same application. In these ways, malicious code can propagate to a growing number of files, programs, and computers.

Virus Particulars   The virus definition is useful, but it's oversimplified. Many different virus types exist, all of which have slightly different *modus operandi*. Viruses usually enter a system with the aid of a person and then spread to the systems of other people with which they interact. For example, boot sector viruses infect files in disk records and are spread from computer to computer as people pass floppy disks back and forth. Macro viruses infect and spread through the exchanged data files of popular application software. E-mail viruses spread in messages that their host's e-mail program sends to other computers. Various other types of viruses hide in Web pages and spread to other Web sites through the browsers that visit them. Hybrids of several of these types also exist.

The increasing sophistication and complexity of viruses has created a difficult problem for security professionals. Perimeter defenses like firewalls do little to stop virus incursions, because unless your organization does not allow e-mail outside to the Internet, the firewall will be programmed to allow it to pass. Virus detection software helps—but only for known viruses, not new ones that the software doesn't recognize.

Viruses are all similar to one another, in that they are programs that give instructions to the computer, and they are written in any number of languages including C, Java, Visual Basic, and Microsoft Office macro languages. Viruses work by inserting themselves into host files that will help them get loaded into the computer's memory. So they may masquerade as a boot sector of a disk or as a system file for the computer's OS; append or prepend themselves to an application program; pose as a macro instruction in a data file or as an attachment in an e-mail; or hide in JavaScript, a Java applet, VB Script, or ActiveX on a Web page. In each case, as the file that hosts them is loaded into memory and executes, the virus program is loaded and executes as well.

Some viruses, called *polymorphic* viruses, mutate and change into a different strain of virus with each infection in a further effort to go undetected and unchecked. No doubt, if history repeats itself, new strains of viruses will invent new attributes. Mutating viruses make it difficult for virus protection software to keep up, because virus scanning software searches through files for *signatures*, which are the key program instructions that characterize the virus. When those signatures change as the virus mutates, the virus is not detected until the software is updated again.

CHALLENGE

Virus Case Study: W32.Simile   This case study was derived from the work of Symantec Corp., (© 2001). The W32.Simile virus infected executable files in folders on all a victim's fixed drives or on any remote drives that were mapped to the victim. The virus did not contain a massively destructive payload, but it infected executable files in a way that caused them to display messages on certain dates.

The virus carried a string *"Metaphor v1 by The Mental Driller/29A."* The string would be displayed on the 17th of March, June, September, and December, whenever an infected executable was run. On the 14th of May on systems with Hebrew character support, the virus would display a message box saying *"Free Palestine!"*

W32.Simile was believed to have been originally distributed through e-mail. Once it infected a computer from an intranet, W32.Simile could be spread to an IIS Web server if the infected computer had a drive mapped to the Web server. W32.Simile could spread to a Web server over the Internet if the infected program was run on the server after being inserted through a buffer overflow.

This virus was polymorphic and used entry-point obfuscation techniques. Specifically, it would insert itself into a seemingly random location and encrypt the message string so as to be difficult to detect. The virus rebuilt itself as it executed to change its signature. This process could both shrink and expand its code to avoid the uncontrolled growth that is common for other metamorphic viruses. The virus contained many other checks to avoid infecting "goat" files (files that are commonly used to capture viruses).

After the rebuild was complete, the virus searched for .exe files in the current folder and then in folders on all fixed and remote drives. Generally it infected other Win32 executable files on the system written in the C language and was more likely to hit OS files than normal applications.

Worm Particulars   A worm is similar to a virus. Sometimes the term is used interchangeably with virus because some viruses have worm-like propagation mechanisms. Technically, a worm is different, however, because it is a self-contained program rather than a program attached to another. In addition, whereas viruses, such as those hiding in e-mail attachments, require a person to open the e-mail before they activate, most worms attack through fully automated procedures. In other words, when they successfully penetrate a system, they fully install and load themselves as part of the attack. Then they automatically spread themselves.

The fully automated properties of worms give them the ability to do a great deal of damage in a short amount of time. The Code Red worm, whose propagation mechanism used a broadcast scan to identify other vulnerable IIS servers, exemplified the havoc a successful worm can cause. Worms can spread exponentially, as one victim passes it to several others, which pass it on to several others. Figure 2-5, from the Cooperative Association for Internet Data Analysis (CAIDA.org), shows how Code Red affected more than 350,000 servers in a 13-hour period as it spread from server to server.

Because a worm is a stand-alone program, it will almost certainly take steps to preserve itself. Hiding is an effective preservation technique. The worm's author will try to make a worm look like any other process running in the system. So the files that the worm adds to the system may be given common sounding names (MS Windows

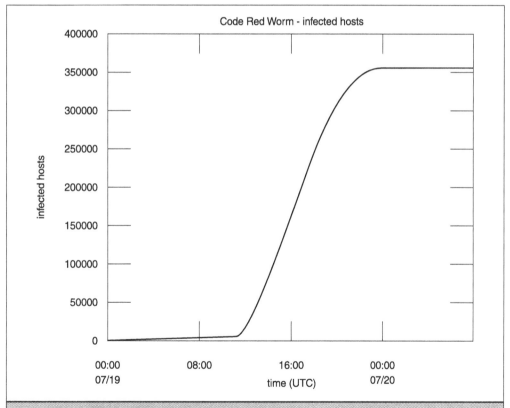

Figure 2-5. The spread of the Code Red worm affected more than 350,000 servers in a 13-hour period.

has scores of files that end in .vxb, .vxd, and so on, for example) or the files may even replace legitimate executable files so that it appears that no new files are on the system. The author may also make it difficult to kill a worm by requiring higher privileges than the user level at which it was installed.

As with viruses, a worm can be polymorphic, changing with each occurrence to stay a step ahead of its pursuers. Toolkits such as the VBS Worm Generator, which is posted on the Internet, make it relatively easy to create mutations of previously released worms. The damage done by a polymorphic worm can be extensive, as is outlined in the following case study.

CHALLENGE

Case Study: The Nimda Worm   This case study was derived from SANS Institute's "Nimda Incident Report," (© 2001). In September 2001 a worm called Nimda attacked Microsoft IIS Web sites, causing DoS incidents on thousands of sites.

Nimda severely compromised the integrity and security of the systems it attacked, providing attackers with full Administrative authority over the victim and access to the entire file system, making numerous modifications to system files and Registry settings.

The worm propagated itself to new victims via four distinct mechanisms:

- The worm scanned the Internet looking for Web servers and attempted to exploit a number of Microsoft Web server vulnerabilities to gain control of a victim, including the "IIS/Personal Web Services (PWS) Extended Unicode Directory Traversal Vulnerability," the "IIS/PWS Escaped Character Decoding Command Execution Vulnerability," and utilization of back doors left behind by the Code Red II (see the next case study) worm. Once in control of a victim IIS/PWS server, the worm used FTP to transfer its code from the attacking machine to the victim.

- The worm gathered e-mail addresses from the Windows Address Book, user's inboxes/outboxes, and local HTML/HTM files and sent itself to all addresses as an attachment named readme.exe.

- If the worm successfully infected a Web server, it used the HTTP service to propagate itself to clients that browsed the Web server's pages. Upon infecting a victim server, the worm created a copy of itself named README.EML and traversed the directory tree searching for Web-related files such as those with .HTML, .HTM, or .ASP extensions. Each time the worm found a Web content file, it appended a piece of JavaScript to the file. The JavaScript forced a download of README.EML to any client that viewed the file via a browser.

- The worm was network aware and propagated via open file shares. It copied itself to all directories, including those found on a network share, for which the user had Write permission. The worm searched the shared drives for executables and attached itself to each executable it found. Any other host that accessed the share and loaded one of the files became infected.

The IIS propagation mechanisms described above require an infected system to scan the Internet in search of vulnerable IIS servers. This worm prefers to target its neighbors in IP. The worm chooses targets having the same first or second octet (that is, an address with the same value in its far right fields such as *xxx.xxx*.654.3210. This behavior can lead to massive amounts of network activity at sites having several infected machines. In particular, Address Resolution Protocol (ARP) flooding effects may be observed, depending on the topology of the target network.

The worm makes numerous changes to the victim's file system, including creating a large number of copies of itself with various names. In some cases, so many worm copies are created that all available disk space is consumed. File names for the worm include Admin.dll, Load.exe, MMC.EXE, readme.exe, Riched20.dll, and MEP*.TMP.EXE.

It should be noted that the behavior of the worm depends on the victim's OS, the file name that the worm is running under, and the command-line options used to invoke the program. When infecting a victim, Nimda creates network shares for each local drive. On Windows 95/98/Me systems, each drive is configured as a full share with no password. On Windows NT/2000 systems, the user Guest is given permission to access all shares and is added to the Administrator's group. The worm removes all share security on Windows NT/2000.

The worm launches up to 200 threads to perform network scanning. This activity can place considerable load on the infected machine as well as the network. ARPs generated by a machine that is scanning, or DNS requests generated by a machine sending Nimda e-mails, can cause problems that manifest as apparent DoS attacks. Further analysis with a disassembler showed that Nimda re-enters its e-mail propagation phase every 10 days.

Trojan Horse Particulars   A Trojan Horse is a program that is placed on a system to be used at a later date. The term, from Greek mythology, is a reference to a gift of a giant horse given the city of Troy that was secretly packed with Greek soldiers, who attacked the city. The analogy is a good one, because a Trojan Horse is generally used as part of a cracking attack to help "open the doors" to a system, or it is installed after a successful crack as a back door that allows the hacker to return.

Trojan Horses can also be installed physically from inside a network (there's that internal threat again) or through the use of an e-mail or Web page that is unwittingly opened by the recipient. Sounds a lot like a virus attacks, doesn't it? You could say that an e-mail or a Web page that introduces a Trojan Horse contains a virus or worm with a specific type of payload (the Trojan program). However, with a virus, the damage is usually done as soon as its program is executed the first time. Trojan Horses, on the other hand, will hang around for a while until the right opportunity for a strike presents itself.

No matter how it is delivered, unless you discover and remove it, the Trojan Horse remains on your system until it removes itself or the hacker decides it's not needed anymore. While it's there, it will be at the hacker's beck and call.

Trojan Horses can be used in many different ways. Some are one-time, destructive programs, set to go off at a specified time. Others are facilitator programs, called *agents*, that assist a hacker in accomplishing other tasks.

One common type of agent is a *sniffer* program that monitors e-mails, network packets, keyboards, computer memory, and other system components for information about its target's environment that will help the hacker accomplish an objective. Another common agent is called a Remote Access Trojan (RAT). A RAT allows the hacker to take over a computer or server and issue commands remotely. Many of the Trojan Horse tools in the hacker community combine elements of both sniffers and RAT features. In fact, some of the tools are essentially toolkits that contain a variety of applets that perform specialized tasks.

It's not uncommon for a Trojan-based attack to use both sniffing and remote control. The role of the sniffer is to discover log-in IDs and passwords. It can monitor and record the keys people type or the packets the computer sends on to the network. The recording mechanism depends on the sniffer program. One mechanism used by sniffers stores the data in a log that the hacker can check. That's where the remote control part of the attack is needed. The RAT would be used as the back door to enter and check the log file. When a back door is not planted, the sniffer may instead send the log to the hacker at an e-mail address. In any case, by inspecting the log, the hacker can find the information he seeks.

A sobering reality of a Trojan attack, when it uses one of the hacker community's tools or toolkits, is that the hacker responsible for a specific attack is not the only person who can use the Trojan after it's loaded on the target computer. The tools are preset to use specific ports. Thus a port scanner can find remote-control Trojan Horses already planted on systems. Anyone who discovers the presence of the Trojan Horse has access to the resources it exposes, even if he or she did not originally put it on that machine.

CHALLENGE

Case Study: Code Red II Worm Analysis Update   This case study was derived from CNET News.com (© 2001). In July 2001, a worm called Code Red attacked and infected thousands of Windows 2000 servers. Several weeks later, in August 2001, a mutation of the original worm called Code Red II used the same mechanism used by the original Code Red worm to infect vulnerable IIS servers that had not patched the unchecked buffer vulnerability in idq.dll or removed ISS ISAPI script mappings.

TIP   You will learn how to fix the unchecked buffer vulnerability in Chapter 3.

Except for using the buffer overflow mechanism to get the worm code executed on a vulnerable IIS server, the Code Red II worm was entirely different from the original Code Red CRv1 and CRv2 variants.

Code Red II had several ominous properties. The most damaging property of this new worm was that the worm created a back door by placing a Trojan Horse called CMD.EXE on an infected server, leaving the system wide open to any attacker.

The worm copies %windir%\CMD.EXE to the following locations:

- c:\inetpub\scripts\root.exe
- c:\progra~1\common~1\system\MSADC\root.exe
- d:\inetpub\scripts\root.exe
- d:\progra~1\common~1\system\MSADC\root.exe

The back door created by CMD.EXE provided a means for a remote attacker to execute arbitrary commands on the compromised server.

In addition, the worm placed a second Trojan Horse on the victim, a modified copy of explorer.exe (the Windows Desktop Manager), which made the C: and D: root directories accessible to a remote attacker when the next user logged into the system—unless the system had been patched against the "Relative Shell Path" vulnerability—because of the way Windows searches for executables by default.

TIP   Chapter 3 will discuss how to remove the "Relative Shell Path" vulnerability.

CHALLENGE (continued)

After the infection-spreading interval, the system was forcibly rebooted. The reboot flushed the memory resident worm and left the back doors and the explorer.exe Trojan in place.

When the worm first arrived on a target and began execution, the worm checked to see whether the host has already been infected, and if so, disabled itself. After the worm created the explorer.exe Trojans, those creation processes went to sleep. But they woke every 10 minutes and looped through their routines again so that even if an administrator noticed the Registry settings that exposed the C: and D: drives and deleted them, the Trojan would reinstate the settings a few minutes later.

The worm selected its targets by automatically scanning systems to determine whether patches had been installed to fix the previously mentioned idq.dll and ISS ISAPI script mappings vulnerabilities that could be exploited with a buffer overflow. After making a successful connection with a target, the worm thread uploaded all the worm code at once, looked for an acknowledgment, and then moved on to find and infect other hosts.

Script and Java Applets

Interactive Web pages that are vulnerable to malicious script and applets are relatively new issues in Web security. The vulnerability relates to the ability of Web servers to use CGI. It also relates to the ability of servers to customize the presentation of their content with server-supplied code (Java or Visual Basic) that is pushed down and executed inside the Web browser. Finally, the category can include JavaScript and VBscript that is embedded in a Web server's HTML pages.

Malicious code that comes from Web servers has possibly even more destructive potential than viruses and worms, particularly if it's Java code, because on the client side much of the code is platform independent and will affect Windows, UNIX, Mac, Palm devices, or any other computer that runs a Java-compatible browser. All a browser has to do to execute some applets or JavaScript is visit the host page for the applet.

Cross Site Scripting   CSS is manifested in interactive Web pages. This category of vulnerability allows malicious code to be inserted into an interactive Web page in a way that causes a Web browser that is reading that page to execute the code. The result is that the malicious program has the ability to do anything on the computer that is allowed by the current user and his or her current set of privileges, including reading information, deleting files, sending e-mails, or performing any of the other damage ascribed to malicious code throughout this chapter.

The following case study from the SANS archives gives an example of a real-world CSS attack, which in this case was not vicious but could well have been.

CHALLENGE

Case Study: The Zkey Exploit   This case study is derived from a SANS article by David Rothermel (August, 2000). In August 2000, a hacker completed an exploit of a dot-com information storage portal called Zkey by using malicious JavaScript code to capture user names and passwords of Zkey e-mail users. This exploit is an example of a CSS attack.

The exploit began when malicious JavaScript code was embedded in an e-mail and sent from a Zkey account used by the hacker to another Zkey user's e-mail account. It tricked Zkey users into logging in, whereupon they revealed their account names and passwords.

The e-mail that carried the malicious code was in HTML format, and the code was embedded inside a `<textarea>` tag. Overlaying the message was a transparent GIF that used an `onMouseOver` command to trigger the embedded code.

The code used a spoofed approach to capture account names and passwords by displaying a log-in box with a message indicating "You timed out of your session, please re-login." When the user provided his or her user name/password, the data was forwarded to a database on the hacker's server instead of the Zkey server. To maintain the appearance of normality, the code sent the user back to the Zkey server and logged him or her in to continue the session.

The potential for damage was immense. By gaining full control of an account, the hacker gained the ability to

- Download files from the victim's Zkey z-drive
- Delete/replace files from the z-drive
- Access/alter the victim's contact information
- Access/alter the victim's calendar/scheduling information
- Change the victim's user name/password, locking the user our of his or her account
- Access any shared z-drives from secondary accounts
- Read/delete the victim's Zkey e-mail or send Zkey e-mail in the victim's name
- Access e-mail from any secondary e-mail accounts configured for mail checking

After publicity, the hacker embarrassed Zkey by going public with the vulnerability. He bragged that even though the site used SSL and the e-mail service had filters in place to strip out malicious code from the body of e-mail messages, both security measures were defeated.

Distributed Denial of Service

DoS vulnerabilities have existed in computer systems since their invention. Through a physical exploit such as knocking out power, or through any number of intrusive exploits, hackers have been able to deny service to vulnerable systems. The attackers have come from both the inside and the external side to the system.

External DoS attacks use the Internet to deny service to a site. For example, in one known exploit, called a *Smurf* attack (named for the automated tool used to launch it), the hacker sends a large amount of ICMP ping traffic at IP broadcast addresses. It works because most Internet facing routers and hosts will reply to the ping with a broadcast ECHO reply. Thus the hosts saturate the Net and its systems with exponentially increasing volumes of packets.

In the last couple of years, a new DoS vulnerability has surfaced. Through a method called a *Distributed Denial of Service (DDoS)* attack, a large number of network systems can be focused on a target to overwhelm and cripple a Web site. The DDoS attack had been a theoretical exploit for a long time. But over a two-day period on February 7 and 8, 2000, the sites of Yahoo!, Amazon, eBay, Buy.com, CNN, E*TRADE, and ZDNet were successfully attacked and the DDoS attack hit the headlines.

Like malicious code attacks, DDoS attacks fall into the category of exploit that is difficult to defend against, because DDoS attackers don't need to penetrate a network to succeed. These attacks have the potential to frustrate security people for a long time to come.

DDoS Attack Strategies

Known DDoS attacks fall into either the flood attack or malformed packet attack category. Flood attacks hit Web sites by exploiting the TCP protocols to overwhelm the routers and servers that support the site. The effect is that there is no more bandwidth to serve legitimate users who try to visit the site.

Malformed packet attacks try take out vulnerable servers that do not appropriately handle error conditions. Through means such as sending packets that are larger than the allowed maximum IP packet size, or sending packets with the same source and destination IP address, the attacks can confuse or crash systems with these vulnerabilities.

To create the greatest chance of success, a DDoS attack plan will usually involve a number of systems that cooperate to besiege the target jointly. Sometimes the plan involves a team of hackers. Each system in such an attack has an assigned role. One attack model, shown in Figure 2-6, employs systems playing two different roles to gang up on an unfortunate victim.

In this attack model, the lead attacker commands handlers and the handlers control a troop of agents to generate network traffic. When the hacker has to enlist his helpers involuntarily, he must use the various scanning and infiltration techniques discussed earlier to take control of the systems he wants to use and then install the tools he will use for the attack.

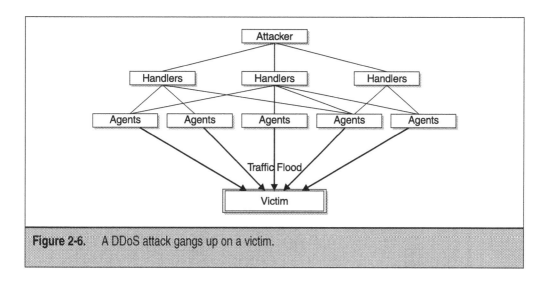

Figure 2-6.   A DDoS attack gangs up on a victim.

Defending Against DDoS

The defenses against DDoS attacks require just as much coordination across a number of different systems as the assault. For example, organizations that connect to the Internet should use firewalls and configure those firewalls to recognize ICMP storms and respond accordingly. Your ISP is the entity that can do the most to manage the problem.

However, there are other things that you can do as well. For starters, make sure you don't have any DDoS attack tools planted on your system. Also, make sure you have applied the Microsoft Service Packs and patches that correct the vulnerabilities in the SANS/FBI Top 20 Vulnerabilities List. This can help you avoid becoming one of an attacker's involuntary DDoS attack agents.

CHECKLIST OF KNOWN VULNERABILITIES

- ☐ Default installs of operating systems and applications
- ☐ Accounts with weak or nonexistent passwords
- ☐ Large number of open ports
- ☐ Lack of address filtering
- ☐ Bad or no logging
- ☐ CGI program holes
- ☐ Malicious or hostile code

☐ Web server folder traversal

☐ Buffer overflows

☐ NetBIOS and Null session log-ins to SMB shares

☐ Weak password hashing in SAM

☐ Microsoft Remote Networking and Data Services

CHAPTER 3

Preparing and Hardening Your Web Server

Installing Microsoft IIS is a straightforward process, and it's almost automatic using the Microsoft installer. However, you shouldn't simply install Microsoft IIS and assume that it is ready for prime time on the Internet. You need to perform a number of tasks to make sure your server is secure before you put it into production. This chapter will walk you through a set of installation and configuration procedures that will help you eliminate potential security problems. Even if you have already finished the installation, you can follow these security procedures to correct your configuration.

PLAN AHEAD

Like any project, your secure Web server installation and configuration should be planned carefully ahead of time. It may help you to think of a secure installation in a series of stages:

- *Identify and assemble required installation prerequisites.* Plan, acquire, and schedule the hardware, software, personnel, support, time, and other resources that will be needed to complete the installation successfully. You need, for example, the computer that will be your Web server and a secure location in which to place the server. You need the appropriate Microsoft software packages and licenses, the networking hardware that will eventually connect the server to the network, and enough time to properly configure it all. The amount of time this takes will depend on your experience. Give yourself a couple of days if this is the first time you are attempting a Web server installation—don't try to do it in a rush.

- *Install and configure components.* Perform the installation. With Microsoft IIS, you can install from a CD-ROM directly on the server, install over the network from a server with the binaries on its disks, or install using a combination of the two. For maximum security, you can install a custom configuration rather than the default, so that you can choose the components you want installed (or not installed). This chapter will walk you through the choices and explain the tradeoffs.

- *Harden the system.* Hardening is the process of fixing vulnerabilities to minimize the possibility of falling victim to a hacker. Hardening generally entails locking down or removing everything in an operating system that you don't need to run your desired service configuration and ensuring that you have configured the appropriate sets of policies, rights, and permissions.

- *Enable audit and recovery capabilities.* Secure computing systems such as Microsoft Windows 2000 and IIS are packaged with a set of system and activity logs that record events and activities. These logs must be properly configured to be used as one of the tools to help identify and diagnose security breaches and provide a way to reverse any damage from a breach.

A verification process should always follow these stages of installation and configuration. Testing procedures are explained in Chapter 7.

SECURE INSTALLATION REQUIREMENTS

Each organization has its own set of needs. Some organizations use a Web server on an intranet for distribution of public information where security is not a primary concern. Others need security even on their intranet because their site is used to manage human resource information and employee benefits. Still others put their site on the Internet for marketing purposes, e-commerce activities, and product support. Each of these scenarios has its own configuration and security requirements.

 SECURITY ALERT   The machine on which you are installing IIS should never be connected to the Internet until you have completely finished installation and verified that the server is secure. For now, this discussion will assume that your server is on a secure intranet (not on the Internet) or is not connected to a network as you begin the install.

General Recommendations

Many of us like to skip the planning steps and dive right in. But keep in mind that it takes only one mistake or omission to leave a large security hole. Working from a checklist will help you reduce the likelihood of error. To get you started, here's a list of recommendations that should be followed for every secure Web server install.

- *Provide a physically secure location for your server.* Many technical security measures are pointless if they can be compromised by someone who has physical access to the server console.

- *If you can, make the Web server a single function server.* In other words, try not to put the Web server on a computer that is also a file server or some other critical part of your operation. The more functions you configure on a server, the greater the likelihood that a configuration error or combination of software components will introduce a security vulnerability. Higher complexity equates to higher risk in a security situation. The most secure configuration you can have is a single-purpose system.

- *Do not, under any circumstances, make a computer running Microsoft IIS a Windows network domain controller.* A Windows domain controller manages the account security for your entire Windows networking domain. Any Web server vulnerability that could be exploited to gain control of the Web server would also give a hacker control of the domain controller and thus compromise your entire network.

- *Use two network interface cards if your Web server will be put on the Internet.* One card will face the public Internet, and the other card will face your intranet or a trusted network of some kind. You will use the interface on the trusted network to manage your server and let Internet traffic access the computer through the other interface. Through the interface on the trusted network you can even perform many site maintenance tasks while the site is in live operation. Never try to manage a live server through the same interface used by the Internet traffic.

- *If your Web server will be on the Internet, plan to isolate it from your intranet.* Do not include the Web server in a workgroup or trusted domain. Do not enable routing between the two interfaces on the server. Use a router and/or firewall to filter traffic between the Web server and intranet (this is covered in detail in Chapter 6).

- *Install multiple drives or drive partitions on your Web server so you can put the Web folders on a drive other than the system drive.* This will reduce the chances that an attack can be mounted on the server through the file directories, such as the Unicode vulnerability explained in Chapter 2, that can traverse beyond the Web content root. Additionally, should a traversal attack of some other kind succeed, this will reduce the likelihood that the attack can move across all the other drives. It's usually a good idea to install more drives or create more partitions than you think you need, because situations eventually appear for which a separate drive comes in handy.

- *Use NTFS on all IIS hard drives.* Windows 2000 drives with NTFS have a robust set of file permissions. The FAT 32 and FAT 16 file systems do not have the same security capabilities and should not be used on a critical system—especially one that is on the Internet.

- *Do not install application software or development tools on the Web server.* Developer tools usually have sophisticated data management capabilities and high levels of privilege on a system. If an attacker is able to penetrate the system and launch the developer tools, he may acquire the power to do significant damage. Do your Web page development and testing on a different machine and transfer the finished content to the production Web server.

- *Do not install a printer on the IIS machine.* Print buffer overflows (and lots of other buffer overflows, too) are classic vulnerabilities. They are popular with attackers because they frequently allow the hacker to gain Administrator level control. Since a printer at your server location doesn't really benefit an Internet user at his or her location, you shouldn't have any need for a printer. So don't take the risk.

- *Create a list of people who will be granted system-level access to your server for tasks such as updating site content and backing up data.* Also decide who else will have the responsibility and authority to create and manage user accounts on the server. Don't plan on giving anyone any more authority than necessary. Not everyone needs to have Administrator privileges to accomplish tasks.

Component Installation

Microsoft IIS is integrated into Windows 2000. The installer is a highly automated program that jointly installs both the Windows 2000 operating system and IIS. The installation program is a wonderful convenience tool for streamlining the installation process, but it cannot be all things to all people. You should not assume it will accommodate your security requirements in its default configuration. You must manage the installation according to your own needs and plan.

Keep It Simple

A secure Web site should be set up in a minimized configuration. The security principle behind this rule is that any services beyond the minimum represent a potential vulnerability or future point of attack. So as you install your system, choose to install a *custom* configuration, and then install only the basic set of components that make it perform the functions you need.

Services Component Selection

The following illustration shows the Windows Components Wizard, where you can select components. If your system is already installed and you want to add or remove components, you can access this wizard through the Add/Remove Software Wizard from the Windows 2000 Control Panel folder.

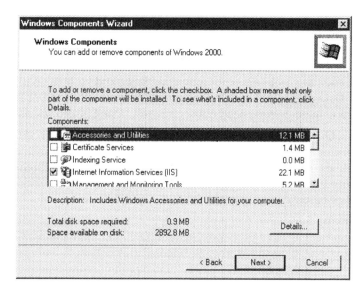

Here is a full list of components and their functions:

- **Accessories and Utilities**   Contains all the standard Windows games, accessories, and utilities such as a calculator, phone dialing program, paint program, CD music player, and so on. These components are not required for a Web server.

- **Certificate Services**   A certificate server, which is used by a certificate authority to issue certificates for use with public key security applications and services such as Secure Socket Layer (SSL) encryption. Your organization might want to use SSL and might want to have a certificate authority for that and other purposes, but this should *not* be installed on your Web server. The certificate server should be a secured, stand-alone system because it is the machine that vouches for the trust of other servers. Certificate services will be covered in detail in Chapter 8.

- **Indexing Service**   Indexing is a method for cataloging stored data. Indexing Service provides an engine that can be used to provide search capabilities on a Web site. Indexing should be done only on a Windows 2000 NTFS (NT file system) disk so that it will inherit the security of NTFS permissions. A database server probably needs indexing services to improve performance. A Web server probably does not need them.

- **Internet Information Services**   A family of services related to managing a Web site and publishing or connecting to other information services on the Internet, such as Web, FTP, news, e-mail, and so on. Naturally, you're going to choose this for the IIS Web server. You might not need the other services, or if you do, you might consider putting them on a different server to improve security.

- **Management and Monitoring Tools**   Tools for monitoring and improving network performance. The Simple Network Management Protocol (SNMP), which is used to send information from a Microsoft server to an SNMP management console such as Tivoli (a tool for managing large and complex networks), is *not* secure. Using SNMP is not recommended on your Web server unless some compelling management need makes it worth taking a security risk.

- **Message Queuing Services**   A message engine that can be used by applications that communicate asynchronously with client and server components or other applications. Are you building a custom Web application on top of IIS? If so, you might need this. But if it's installed, it introduces a potential vulnerability to a message-based attack. Don't install it if you don't need it.

- **Networking Services**   Contains a variety of network-related services and protocols such as Domain Name System (DNS), Dynamic Host Configuration Protocol (DHCP), and Internet Services Proxy. These are all potentially valuable components on your network, but they should be run on one of the network's other servers and not the Web server.

- **Other Network File and Print Services**   Services that will allow Windows 2000 to share files and printers with other, non–Windows computers. You don't need these services on a Web server because the Web protocols (HTML and HTTP) already work on non–Windows systems.

- **Remote Installation Services**   Offers the ability to remotely install Windows 2000 Professional on client computers with remote boot capability. Again, this could be a valuable service if you are managing a large and geographically diverse network. But in that case, you are sure to have plenty of other servers on which you could install this service. Don't put this on your Web server.

- **Remote Storage**   Enables a Windows 2000 server to migrate files to another disk or other media such as tape if the files are used infrequently. It's used on file servers where people frequently place files and space becomes a problem, because remote storage will free space when it moves the files to the remote storage media. Your Web server is used for a completely different purpose. You place and manage its content, and it's unlikely that your Web server needs this.

- **Script Debugger**   This tool helps you diagnose problems with the scripts you write on your server. Use it on a development system but do *not* put it on your production Web server.

- **Terminal Services**   Provides a terminal environment, allowing a Windows 2000 server to host multiple-user clients of Windows applications. In a distributed network environment, Terminal Services can also be used for remote management. However, there is risk associated with running the service because it opens up another port. You will learn how to use it securely in Chapter 6 for remote management, but you should disable it in your initial installation if you don't already know how to configure it.

TIP   Don't select the component for Terminal Services Licensing, because the licenses are for use of Windows 2000 as a remote application server. The only reason you should run Terminal Services on your Web server is for remote management, and you do not need the Terminal Services Licensing to do remote management.

- **Windows Media Services**   Enables you to stream multimedia content over the network. Content can be delivered either live or prerecorded, and either multicast or unicast. If you use this, you should be aware that some known vulnerabilities exist for which you should acquire Microsoft's security patch. The topic will be covered in Chapter 10.

IIS Components

In addition to the basic operating system (OS) features, network protocols, and the Client for Microsoft Networks, the only service that is absolutely necessary to run a functioning Web server is Internet Information Services (IIS). IIS has a number of components within its family of services. As you continue with the Microsoft installer, if you click the Details button in the wizard dialog box while Internet Information Services is selected, you will see a new dialog box, shown next, with all of the IIS services.

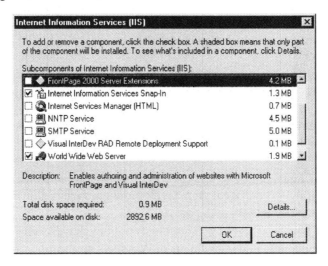

Here are the IIS components:

- **Common Files**   Common, shared files used by a number of IIS components
- **Documentation**   IIS documentation and help topics
- **File Transfer Protocol (FTP) Server**   A service that provides support for FTP file transfers on your Web server
- **FrontPage 2000 Server Extensions**   Allows the Web to be dynamically managed and updated with Microsoft's FrontPage Web authoring tool.
- **Internet Information Services Snap-in**   A Web management component for the Windows 2000 Microsoft Management Console (MMC)
- **Internet Services Manager (HTML)**   A browser-based administrative interface for managing your Web server from a remote location
- **NNTP Service**   Internet News server
- **SMTP Service**   Simple Mail Transfer Protocol for providing the network with Internet e-mail connections
- **Visual InterDev RAD Remote Deployment Support**   Used to deploy applications from a remote location
- **World Wide Web Server**   A service providing HTTP support for HTML browser access

When you select World Wide Web Server, the installer will also select Internet Information Services Snap-in and Common Files because the Web server has a dependency on those resources. But that is all you need for a basic Web server. Security for some of the other services within the IIS family, such as FTP services, will be discussed in Chapter 10, but the discussion for now will be concerned with the basic World Wide Web server.

Network Components

The Microsoft installer will ask you to set up a computer name and will then ask whether the computer will be on a network. If your Web server will be on the Internet, choose Is On A Network Without A Domain, because you should keep the Web server separate from your intranet. You can put in whatever workgroup name you want.

As the installation wizard continues, or immediately after it runs if you miss the opportunity, you will be configuring your network interfaces for the network services your Web server will use. The dialog box for setting network connection configuration is shown in Figure 3-1. The same dialog box can be reached by selecting Network Dialup and Connections under Settings in the Windows Start Menu at any time after you finish the install process.

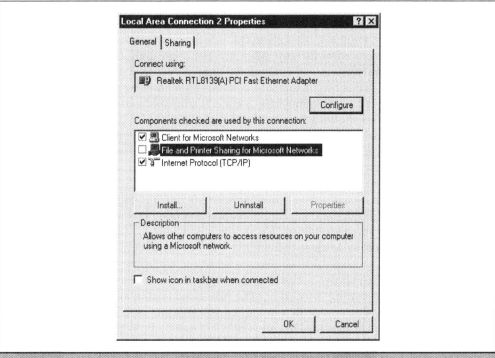

Figure 3-1. Use the Connection Properties dialog box to select the network services you'll use.

TIP If your network settings have already been configured and you want to change them to match these recommendations, you can change the computer name and Windows domain settings through the Properties dialog box settings for the My Computer icon and change the TCP/IP setting through the Properties dialog box for the My Network Places icon.

The only services you need to run IIS over a network interface are Client For Microsoft Networks and the Internet Protocol (TCP/IP), so check marks should appear next to those items. Turn off all other protocols and services, such as File And Printer Sharing For Microsoft Networks, unless there is a compelling need to run them on an intranet Web server. Do *not* share the Internet connection and never use file sharing on the Internet.

Next you need to configure the server's TCP/IP stack. You will need to provide the IP network addresses your server will be using. Even on your intranet, although Windows 2000 has a DHCP client, you should use a fixed IP address for your Web server. It's partly a matter of reliability (if something ever goes wrong with your internal DNS or WINS configuration, you can still access the server by its fixed address), and some of the networking and security features of Windows 2000 Server require it. Make sure you use an address that is in the appropriate subnet for the trusted network from which you will be performing Web site administration.

Select Internet Protocol (TCP/IP) and click the Properties button to see the Properties dialog box shown in Figure 3-2. Then add the appropriate address and subnet mask information, assuming you have been given this information by your Internet service provider (ISP) or network administrator. Microsoft has some good tutorial information on its Technet Web site (www.microsoft.com/technet) if you need a primer on the topic.

For a Web server that is on the Internet, assuming you followed the advice to use two network interface cards, you must use a fixed IP address on the interface that faces the Internet. Figure 3-3 shows a two-card configuration for an Internet Web server configured for hypothetical intranet and Internet subnets. An Internet Web server is most secure with two network interfaces. As you configure the addresses, take care to ensure that you have selected the proper interface card for the address you are configuring, by watching the name at the top of the dialog box shown in Figure 3-1.

You must perform several other procedures on the Internet-facing card to secure the configuration. Through the Connection Properties dialog box for this card (the Internet-facing card), shown in Figure 3-1, remove the Client for Microsoft Networks, because the instance of it you already installed for your intranet interface is sufficient to allow IIS to run.

You should also turn off the NetBIOS protocol for the Internet interface (the protocol Microsoft uses for file sharing) by clicking the Advanced button at the bottom of the TCP/IP Properties dialog box shown in Figure 3-2, and then selecting the WINS tab and selecting the radio button for Disable NetBIOS Over TCP, as shown in Figure 3-4. NetBIOS, which uses ports 137 and 139, is used by Windows networking on an intranet for WINS name resolution and services such as file and printer sharing. Activity on those ports is one of the first things that a hacker usually checks for as he scans a system. If the hacker finds that a host is listening on those ports, he will probably guess that the host is running a Microsoft OS.

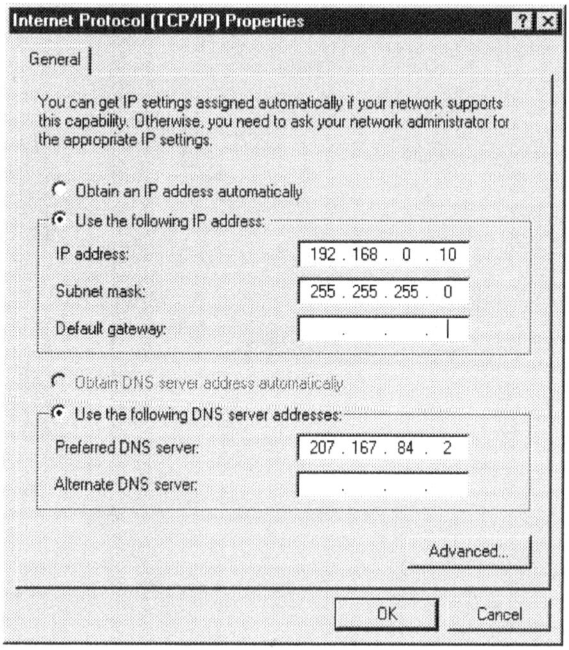

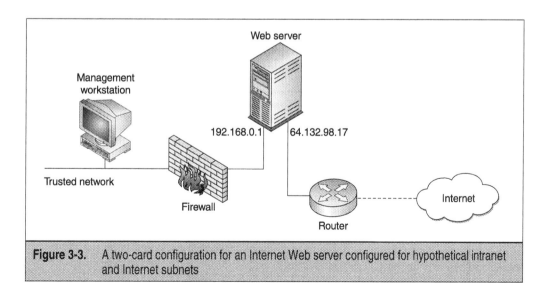

Figure 3-2. Use the Internet Protocol TCP/IP Properties dialog box to set your address and subnet mask information.

Figure 3-3. A two-card configuration for an Internet Web server configured for hypothetical intranet and Internet subnets

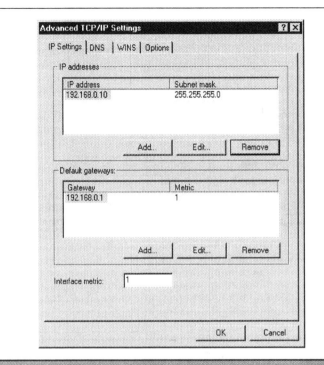

Figure 3-4.   Use the Advanced TCP/IP Settings dialog box to set additional configurations.

Service Packs and Security Patches

Immediately after the Windows 2000 installer finishes its work, you should install all the Microsoft service packs and security rollup packages. These service packs and patches are critical! They contain the fixes for newly discovered vulnerabilities. You must install them before you expose a Web site to the public Internet or even to your intranet.

TIP   You can download the service packs from www.microsoft.com/technet/ or from http://vx.windowsupdate.microsoft.com and install from another network server or from CDs that you order.

Hot fixes and *security rollup packages* are the mechanisms Microsoft uses to address security issues between releases of the service packs. Hot fixes, which Microsoft posts frequently on the Web, are patches that address specific security issues for specific configurations. Security patches are rollups of all the individual Microsoft hot fix releases. These are also available on the Microsoft Technet Web site. Therefore, you should always check the Web site at www.microsoft.com/technet/security for the latest patches whenever you install a service pack. The site also lets you sign up to receive future security bulletins and automatic notification of new hot fixes. These notifications can be important to your network's security, and you should apply a new security hot fix every time one is released.

While on the Microsoft Web site, you should also visit the Recommended Updates link to check for any patches or updates that are relevant to your configuration that Microsoft did not include in the latest service pack release or did not package as a security patch or hot fix. For example, for quite a long time, the Windows 2000 High Encryption Pack was not part of any current service pack or security patch. If you wanted 128-bit encryption strength when you used SSL encryption, you needed to have this patch installed. The High Encryption Pack has now been rolled into Windows 2000 Service Pack 2.

HARDENING THE SYSTEM

The service packs and patches will certainly eliminate some of the obvious opportunities that anyone might have to hack into your site. However, it would be unwise for you to assume that the patches alone will be enough to keep your system out of harm's way. The world does not stand still. These updates are reactive fixes for holes that have already been discovered. You can be sure that plenty of people are burrowing away on patched systems trying to find new vulnerabilities and holes. Therefore, when preparing your server, you should take additional measures to minimize the likelihood of becoming someone's victim.

All systems should be *hardened* before being deployed in a production environment. Hardening is a process that, in addition to applying service packs and security patches to fix known vulnerabilities, removes unused features of the operating system and its services to limit the possibility of a new vulnerability being found in a feature you are not even using. During the hardening process, if you follow best practice security procedures, you should also be able to make sure your Microsoft configuration is as secure as possible.

Is it possible to eliminate completely all the potential problems? Probably not, as there are too many variables, but that is not the point. Your goal is to make the system so difficult to crack that the cost and effort of trying is greater than the hacker's potential gain.

Hardening Tools

A commonly accepted best practice when you are hardening a system is to restrict all operating system functions, services, accounts, and access rights to attain the maximum level of security that still allows the system to run effectively. The settings required to achieve that goal will vary depending on the application that is running and an interpretation by administrators and users as to what it means to "run effectively." For example, some organizations make it a policy to log every event that happens on a server. While this is a good security goal that is feasible in a high-security/low-traffic situation, doing this could significantly hinder performance on a high-volume Web site. In the end, a balance must be found between the level of security and system usability.

Name	Location
HisecwebSecurity Template (Hisecweb.inf)	support.microsoft.com/support/misc/kblookup.asp?id=Q316347
IIS Lockdown Tool	www.Microsoft.com/technet/security/
IIS 5.0 Baseline Security Checklist	www.Microsoft.com/technet/security/
Secure Internet Information Services 5 Checklist	www.microsoft.com/technet/security/
NSA Guide to the Secure Configuration and Administration of Microsoft Internet Information Services 5.0	http://nsa2.www.conxion.com/win2k/download.htm

Table 3-1.   Useful Hardening Tools

Microsoft has made its recommendations for that balance in a set of tools and configuration guidelines for IIS that are available on its Technet Web site. The United States National Security Agency (NSA) has also created an exhaustive hardening guide that contains its recommendations. The respective tools can be found at the Web locations shown in Table 3-1 above.

Hardening Procedure Overview

After you've downloaded the tools you're ready to go. The NSA guidelines and the Microsoft checklist give you topic-oriented guidelines organized by the menus you use to perform tasks.

Following the menu-driven guides requires a certain amount of blind faith on your part because they lack context. They tell you all the settings to change on a particular screen regardless of where you are in your own working process. You end up just doing what you're told as you jump from menu to menu, and your not sure why you're doing things. The following discussion will follow a process-organized task flow. That way you can jump from heading to heading if your own task flow follows a different order without losing the context of why you are doing things.

This discussion includes some recommendations not included on the Microsoft and NSA lists; these recommendations come from information culled from various sources in the security industry. What follows is a blending of the best ideas, organized by process, that should be performed before putting a Web server online.

The following operations will be covered:

- Stopping or disabling all nonessential Windows 2000 services.

- Modifying the default IIS server environment to prepare for eventual Web deployment. This includes changing the default Web server directory and disabling or removing all unnecessary system contents such as sample code, command utilities, script mappings, and so on.

• Changing miscellaneous Windows 2000 settings to mitigate a number of known and theoretical security vulnerabilities.

Using the Microsoft IIS Lockdown Tool

The IIS Lockdown tool, or IIS Lock, is a Microsoft utility that will automate the configuration of security settings on your Web server. It has a set of screens that allow you to make selections to describe your intended Web server configuration. At the end of the process, it will produce a Windows 2000/IIS policy template and deploy the template policy settings on your server.

The tool is a great time saver. Here you'll learn how to use it, but this discussion will not take the configuration it generates for granted. You'll also walk through the procedures for performing everything in IIS manually, because with an automated tool, there's no guarantee that you'll automatically get the optimal settings for your specific needs. Sometimes you can fine tune to improve on it.

Here are the general procedures to use the IIS Lockdown tool:

1. Start the tool to start the wizard, and choose the configuration that most closely matches your plan, as shown in the following illustration. Check View Template Settings in the lower part of the window so you will see all the options as you proceed through the wizard. Click Next to open the Internet Services screen.

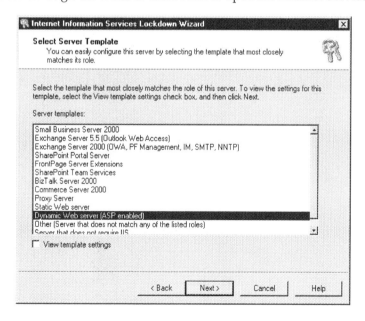

2. On the Internet Services screen (not pictured), select the services you want to enable or disable (those you would want to disable are probably already grayed out if you followed the advice in the "Component Installation" section). Naturally, the HTTP Service option must be selected. In the lower-left corner, you can choose the Remove Unselected Services button, which will perform exactly what it says if you choose to have the services removed at this time. Then click Next.

3. The Script Maps screen, shown in the following illustration, will ask you to choose from a list of mappings to disable. Look ahead to the section "Remove Unnecessary Application Mappings" if you don't know what each of these means and aren't sure what to do here. Click Next after you've made your deletions.

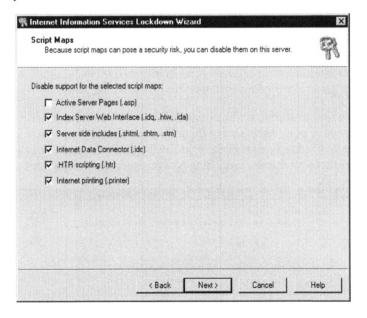

TIP In this example, we have chosen to install a server that will contain Active Server Pages, so we are not removing those mappings.

4. The Additional Security page, shown in the following illustration, requires that you make a couple of miscellaneous selections for removing virtual directories and sample scripts. It also lets you set some file permissions on the anonymous guest account. Finally, you can disable the feature that allows Web content authoring to be done remotely (definitely something you shouldn't do on a production server). You will learn about securing the Internet Guest account

in Chapter 4 and the settings you specify now may become irrelevant—but go ahead and check all the boxes on this screen and click Next.

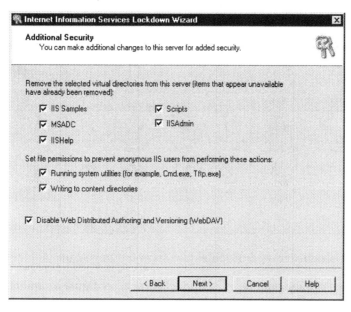

5. A final configuration wizard page will ask if you want to install URL scan (not pictured). Don't do this now unless you already know how to use it. It will be covered in Chapter 7. Uncheck the box next to the option labeled Install URL Scan? and then click Next.

6. You have one last chance to look over the settings to make sure they are the ones you want. Then click Next and you'll see an Applying Security Settings page, where you can view a report of your choices. Finally, click Next to implement them and then click Finish to save your changes and exit the Wizard.

Manual Hardening Procedures

Now it's time to harden your system. As you proceed, you may find that some settings recommended in the remaining part of this chapter have already been implemented by the IIS Lock tool. But you may also find that you want to modify some of the settings because of the new information that you learn here. In any case, it would be a mistake to assume that you are done just because you ran IIS Lock.

To configure manual settings you will use a variety of tools with the Microsoft Management Console (MMC). The MMC is the primary platform management application for Windows 2000 and IIS and is installed, along with a number of default snap-ins, by the Microsoft Installer (you don't get a choice) when you install Windows 2000 and IIS. The MMC modules and default MMC snap-ins are available under

Administrative Tools under the Windows Start Menu. You can also access all the MMC modules and snap-ins through the My Computer icon on the Windows 2000 desktop, where you'll find a group of icons in the Administrative Tools folder in the Control Panel, as shown here:

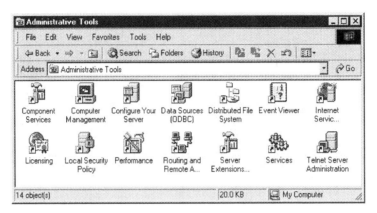

The default security related modules and snap-ins consist of:

- **Computer Management**   Used to create and configure accounts, groups, storage resources, and removable media and to monitor system information

- **Event Viewer**   Used to monitor system, event, and security logs

- **Internet Services Manager**   Used to configure IIS security settings

- **Local Security Policy**   Used to configure Windows 2000 security settings

- **Services**   Used to manage services running on the server

Disable Nonessential Services

The Microsoft Windows 2000 installer, as it loads many of the services you selected for installation, sets those services to start automatically whenever the system boots. Some of the services that are set this way are critical to IIS and some are not. Only the essential services should be set to start automatically.

Services are managed through the Services snap-in to the MMC, which is launched by choosing Start | Programs | Administrative Tools | Services.

The Services management console, like that shown in the following illustration, presents a list of all the services that are installed on your system, a description of each one, the status of each, the startup setting, and the user level under which the service is logged on. You will use this console to stop and disable the services that you don't need.

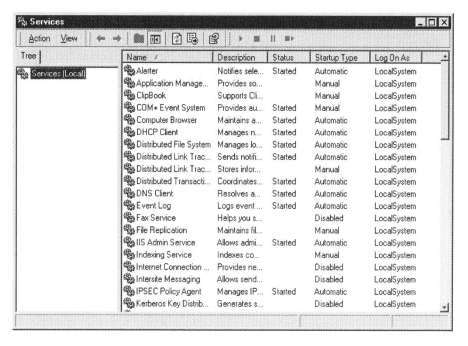

Table 3-2 shows a list of the services that are installed even if you follow our recommendations for a minimized Internet Information Services installation. New services will be added to the list, or some of the disabled services may need to be activated if you install additional components (that is, if you install more than the basic WWW services for IIS).

To function properly, your IIS Web server does not need any of the services listed in the table's left column, and you should disable them on a production Web server. (You probably don't want to disable them on a test, development, or standard Windows file server, however.) As you disable those services you should also change their Startup setting to Manual so that the next time you reboot the server, they do not automatically start. The only services you really need are the ones listed in the table's right column.

To disable any of the services, using the MMC Services console depicted in the previous illustration, follow these procedures:

1. Right-click the service you want to disable and select Properties from the pop-up menu. This will open the service's Properties window, shown in Figure 3-5 for the Alerter service.

2. Click the Stop button and the service will be disabled.

3. In the middle of the window, in the Startup Type drop-down menu, click the arrow button and select Manual from the list of choices. Then click OK.

Nonessential Windows2000 Services	Essential Services for IIS
Alerter	COM+ Event System
ClipBook Server	Event Log
Computer Browser	IIS Admin Service
DHCP Client	IPSEC Policy Agent
Distributed File System	Logical Disk Manager
Distributed Link Tracking (Client and Server)	Network Connections
Distributed Transaction Coordinator	Performance Logs and Alerts
DNS Client	Plug and Play
FTP Publishing Service (unless users require FTP services)	Protected Storage
Licensing Logging Service	Remote Procedure Call (RPC)
Logical Disk Manager Administrator Service	Remote Registry Service
Messenger	Security Accounts Manager
Net Logon *	System Event Notification
Network DDE	Uninterruptible Power Supply
Network DDE DSDM	Windows Management Instrumentation (WMI)
Print Spooler	WMI Driver Extensions
Removable Storage	World Wide Web Publishing Service
Remote Access Connection Manager	
Routing and Remote Access	
RPC Locator (required if user is doing remote administration)	
RunAS Service	
Server Service (unless server will run the SMTP or NNTP)	
Task Scheduler	
TCP/IP NetBIOS Helper	
Telephony	
Telnet	
Windows Installer	
Windows Time	
Workstation *	

* Services required if running as part of a Windows domain (for an intranet)

Table 3-2. Essential Versus Nonessential Services

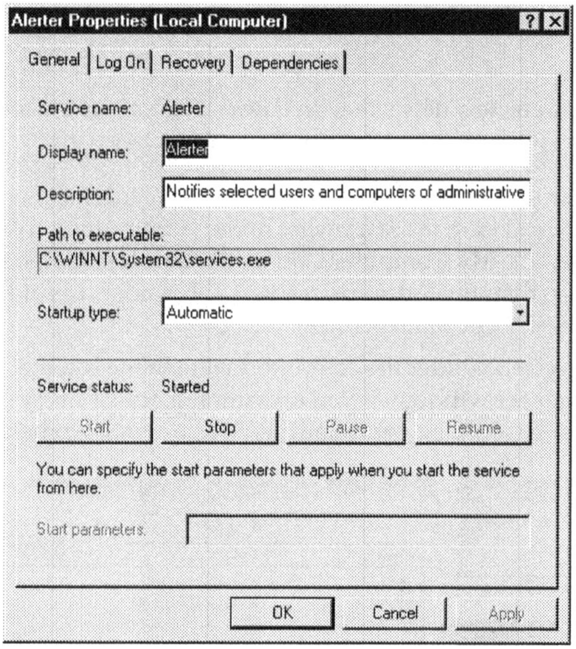

Figure 3-5. Use the Service Properties Window to disable services.

Modify the Default IIS Server Environment

A number of settings in the default Windows 2000 configuration, from a security point of view, are not recommended for a Web server. The following discussion will show you how to change those settings.

Create a New Site and Root Directory for Web Content   To guard against the directory traversal type of attack described in the vulnerabilities list in Chapter 2, a recommended security best practice is to put the root directory of your Web site's content on a disk or logical partition different from the disk that contains the server's operating system. If you run more than one Web site on the server, use a different disk or partition for each Web site if it's practical.

IIS configures a default Web site when it's installed. Some experts recommend that, even if you run only a single Web site on the server, you should create a new site with a different name to run as the active Web site (that is, don't use the default site) and use a new location for the site's root directory. This is good practice. The security advantage to changing the default Web site is that if an automated exploit is written to attack the default site, you may be able to thwart the attack if the default site is inactive.

TIP You should leave the default setting there as a decoy, but you should activate a new site in its place as the *active* site.

The procedure to create a new site with a new location for the root directory is as follows:

1. Stop the Web site so you can modify it using the Internet Services Manager, which is accessed from the Start menu under Administration Tools. Alternatively, you can open the My Computer icon on the desktop and go into the Control Panel folder, then the Administrative Tools folder, to find the Internet Information Services Manager icon.

2. Select the Web site under the computer name in the Internet Information Services Manager window. If you are running only a single Web site on the server, the site would be the Default Web Site, as shown here:

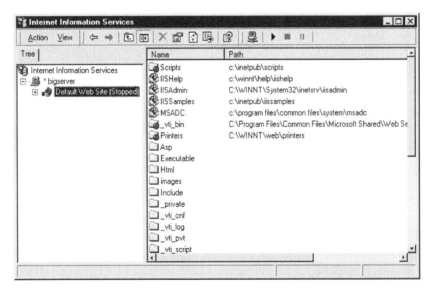

3. Right-click the site name and select Stop from the pop-up menu that appears to disable the default site.

4. Create a new site with the content stored in a directory different from the default directory. This works best if you've created the directory on the appropriate partition ahead of time. Microsoft recommends that you configure a separate directory for each file type so you can easily set Access Control permissions. This is a good practice, and you should follow it if you can. For example, you set up your Web site like this:

```
Root = D:\my_website
D:\my_website\static (.html)
```

```
D:\my_website\include (.inc)
D:\my_website\script (.asp)
D:\my_website\executable (.dll)
D:\my_website\images (.gif, .jpeg)
```

TIP   If you don't want to create a new site, you should still change the default contents directory of the site by right-clicking on the Default Site in the Internet Services Manager window and choosing Properties from the pop-up menu. The default directory can be changed on the Home Directory Tab.

To create your new Web site do the following:

1. In the Internet Information Services Manager window, select the Default Web Site (as shown in the previous illustration), and right-click it. Select New Site from the pop-up menu to start the Site Creation Wizard.

2. In the first input screen of the Wizard type in the name of the Web site in the Description box when requested by the wizard. Click Next when you're finished.

3. You should now be at the IP address and Port Settings window shown in the following illustration. Select the appropriate, previously configured IP address from the drop-down box at the top of the screen. Take care to choose the address that corresponds to the Internet-facing interface (assuming you have two cards in the server). You can continue by selecting the All Unassigned option here if you haven't previously configured your network interfaces.

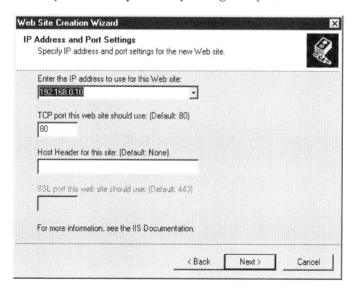

4. Add the TCP port address for your server. If your site is on the Internet, it's unlikely that you would change from port 80 unless you are using this Web site

for some special purpose application. For now, skip the host header information, as it's not required. Click Next when you finish.

5. In the Web Site Home Directory window add the new location of the directory in which you want to store the content for your new Web site. Choose a path that is not in the same partition as your server's operating system.

TIP   Make sure that you choose a different name than the default *pathname* of Inetpub. Why make it easy for a hacker who has written an automated attack?

---

6. If your site is on the Internet, you probably want to leave the Allow Anonymous Access To This Web Site option selected. This will eliminate the requirement to log in as users visit your site. Uncheck the box if you do want to require a log-in. It's a pretty common practice to require log-ins on an intranet. Click Next when you are ready to move on.

7. The final task is to set the directory permission on your new content directory in the Web Site Access Permissions window shown in the following illustration. Set the permissions to the lowest level you can. If you are not going to use Active Server Pages (ASPs) on your site, do not enable permissions for them. The same goes for Common Gateway Interface (CGI) programs. If you are not going to use them now, but plan to use them in the future, do not enable permissions for them now. Set them later as you are ready to deploy.

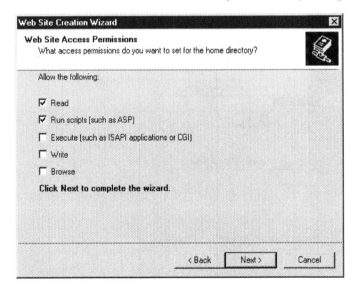

8. Click Next and to proceed with your changes and then click Finish to close out the Wizard when the changes are complete. You should repeat all the above (and following) steps for all other Web sites that you maintain on your IIS server.

TIP Now that you have created a new Web site, you *could* remove the Default Web Site from the Internet Information Services Manager. But, as mentioned, you might keep it up as a decoy. If you do retain the site, keep track as you reboot to make sure you haven't restarted the default site.

Disable Parent Paths   Parent paths are a feature of the Windows operating system that allows command-line instructions and programs to refer to a parent directory with two dots (".."). This feature provides a convenient way for system administrators and programmers to give instructions to traverse a directory hierarchy independent of their location in the directory tree. In other words, a command or program does not have to list the name of the specific parent directory the administrator wants to move to; instead, it needs to use the two dots in place of the directory name. This works no matter for what directory a program context is currently set.

Unfortunately, this feature is dangerous from a security point of view. It makes it too easy for a hacker to write an automated exploit that will traverse up to the root directory of the disk partition and then target other resources. That's why you want to disable parent paths.

Parent paths are disabled through the Web Site Properties window for a Web site. To perform the task, follow these steps:

1. Start Internet Information Services Manager. In the left panel of the Internet Information Services Manager window, shown in the following illustration, right-click the name of your Web site and choose Properties.

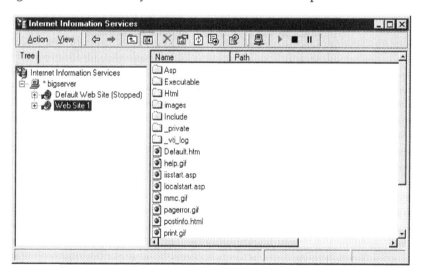

2. Open the Home Directory tab in the Web site Properties window, shown in the following illustration, and click the Configuration button to open the Application Configuration window.

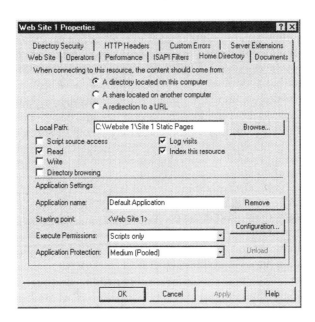

3. The Application Configuration window has a set of tabs. Open the App Options tab, and you'll see a check box next to Enable Parent Paths, as shown in the following illustration. Because you do not want these paths enabled, uncheck this box and click OK.

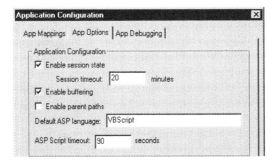

4. If you have installed other IIS services, such as IIS Help or FTP, you will need to make a decision about inheritance of the disabled parent paths setting you just configured. In that situation, after you click OK to close the Application Configuration window, you'll see an Inheritance dialog box that asks whether you want to apply the parent paths to all the services associated with your Web site. You should say yes to this option and click OK to close the window and confirm your settings.

Extension	Use
.asp	Active Server Page
.htr	Web-based password resets
.idc	Internet database connector
.stm, .shtm, .shtml	Server-side includes
.printer	Internet printing
.cer	Represents a certificate
.cdx	Active channel definition file
.asa	Active server application
.htw, ida, .idq	Index server

Table 3-3. Common Application Mapping Settings

Remove Unnecessary Application Mappings   By default, IIS is configured to support many different common file name extensions that are related to a variety of features in IIS. For example, an .idc file is a database connector that is used to help transfer data between a database and a Web-based query or display form. Through a configuration called Application Mapping, which associates the .idc file to the IIS HTTP-enabled open database connectivity (ODBC) driver called httpodbc.dll, IIS can be configured to read formatting information from the database connector so that it can properly execute the data transfer.

The information in Table 3-3 is from the NSA's guide for securing IIS. It lists some common application file name extension mappings along with their uses.

Some Web sites do not use many of the advanced IIS features, such as connections to databases, and including the mappings for features that are not used is unnecessary. As with the nonessential services that were disabled on the Web site, nonessential application mappings should be removed to minimize the possibility of their being exploited in an attack.

The procedure to remove applications mappings follows:

1. Open the Internet Information Services Manager.

2. In the left panel, right-click the name of your Web site and select Properties. Then open the Home Directory tab in the Web Site Properties window and click the Configuration button to bring up the Application Configuration dialog box.

3. Click the App Mappings tab to open it, as shown in the following illustration. This tab contains a listing of the default mappings. If you are not using any of

the features shown in Table 3-3, you should remove the mapping by selecting it and clicking Remove. Click OK to close the window and save your changes.

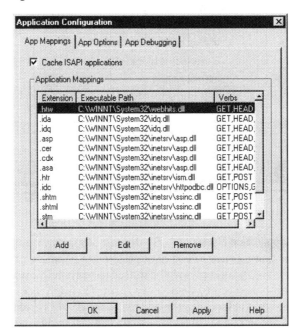

CHALLENGE

Using Application Mappings

Web applications (that is, applications that run on the Web server) can be developed in a number of programming and scripting languages. Organizations use Web applications for a variety of reasons, such as performing live data searches and gathering customer information.

IIS uses the file name extension of a requested resource on your Web site to determine which Internet Services Application Programming Interface (ISAPI) or CGI program to run to process a request. For example, a request for a file ending with an .asp extension causes the Web server to call the ASP program (Asp.dll) to process the request. The association of a file name extension with an ISAPI or CGI program is called *application mapping*.

Mapped applications can make your Web site vulnerable. A hacker might force the execution of one of the mapped applications by passing it a file with its type of mapped extension. The hacker tries to cause an application buffer overflow when the application loads the file, or he might try to perform some other behavior that compromises the system so that he can take control. By removing the mappings, you can limit the potential for this type of security breach.

Remove IIS Internet Printing Folder   You may have already disabled the Windows 2000 Print Spooler Service if you followed the advice to install a minimized Web server configuration. However, the NSA's guide says the IIS \printers folder will restore itself upon reboot, so you must still perform the following tasks. (Note that when we tested this, we didn't see it reappear, so the NSA may have been using an older version of Windows 2000 or perhaps IIS Lockdown.)

1. Open Internet Information Services Manager.

2. Select the name of your Web site in the left panel. The sites folders will appear in the right panel.

3. Delete the Printers virtual folder, if it exists, as shown here:

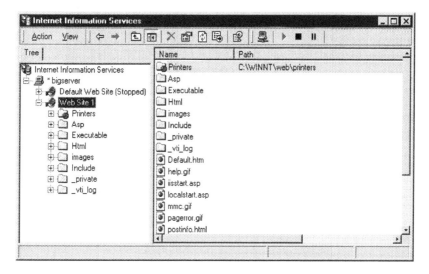

The printers folder is actually a virtual folder. Virtual folders (or directories) are a feature of IIS that hides the actual location of the information from Internet browsers by showing the alias in the URLs rather than the real directory. The actual location of the Printers folder is winnt\web\printers on the bootable system drive of your server. (Your system drive is often referred to as %systemdrive% in the Windows 2000 documentation, so the directory is often represented as %systemdrive%\winnt\web\printers.)

Delete All Sample Directories, Help Files, and Scripts   You had the option of omitting the samples when IIS was installed. But if you elected to install them, you can delete them now—it is highly recommended that you do so. Use the following steps to delete all the sample directories and scripts.

1. Open the Internet Services Manager, and in the left panel, select the name of your Web site. The Web site's folders will appear in the right panel.

2. Delete the appropriate folders. In the Internet Services Manager, you can delete the virtual folders. Table 3-4 shows the actual names and locations of folders that may appear on your system and should be deleted.

TIP   In Table 3-4, *%webroot%* is the root directory where your Web content is installed, and *%systemdrive%* is the bootable drive where your operating system is installed.

Disable IP Address in Content-Location Header   When you use static HTML pages (for example, Default.htm), a Content-Location header is added to the Web server's response to a browser's request for the page. By default, the Content-Location references the IP address of the server rather than the Fully Qualified Domain Name (FQDN) or host name. The Content-Location header can expose internal IP addresses that are usually hidden or masked behind a Network Address Translation (NAT) firewall or proxy server.

The following instructions are paraphrased from a Microsoft Knowledge Base article (#Q218180) that describes how to set a value to disable the Content-Location header in Internet Information Server 5.0.

1. Open a command window. To do this, select Command Prompt from the Accessories group of the Windows Start menu.

2. Change the directory to the admin scripts directory with this command:

   ```
   cd c:\inetpub\adminscripts.
   ```

Directory	Location
IIS Samples	%webroot%\iissamples
IIS SDK	%webroot%\iissamples\sdk
Admin Scripts	%webroot%\AdminScripts
Scripts	%webroot%\scripts
Data access	c:\Program Files\Common Files\System\msadc\Samples
IIS HELP	%systemroot%\help\iishelp
IIS adpwd	%systemroot%\system32\inetsrv\iisadmpwd

Table 3-4.   Sample and Script Directories and Locations

Note that the name of this directory may differ depending on the name you assigned if you changed the Home directory.

3. Type the following syntax:

```
adsutil set w3svc/UseHostName True
```

By default, this value is set to False, so it returns only the IP address of the IIS computer. Setting this value to True returns the FQDN for the IIS computer.

4. It is recommended that the Inetinfo service be restarted or rebooted after making this modification. To stop and start the Inetinfo process without rebooting, type the following at the command line:

```
net stop iisadmin /y
```

5. To restart, type the following:

```
Net start w3svc
```

Reconfigure How System Data Is Handled   The Recycle Bin and Virtual Memory functions of Windows 2000 can expose information that should no longer be available, unless you configure them to flush the data immediately.

By default, the Recycle Bin is configured to save a copy of every file deleted from the Windows desktop or though the Windows 2000 Explorer. This should be reconfigured to destroy the data immediately.

Here's how to reconfigure the Recycle Bin:

1. From the server's desktop, right-click the Recycle Bin icon and select Properties.

2. Check the radio button labeled Use One Setting For All Drives, and also select the box labeled Do Not Move Files To The Recycle Bin. Remove file Immediately When Deleted Then click OK.

The data vulnerability in the Windows 2000 Virtual Memory function comes from the default security setting for the System Page file that is used to swap contents from memory as the function moves data on and off disk. Windows 2000 has a security setting that should be enabled to clear out the data in the System Page file when Windows 2000 shuts down.

The procedure to enable the setting is as follows:

1. Select the Local Security Policy Tool from Administrative Tools in the Start menu, or open the My Computer icon on the desktop and find the Local Security Policy icon in the Administrative Tools folder of the Control Panel.

2. In the Local Security Settings window, open the Local Policies folder, and then open the Security Options folder, as shown here:

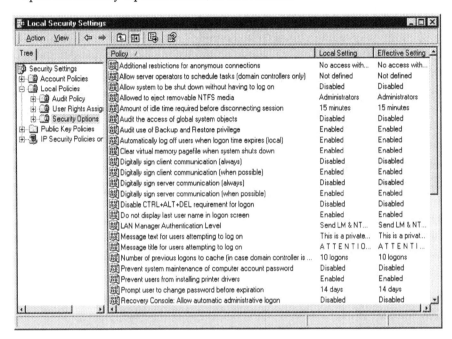

3. The right pane shows a list of options. Double-click Clear Virtual Memory Pagefile When System Shuts Down, and the Local Security Policy Setting dialog box opens.

4. Click the Enabled radio button, as shown next. Then click OK to close the window.

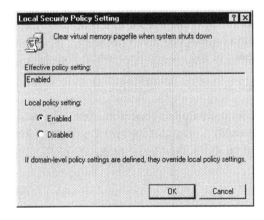

Miscellaneous Procedures

Following are a few more recommended hardening procedures. Not all of them may apply to your configuration, depending on whether you upgraded from previous versions of Windows and IIS or whether you have run the latest security patches and service packs. Although these procedures do enhance IIS security, they are not essential in low- or medium-security environments.

Remove Leftover Directories   If you upgraded your server from an NT system, you should remove a directory called IISADMPWD from the IIS root directory folder. According to Microsoft's Security Checklist for IIS 5.0, this directory allows you to reset Windows NT and Windows 2000 passwords. You want to make sure you don't leave any holes on your server that might be used to attack your IIS 5.0 password security.

The IISADMPWD directory is designed primarily for intranet scenarios and is not installed as part of IIS 5, but it is not removed when an IIS 4 server is upgraded to IIS 5. It should be removed if you don't use an intranet or if you connect the server to the Internet.

Several other miscellaneous directories are leftover on an upgraded server in addition to IISADMPWD, including the following. These should be removed:

- <System Root>\DOS
- <System Root>\Cookies
- <System Root>\History
- <System Root>\Temporary Internet Files

Remove the SAM File from the WINNT/REPAIR Directory   The Security Accounts Manager (SAM) database is the storage point for user passwords in Windows 2000. When a session is established on the Windows server, the user account database or SAM database is used to validate the credentials based on certain rules. Your Windows passwords are only as secure as the SAM file. Consequently, Windows 2000 takes measures to secure it by restricting permissions to the file and by encrypting the file with a protected key stored in the system Registry. You further protect it through measures such as setting the local security policy of you server to clear the system memory pagefile.

You can further protect your passwords by removing an extra system copy of the SAM file that is found in the following directory (*%Sys Volume%* is the root of your boot drive):

%Sys Volume%\WINNT\Repair

By default, the SAM file, along with the Windows Registry keys and a log of all other system files, is copied to this directory so that Windows 2000 can create an

Emergency Repair Disk (ERD). After you make the ERD, which you do through the Backup command in the Start menu Accessories folder, store the disk in a safe place and delete the SAM file from the repair directory. Repeat the process each time you update the ERD.

Disable the MS DOS, POSIX, and OS/2 Subsystems   The NSA Windows 2000 configuration guide suggests that you remove subsystems for the OS/2 and POSIX operating systems. The Microsoft IIS operations guide additionally recommends removing a set of legacy utilities related to DOS that are effectively a DOS subsystem. *Subsystems* is just a fancy name for the various commands and utilities that are included in Windows 2000 to provide compatibility with older software or to provide a capability for system management from a DOS command line as was possible with older Microsoft OS versions. These subsystems represent a potential vulnerability on your Web server and you should disable them and remove the commands.

TIP   Editing the Windows Registry is not for beginners. If you do it wrong, you can disable your server. Before attempting to edit the Registry, you should always make a set of ERDs for your system. The procedure to do that is discussed in Chapter 6.

You can disable these subsystems by deleting their strings from the Win2000 Registry. You will have to run a Windows 2000 utility called REGEDIT to do that with the following procedures:

1. From the Start menu, choose Run, and type **regedit**, which will open the application window shown next. In this window, open the folder for HKEY_LOCAL_MACHINE and find the SOFTWARE folder, and then the MICROSOFT folder.

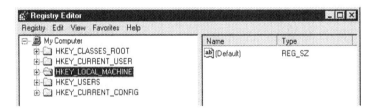

2. Delete all the subkeys under \HKEY_LOCAL_MACHINE\SOFTWARE\ MICROSOFT\OS/2 Subsystem for NT.

3. Now open the Folder for HKEY_LOCAL_MACHINE and find the SYSTEM folder, then the CurrentControlSet Folder, and then the Control folder. Under the Control folder:

- Open the Session Manager Folder, and then the Environment folder. Delete the value Os2LibPath.

- Open the Session Manager Folder, and then the Subsystems folder. Delete the Os/2 and Posix subkeys.

Your changes will take effect when you reboot.

Next, you can remove the subsystem commands because they were intended for application compatibility on a file server. You shouldn't run any old applications that would need this compatibility on your Web server. The location of these files is %Sys Volume%\ (%System Root%\system32).

- os2.exe

- os2ss.exe

- os2srv.exe

- psxss.exe

- posix.exe

- psxdll.dll

- All Files in the \os2 folder (Leave the nested DLL folder and its contents. The Windows 2000 command executor, Command.exe, will reportedly stop working if you remove it.)

Next, remove old DOS, Win98, NT, and Windows 2000 command-line utilities that are in the server's system directory; otherwise, these utilities might become weapons in the hands of an attacker who might gain access to your server. They can be found in the Windows 2000 installation directory at %System Root%\system32, where *%System Root%* is the root directory of your server's bootable system disk. If you ran IIS Lock, the rights to the system folder were restricted to make it impossible for normal Internet users to access them, but that won't help if someone gains a higher level of privilege on the site. You can be a little safer if you move them off the server.

Do you keep a floppy disk set of utilities for emergency repair of systems? Those utility floppies would be an ideal place for them. Here is a list of the commands that should be removed:

AT.EXE	DEBUG.EXE	ISSYNC.EXE
CACLS.EXE	EDLIN.EXE	NBTSTAT.EXE
CMD.EXE	FINGER.EXE	NET.EXE
CSCRIPT.EXE	FTP.EXE	NETSH.EXE

POLEDIT.EXE	REXEC.EXE	TELNET.EXE
RCP.EXE	RSH.EXE	TFTP.EXE
REGEDIT.EXE	RUNAS.EXE	TSKILL.EXE
REGEDT32.EXE	RUNONCE.EXE	WSCRIPT.EXE
REGINI.EXE	TRACERT.EXE	XCOPY.EXE
REGSRV32.EXE		

You need to manipulate the files in two places. Windows 2000 has a self-repairing feature called the System File Checker that will replace many system files from a backup directory location which is \%System Root%\system32\dllcache. In addition to removing the files from the system32 folder, you should delete them from this directory, rather than move them or rename them.

TIP   If you deleted the Regedit.exe command too soon, you couldn't have edited the Registry to remove the OS/2 and DOS subsystems. You never know when you might need them again. So the commands in the system32 folder should just be moved and/or renamed and *not* deleted. If you can move them on to a floppy disk, you probably don't even need to rename them.

Move the Metabase and Change the Registry Key   Finally, also from the NSA Guide comes a recommendation for securing the IIS alternative to the Windows 2000 Registry. IIS stores much the same information as the Windows 2000 Registry in a specialized data store called the metabase. The metabase stores IIS configuration parameter values in a fast-access, memory-resident data store. The metabase is specifically designed for use with IIS and is faster, more flexible, and more expandable than the Windows 2000 Registry.

CAUTION   Refer to the NSA Guide on the Web at the location shown in Table 3-1 for your evaluation of its recommendations and the instructions for this procedure. This procedure has great risk for all but the most experienced system administrators.

SECURE PHYSICAL, BOOT, AND MEDIA SETTINGS

The last (but not least important) settings of your Web server that must be secured as part of the installation process are the attributes that control how the server boots. After you've provided a secure location and made all the previously discussed changes to IIS and Windows 2000 security settings, it would be a tragedy if they could be circumvented by an attacker who gained physical access to the server and booted into a different OS image, where he had administrative privileges to do anything he wanted.

The vulnerability to this scenario is not unique to Web servers. Most security-conscious organization might already have the following Windows 2000 server setting recommendations specified in their security policies and implemented on their other Windows 2000 servers.

BIOS Boot Settings

You should modify the boot options in your server's BIOS to prevent booting from removable media, which is a method some attackers use in physical attacks to try and bring the system up into a different OS than the one installed on the server. If an attacker succeeds with this kind of attack, he can bypass the file system's access control.

The procedures to change the BIOS settings will vary from computer to computer, depending on the computer and BIOS manufacturers. The general process is as follows:

1. Watch the information that streams across your monitor before Windows 2000 loads when you power up the computer. Press the key that your system tells you to use to enter the Setup options.

2. In your BIOS Setup menus, first enable the administrator password for either booting or for changing the menu options, depending on which method of security your computer uses. You can use the same Administrator password you use for Windows 2000 if you want. Then, if your computer has the option, disable the user password. Note that you want to set a boot password but not a power-on password as some systems allow because the power-on password will prevent the system from automatically rebooting in the event of power failure.

3. If the option is available, set the computer CMOS to disallow removable media booting. When the option of defining which drives are bootable is not available in the system, the boot password you created will at least provide reasonable protection.

Media Settings

Configure Windows 2000 to prevent other types of physical attacks, such as the introduction of malicious code, by restricting access to the floppy or CD-ROM drive if a user isn't logged on locally. Two procedures should be performed to secure the media:

- Restrict CD-ROM access to users who are logged on locally
- Restrict floppy access to users who are logged on locally

The settings to control the media are part of the server's Local Security Policy. To confirm a secure policy or adjust the local security policy settings, use these steps:

1. Select the Local Security Policy snap-in from the Administrative tools in the Windows Start menu.

2. In the Local Security Settings window, open the Local Policies folder, and then open the Security Options folder as shown here:

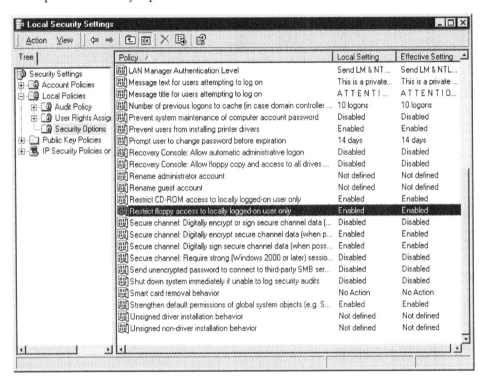

3. In the Security Options folder, the right panel of the split screen Security Policy tool will show a list of options. One by one, you will enable the required media restrictions:

   • Open Restrict CD-ROM Access To Locally Logged On Users to bring up the dialog box that allows you to enable the setting.

   • Click Enabled and then click OK.

   • Open Restrict Floppy Access To Locally Logged On Users to bring up the dialog box that allows you to enable the setting.

   • Click Enabled and then click OK.

INSTALLATION PLANNING CHECKLIST

- ☐ Place the Server in a physically secure location.
- ☐ Do not install on a Windows Domain Controller—make the server stand-alone.
- ☐ Use multiple disks or partition volumes and do not install the Web server home directory on the same volume as the operating system folders.
- ☐ Use two network interfaces in the server—one for admin and one for the network.
- ☐ Keep it simple—minimize your service configuration—omit unnecessary services.
  - ☐ Do not install a printer.
  - ☐ Do not install Data Access Components unless specifically needed.
  - ☐ Do not install the HTML version of the Internet Services Manager.
  - ☐ Do not install the MS Index Server.
  - ☐ Do not install the MS FrontPage Server extensions on a production server.

HARDENING RECOMMENDATIONS CHECKLIST

- ☐ Install service packs, patches, and hot fixes
- ☐ Run IIS Lock
- ☐ Create a new site and disable the default site
- ☐ Create a new content directory
- ☐ Verify secure configuration through manual hardening procedures
- ☐ Disable parent paths
- ☐ Remove unnecessary application mappings
- ☐ Remove the IIS Internet Printing virtual directory
- ☐ Delete sample directories and scripts
- ☐ Remove IP address in header for Content-Location
- ☐ Reconfigure Recycle Bin and Pagefile system data policies
- ☐ Remove leftover directories (only required after upgrade)
- ☐ Secure CMOS settings
- ☐ Secure physical media (floppy drive, CD-ROM drive, and so on)

CHAPTER 4

Accounts, Authorization, and Security Policy

A s soon as you finish the hardening process described in Chapter 3 you should immediately begin to set up your administrative and user accounts and configure the Windows 2000 and IIS security properties for those accounts. You should also immediately disable default accounts that won't be required for the way you are using your server. In fact, you need to examine and/or change dozens of settings to make a system secure for a Web server. Many security professionals would consider these processes inseparable from the hardening process discussed in the previous chapter. However, these processes are so important that they deserve a chapter of their own.

APPLYING SECURITY POLICY

The privileges and restrictions you give to others to use your system's resources let you map your security policy to the management and distribution of information through your Web server. A lot of organizations pay only lip service to creating and maintaining a policy. To do it right, you need to become familiar with some of the issues you will have to address to secure your server's resources in a serious and meaningful way. Some examples are listed in Table 4-1.

The list Table 4-1 is greatly abbreviated—but you get the idea. Are you comfortable with each of the decisions and tasks described? You are going to need to address them, because they control the access to your data; this discussion shows you how. Before we

Issue	Description
IP Security Rules	Sets filters for passing or blocking IP traffic. Tells if and how to encrypt packets.
Assign/Create Delegated Administrative Responsibilities	Sets administrator responsible for content and security of the server. Sets pseudo-administrative roles such as backup operators.
Assign/Create User Accounts	Sets anonymous account and authenticated accounts.
Account Security Rules	Indicates groups to which accounts belongs. Indicates whether lockout for incorrectly entered password is used. Specifies allowed attempts before lockout and length of lockout. Specifies length of lifetime for Kerberos user ticket.
Group Security Rules	Indicates what are the groups, members of groups, and which rules are applied at the group level.
Define Password Security Rules	Sets minimum length of passwords and whether blank passwords are allowed. Establishes deny permission to reuse passwords. Sets requirements for alphanumeric passwords. Ses user rules for periodically changing passwords (if at all).
Data Confidentiality Rules	Sets directory permissions and file permissions.

Table 4-1.   Policy Issues for Web Server Security

start, a quick review of Windows 2000 security concepts and terminology is in order to set the context and make sure that you understand the discussion that follows.

WINDOWS 2000 AND IIS SECURITY CONCEPTS

Internet Information Server is integrated into Windows 2000 and the security of IIS is inextricably bound to the security of Windows 2000. Managing Windows 2000 security requires an understanding of five concepts:

- Trusted relationships
- Workgroups and domains (and Active Directory)
- Authentication of accounts and groups
- Access control (rights, permissions and restrictions)
- Inheritance

Everything in Windows 2000 security is built on these concepts. They all work together to provide security by preventing, restricting, and allowing access to data and resource on an IIS Web site.

Trusted Relationships

The security of a system such as Windows 2000/IIS is based on rules and settings that say what the system should allow or not allow. A critical part of this system is the mechanisms used to uniquely identify individuals, computers, and resources. In Windows 2000, IP networking address, user name, certificates (digital IDs), and Kerberos identity credentials are some of the ways identity is established. Rules of trust can be established between computers and individuals or other computers based on the confidence placed in the means of identification. In Windows 2000, at the highest level of trust, two computers are willing to accept all log-ins and other information from each other as legitimate.

Workgroups and Domains

Workgroups and domains are collections of individuals and resources on the network. The resources consist of storage devices, printers, data files, and other components of information systems that are associated with servers.

One difference between a workgroup and a domain is that in a domain, the servers have a trust relationship and share a common management database, while in a workgroup, each server maintains its own unique management database. When an organization requires more than one server, although the network could be configured in a workgroup arrangement, it often becomes advantageous to use a domain. The trust relationships between the domain's servers make life easier for both users and administrators. When users log in to a domain they log in to all of the servers at the same time and don't have to log in to each one individually. Administrators also benefit because the domains shared database saves them from having to create and maintain redundant user identities in each server.

Figure 4-1 depicts a group of servers in a domain. You will notice that the domain has a system designated as a domain controller, which "owns" the user database that it shares with the other servers.

Organizations that use domains frequently make use of a Windows 2000 service called *Active Directory*. Active Directory is a database that not only manages the users, it manages all of the network resources in a logical model. In other words, resources such as printers can appear to users as though they are attached to the network—regardless of the specific server to which they may actually be attached.

The intranets of many large organizations realize great benefits from Active Directory technology because the centralized management capabilities make it easier to manage servers, resources, accounts, groups, and other details without having to repeat the same procedures over and over again at each individual server's console. Active Directory also allows network resources to be physically reconfigured without changing their appearance in the graphical user interface (GUI) in which they are viewed.

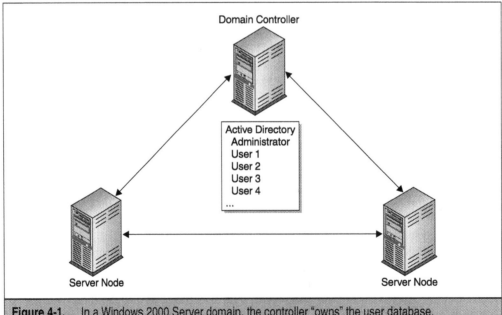

Figure 4-1. In a Windows 2000 Server domain, the controller "owns" the user database.

Authentication

Windows Domains (and Active Directory) also make it easier for users where authentication is concerned. *Authentication* is the process of verifying a computer user's identity, most often through the use of an account name and a password, and the centralized maintenance of accounts and passwords for a Windows domain (in Active Directory) eliminates the need for users to log in individually to each server.

Intranet vs. Internet

Ironically, some of the security goals of a Web server are often in conflict with the benefits associated with Windows domains and Active Directory. For example, if your Web server is on the Internet, it should not have trust relationships with other systems. If that's the case, would you ever want a Web server to be part of a Windows domain? Well, yes, sometimes—as long as its hardended. On the other side of a firewall, on an intranet, an organization could include the Web server in a domain if authenticated access to the Web server was required. The domain would eliminate the need for the organization to retype all the user identities, passwords, and so on, on the Web server—a very big deal on a big network—that already exist in the Domain Controller's database.

Any time you create trust links between systems, you make them all more vulnerable to the security failure of any single one of them, so Internet Web servers are most securely managed as stand-alone systems. In addition, Web servers on the Internet are often set up for a special type of authentication called an *anonymous log-in* that doesn't require a unique account identifier. The use of anonymous log-ins is a common difference between Internet and intranet Web server configurations. Other than that, most of the security management issues are pretty similar.

TIP   There are exceptions to every general statement. Some intranet Web servers do use anonymous log-ins and do not require the visitor to provide an ID and password. Conversely, some Internet Web servers require traditional authentication. In the latter case, if the managing organization also uses FTP, News, and other servers simultaneously, it may put all of these Internet servers together in an isolated management domain. But we're going to ignore the exception cases for now so as not to complicate the point.

Local Security Management

Most security issues, other than authentication management, are similar for Internet and intranet Web sites. Both types of Web servers have a variety of settings that must be managed uniquely on the server. Even if the Web site is part of an intranet Windows domain, the server will require a number of security measures that are different from the rest of the domain. Greater security efforts are required on a Web server, as opposed to a file server, because Web technologies are inherently full of vulnerabilities. Therefore, a Web server should manage the majority of its security through local security settings.

The local security settings on an IIS Web server, or any Windows 2000 computer, manage all the security policy issues that are unique to the server.

Access Control Lists

Access to Windows 2000 servers is enforced through a system of user accounts and groups to which accounts belong. Once a user is authenticated on the server, the user is authorized to use its resources based on rights and permissions they are given to use the server's resources. The rights and permissions settings for accounts and groups in a workgroup server are locally managed and stored on a server in its local *Access Control List (ACL).* The settings in the local ACL determine what an account or group can do on that server and is not shared with other systems, even if the computer is on a Windows domain.

Rights and permissions are defined as follows:

- **Rights**   In general, a right is the ability to do something, often something administrative-related or otherwise restricted, such as starting and stopping the system and creating new user accounts and groups.

- **Permissions**   Alternatively, permissions grant the user the ability to access resources such as directories, files, and printers. With directories and files, permissions can be any combination of the ability to list, read, modify, write, and execute.

TIP   With domains managed by Active Directory, the resources belong to the network rather than to a server and the authorization is not managed locally—it's managed by the Domain Controller.

Some of the local security administration of your IIS Web site, if not most, will entail making modifications to local ACLs to deny, extend, or delegate the rights and permissions that the groups and accounts have to the server's resources. Beyond that, you will need to define password rules, IP security rules, auditing rules, and other miscellaneous settings as discussed in Table 4-1 at the beginning of this chapter.

Filters

Filters are settings that compliment ACLs. They enforce access restrictions. Though less commonly used, filters can also be an important part of a security policy, because they can enforce rules that ACLs cannot handle. For example, an IP filter can be used that restricts all visitors attempting to access the site from a particular IP address or Internet Domain Name Server (DNS) domain. In a way, filter restrictions are kind of like reverse permissions. Firewalls, which will be discussed in Chapter 6 and Chapter 9, make extensive use of filters. For example, one commonly used filtering rule is that a firewall blocks all traffic to a Web server except port 80 traffic via HTTP.

Inheritance

After you set rights permissions on a folder in Windows 2000, by default, new files and subfolders that are created in the folder *inherit* the same ACL properties. In other words, the new files and folders (called *child objects*) will be given the same account- and group-related rights and permissions as the folder they are created in (called the *parent*). You can change this condition if you want by explicitly overriding the inheritance properties. You'll be shown how to do that as this discussion proceeds.

TOOLS FOR LOCAL SECURITY MANAGEMENT

The concept of managing local settings and policy is the same whether you are working with a stand-alone server or working with a server that is part of an intranet domain and/or using Active Directory. The local settings and policy apply only to the computer where you set them. Even when the computer is in a domain, the other systems in the domain have no knowledge of any individual computer's local settings and are not affected by its local policy.

Windows 2000 and IIS use three basic toolsets to configure and manage local security settings on a server:

- The Microsoft Management Console (MMC) tool suite
- The IIS Lockdown tool (IIS Lock)
- The MMC Security Configuration and Analysis Snap-in and templates

The MMC tool suite is the set of general purpose, everyday management tools used for day-to-day security configuration and maintenance tasks, including authentication settings, creating users and groups, ACL management, and so on. IIS Lock and the Security Configuration and Analysis snap-ins are specialized tools. IIS Lock is used to automate security settings during the initial setup or the reconfiguration of an IIS server. The Security Configuration and Analysis snap-in and its associated Security Templates tools are used to build and deploy customized local security policies.

You read about and used both the MMC and the IIS Lock tool in Chapter 3 as you hardened your Web server. You'll use IIS Lock again when you install new Service Packs or add a File Transfer Protocol (FTP), Network News Transfer Protocol (NNTP), or Simple Mail Transfer Protocol (SMTP) service to your site. You will use the MMC over and over, not just for security, but for all aspects of IIS maintenance.

The Microsoft Management Console

The tools in the MMC tool suite are found under Administrative Tools in the Windows Start menu. In a stand-alone server, all local user accounts, group accounts, passwords, and many other settings are managed through the MMC and stored in the server's local *Security Accounts Manager (SAM)* file.

Some of the security administration tools in the Active Directory MMC are a bit different than those for a stand-alone server. For example, to manage users and groups on a stand-alone server, you would use the Local Users and Groups folders in the MMC Computer Management tool. In a Domain/Active Directory environment you would use the Active Directory Users and Computers Snap-in. Active Directory keeps the domain information in a different file than the SAM file that stores local information. It's called NTDS.DIT and it gets replicated onto other domain controllers.

Readers whose Web sites are only on the Internet, if the recommendations in Chapter 3 were followed, should have kept their Web servers out of domains and thus will be using only the local management MMC tools for Windows 2000 and IIS. But guess what? Most of the local security settings of a Web site that is in a domain also are managed through the MMC local management tools. It's the management of intranet Users and Groups that are the big exception, as they are managed by MMC Active Directory tools, because they can be integrated across all of an intranet's servers. But we won't be talking about those Active Directory tools in this chapter. This discussion will cover only management of the server's local security policy. Table 4-2 contains a list of the Windows 2000/IIS local MMC local security management tools.

Tool	Function
Computer Management	Manages local or remote computers in a single tool. Includes functions for managing server attributes such as system events, storage properties, users and groups, device configurations, and services.
Internet Services Manager	Manages the security properties of the IIS World Wide Web server including home directories permissions, authentication methods, anonymous access, and operator rights.
Local Security Policy	Manages local security policy on a server for parameters such as IPSec properties, password properties, group properties, and lockout properties.
Security Configuration and Analysis Snap-in	Analyzes and configures local computer user rights, restricted groups, the Registry, the file system, and system services using a security policy template.
Security Templates Snap-in	Defines security policy that can be applied to a group or a computer.

Table 4-2. Tools for IIS Server Local Security Management

Customizing Security Policy with Templates

Security templates provide a centralized method of defining security settings when used with the Security Configuration and Analysis and Security Template MMC snap-ins. Microsoft provides a security policy template on its Technet Web site, which contains baseline security settings for IIS that Microsoft deems applicable to most secure Web sites. The template is a file named Hisecweb.inf that can be downloaded from the Microsoft Web site at

> http://support.microsoft.com/support/misc/kblookup.asp?id=Q316347

The security template is indeed a good starting point for securing your server. When you ran IIS Lock in Chapter 3 as you hardened your sever, it implemented the settings in the Hisecweb.inf file among its procedures.

Templates also provide an efficient way to deploy a customized local security policy. You can use the Hisecweb.inf security template as a starting point, make changes, and save it under a different name to create your custom policy. With this technique, a range of system security settings can be viewed, adjusted, and applied to a local computer. It's a good way to predefine changes you want to make to the default Microsoft IIS security policy settings and then deploy them without have to click through window after window after window.

The Security Policies in the Hisecweb.inf template include settings for the following:

- **Account Policies**   Security for passwords, account lockouts, and Kerberos authentication
- **Local Policies**   Logging for security events and user/group rights assignment
- **Restricted Groups**   Local group membership administration
- **Registry**   Security for local Registry keys
- **System Services**   Security and startup mode for local services
- **Security Options**   Rules for numerous and miscellaneous security settings

Unfortunately, even though we are going to show you how to use templates now, you probably won't know what a lot of the settings mean until you get farther into this book. But there is a method to this madness. As part of the process we are about to take you through, you will be setting up the snap-in tools, because you will need them in subsequent chapters. As far as the template deployment goes, you can skim through it now and come back later when you have a deeper understanding and are ready to use it.

Installing the Security Configuration and Template Snap-Ins

To use the template, you first have to copy it onto your Web server's system volume and then install the MMC Security Templates and Security Configuration and Analysis Snap-ins so you can use it. The following procedures are required.

1. Copy the template (the template is the Hisecweb.inf file) to the security templates directory of your server's system volume, which is typically c:\WINNT\security\templates.

2. To install the snap-ins, you have to open up the MMC in Author mode. You can create a new MMC console for the snap-ins or you can add them to an existing tool such as Computer Management.

To add them to the existing Computer Management console tool:

1. Find Computer Management under Administrative Tools in the Windows Start Menu.

2. Right-click Computer Management and select Author from the pop-up menu. The Computer Management Console will open in Author mode. Install the tools under Computer Management rather than under the Console Root.

To Create a new Console tool:

1. Select Run from the Windows Start Menu.

2. Run the MMC command executable by typing in **MMC.EXE** into the Run dialog box. A blank console window will open in Author mode, as shown here:

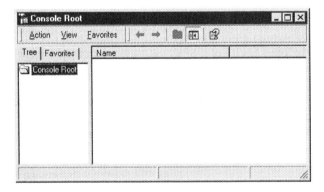

3. Pull down the Console menu and select Add/Remove Snap-in to open the Add/Remove Snap-in dialog box, shown next. Click the Add button. This will open the Snap-in Selection list.

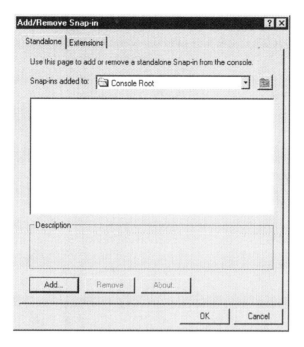

4. Choose Security Configuration And Analysis from the list shown in the
    following illustration and then click Add. Repeat the process for the Security
    Templates tool. Then close the Snap-in window and the snap-in will be added
    to the console.

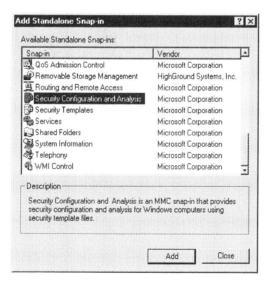

5. Click OK to close the dialog box and save your changes. If you created a new console tool you will have to save the tool by giving it a name when you close the tool. It will be added to the Windows Start Menu under Administrative Tools.

Modifying and Implementing the Security Templates

You will use the Security Templates snap-in and the Security Configuration and Analysis snap-in that you just added to your MMC console tools to modify and apply the template settings to your server.

To examine and modify template settings, you first need to open the template with the Security Templates snap-in. The procedures are as follows:

1. Open the MMC console tool that has the Security Templates snap-in.

2. Click the snap-in to expose the nested items underneath. Click the Security Templates folder to expose the individual templates that are nested under the folder. Double-click the template named hisecweb to open (or right-click the template name and select Open), as shown here:

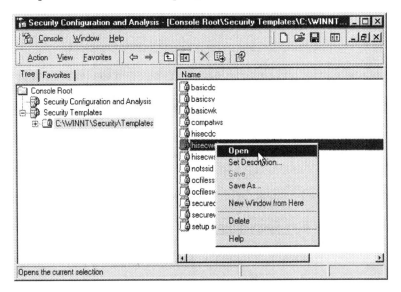

3. Now save the template under a new name so you can modify the settings. Right-click the hisecweb icon and choose Save As. Choose the name you want to use and click Save when you are finished. You should then see your new policy in the templates directory.

To view and edit the new policy you just saved, locate it, right-click it, and select Open to expose the settings in the policy in the right windows of the MMC. Right-click any policy you want to change and select Security. You can change any of the templates settings in this way.

Now you are ready to deploy. But before you actually run the configuration tool, do a comparison between the new templates settings you created and your current server settings so you can see the differences. The Security Configuration and Analysis Tool can do that for you and put the output into a log file (it uses the term *database*). Here's how you do it:

1. In the MMC console tool that has the Security Configuration and Analysis snap-in, right-click the snap-in and select Open Database, as shown here:

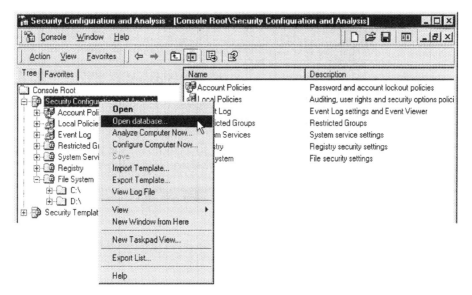

2. The Open Database dialog box will open, requiring that you name the database where your comparison output will be stored. Type any name that you want. If some database files already appear in the window, from previous comparisons, you can ignore them. A name like "test" would be fine (the database file will be given a .sdb extension). Then click Open.

3. Now you should see the Import Template dialog box, as shown in the following illustration. A list of templates should appear in the central window. Select the template you created and click Open. That will return you to your MMC console. It might not look like anything happened, but if your new

template is now nested among all the default Microsoft templates, you're ready to run your comparison.

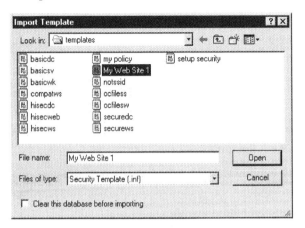

4. Now pull down the Action menu at the top of the MMC console and select Analyze Computer Now. It will run the comparison of the templates settings to the settings currently on your server and store the output in the database you created. Data output will be displayed in the right window of the console. Any settings on your server that are different than those on the template will appear with an X on their icons, as shown for the Password Policy example here:

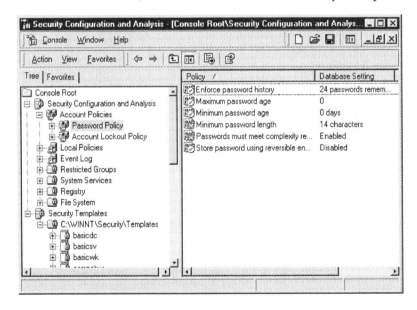

TIP   You will be prompted for an error log file location as you execute the analysis. This log can help you keep track of your setting changes. It's your choice as to the location where you want it stored.

TIP When you run the configuration procedure, it will change numerous configuration settings and disable the nonessential services we discussed in Chapter 3 without any prompting. Our editor found this out the hard way when he ran it on his development network server and it disabled his DHCP client process. So look over the template carefully, if you are not using the stand-alone, minimized configuration we recommended in our hardening chapter, before you apply it.

---

5. At your convenience, you can deploy. Right-click the Security Configuration and Analysis snap-in in the left window of the MMC console and choose Configure Computer Now. You'll see it processing; when it stops, you're done.

That will do it. If you rerun the configuration comparison in step 4 you should not see any more red Xs, because all of the template's settings were put into effect.

CONFIGURING WEB SERVER ACCESS CONTROL FOR WINDOWS 2000

You may have noticed in looking at the settings of the Hisecweb.inf security template that the settings for access control were largely undefined. You are going to have to provide these settings yourself. In a local ACL, any group or any user account can be given any combination of rights and permissions. That characteristic makes Windows 2000 security very flexible and powerful, but it also creates vulnerability if the rights and permission are not configured properly.

Modifying Default Groups and Administrator Settings

The first thing you should do to manage the ACLs on your Web server is lock down the ability to control storage resources. In other words, you should be specific about designating who has rights for the storage and equally as specific about who does not have rights.

Windows 2000 installs a number of default administrative accounts, groups, and user accounts. The installation of IIS does nothing to change those. In a stand-alone installation, these default accounts and groups are as shown in Table 4-3.

The settings for Rights and Permissions of Administrators are very broad. An Administrator has complete authority over the system and is given full control—and that is appropriate. The list of Administrator Rights and Permissions is shown in Table 4-4.

It is usually not appropriate for accounts and groups other than Administrators to have full control in a Web server's ACL unless they have some kind of delegated administrative authority. Even then, the authority is usually constrained to some subset of full control and some subset of the resource. For example, a Web manager might be

Default *Groups* that Appear in Local ACL	Default *Groups* that *Do Not* Appear in ACL	Default *Accounts* that Appear in Local ACL
Administrators	SYSTEM	Administrator
Backup Operators	CREATOR OWNER	Guest
Guests	AUTHENTICATED USERS	IUSR_*computername*
Power Users	ANONYMOUS LOG-IN	IWAM_*computername*
Replicator	BATCH	TsInternetUser
Users	SERVICE	
Everyone	CREATOR GROUP	
Web Anonymous Users	DIALUP	
Web Applications	INTERACTIVE	
	NETWORK	
	TERMINAL SERVICE USERS	

Table 4-3. Windows 2000 Default Accounts and Groups

Right or Permission	Description
Traverse Folder/Execute File	Traverse Folder allows users to move through a folder to access other files or folders, regardless of permissions the user may or may not have on that folder (folders only). This permission has meaning only when the user has not been granted the Bypass Traverse Checking user right. The Execute File permission allows a user to run program files (files only).
List Folder/Read Data	List Folder allows the reading of file names and subfolders within a folder (folders only). Read Data allows file data to be read (files only).
Read Attributes	Allows viewing of a file's NTFS attributes (such as Read only or Hidden).
Read Extended Attributes	Allows viewing of a file's extended attributes, which may vary as they are defined by specific programs.
Create Files/Write Data	Create Files allows the creation of files within a folder (folders only). Write Data allows modification and/or overwriting of files (files only).
Create Folders/Append Data	Create Folders allows the creation of folders within a folder (folders only). Append Data allows making changes to the end of file (files only).
Write Attributes	Allows the modification of a file's NTFS attributes (such as Read only or Hidden).
Write Extended Attributes	Allows the modification of a file's program-specific extended attributes.
Delete Subfolders and Files	Allows the deletion of subfolders and files regardless of whether the Delete permission was granted on the subfolder or file.
Delete	Allows deletion of a file or folder.
Read Permissions	Allows viewing of the permissions on a file or folder.
Change Permissions	Allows the modification of the permissions on a file or folder.
Take Ownership	Allows taking ownership of a file or folder.

Table 4-4. The Complete Set of Windows 2000 Rights and Permissions

given the following permissions in the root content directory of the Web server's home directory disk (but not for any other directory on any other disk):

- **Modify**   The ability to make changes in the directory
- **Read & Execute**   The ability to run executable programs
- **List Folder Contents**   The ability to see the directories file list
- **Read**   The ability to read data files in the directory
- **Write**   The ability to save new files in the directory

This set of permissions is close to full control but differs in some subtle ways. Table 4-5, from Microsoft's IIS documentation, shows how the subset of full rights and permissions given to the Web manager differ from full control.

The accounts of other users on the Web server (nonmanagers and nonadministrators), compared to Web managers, are generally quite restricted, usually allowing only Read permissions in the case of anonymous user access.

Remove Storage Administration Rights for Group "Everyone"

It just so happens that one of the default security settings that results in the combination of Windows 2000 and IIS leaves a Web server's storage drives in a possibly vulnerable configuration because the group Everyone is given Full Control. You must remove the ability of the default group Everyone to control and manage the server's drives. This group has those rights by default when you install Windows2000 and IIS. Since the

Full Control Permissions	Modify	Read & Execute	List Folder Contents	Read	Write
Traverse Folder/Execute File	✓	✓	✓		
List Folder/Read Data	✓	✓	✓	✓	
Read Attributes	✓	✓	✓	✓	
Read Extended Attributes	✓	✓	✓	✓	
Create Files/Write Data	✓				✓
Create Folders/Append Data	✓				✓
Write Attributes	✓				✓
Write Extended Attributes	✓				✓
Delete Subfolders and Files					
Delete	✓	✓			
Read Permissions	✓		✓	✓	✓
Change Permissions					
Take Ownership					

Table 4-5.   Permission Subcategories Compared to Full Control

Everyone group consists of all users, including anonymous users, this setting is way too broad. Only individuals designated as Administrators or some other level of delegated group and account responsibility should have these rights on a Web server that goes in to production.

Presumably, if you have followed previous advice to create a separate partition for the Web content, you will be performing the operation to disable the management rights of the group Everyone on more than one drive. Here's how to make this change:

1. Use Windows Explorer (Start | Accessories Windows Explorer), or open the My Computer icon on the desktop and find the drives you will be working with.

TIP   You could also use the MMC Computer Management console program to set access-control permissions at a drive's root level. But the console is not nearly as flexible for this task as using Windows Explorer.

---

2. Right-click the appropriate drive and select Properties. The Local Disk Properties window will appear. Select the Security Tab, shown here:

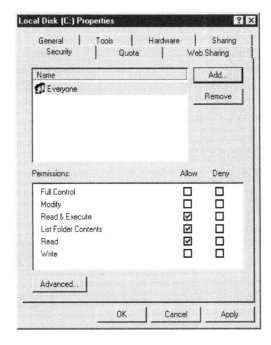

3. Remove the group Everyone by selecting it and clicking the Remove button. If your server storage drives have been configured along the way to have other groups or accounts besides Everyone in their ACLs, delete them, too. Then click Apply so that the system saves your changes.

4. Repeat steps 1–3 for your other drives.

Give Full Control to Administrators Group and System Group

Now that you have eliminated the unwanted groups from your storage drive ACLs, you can add the groups and accounts that you know you want and set the appropriate rights and permissions for them.

The default groups of Administrators and System should definitely be added. The System group refers to the operating system, which should reasonably be allowed access to all of the computer's resources. Administrators is the group whose members are in charge of managing the server. You could add others if your management strategy and organizational security policy make use of subadministration roles that have delegated administrative authority. That topic will be covered shortly.

To add the desired groups follow these steps:

1. Choose Start | Administration Tools | Computer Management and find the computer's disks in the tool's resource tree, or use Windows Explorer to navigate to the appropriate drive.

2. Right-click on the appropriate drive and select Properties to bring up the Local Disk Properties window as you did in the previous section. Select the Security tab and click the Add button to add new groups to the ACL.

3. Select the Administrators (plural) and System groups and click the Add button, shown next, to make your change. Click OK to save the change and return to the Local Disk Properties window.

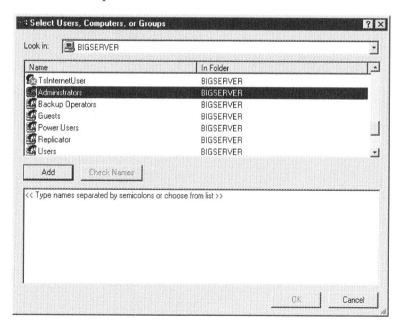

After successfully adding the groups and accounts, you can set the rights and permissions. You should give the Administrators and System groups full control of the drive, and you should also set the drive to inherit permissions as you create new directories on the drive.

Here's how to set the permissions for each group or account you have added to the ACL list:

1. In the Security tab of the Local Disk Properties windows, select the Administrators group in the upper window and you will see the groups rights and permission settings in the lower window, as shown here:

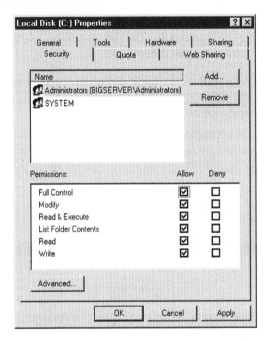

2. Click the Full Control Allow check box to enable all the file permissions for the group and then click Apply to save the settings. That's the shortcut. On a new account, you need to take an additional step to enable inheritance on the object.

3. Click the Advanced button at the bottom of the dialog box to bring up the Access Control Settings for Local Disk window, shown here:

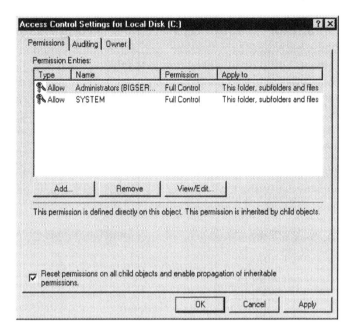

4. In the Permissions tab, check the option *Reset Permissions On All Child Objects And Enable Propagation Of Inheritable Permissions*. Then Click OK so your server can update the Windows 2000 Registry with your new permission settings. You will be asked to confirm with a dialog box requiring you to click Yes to continue before the operation is completed.

TIP As the procedure completes, you may see an error message indicating the permissions on Pagefile.sys could not be updated because the file is in use. This file is used by your system's virtual memory process and you will always get that error when virtual memory is enabled. Ignore it.

---

5. Repeat steps 1–4 for each storage drive.

TIP Make sure all other applications and files are closed before you click OK to reset permissions on all the objects or you may get error messages as the Registry updates.

Rename Administrator Account and Create a Strong Password

Since the Administrator account is a default account, it is frequently used in attacks, because hackers know it's there. You'd be surprised how often these attacks are successful when poorly chosen passwords are used. One frequently used defense against this vulnerability is to rename the account. When you do this, you should also make the Administrator password a *strong password* (a combination of alphabetic, numeric, and punctuation at least eight characters long), to guard against brute force and dictionary attacks on the password. Both procedures are easy to do:

1. In the MMC Computer Management console program, find the Local Users and Groups folder in the tool's resource tree and open it to expand the list shown here:

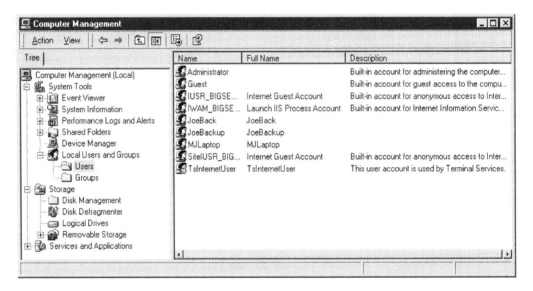

2. Click Users to display the list of user accounts on the server in the right window.

3. Right-click the Administrator account and choose Rename. Give the account a name of your choice.

4. If the Hisec.web template was applied, strong password requirements will be enforced on your server. Even if this is not an enforced policy, you should use a strong password on your Administrator account. Right-click the renamed Administrator account and choose Set Password to change the password to a strong password. Click OK and your changes will be saved.

Delegating Administration

You may want to delegate the ability to manage functions of your Web site, such as content management or FTP directory maintenance, to individuals other than an administrator. For example, you may want to delegate some of the tasks of day-to-day site content management to a Web manager, in which case you may create a type of account that has a set of rights that are greatly expanded from a normal user but more limited than the system administrator. The Web manager permissions in the Web server's content directory should minimally allow the manager to Read, Modify, and Write to files. IIS comes with a default role called an Operator that additionally allows the individual to set site access permissions, enable logging, set directory security, and change the default document.

If you do delegate content administration, it's a good idea to a have a specialized Windows 2000 group to which you can add the accounts of individuals who will be performing these tasks. While you could make each of those individuals an Administrator, and use the default Windows 2000 group called Administrators, creating a new group for this purpose is a better security practice because the full authority of an Administrator is not required for a task such as site content management, so full authority should not be granted.

The benefits of delegating and partitioning site administration become apparent when a single server is used to manage several Web sites. This would allow organizations to distribute the workload of site maintenance, while not permitting any one group total control over all sites on the server, and once again not granting full Administrator authority unnecessarily.

Creating a Delegated Administration Group

To create a delegated administration group, you must perform the following steps:

1. Open the MMC Computer Management tool, and find the Local Users and Groups folder in the tool's resource tree, and open it to expand the list, as shown in the following illustration. Right-click the Groups folder (under Local Users and Groups) and select New Group.

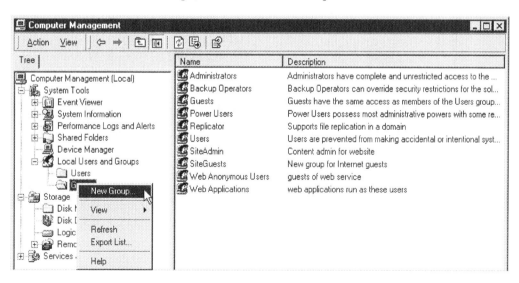

2. Name the group in the New Group dialog box that appears, as shown next. You can use any name you want. Put in a description if you want—something like "Siteadmin" for the group name would be descriptive enough to be self explanatory on a single site server. If you are running multiple sites on the server, also add the name of the site to the name of the group.

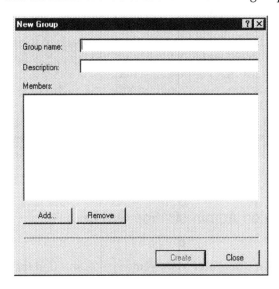

2. The Members window lets you assign the individuals who will have the management responsibility to the group. If your Web server is on the intranet, in one of its existing domains, you can choose the individual's account name from the domain account list that shows up in this window. However, no account names may appear in the list if this server is a stand-alone server and you haven't created the accounts yet. This is no problem, of course, because as you do create accounts, you will assign the account to this preexisting group when appropriate.

3. Click Create and then close the window when you are finished.

Assign Rights and Permissions to a Delegated Administration Group

The minimum set of rights the site manager would need to manage content on the Web site would be directory access permissions to modify the Web site's storage directories and perhaps grant the same ability to other people the manager supervises. If you would like the members of the delegated administration group to have the full rights of the default IIS operators group then you can use the MMC Internet Services Manager to add the group to the Operators ACL. But, if you want to give the group a more restricted set of rights you will need to explicitly set them through Windows 2000 ACLs.

The following procedures are used to grant rights and permissions in the local ACL of your server:

1. Use Windows Explorer to find the root directory of your Web site's content folders in the My Computer window.

2. Right-click the root content folder, choose Properties to open the Properties dialog box, click the Security tab, and once again you will see a Properties configuration dialog box that looks something like this:

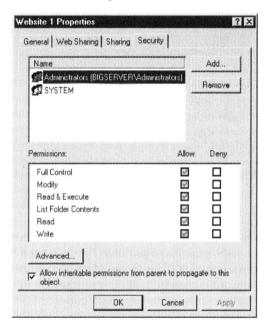

3. In the Security tab are the Administrators and System groups to whom you previously gave full permissions for your entire hard drive. Now, here at the root for the content directories, you will be adding a new group with rights to the directories.

4. Click the Add button to open the Select Users, Computers, or Groups dialog box shown in the following illustration. Scroll down the list of groups until you find the new administrative group that you created for Web content management. Select the new group you created as your delegated Web manager group and click the Add button.

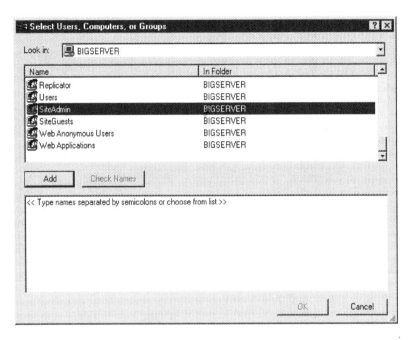

5. Click OK to save your changes and close the window. You will be returned to the Properties dialog box for your Web site root directory.

6. Now, back in the Properties dialog box for your root content directory, you can see your new administration group in the directory ACL. If you select the group, you will see the properties assigned by default to the directory (make sure the correct group is selected). These permissions to which IIS defaulted are not enough to permit content management, and you will need to expand them.

7. You will need to add the ability to Modify and Write in this directory by checking the box next to those permissions. Click Apply to save your changes.

CAUTION In the lower-left corner of the Properties dialog box for the root directory of your Web site shown in step 2, you will see a check box next to Allow Inheritable Permissions From Parent To Propagate To This Object. Make sure this box is checked. This is not an account-specific setting; it is a setting that affects the entire directory. If you remove inheritable permissions, all of the accounts that had rights and permissions in parent directories will be denied rights in this directory. That's not what your trying to do. That would deny rights in this directory to the Administrators and System accounts to whom you gave Full Control rights for the entire disk volume in an earlier procedure. You don't want to override those now.

Repeat the above procedures for the Home directory of each of your server's Web sites if that is all the authority you want to give to your Web managers. Whether you add additional rights and permissions to their profile depends on your organization's security policy. Consult Table 4-1 and Table 4-2 for a listing of the other permissions you could give or deny to your delegated administration groups.

The procedures below should be performed if you do want to modify the default windows permission subcategories:

1. Click the Advanced button at the bottom of your Web site's Home directory Security tab window (shown in step 2 in the last procedure). This will open a new dialog box for Access Control Settings, as shown in the following illustration. You will make your changes in the Permissions tab of this dialog box.

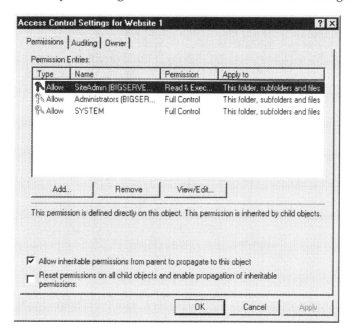

2. You will see two check boxes in the bottom-left corner that apply to all of the accounts in this directory. Take the following actions as long as they are consistent with your organization's security policy:

   • Check the box next to Allow Inheritable Permissions From Parents To Propagate To This Object so that the accounts that already have rights to the parent directories of this account have their rights inherited by this account.

   • Check the box next to Reset Permissions On All Child Objects And Enable Propagation Of Inheritable Permissions. This will ensure that the permissions you give to an account in this directory are also applied to all of the subdirectories.

3. Select the group from the ACL in the center of the screen for whom you want to modify the access control settings, and click the View/Edit button.

4. You'll see the complete list of Rights and Permissions for Windows 2000, as shown next. Make your selections by checking the boxes next to the permission types. Then Click OK to save your changes and exit the window.

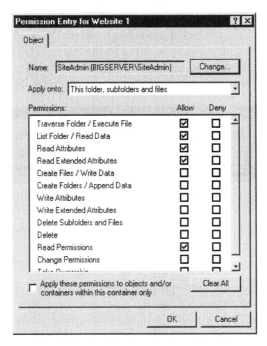

TIP Notice the option Apply These Permissions To Objects And/Or Containers With This Container Only at the bottom of the Permission Entry dialog box. This would, in the terminology of Windows 2000, keep the change you are making to your admin group confined to the Active Directory container you are working in if your server is in a Windows domain. If you are not using domains, it doesn't apply.

---

5. Click OK to save your changes and close the window. You will be asked to confirm with a dialog box that wants you to click Yes to continue.

Modify Default User Account Settings

Default accounts, set up when you install Windows 2000 and IIS, should be examined for compliance with your security policy and adapted to commonly accepted best practices. The following set of recommendations will help you further secure access control and authorization on your Web server.

Disable and Deny Rights and Permissions to Windows 2000 Guest Account

Windows 2000 always installs a default Guest account. By default, in a clean install, the Windows 2000 Guest account should have been disabled when you installed IIS.

Make sure this is the case on your server if you upgraded the server from NT or if you turned a previously existing Windows 2000 server in to a Web server.

Here's how you can verify that the Guest account is disabled:

1. In the Computer Management tool, find the Local Users and Groups folder in the resource tree. Open it, and then open the Users folder to show the names of all the user accounts displayed in the right window.

2. If the guest account is disabled, you will see that it is marked with a red X.

3. If the Guest account is not disabled, right-click it and choose Properties. This will open the Properties dialog box shown next. Click the Account Is Disabled option and then click OK to save your changes and close the window.

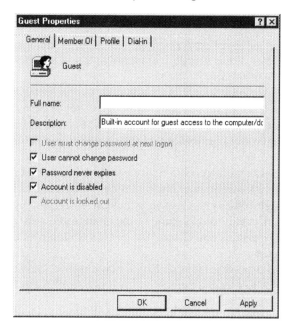

Securing the Windows 2000 Guest Group

A Guest group is also installed by default in Windows 2000. You must keep the two Guest accounts straight. The Windows 2000 Guest account is always a member of the Guest group, as are several other default accounts.

Like the Guest account, the Guest group frequently comes under attack by hackers who know that it's a default. Their attack is usually based on the hope that they can penetrate a system because the Guest group's rights and permissions are insecurely configured and will allow them to use one of the member accounts to gain access.

A highly effective defense against Guest account attacks is to remove the account from the Guest group. But wait, don't rush off and delete it yet. The Internet Guest account (*IUSR_%computer name%*) is critical for anonymous log-ins. You should actually rename it and move it instead of deleting it. So read the next two sections before you do anything else.

Secure the Internet Guest Account for Anonymous Log-Ins

Most Web sites on the Internet that are used for marketing and distribution of information do not require user log-ins because it's not practical to try to manage accounts and passwords for casual visitors and browsers. Instead, most sites use the Anonymous Login, which was discussed briefly in Chapter 3. Anonymous Login is a feature that automatically authenticates users with a generic account name called IUSR. (Actually, it's *IUSR_%computer name%* in your server's ACL.) This account is sometimes referred to as the Internet Guest account. It sounds like the Windows 2000 Guest account, but it's a distinctly different account.

 SECURITY ALERT If you do not use Anonymous Login, perhaps because your Web site is on an intranet and you want users to authenticate, make sure it's not selected in the IIS Directory Service tab and disable the Anonymous Guest Account.

The Internet Guest account should have a restrictive set of permissions that can safely be granted to everyone who visits your site. Basically, to have maximum security, the accounts should not have any permissions on the server except Read in some of the Web site directories.

For a couple of reasons, it's good security practice to create a new Internet Guest account rather than use the default one. The first reason is to mitigate the vulnerability of a default account name. The other good reason is that currently, when your Windows 2000/ IIS server reboots, it ordinarily resets some of the changes you are going to learn in the next several pages. However, if you change the default IIS Internet Guest Account, your changes will not be reset.

The recommended procedure for creating a new Internet Guest account is a lot like the procedure you used to create a delegated Web site Administrative account.

1. Create a new group to which the account will belong. Open the MMC Computer Management tool.

2. Find the Local Users and Groups folder in the resource tree and open it to expand the list. Right-click the Groups folder (under Local Users and Groups) and select New Group.

3. Name the group when the New Group dialog box appears. You can use any name you want. Something like "Siteguests" for the group name would be descriptive enough to be self-explanatory. Click Create to save your new group settings.

4. Now rename the IUSR account. Back in the MMC Computer Management tool, click the Users folder and find the existing IUSR account in the tool's right window. Right-click it and select Rename. Name the account something like SiteIUSR_%server name%.

5. Modify the accounts properties and make the renamed account a member of the new Guest group you just created by right-clicking the account and selecting Properties. This will bring up a Properties dialog box for the account.

6. On the General tab, make sure the following options are selected: User Cannot Change Password and Password Never Expires, as shown here:

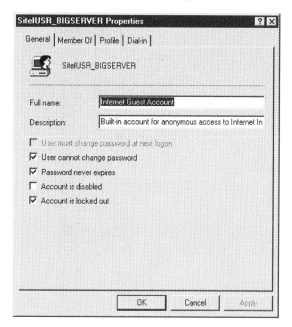

7. Click the Member Of tab and remove the account from the Guests Group. Then add it to your newly created "Siteguests" group. Don't allow the account to be a member of any other group.

TIP   You can remove the Web Anonymous group if you want. We prefer to leave it as a decoy (make sure you deny permissions on the group).

---

8. Click OK to save your changes and close the dialog box.

Directory Access Rights for the Internet Guest

After renaming the Internet Guest account and assigning it to your new group, make sure that you have given the account access to the Web site Home Directory, and double-check its permissions to make sure they are appropriate for an Internet Guest account. It's critical to get this right. If you haven't given the account any access rights, browsers (and users) won't see your pages. If you inadvertently give the account too many access permissions, you have potentially created a large vulnerability.

The permissions the Internet Guest account should have on a Web site that serves only static Web pages are Read permissions in the Web site root directory where the site's static Web pages are placed. If you use dynamic pages and scripts, you should also give Read and Execute permissions in the scripts directory. The Internet Guest account should never be allowed to Write anywhere on the system.

The security best practice to set the permissions for accounts with as much risk potential as the Internet Guest account is to go back to the root directory of the Web site's disk volume, deny all permissions, and then explicitly grant only the appropriate ones in the Web site root directory.

The procedures to deny all permissions are as follows:

1. Use the Windows Explorer or open the My Computer icon on the desktop and find the drives you will be working on.

2. Right-click the appropriate drive and select Properties. The Local Disk Properties window will appear.

3. Select the Security tab to see the accounts in the ACL, as shown in the following illustration. Click the Add button and add the renamed Internet Guest account that you created.

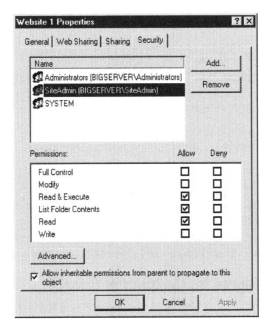

4. Click the Deny boxes on all access permissions so that the account has no rights to the volume. You will be asked to confirm with another dialog box requiring you to click Yes to continue.

5. Repeat these steps for all of the Web server's storage volumes.

Now, to grant rights to the Internet Guest account in the appropriate site directories, take these steps:

1. Find the Web site root directory for static Web pages, right-click it, and then choose Properties.

2. In the Properties window, select the Security tab.

3. The only groups and accounts you should see in the existing ACL for the directory are Administrators, SYSTEM, and the delegated Web administration group you created (it depends on how the rights cascade on your server based on you previous rights configuration selections). Click Add to add your renamed Internet Guest Account to the ACL if its not there already.

4. In the account selection list that appears, shown next, select your renamed account. Then click OK to save your changes and close the list.

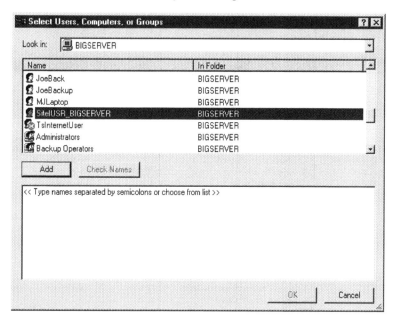

5. Back at the Properties window for the directory, the Internet Guest Account will now appear in the ACL. Select it and click the box next to Read to grant that permission. Uncheck all the other boxes. Click Apply to save your changes.

If your Web site also uses dynamic pages and scripts, repeat the above procedures on the scripts folder and set the permissions for Read & Execute. This will automatically check Read and List Folder Contents, too, but all the other boxes should be unchecked.

Remove Internet Guest Account Rights from Local Security Policy

By default, when IIS creates the Internet Guest account, the account is granted the right to "access this computer from the network," and "log on as a batch job." However, these are rights that should be granted only to administrators or administrator-run scripts, respectively. Now that you are using the account for anonymous log-ins, you should remove those rights in the Windows 2000 Local Security Policy.

Here's how to change these settings:

1. Open the MMC Local Security Policy tool under Administration Tools in the Windows Start menu, or from the Windows 2000 desktop, open the Control Panel folder within My Computer icon and double-click the Local Security Policy icon.

2. Expand the list under the Local Policies item in the Console tree, right-click User Rights Assignment, and select Open (or double-click the item to open it). You'll see the choices for rights assignment policies in the right window of the tool, as shown here:

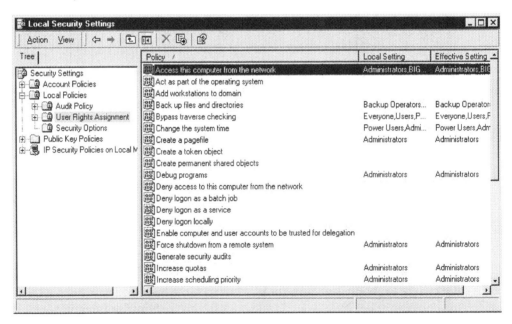

3. Right-click the setting you want to change, and select Security. This will open the Local Security Policy Setting dialog box, shown next, for the policy you are changing. The rights are enabled with a check mark and disabled by removing

the check mark. Uncheck the box for your renamed Internet Guest account and any references to the former Internet Guest account(s) you may have deleted.

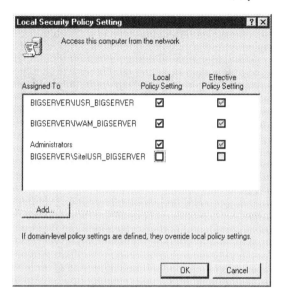

4. Click OK to save your settings and exit the dialog box.

CONFIGURE IIS SITE ATTRIBUTES AND PROPERTIES

Congratulations. You're almost finished. The hardest part is behind you. So far, you have fortified the security of the Administrator account, tightened up the access control on your server's storage disks, delegated administration to Web managers, and secured the Internet Guest account. But you need to address a few more settings through the security properties of IIS before your site is ready for production deployment.

IIS Security Properties

The previous sections discussed Windows 2000 configurations and properties that eliminated security holes and prepared your server for the Internet. Now you must set the properties of your IIS site(s) to match or compliment the configuration of the operating system. You do this through the MMC Internet Services Manager. You can do it site by site or you can set the properties for all the sites on the server through the Master Properties. If you do it site by site, you must repeat each of the procedures for each site.

Master Properties

To access the Security Properties Master tab, select the MMC Internet Services Manager from the Administration Tools of the Windows Start menu. Then, from the console tree, right-click the server site (not a Web site) you want to configure and select Properties from the menu, as shown here:

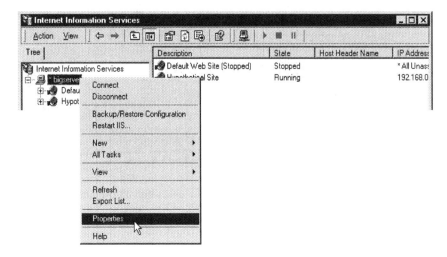

The Master Properties window contains 10 tabs that are used to configure various aspects of the site you selected. If you have multiple sites, you will be configuring the properties individually for each site.

Configure IIS Web Site Properties for Anonymous Access

The configuration you established for the Internet Guest account has prepared it for a production Web environment. Now you must tell IIS you want to use Anonymous access. You may have done this in Chapter 3 as you hardened your server, but it's a good idea to double-check. Besides, if you renamed the account, you also need to specify the new name during this process.

To enable Anonymous access on your site, you use the Directory Security tab (shown next), which when selected gives you the option to edit anonymous access and authentication controls, as well as IP address and domain name restrictions. This tab also contains a grayed out section for "Secure Communications." This is used to configure encrypted communication between the server and its Web clients, through either VPNs or SSL Web sessions. On a stand-alone server encrypted communication is configured on each Web site rather than through Master Properties. Encryption will be covered in Chapter 8.

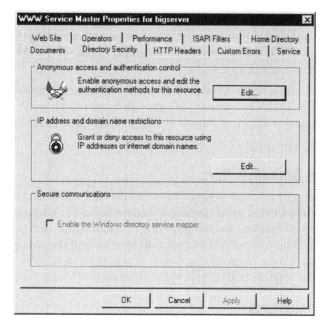

Here's how to do this:

1. Click the Edit button in the Anonymous Access and Authentication Control panel of the Directory Security tab to open the Authentication Methods dialog box, shown next. Select Anonymous Access.

TIP   The other choices for authentication method can be useful in an intranet that uses only Windows clients. In a mixed-client environment, they have some major drawbacks for the non-Windows clients. In Appendix D, we will discuss these alternative authentication methods in more detail.

---

2. Click the Edit button in the top half of the dialog box to open the Anonymous User Account dialog box where you can select the account you want to use as your Internet Guest. Click the Browse button to see your server's ACL and choose the account from the list.

3. The option Allow IIS To Control Password is relevant when you are using more than one authentication method with more than one IIS service. This will be discussed later in Chapter 10. Leave the box unchecked for now.

4. Click OK to save your changes and exit the dialog box.

IP Address and Domain Filters

On the Directory Security tab, you may have noticed two other security property categories you can configure in addition to Anonymous Access. Secure Communications, at the bottom of the screen, allows you to configure certificates for your server used with SSL and VPNs, which will be covered in Chapter 8. IP address and domain restrictions are used to set up filtering rules to prohibit access to your site from specific IP addresses or DNS domains. These settings will be covered in Chapter 6.

IIS Access Permissions

On the Home Directory tab of the IIS Security Properties settings window, IIS offers a set of access permissions that can control access to Web sites, directories, or individual files. These access permissions are IIS access control permissions and not the Windows 2000 permissions you were working with earlier in this chapter. IIS gives you a layer of access control on top of the Windows 2000 OS access control security. These access control permissions are global and not tied to an account or group.

IIS access permissions are enabled for a resource by right-clicking the Web site, directory, or file resource you want to set the rights for in the MMC Internet Service Manager and selecting Properties.

These rights are set at the site level through the Site Creation Wizard when a node is first created. They are modified for all of the server's sites through the Home Directory tab if you bring up the Master Security Properties window at the Web site level, or the Directory tab of the folder or file Properties window, shown next, that opens if you select an individual site's lower level node in the Internet Services Manager console tree.

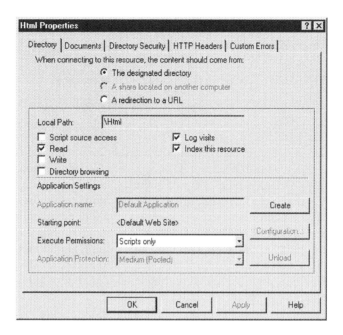

An explanation of the IIS permissions is presented in Table 4-6 (except for the log permissions, which will be covered in Chapter 5). These IIS access controls complement the NTFS access controls and are combined to produce a composite set of permissions. For example, a user denied IIS Directory Browsing to the Home directory of a Web site but given Windows 2000 List permissions would end up with the most restrictive set of permissions (denied the ability to list the file in the directory).

A security best practice, as consistently recommended here, is to use the most restrictive settings that still allow your site to function correctly. Do not allow directory

Access Type	Description
Script Source Access	Users can access source files. If Read is selected, source can be read; if Write is selected, source can be written to. Script Source Access includes the source code for scripts, such as the scripts in an ASP application. This option is not available if neither Read nor Write is selected.
Read permission	Allows the contents to be viewed and passed to the client browser for rendering.
Write permission	Enables clients with browsers that support the "PUT" feature of the HTTP 1.1 standard to upload files to the server or to change the content in a write-enabled file. This is generally not granted unless the administrator has a specific need to make this type of access available.
Directory browsing	Allows a client to view all the files in a directory. Unless this is a public FTP server, this option should be disabled.

Table 4-6.   IIS Access Permissions

browsing on an Internet Web site. Do not assign both the Write and Script/Execute permissions on the same folder.

Managing Multiple Web Sites on the Same Server

IIS has the ability to run multiple Web sites on the same computer. These are called *virtual servers.* Virtual servers can be a good practice if you have a need to segregate different types of information to different groups of users. The security best practice for running virtual sites is to use a different disk volume for each site so that if a hacker should crack one of the sites, he wouldn't automatically gain access to information on all the other sites.

If you are running virtual servers, you can handle delegated Web manager accounts and the Internet Guest account on those Web sites in a number of ways. The method that is both the easiest and the most secure is to use a unique delegated Administration account for each site and a common Internet Guest account across all the sites.

If you follow this recommendation, assuming you are using a different Home directory and associated content directories for each site (as recommended in Chapter 3), each set of directories will have its own unique content manager, as shown in Figure 4-2.

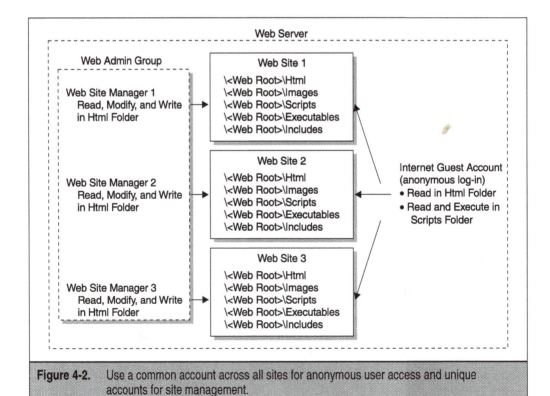

Figure 4-2.   Use a common account across all sites for anonymous user access and unique accounts for site management.

This account configuration allows you to set whatever access control you want for the content managers of the Web sites. You can set the Windows 2000 access control permissions at the group level if you want all of the managers to have the same level of access, or you can set the permissions for each manager in the appropriate directory. As for the Internet Guest account, by using the same account across all the sites you reduce the chances for mistakes and omissions, an important consideration with this critical account.

You create a virtual server with the MMC Internet Server Manager. In fact, you already did this when you created a new site and disabled the default site as you hardened your server in Chapter 3. However, in that scenario, you were only running one site on the server. To run more than one site at the same time, you need to create a unique identifier for each site that DNS can use to direct browsers to the appropriate IIS virtual server. The unique identifier can be a different DNS domain name or it can be a different IP address.

The procedure to set up a Virtual server is as follows:

1. Open the MMC Internet Services Manager tool.

2. Right-click your server in the Console tree and select the New Web Site item from the menu. This will start a wizard that will guide you through the steps to create the site.

3. Name the site on the first wizard screen and click Next. The following screen will ask you for the IP address, port number, or Host Header. Any one of these variables will be enough to make the site identifier unique. If you are using a unique IP address or DNS domain name, you are going to need to coordinate with the appropriate Internet agency or internal network administrator to update DNS databases.

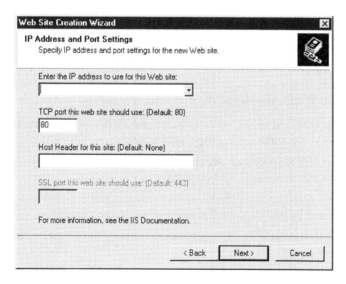

4. On the next several screens you need to give the wizard the location of your Home directory and assign the access control permissions. The access permissions screen is shown next. Select the minimum permissions here. You can go back into IIS properties later to modify them if needed.

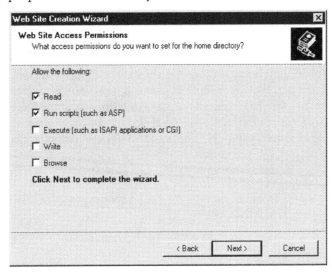

5. When you are through, click Finish and your site will be created.

Using Virtual Directories

IIS allows aliases to be used for the actual directory paths that contain the content you publish on your site. This alias is commonly referred to as a *virtual directory*. The virtual directory feature of IIS hides the actual location of the information from Internet browsers by showing the alias in the URLs rather than the real directory. To the browser, virtual directories look like subdirectories branching from the main /wwwroot directory.

Virtual directories enhance security by obscuring information about the actual physical properties of the server. Use the following procedures to create a virtual Directory for your Web site's Home directory (or any directory, for that matter):

1. Using the MMC Internet Services Manager, right-click the site to which you want to add the virtual directory, and select New | Virtual Directory:

2. A Wizard will help you create the directory. The first screen asks you to name the alias. Choose a name and click Next.

3. The next screen requests that you enter the path of the real directory. You can browse for it by clicking the Browse button. Then click Next.

4. The final screen once again wants you to choose the IIS permissions for the site. Click Next again.

5. Click Finish when you're done and your virtual directory will appear.

CHALLENGE

While Virtual Directories help to protect your site by shielding the actual directory structure of your site from exposure through the browser, they do not provide a defense against URL decoding attacks. There have been several well-known exploits that succeeded in attacking IIS sites using virtual directories that allowed the attacker to access the directory structure under a Web site. The only defense against the known decoding attacks is to update your server with appropriate service packs and security patches.

The lesson to be learned from this history is that you shouldn't allow yourself to have a false impression about directory security. You need to apply all of the protective directory security measures discussed in this book rather than to rely only on a single defense. Furthermore, you should realize that mapped directories from your Web server to other networked servers through virtual directories potentially expose those servers to the same vulnerabilities as your Web site. If your Web server's security is compromised, and a user is able to navigate the Web root without access restrictions, then they can access any folder mapped under that Web root. The consequence is that any file and folder mapped from a Web site is potentially available for downloading or even deletion or alteration.

The best way to prevent this inadvertent compromise is to completely avoid using virtual directories mapped to other servers and to use the techniques described in Part III, "Advanced Topics," when you create connections from your Web server to other systems.

CHECKLIST FOR WINDOWS 2000 ACCOUNT AUTHORIZATION

- ☐ Remove storage administration rights for the Everyone group
- ☐ Give full control of resources to Administrators group and System group
- ☐ Rename Administrator account and create a strong password
- ☐ Create a delegated Administration group for Web content (optional)
- ☐ Disable default Windows 2000 Guest account and deny access rights
- ☐ Rename default Internet Guest account
- ☐ Remove default Internet Guest account rights from Local Security Policy
- ☐ Set renamed Internet Guest account to Read Only access permissions

CHECKLIST FOR IIS SITE PROPERTIES

☐ Configure site to allow Anonymous access or Integrated Windows Authentication

☐ Set IIS Access Control to Read Only in content directories and Read and Execute for scripts

☐ Disable directory browsing

☐ Use virtual directories for additional site security

CHAPTER 5

Security Auditing and Logging

After a Microsoft IIS Web site has been hardened and securely configured, you need to take measures to ensure that you can identify the symptoms and events of a security incident. You need to be able to monitor your system to look for signs that might indicate you have experienced an attack or an intrusion.

Tracking activity on mission-critical systems is a normal and necessary part of the routine of any system administrator (or Web site manager). To track IIS Web site activity, you must use and properly configure the Windows 2000 and IIS logging and auditing features. Your site maintenance procedures should include regular inspection, analysis, and review of logged information to observe or detect anomalous activity that shows a failed or successful attack was launched against your site. If a problem is discovered, you need to perform a security audit to determine what damage was done and how it happened.

Presumably, your organization's security policy has outlined processes and standards for all of these issues. You shouldn't even consider putting your site into production until you have implemented those policies. This chapter will cover the steps required to set up logging, auditing, backups, and restores so that you can ensure that your Web site will comply with your organization's security policy and you can be confident that the site can be securely and reliably operated.

SITE MONITORING OVERVIEW

You monitor a Windows 2000/IIS Web server by examining and analyzing log file information, which primarily consists of messages sent to the event log service by another service, an application, or some other part of the operating system. These messages are used to track the events that occur on the system, such as shutting down, starting up, creating a new account, and so on. In addition, IIS tracks a long list of events that occur within its suite of services. For example, IIS can track and list every request made to the server to log on anonymously by visitors to the site.

Windows 2000 has six different kinds of logs in which it records events and activity. You may already be familiar with some of them if you have previous experience with Windows 2000 system administration. IIS keeps its own log separate from the Windows 2000 logs. The full list of log file types that could be on a server is shown here:

- **System Log** Captures system component events, such as when a service is stopped or started or when a failure occurs.

- **Security Log** Records security issues such as user logons and resource usage such as creating, opening, and deleting files.

- **Application Logs** Logs events related to the applications that might be run on the server.

- **Directory Service Log** Stores information regarding the Active Directory Service, such as problems connecting to the global catalog.

- **DNS Server Log** Records events related to running the Windows 2000 Directory Name Service in your Active Directory.

- **File Replication Service Log** Records any notable events that took place while the domain controller attempted to update other domain controllers.

- **IIS Log**   IIS keeps a separate log that tracks the events generated by use of IIS services (WWW, FTP, and so on).

Some of the logs are of no consequence to an IIS Web server. For example, your server should not be running as a Domain Name Service (DNS) server or a domain controller on a Web site, so the DNS Server Log and the File Replication Service Log don't need to be run. The Directory Service Log would apply only if your server is part of an Active Directory Windows domain, and the log could be kept on another server. Therefore, the logs you will most likely manage on your Web server are the System Log, the Application Log, the Security Log, and the IIS Log.

Tracking in the Windows 2000 System Log and the Application Log are activated by default when IIS is installed, so that system and application events are automatically recorded. All other tracking ordinarily runs only if expressly configured and/or started. On your Web site, if you ran IIS Lockdown as you hardened your server in Chapter 3, tracking in the Windows 2000 Security Log and the IIS Log was activated for you.

Site Monitoring Information

The log features of Windows 2000 and IIS can be configured to record a great deal of activity. IIS stores its log files in text format by default, and you can view them in any application or reader than supports text. Typically, the files are analyzed by loading them into a report-generating software tool that can filter, sort, and manipulate the data in any number of ways. The following illustration shows a sample readout of the IIS Log file.

Windows 2000 System Log files are stored by default in a proprietary format with an .evt extension. The Windows 2000 Event Viewer, accessed via one of the Microsoft Management Consoles (MMCs) under Administration Tools in the Windows Start menu, allows you to read the messages in the Windows 2000 log files and organize them by filtering or sorting on date, time, source, severity, or other variables. You can use the Event Viewer to convert the log files to text format and view them in another program if you prefer. The following illustration shows the console of the Event Viewer.

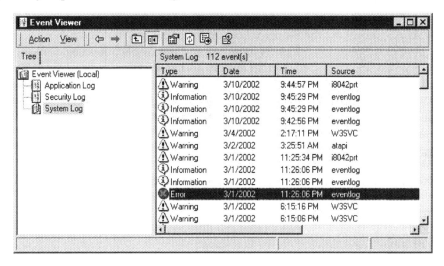

Spotting security issues with the log files requires a little study on your part. You'll need to review the message types and make sure you understand what they mean. When you deploy, you should closely observe your server for awhile and establish benchmarks for "normal" activity, so that in time you can identify events that indicate a departure from the norm (often a signal of a problem).

Each of the five categories of log entry messages is identified by its own icon. Each message includes an event ID, the date, time, object, computer name, category, and event number type of the message. The message categories and their functions are listed here:

- **Information Event Messages**   Describe the successful completion of an operation, such as a service starting

- **Warning Event Messages**   Describe the unexpected behavior that might indicate a problem, or point to a future problem if not corrected

- **Error Event Messages**   Describe errors that mean a task failed

- **Success Event Messages**   Describe an audited security event that Windows 2000 completed as requested

- **Failed Event Messages**   Describe an audited security event that Windows 2000 could not complete as requested

Figure 5-1 gives you a look at an error message example from the System Log of a Windows 2000 server that recorded the sudden shutdown of the server. An unexpected shutdown certainly falls outside the boundaries of normal operation and is the kind of event you would usually want to investigate further. The event ID is the easiest way to research the event in the Microsoft Knowledge Base if you don't understand what a message means.

Auditing

Windows 2000 and IIS have a specialized security monitoring feature called *Auditing* that helps you track specific events in the Security Log that are associated with specific IIS or Windows 2000 resources or system management objects. But auditing is also a process. It's what you do with the information you collect and the tools you use to analyze and diagnose security issues on your site.

Windows 2000 provides three types of object and resource auditing features, and several more are unique to IIS. Table 5-1 shows the auditing types and the system to which they each apply.

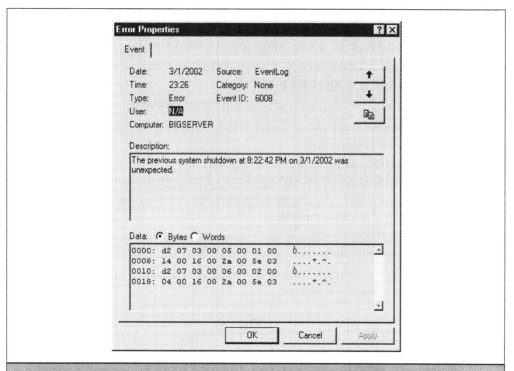

Figure 5-1.   A sample message from the Windows 2000 System Log indicating an unexpected shutdown.

Auditing Type	Applies to
System & Registry	Both Windows 2000 and IIS
File System	Both Windows 2000 and IIS
User Account	Both Windows 2000 and IIS
Home Page Visitors	IIS only
Application Processes	IIS only
Authoring	IIS only

Table 5-1.   Auditing Types in Windows 2000 and IIS

Auditing features track events according to auditing rules defined in the server's Local Security Policy and/or the property settings of the Web site. You can audit the following nine event categories:

- **System events**   Events related to security, such as system shutdowns and restarts; events that affect the security log.

- **Process tracking**   Detailed tracking of process invocation, duplicate process handles, indirect object access, and process termination.

- **Policy change**   Security policy changes, including privilege assignments, audit policy modifications, and trust modifications.

- **Privilege use**   Use of a privilege; assignment of special privileges.

- **Account management**   Creating, modifying, or deleting users and groups; password changes.

- **Directory service access**   Record access to Active Directory. Must be enabled to permit auditing specific directory objects. Works on domain controllers only.

- **Account logon events**   Authenticating (account validation) on the local computer at the console or across a network.

- **Logon events**   Interactive logons or network connections to the local machine that are generated where the logon occurs.

- **Object access**   Access attempts on specific objects. These include files, directories, user accounts, and Registry keys.

An audited event can have two outcomes: *success* or *failure*. For each event category, you can indicate whether to audit for success, failure, or both. A high concentration of events in a log that you examine, or an unusual usage pattern, can indicate a problem. For example, a large number of invalid password events could indicate that a password-cracking attack might have been attempted on the server.

LOGGING SETUP AND MAINTENANCE PROCEDURES

Logging and auditing features work together to enable system monitoring, but they are not sufficient by themselves to support security audits. To produce a credible security audit, a process and procedures must exist to review the log files regularly to make sure they are secured, archived, and working properly. Only when the logs are properly defined, enabled, and regularly maintained can security audits be confidently performed and trusted. When logs can be trusted, they can help you reconstruct the events of security incidents and provide legally enforceable evidence if you ever need to take action in the courts to seek remedy for a security breach.

The logging and auditing features of Windows 2000 and IIS can be configured to record a great deal of activity. Windows 2000 event logs tend to fill up quickly when a system is configured to collect too much information. What's the point of collecting information you will never use? Conversely, if only a few kinds of events are logged, important information could be missed. Therefore, your decision of what to log and what not to log has far-reaching consequences.

Auditing Goals and Objectives

Planning, policy, and maintenance are key to ensuring that the critical information that logs collect will be there when you need it. If you have clear goals, it will be easier for you to determine exactly what type of information you want to capture and then configure the logging mechanisms to log the necessary number of events to collect that information. The settings put in place by the IIS Lockdown utility (IIS Lock) and/or Hisecweb.inf template used in hardening your server provide a pretty good policy baseline. You can modify those settings to capture any additional information you want to collect.

You also need to think about the resources and management objects you are going to audit. Then, for each class of resource or object, you need to decide which events and instances you are going to audit. The information shown in Table 5-2 was taken from a white paper entitled *Security Auditing in Windows 2000* that can be found on the Microsoft Technet Web site (www.Microsoft.com/technet). The table contains some examples of the events that can help you spot a security problem for a variety of resources and objects. You'll learn how to implement this list in the discussion that follows.

Table 5-2 illustrates how you can target your approach to auditing, but don't assume that this list is the right one for your organization. You must make your own decisions when it comes to audit objectives. As you plan, decide on the resources that you must audit and then determine the events you must monitor to detect a problem. For example, when trying to ascertain whether an audited object has come under attack, the best indicators would be failure events, because they imply attempted access by someone who does not have access permission.

Potential Threat	Audit Type	Events Outcomes
Random password hack	User Account	Failure audit for logon/logoff events. A large number indicates repeated attempts that are frequently the result of a systematic attack.
Stolen password break-in	User Account	Success audit for logon/logoff events to identify users of the system to identify where they came from.
Improper access to sensitive files	File System	Success and failure audit for file-access and object-access events on high security resources. Success and failure audit of read/write access by suspect users or groups for the sensitive files.
Misuse of privileges	File System & Registry	Success audit for user rights, user and group management, security change policies, restart, shutdown, and system events to observe who made changes and what changes were made.

Table 5-2.   Events That Can Help Identify a Security Problem

Log Management

Several configuration parameters are associated with every Windows 2000 log file. They allow you to change the amount of space the log files consume on disk and to specify system behavior when the log files fill up. The Windows 2000 configurable parameters are shown here:

- **Maximum log file size**   This can be configured in the Event Viewer application, and defaults to 512KB.

- **Overwrite behavior when log is full**   Three choices are available: overwrite events as needed, overwrite events older than a certain number of days, and do not overwrite.

- **Shut down on audit failure**   This security policy setting will cause the server to stop if the security log is full and the overwrite behavior is set not to overwrite events. Sometimes, this setting is also referred to as "CrashOnAuditFail" in various pieces of Microsoft documentation and technotes, which refers to the value in the Windows 2000 Registry that the policy sets.

IIS has similar, though slightly different, log file parameters, as IIS will automatically create a new file when the current log file fills up or based on some kind of simple rule. The log file parameters are shown here:

- Allow the log file to have an unlimited size.
- Create a new log file when the file reaches a certain size.
- Create a new log file based on a define period of time (hour, day, week, month).

To manage the log files, you need to specify the appropriate values and behaviors for these settings. You also need to make sure the log files are secure and to archive the files on a periodic basis to make room for new log entries and to ensure that you have an historical record of site activity.

Configuring Log Parameters

You can use the Windows 2000 MMC Event Viewer to interpret log information and to set and control the configurable Windows 2000 log parameters. The Event Viewer allows you to set the log file size, choose the overwrite behavior, and set the "CrashOnAuditFail" to on or off. To manage IIS log files, you use the MMC Internet Services Manager.

Set Windows 2000 Log File Size and Overwrite Behavior   The procedures to set the log file size and overwrite behavior properties for the Windows 2000 logs is the same for each log file type:

1. Open the Event Viewer, located in Administrative Tools in the Windows Start menu. (The Event Viewer Console).

2. In the left window of the Event Viewer console, right-click the Security Log entry and select Properties. The Security Log Properties window shown in Figure 5-2 opens.

3. On the General tab, you can specify the size of the Security Log file in the Log Size section. The default value is about 10MB (10240KB). Change this value to a number you are comfortable with, depending on the size of your server's disk or volume and the amount of traffic your site gets. Watch the log over time and you'll get a good idea of the right size to specify here.

4. Define the overwrite parameter for the file by selecting one of the options. What you choose here may depend on the frequency with which you expect to maintain and archive the log data. The safest choice for a site with a high availability requirement is to use select "Overwrite events as needed" and not allow the log to fill up, because full log conditions will miss activity you should be recording and have been know to cause server crashes. That it is certainly not acceptable behavior for a Web site that promotes your organization's brand and image to the public.

5. Click OK after you make your selection to save your changes and close the window.

Using the Windows 2000 "Shut Down on Audit Failure" Policy   Believe it or not, having the server shut itself off if the log file fills up is a preferred reaction for some high-security Web applications, when it's better that the application not run than run without auditing. The server will shut down if the shutdown setting is enabled in the Local Security Policy

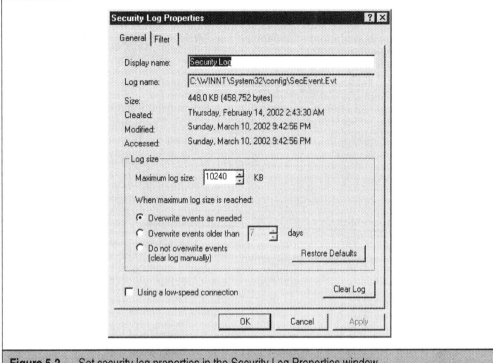

and the log file overwrite parameter is set to "do not overwrite." This capability is disabled by default.

To turn on the shut down on audit failures policy, you should use the Local Security Policy MMC. The procedure for turning off the policy is shown here:

1. Open the MMC Local Security Policy console tool under Administration Tools in the Windows Start menu; or from the Windows 2000 desktop, open the Control Panel Folder in My Computer, and double-click the Local Security Policy icon.

2. Expand the list under the Local Policies item in the left pane, right-click the Security Options folder, and select Open (or double-click the folder to open it). You'll see the choices for security policies in the right window of the Local Security Settings tool, as shown here:

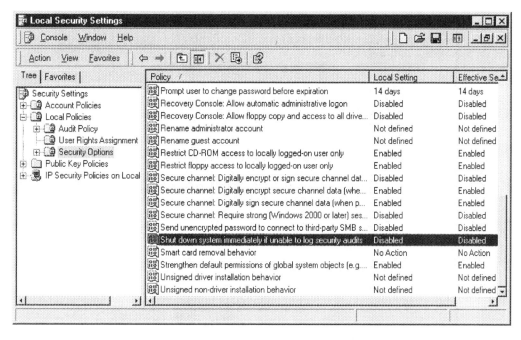

3. Right-click Shut Down System Immediately If Unable To Log Security Audits in the right window of the console and select Security from the pop-up menu to bring up the Policy Setting dialog box.

4. In the Policy Setting dialog box, you can enable the policy by selecting the Enable button.

Changing the IIS Log File Properties   As stated, the IIS log file properties are similar to Windows 2000 log file properties, but IIS properties control slightly different behavior. IIS log file properties can be set globally for all Web sites on the server, or they can be customized on a site-by-site basis. Here's how to set IIS log file properties:

1. Open the Internet Services Manager under Administration Tools in the Windows Start menu to open the console. Alternatively, you can open the My Computer icon on the desktop, open the Control Panel folder, and then open the Administrative Tools folder and find the Internet Services Manager icon.

2. Select the server name in the window if you want to set the properties globally for all Web sites. Or select a specific Web site in the left panel. Right-click the server or site and select Properties from the pop-up menu.

3. In the Properties window shown next, select the Web Site tab. At the bottom panel of the tab, make sure the box labeled Enable Logging is checked.

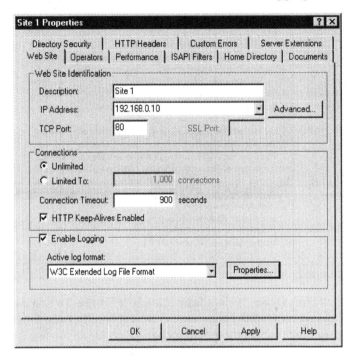

TIP   On the Web Site tab, you can change the log file format. The choices are W3C Extended Log File Format, ODBC Logging, and NCSA Common Log File format. W3C Extended format is a standard defined by the Internet's World Wide Web Consortium. ODBC (Open Database Connectivity) Logging would allow you to store the log information into a database on another server, rather than in the IIS log file. Organizations with heavy Web traffic sometimes do this to help manage the log data. NCSA format is another text log file alternative from another standards organization. Many UNIX servers use NCSA format, and you could use it if you want the log files to be compatible with those types of systems.

---

4. Click the Properties box in the lower-right corner of the tab to open the Extended Logging Properties window shown here:

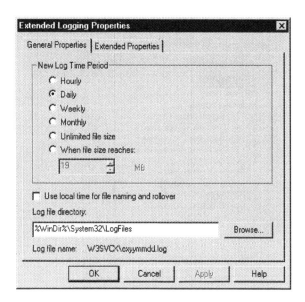

5. On the top of the General Properties tab, you can specify whether you want the log file to have an unlimited file size, specify a maximum file size, or specify that you want a log file to be closed automatically at the end of a specific time period. In each case, IIS will create a new log file when the current file has reached its limit. IIS will choose the new file's name based on the "yymmdd" date convention if you use W3C format. The date format changes if you use a different format.

6. Check the option for Use Local Time For File Naming And Rollover if you want the day to start at 12:00 A.M. local time (use the time and date from your local machine) rather than the Windows 2000 default of 12:00 A.M. Greenwich Mean Time.

7. IIS also has a set of extended properties that you can configure. These properties allow you to control the detail of the information the IIS log collects. Click the Extended Properties tab, shown next, if you want to have a look at the choices. The defaults that Microsoft has chosen and that you implemented by running IIS Lockdown are quite comprehensive, but you can track additional detail if your situation requires it.

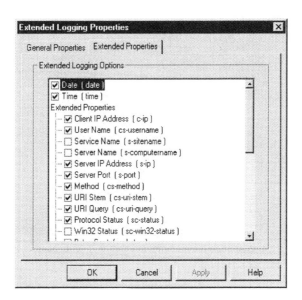

A complete list of extended logging properties is shown in Table 5-3. The name of the field is in the left column of the table. The way the field is listed in the log file is in the center column.

Field	Appears As	Description
Date	`date`	The date on which the activity occurred.
Time	`time`	The time the activity occurred.
Client IP Address	`c-ip`	The IP address of the client that accessed your server.
User Name	`c-username`	The name of the authenticated user who accessed your server, not including anonymous users, which are represented by a hyphen.
Service Name and Instance Number	`s-sitename`	The Internet service and instance number that was running on the client computer.
Server Name	`s-computername`	The name of the server on which the log entry was generated.
Server IP	`s-ip`	The IP address of the server on which the log entry was generated.
Method	`cs-method`	The action the client was trying to perform (for example, a `GET` method).
URI Stem	`cs-uri-stem`	The resource accessed; for example, Default.htm.
URI Query	`cs-uri-query`	The query, if any, the client was trying to perform.
HTTP Status	`sc-status`	The status of the action, in HTTP terms.
Win32 Status	`sc-win32-status`	The status of the action, in terms used by Windows 2000.

Table 5-3. Extended Log File Properties

Field	Appears As	Description
Bytes Sent	`sc-bytes`	The number of bytes sent by the server.
Bytes Received	`cs-bytes`	The number of bytes received by the server.
Server Port	`s-port`	The port number the client is connected to.
Time Taken	`time-taken`	The length of time the action took.
Protocol Version	`cs-protocol`	The protocol (HTTP, FTP) version used by the client. For HTTP this will be either HTTP 1.0 or HTTP 1.1.
User Agent	`cs(User-Agent)`	The browser used on the client.
Cookie	`cs(Cookie)`	The content of the cookie sent or received, if any.
Referrer	`cs(Referer)`	The previous site visited by the user. This site provided a link to the current site.

Table 5-3.   Extended Log File Properties *(continued)*

CHALLENGE

If you know how to read the logs, you can discover a great deal about the activity of users who visit your site. A well-known case a few years back involved a hacker by the name of Kevin Mitnick, who was prosecuted and convicted in a trial in which log file information was a major part of the evidence. It showed what he did on the systems he cracked.

The example below shows lines from a log file using the following fields: Time, Client IP Address, Method, URI Stem, HTTP Status, and HTTP Version.

```
#Software: Microsoft Internet Information Services 5.0
#Version: 1.0
#Date: 1998-05-02 17:42:15
#Fields: time c-ip cs-method cs-uri-stem sc-status cs-version
17:42:15 172.16.255.255 GET /default.htm 200 HTTP/1.0
```

The line beginning with *#Software* is the server software. The *#Version* line indicates the log is using W3C extended log file format. The *#Date* line is self-explanatory. You need to understand the shorthand to know how to read the rest of the log file:

Prefix	Meaning
s-	Server actions
c-	Client actions
cs-	Client-to-server actions
sc-	Server-to-client actions

CHALLENGE (continued)

Therefore, the translation of the last two lines in the log file listing (the #*Files* line and the line with the data that follows) is presented below:

Field	Field Data	Translation
time	17:42:15	The time is 5:42 and 15 seconds in the P.M.
c-ip	172.16.255.255	The client IP address was 172.16.255.255
cs-method	GET	The client requested HTTP GET on the server
cs-uri-stem	/default.htm	The resource requested was the home page
sc-status	2000 HTTP/1.0	The HTTP v1.0 status code 2000 indicates the request was successfully fulfilled

This particular excerpt doesn't show it, but a large number of fields can be selected for logging as you configure the log file properties. When the logging fields do not have information recorded for an action, a dash (—) appears in the field as a placeholder.

Securing the Logs

Securing the logs is just as important as auditing and reviewing them. Only the appropriate personnel should have access to the files. Keeping records of system events does no good if someone can tamper with them. The log files must be protected to prevent experienced hackers from modifying the information to try to cover their tracks.

Event log data is reported to the Windows 2000 Event Log service by other parts of the system or by applications running on the system. The Event Log service stores this data in .evt files in a default directory. The specific paths to each log file are listed in the following table:

Log	Path
System Log	<SystemRoot>\System32\Config\SysEvent.Evt
Application Log	<SystemRoot>\System32\Config\AppEvent.Evt
Security Log	<SystemRoot>\System32\Config\SecEvent.Evt
IIS Log	<SystemRoot>\System32\LogFiles\W3SVC2\exyymmdd.log*

*IIS will automatically assign the file name using the date to replace *yymmdd*.

Two procedures can be used to secure the log files. The first procedure, which is critically important, is to restrict access to the Windows 2000 log files to all except the Administrators group and the System account. The second step, a good idea but less critical, is to move the location of the log files. The best location would be to another volume—not the system volume—that has nothing else on it and has plenty of space for large log files.

If you move the log files to their own volume, it's easy for you to change the access permissions to prevent others from seeing or tampering with the files. So let's first discuss the procedure for moving the log files.

Moving the Log File Location   Moving the location of the IIS log file is simple. You change the properties of the server in the MMC Internet Services Manager on the same tab where you set the IIS log file properties. Refer back to the section "Changing the IIS Log File Properties " to see the console and windows used to change the log file directory.

To modify the location of the Windows 2000 log files, you need to modify a string in the Windows 2000 Registry that specifies where the event log is currently located. To edit the Registry, you will use the Windows 2000 Regedit utility.

TIP   Editing the Registry incorrectly can cause serious problems that may require you to reinstall your operating system. It might be a good idea to look ahead to Chapter 6 at the procedure for backing up the Registry and make an Emergency Repair Disk before you attempt this.

---

1. Select Start | Run to open the Run dialog box.

2. Type **Regedit**, and then click OK. This will launch the Regedit program.

3. In the Regedit window, make sure you are working on the local machine. Click the folder called HKEY_LOCAL_ MACHINE to open it and expose the nested folders.

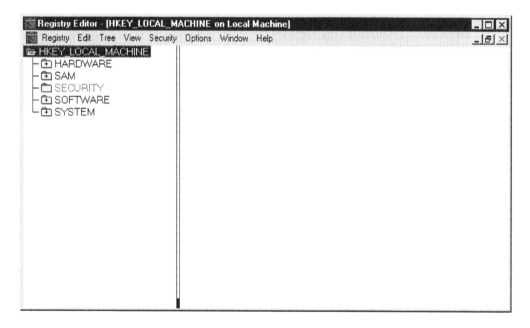

4. Click the following succession of folders to open them: System\
CurrentControlSet\Services\EventLog\. The contents of the EventLog
folder reveal the folders of the Windows 2000 Application, Security, and
System event logs, as shown here:

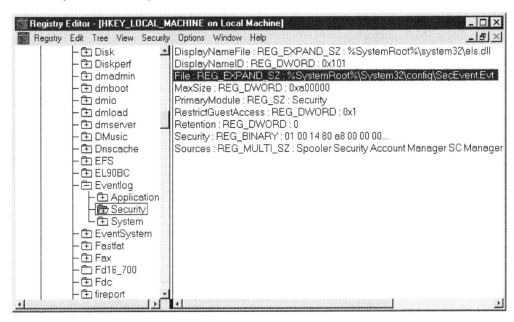

5. Select the Security Log. You should see information in the right pane that
displays the values for the security log.

6. Double-click the File value to open the String Editor dialog box, shown next.
Type the new drive and path in the box for the new volume and directory, but
use the same file name \SecEvent.Evt. Then click OK.

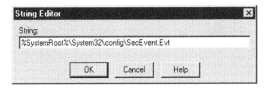

7. Repeat the steps for the other log files. Then quit Regedt32, and restart the
computer.

Remove the Everyone Group   With the log files stored on a volume of their own, you can change the access control permissions on the volume by removing all users from the access control list (ACL) of the volume except for the Administrators Group and the System user account. If you have not put the log files on a volume of their own, you can modify the ACL of the directory where all the files are stored. The procedure to make those changes follows:

1. Use Computer Management under Administration Tools in the Windows Start menu and find the computer's disks in the tool's resource tree. Or open the My Computer icon on the desktop and find the drives you will be working on. Right-click the appropriate drive and select Properties. The Local Disk Properties window will appear.

2. Select the Security tab, shown in the following illustration. Remove the group Everyone if it's present in the ACL by selecting it and clicking the Remove button. If your server storage drives have been configured to include other groups or accounts in addition to Everyone in their ACLs, delete them, too.

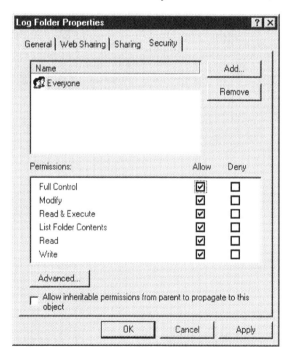

3. Click Apply so that the system saves your changes.

Give Full Control to System Users and Auditors   Now that you have eliminated the unwanted groups from your storage drive ACLs, you can add the groups and accounts that you do want and set the appropriate rights and permissions. The default group of System should be added and given full control. Some user or group of users with the authority to perform audits should also be given full control rights and permissions.

SECURITY ALERT   You do not want the auditing group to be the Administrators group. Somebody has to audit the administrators, too. If you have a large Administrators group, you may want to create a separate group called Auditors that is the only set of users in addition to the System account to have full control rights. Otherwise, at least create a separate account.

1. In the Security tab of the Local Disk Properties window, click the Add button to add new groups to the ACL.

2. In the next dialog box, shown in the following illustration, select System and your audit group and click the Add button to process your change.

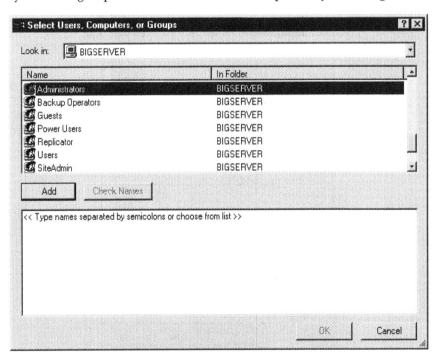

3. Click OK to return to the Local Disk Properties window.

After you successfully add the groups and accounts, you can set the rights and permissions on the log file volume or directory. You should give the System user and auditing groups full control of the volume or directory, and you should also set it so that as you create new subdirectories, System and auditing users will inherit permissions on those directories as well.

Archiving the Logs

Log files can grow to be quite large. Archiving procedures will move the files onto a backup media, saving them for future reference and clearing room in the logs for new information. You should regularly archive log files just as you should regularly review them to look for abnormal activity.

Archiving a Windows 2000 Log File   To archive a Windows 2000 log file:

1. Open the Event Viewer and right-click the log file you wish to archive. Choose Save Log File As.

2. In the Save As dialog box, enter a path and file name for the archive. Ideally, you should have a resource and a process for storing and maintaining the archived logs on a long term basis, because you never know whether at some point in the future you might find you have been hacked, and want to trace how far back the original breech occurred. A network drive on an internal server makes a good archiving repository. Be sure to save the archive in .evt (event log) format—this preserves the binary information in the log's detail records (so you can continue to read them with the Event Viewer).

3. After you archive the files, if you did not choose to overwrite the events as needed in the log file properties, you should also use the Event Viewer to clear the log files to make room for new entries. To clear the log files, right-click the log file you wish to clear and choose Clear All Events from the pop-up menu.

Archiving an IIS Log File   Archiving IIS log files can be an automated process, depending on how you set up the IIS Extended Logging properties. IIS Log file properties can be set so that a new log file is started, with a new file name, according to any of the following choices:

- On the hour
- At the end of every day
- At the end of every week

- At the end of every month
- When the file reaches a certain size
- Never (i.e., the log file can be allowed an unlimited file size)

What happens in all of the properties choices, except Unlimited File Size, is that the old log file will be saved and a new log file will be automatically created when the end of the period is reached.

Here's how to archive IIS log files:

1. Open the MMC Internet Services Manager and right-click on the Web site whose archiving properties you want to change, or right-click at the server level if you want to edit the properties globally for all sites, then select Properties from the pop-up menu.

2. On the Web-site tab of the Web Site Properties window (or the Master Properties window if done at the server level), select the Properties button at the bottom of the window next to the selection box that specifies your log file format.

3. When the Extended Logging Properties window opens, on the General tab, make your selection for the Log Time Period. Just below those choices is a box labeled "Use local time for file naming and rollover" you can check to use the local time to determine the end of the log period. The default is 12:00 A.M., Greenich Mean Time.

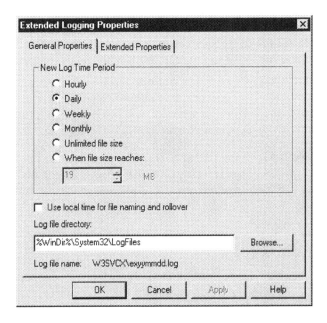

4. At the bottom of the General Properties tab you can specify a new location to store the log files. Change the directory as appropriate (once again this is preferably a network drive on a different server) and then click OK to close the window and save your changes.

TIP   The names of the new log files IIS creates will change depending on the Log Time Period that you choose. The file name will use the format *exyymmdd.log* if you chose daily, exyymm.log if you chose monthly, and so on. If you click on the Log Time choices in the General tab of the Extended Logging Properties window you can watch the name format change at the bottom of the screen. Remember that the old files will be preserved as new files are created in the directory so you will need to manually move the old files to your long-term archive repository from time to time.

AUDITING

With your log files configured and secured, you have the necessary and trusted infrastructure in place to audit your Web site. Auditing features in Windows 2000 and IIS will provide information for the logs that can record specific activity about resources, objects, and users so that you can tie events to their sources and targets and track the history of the activity. In other words, the auditing features will track information that establishes an *audit trail*. The audit trail can show who performed the actions and who tried to perform actions that were not permitted, depending on how you define the audit policy.

Setting Auditing Policy

Auditing policies determine what event message categories are tracked and stored in the Windows 2000 and the IIS logs. Audit event settings obey standard group policy application rules. The hierarchy of Windows 2000 audit policies is

1. Domain policy settings
2. Site policy settings
3. Local policy settings

A stand-alone server's local policy will be the effective policy. However, if your Web server is in an intranet domain and a policy element higher in the hierarchy is defined (and the group policy has been configured to disallow local overrides), that definition will override the local one. Therefore, as you read the following discussion, bear in mind the context of your server if it is part of an Active Directory because you may need to set the policies at the group level rather than the local level.

Auditing policies are set locally on a system via the MMC Local Security Policy tool. You can view and edit the auditing policy currently in your system through the following procedure:

1. Open the MMC Local Security Policy tool under the Administrative Tools in the Windows Start menu to open the console shown here:

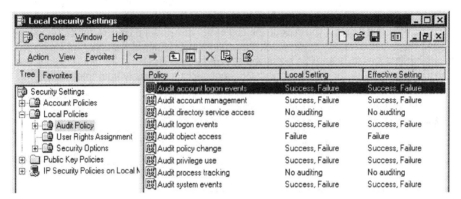

2. In the left pane, click Local Policies to expose the nested folders. Click the Audit Policy folder to expose the individual audit policy settings in the right pane of the console.

3. In the right pane, right-click the policy that you want to set or change, and select Security from the pop-up menu (or just double-click on the policy) to open the dialog box.

4. Each of the auditing policy settings will have the same Success (an audited security access attempt that succeeds) and Failure (audited security access attempt that fails) choices, which you can set. Click the Success and Fail check boxes as appropriate for your audit policy.

TIP   If you want to apply the same audit settings to multiple servers, it may be more efficient to use a Security Policy Template to store the settings that you can copy onto other servers and apply. Using the Security Configuration snap-in and the Security Templates snap-in was discussed in Chapter 4.

Table 5-4 contains the configuration of audit policy settings that are implemented when you run the IIS Lockdown tool or the High Security Template (hisecweb.inf) described in Chapters 3 and 4.

TIP   This discussion will adhere to the Microsoft recommendations for Windows 2000 audit policy settings, but you can refer to Appendix C for a more detailed list of settings if you want to depart from those recommendations.

Property	Success	Failure
Account Logon	On	On
Account Management	On	On
Directory Service Access	Off	Off
Logon	On	On
Object Access	Off	On
Policy Change	On	On
Privilege Use	On	On
Process Tracking	Off	Off
System	On	On

Table 5-4. Latest Settings for IIS Audit Policy Implemented in IIS Lock

Auditing Windows 2000 Objects and Resources

Windows 2000 auditing capabilities will collect information about the use of file system resources, user accounts, Registry keys, and other system resources. Auditing of the objects is not enabled by default and must be turned on and configured through the Properties settings of the resource that is to be audited.

Auditing is performed on a per-object basis. You specify which objects to audit and what to audit. Object auditing can be useful in identifying unauthorized attempts to use files. Note that Microsoft recommends turning off your audit policy for successful Object Access in Table 5-4 for a server running IIS 5. That's generally OK because IIS auditing is pretty detailed; however, some people like to at least track Administrator access on the system folder of any bootable system drive that occurs through the use of basic operating system utilities. Under ordinary circumstances, that traffic will be low so it won't overload the log with data and will also show whether other authorized (or nonauthorized) Administrators have been in there.

TIP If you decide to audit any of your directories or other system objects, you must enable at least one ACL permission setting for any account you are specifically auditing in the object's security properties or you will get error messages when you try to set the audit properties on the object. In other words, if you try to audit an account's activities on an object to which it has no permissions, Windows 2000 will object.

Auditing Administrator's access to the default system folder makes sense and is a good practice when setting up file system object auditing properties if administrative duties for the server will be shared. The properties can be set with the server's local management tools. A Security Template is useful when you need to repeat the security settings procedure for more than one server (assuming the settings on all the servers will be the same).

TIP   To use a security template to set the audit properties for a file system object, open the MMC, where you previously added the Security Analysis and Configuration snap-in and the Security Templates snap-in. Then find the security template file where you want to make the policy setting, open it, and then open the nested folder called File System. Right-click the folder and choose Add File. From there, you can follow along from step 2 in the following procedure.

The procedure for setting up auditing on a Windows 2000 file system object (with the local management tools), such as the system directory, is as follows:

1. Open Windows Explorer, or alternatively open the *My Computer* icon on the desktop, and then navigate to the default system folder of your Web server.

2. Right-click the folder and choose Properties. In the Properties dialog box, open the Security tab. You will see a configuration screen that looks like the one shown here:

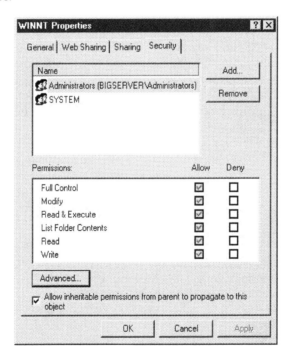

3. Click the Advanced button at the bottom of the dialog box to open the Access
   Control Window for the object. Open on the Auditing tab to see auditing
   properties shown in this dialog box:

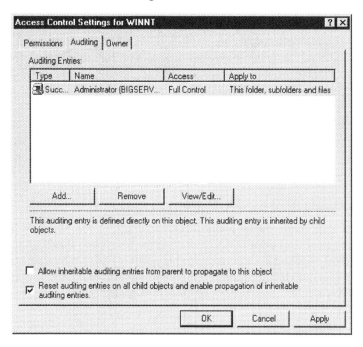

4. At the bottom-left corner of the window, select the option Reset Auditing Entries
   On All Child Objects And Enable Propagation Of Inheritable Auditing Entries so
   that the auditing will apply to all objects in the directory.

5. Click the Add button in the middle of the window to select the Administrators
   group from the ACL. Choose the appropriate rights and permissions in the
   Audit Entry dialog box that pops up, and then click OK. When you click
   the Apply button, your changes will be implemented.

Auditing for IIS

IIS auditing complements the auditing features of Windows 2000 with a broad range of
capabilities, flexible options, and a wealth of detail. IIS auditing can be set up globally for
all sites on a server, or it can be enabled or disabled for individual Web sites. You can
choose which events you want to audit for any site, directory, virtual folder, or file. If
logging is enabled on a site, you can disable it for specific objects.

IIS logging and auditing monitors IIS-specific events related to HTTP traffic (or FTP and NNTP) in and out of the server and tracks IP address information that is not available through Windows 2000 logging and auditing mechanisms. Consequently, IIS auditing can help you track the behavior of visitors to your site and identify them by the IP address they visited from. You can track any visitor's attempts to access your Web pages or any other part of the server and know what the visitor did.

For example, IIS auditing can help you spot any of the following visitor behaviors that often signal a break-in or attempted attack:

- Excessive failed logon attempts from a single IP address

- Failed attempts to access and modify .bat or .cmd files or run executable files or scripts

- Unauthorized attempts to access secured directories or to upload files to a folder that contains executable files

Configuring Properties for IIS Auditing

The terminology in IIS blurs the distinction between logging and auditing, and that can be confusing. The easiest way for you to reconcile the terms and conceptualize the steps required to support auditing is to think of first enable logging, which allows you to audit. IIS auditing is configured through the property settings for your Web site. IIS auditing settings are complementary to Windows 2000 auditing settings. IIS auditing settings monitor the following objects:

- **Home directory**   Tracks visits to the site's home directory and its pages.

- **Application processes**   Records unsuccessful client requests to event logs.

- **Authoring server extensions**   Tracks changes made to site with FrontPage server extensions.

TIP   Chapter 3 recommended that you not use the authoring server extensions on a production server, but they are a useful tool on a development server.

Setting IIS Object Properties   To set the properties to log and audit these objects, you use the Internet Services Manager. In general, you can set the properties for all Web sites on your server or you can customize the properties on a server-by-server basis. Authoring server extensions are an exception because you can set them only on an entire server.

1. In the MMC Internet Services Manager, right-click the server name if you want to set the properties globally for all Web sites, or right-click a specific Web site from under the server name, and select Properties. If you are setting the properties globally for all Web sites you will see the server Properties window shown here. For individual sites, you'll go straight to the Properties windows shown in step 4.

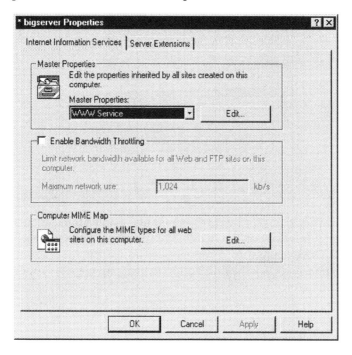

2. To set the properties for authoring server extensions, select the Server Extensions tab in the server Properties window and check the box at the bottom of the screen that says Log Authoring Actions, as shown here:

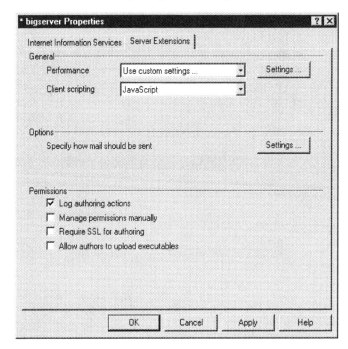

3. To set the properties for home directory and application processes, select the Internet Information Services tab of the server Properties window shown in step 1. Then, make sure WWW Service appears in the Master Properties selection box, and click the Edit button to bring up the site Properties window.

4. Select the Home Directory tab and make sure the Log Visits box is checked, as shown here:

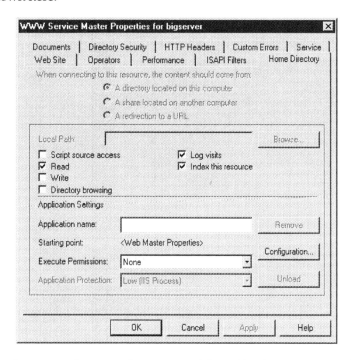

5. To set the properties to track unsuccessful application processes, click the Configuration button in the bottom panel of the Home Directory tab to open the Application Configuration window.

6. Open the Process Options tab and check the box that says Write Unsuccessful Client Requests To Event Log, as shown here:

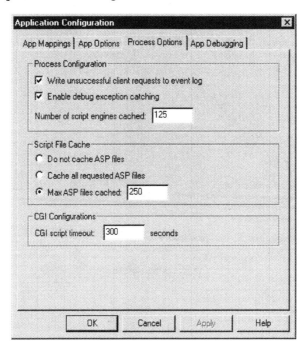

TIP The option in step 6 is available only when High Isolation protection is set on the application. This setting isolates the memory space in which the application is run to try to prevent a rogue application being able to seize control of the system.

Auditing Events Captured by Settings for Extended Logging Properties Extended logging properties were briefly discussed in the Changing the IIS Log File Properties section, as you were enabling logging on your IIS Web site. The extended properties are set through the Web Site tab of the server Properties window.

The list below contains the National Security Agency (NSA) recommendations for the extended properties you should use to audit your Web server:

- **Date and time event occurred** Helps to pinpoint the time of the event.
- **IP address of the client** Indicates where the client was coming from.

- **User name accessing your site**   Reveals the name of the authenticated user who accessed your site. This does not include anonymous users.

- **HTTP method**   Indicates the action the client was trying to perform (for example, a GET method, which indicates a download or a form action).

- **URI stem**   Records the resource accessed by the client (HTML page, script, or ISAPI application).

- **URI query**   Shows the query the client was making.

- **Time taken to process the request**   Indicates how long the visitor was on the site or at least how long it took to accomplish an event.

- **Status of the request**   Displays the status, in HTTP terms and/or in the terms used by Windows 2000.

- **Referrer**   Lists the URL of the last site visited by the client (indicates the path followed to an event).

- **Server port**   Captures the port number to which the client was connected.

Auditing for Backups

The right to perform backups is a powerful privilege. Backup and restore rights override Windows NTFS file access restrictions while a backup is being made, allowing backup operators to read and write to any file in the system so that the files can be copied to the backup media or restored to hard disk.

Consequently, backup activities should be audited. Auditing backups, which translates to auditing the activities of a user group called Backup Operators, gives security administrators the ability to identify activity that is not normal. The setting to audit backups was enabled when you ran IIS Lockdown during your hardening procedures.

To set or verify the enabled setting, you use the MMC Local Security Policy tool on your server. The procedure follows:

1. Open the MMC Local Security Policy console tool under Administration Tools in the Windows Start menu; or from the Windows 2000 desktop, open the Control Panel folder under the My Computer icon and double-click the Local Security Policy icon.

2. Expand the list under the Local Policies item in the left pane of the console, right-click the Security Options folder, and select Open from the menu (or

double-click the folder). This will open the choices for security policies in the right pane of the tool, as shown here:

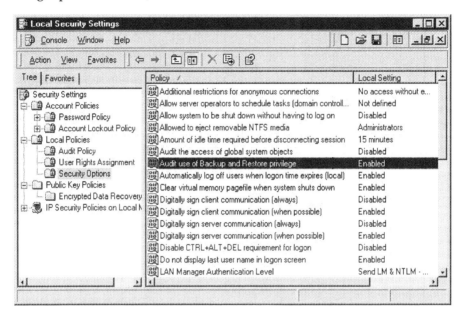

3. Right-click the policy Audit Use Of Backup And Restore Privilege in the right window of the console tool and select Security from the pop-up menu.

4. You'll see the dialog box where you can enable or disable auditing for backups by checking the appropriate option. Make sure the backup and restore policy is enabled.

By auditing, along with enforcing some of the security measures for backup that will be described in Chapter 6, you can manage and monitor a reasonably secure backup process.

LOGGING AND AUDITING CHECKLIST

☐   Manage log files

☐   Set the Windows 2000 log file size and overwrite behavior

☐   Set the Windows 2000 "Shut down on Audit Failure" policy to the requirements of your security policy

- ☐ Set the IIS log file properties:
  - ☐ Format (W3C recommended)
  - ☐ Rollover properties
  - ☐ Extended properties
- ☐ Set up log file security and archives
- ☐ Move the log file location
- ☐ Remove the Everyone group and give Full Control to System and Auditors groups
- ☐ Define policy and procedure for archiving the logs
- ☐ Audit:
  - ☐ Set policy for Windows 2000 in MMC Local Security Policy console
  - ☐ Set Windows 2000 auditing properties for objects you want to audit
  - ☐ Set the IIS auditing properties for objects and events
  - ☐ Set auditing policy for backups

PART II

Administration

PART II

Administration

CHAPTER 6

Deployment Issues

Deployment is the stage at which all your site planning and preparation move out into the real world. After you connect your site to the network, it's exposed and potentially imperiled. So you want to make sure that you give it every advantage possible.

You should consider some environmental and procedural measures to augment the hardening and configuration work you've done so far. In brief, before actually deploying a live site, you should take any of the following steps that apply to your situation:

- Make sure you have a backup of your server content and configuration, and make sure that you possess the tools and resources necessary for restoring your system should something go wrong.

- Set up an appropriately secured network perimeter to keep the Internet separate from your intranet. On the Internet, routers and firewalls play important roles in perimeter defense, and the layout of a "demilitarized zone" (DMZ) can be used to fortify the perimeter.

- Take advantage of advanced IIS directory security and Windows 2000 network filtering features on an intranet where you might not use a firewall to block ports and/or restrict access to or from specific IP addresses and domains that are outside your network.

- If your organization manages its Web site remotely, because the site is hosted at a remote location such as an ISP or at the facilities of Web hosting company, the site needs to be set up for secure remote management.

This chapter discusses all these management and network security measures. You will learn how to back up and repair your system in the event that a destructive security incident occurs. Network filtering, perimeter defense, and the IIS configuration for various network architectures are also covered. Finally, you will learn how to set up a secure remote management configuration.

RECOVERY PLAN

Your should include a site backup procedure and a disaster recovery plan in your organization's security policy and data management strategy. Regularly scheduled backups should be a central part of the plan. In addition, your policy should specify that you perform a backup every time the site is updated, even if the scheduled time has yet to come.

Independent of your Web content, whenever you make modifications to the configuration of the site, you should make a set of emergency startup and repair disks. Emergency Repair Disks (ERDs) allow you to restore your Web site to operational status should it suffer a crippling incident, such as virus intrusion or malicious attack that corrupts or destroys critical operating functions. You should always back up the Registry when you create these disks, as the Windows 2000 and IIS configuration information is stored in the Registry. After all your hard work to secure your site, it would be foolish not to have a restorable image of the configuration.

You can back up site content in numerous ways. Sites with high availability requirements commonly use automatic backup measures, such as *disk mirroring* or *duplexing*. Disk mirroring hooks a second disk up to the server's disk controller so that data is simultaneously written to two disks. Duplexing adds a second controller so that each disk has its own. Such redundant disk systems provide a complete copy of the server's hard drive that can go online in the event that the primary drive goes down. However, even redundant disk systems do not guarantee security, and they won't eliminate the need for manual backups onto removable media, because mirrored disks are equally vulnerable to many attack methods. A virus that affects files, for example, can easily spread to both disks.

Removable media backups will allow you physically to separate your backups from your live system and even to locate a copy offsite in case you have a fire, theft, or natural disaster at your site's facility. It's essential that you store the media offsite, or you have solved only half the problem.

Emergency Repair

Generally, if you suffer damage to you system, you can use your Windows 2000 Setup CD to repair the problem. But to prepare for a worst case scenario, you should make a set of floppy disks that you can use to start the computer and initiate the recovery if the install program on the CD doesn't recognize that a server's corrupted disk has a previous system image you want to save. The floppy disks will consist of setup startup disks for booting the system and an ERD.

Create Bootable Setup Disks

You will use the Windows 2000 Setup CD to prepare the disks. You need four blank, formatted, 3.5-inch, 1.44MB floppy disks for the setup and one disk for an ERD. Label the first four disks Windows 2000 Startup Disk 1–4, and label the fifth disk as a Windows 2000 ERD.

To create Windows 2000 setup floppy disks:

1. With the Windows 2000 Server Setup CD inserted in your CD-ROM drive, choose Start | Run. You'll see the Run dialog box, shown here:

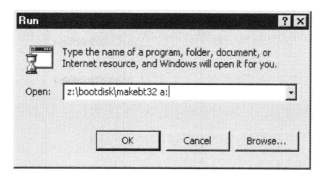

2. Type **Z:\bootdisk\makebt32** *a:* into the command line and click OK (where Z: is the letter that represents your CD-ROM drive and *a:* represents your floppy drive).

3. As the command executes, a console window like the one shown next will instruct you to insert the first floppy disk. Follow the screen prompts and exchange disks until all four setup disks have been prepared.

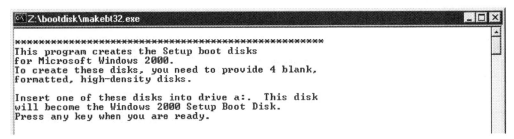

Now you have a set of bootable setup disks in case you can't boot the damaged system from either the hard disk or the CD-ROM drive. These disks, at some point when you need them, will allow you to initiate the Windows 2000 disaster recovery process, which is discussed shortly.

Preparing an Emergency Disk

Your next step is to create the Windows 2000 ERD. If a system failure occurs and an attack has damaged your server, you can sometimes use the ERD to restore core system files from your original Windows 2000 CDs without reinstalling the entire system.

The following repairs are possible with the use of an ERD:

- *Inspect and repair the boot sector.* This function verifies that the boot sector on the system partition still references the operating system loader file, NTLDR, and that it has not been damaged (or modified) by the incident.

- *Inspect and repair the startup environment.* If any of the files on the server that are needed to start Windows 2000 are missing or corrupted, they are replaced from the Windows 2000 Setup CD.

- *Verify the Windows 2000 system files and replace missing or damaged files.* A comparison is made on the Windows 2000 system files on the bootable system drive to verify that each installed file is good and that it matches the file that was installed from the Windows 2000 Setup CD. Any file that does not pass the test is replaced.

TIP   When you performed your initial Windows 2000 and IIS installation, a directory named %systemroot%\Repair was created on the bootable system volume, and information about your system settings was recorded there. In general, you should not change or delete this folder. The exception to the rule, as you were advised during the system hardening process (see Chapter 3), is to remove the Security Accounts Manager (SAM) file. This is a security precaution to minimize your vulnerabilities to attacks that target the files that store passwords. But it will prevent you from restoring passwords and user accounts through the recovery process if you suffer a system failure. If you ever need to restore your user accounts or passwords, you can restore the SAM file from the last total system backup you performed.

Emergency Disk Contents

The Windows 2000 Backup program includes a wizard that helps you create an ERD. The ERD is made by copying several files from the Windows 2000 %systemroot%\Repair directory onto a floppy disk. Table 6-1 contains a list of the files and their purposes.

As you can see, the ERD does not back up data or programs. It just keeps a record of what was installed on your system in the Setup.log file. This file is a text file that records the Windows 2000 components (and their locations) that you have installed on the server. Because Setup.log is a text file, you can view its contents using any text-editing program. Figure 6-1 shows a view of the contents of a sample Setup.log file.

Each line of the log file records a detail about a file or directory in your server's system directory (the directory on the startup volume that contains the operating

File Name	Purpose
Autoexec.nt	Used to initialize the MS-DOS environment.
Config.nt	Used to initialize the MS-DOS environment.
Setup.log	A log of which files were installed files, and Cyclic Redundancy Check (CRC) information for use during the emergency repair process. This file has the read-only, system, and hidden attributes and is not visible unless you have configured My Computer to show all files.

Table 6-1.   Files Stored on an ERD

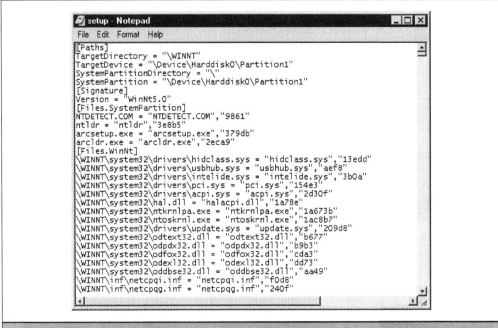

Figure 6-1. Use the Setup.log file to see what is installed on your system.

system executables, drivers fonts, and other files). At the end of every line is a Cyclic Redundancy Check (CRC) value. This is a binary value, calculated by the backup/ recover program, that is a measurement of the file size. When you use the Windows 2000 recovery program along with the ERD, that value is used to determine whether the file currently on the system has somehow been changed (either it's been deleted, corrupted, or otherwise modified); if the current system file has been changed, the recover program will restore the original file.

The ERD does not contain a copy of the Registry files. However, during the process of creating the disk, you have the opportunity to back up the files to the %systemroot%\ Repair directory. It's a good idea to take advantage of this opportunity. If your system Registry files become corrupted, accidentally or otherwise, you can use the files in this folder to repair the Registry without performing a full system restore.

Creating an ERD

You can use the Windows 2000 Backup program to create an ERD. You need to supply a formatted disk, as the program will not format the disk for you. The procedure follows:

1. Select Start | Accessories | System Tools | Backup. This will open the screen shown here:

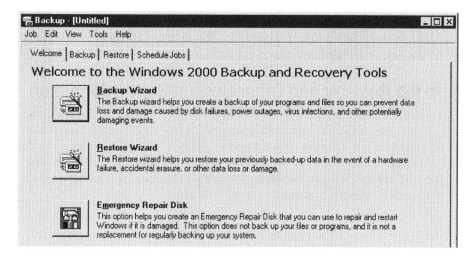

2. Click the Emergency Repair Disk button. The Emergency Repair Diskette dialog box, shown next, appears. As stated, it's a good idea for you to back up the Registry at this point by selecting the Also Backup The Registry… option in this dialog box. This backup can be used to help recover your system if the Registry is damaged.

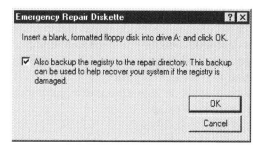

 SECURITY ALERT   The Registry backup copy will actually be created in a directory called RegBack in the %systemroot%/Repair directory of your portable operating system volume. Putting the Registry backup on the same drive as the original leaves it potentially vulnerable to whatever damage the original drive may suffer in an attack. But that's how the option works. For that reason, the Registry copy created by the ERD is a nice convenience, but not a best practice disaster recovery procedure. You should still perform a Registry backup that is physically separated from the server.

3. Click OK and the disk will be prepared. You'll see a dialog box when it's done, asking you to label and date the disk.

That's all there is to creating the disks. You should re-create the Setup disks and ERD each time you update a driver, perform a version upgrade, install a new service pack, or make any other significant configuration change.

Backing Up the Registry and Other System State Information

The ERD is not a replacement for a proper backup. As stated earlier, you should also perform a backup, in addition to re-creating your emergency disks, each time you make significant configuration changes on your server—even if it is not time for a regularly scheduled backup. Although full coverage of the Windows 2000/IIS backup process is beyond the scope of this book, a few things about the procedure for backing up your Web server's *system state* are important to point out here.

TIP   Backup and restore are well covered in the Microsoft online documentation and support literature on www.microsoft.com/technet if you need help with full backup and restore procedures.

CHALLENGE

About Recovery and Repair

Hopefully, you'll never have to use your emergency setup disk and ERD. But if you ever need to recover a damaged system, you need to be aware of an important issue that we learned the hard way. When you run the Microsoft Setup program to repair a system, you are offered two choices for restoration methods. The Setup screen where you make your choice will contain information similar to the following:

```
Windows 2000 Server Setup
        Windows 2000 Repair Options
        To repair a Windows 2000 installation by using the recovery
        console, press C.
        To Repair a Windows 2000 installation by using the Emergency
        Repair Process, press R.
        If the repair options do not successfully repair your
        system, run Windows 2000 Setup again.
```

If you run the Windows 2000 Setup Emergency Repair Process, which is the second option, the copy of the Registry that will be restored is the *original* Registry created during your site installation—not the copy that you created in %systemroot%\Repair\RegBack when you made your ERD. *That's not the one you want to use*, though, because it will wipe out all the efforts discussed in the first five chapters of this book! To use the backup Registry files that contain all your configuration changes for system restoration, you must use the Recovery Console to copy the backed up Registry files to the %systemroot%\System32\Config folder.

If you change only the configuration when you make site changes, you don't have to do a complete server backup. Instead, you can take advantage of the Windows 2000 Backup program feature that allows you to back up only the system state. When you choose the system state backup option, you are backing up the following system information:

- The server's Registry (configuration information)
- Startup files (necessary for starting the computer)
- Operating system files (necessary for running the operating system)
- The COM+ class registration database (information used by Component Services and COM+ applications)

The following procedure is used to perform a backup of a Windows 2000/ IIS Server's system state:

1. Choose Start | Accessories | System Tools | Backup. Then click the Backup Wizard icon at the top of the window.

2. As you run through the wizard, you'll be presented with the screen shown next, where you can select what you want to back up. Choose Only Back Up The System State Data. Then click Next.

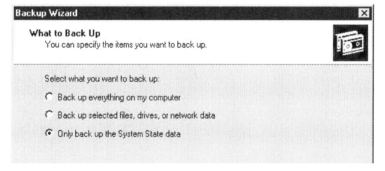

3. Choose the media and location for your backup from the window shown next. It's a good idea to save the backup on a removable media so you can store it offsite or at least off the system. Name the file and click Next.

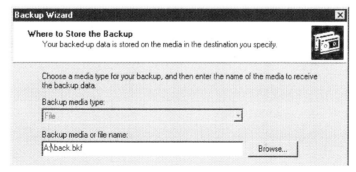

4. When you get through all the settings screens, click Finish and the backup will begin.

You can set some advanced properties before proceeding with the backup, such as backing up only the changes, but chances are you won't need those unless your system state backup is a very large file. The following illustration shows a report from a sample system state backup. The backup file was about 250MB and took less than 2 minutes to back up to a remote hard disk drive over the network.

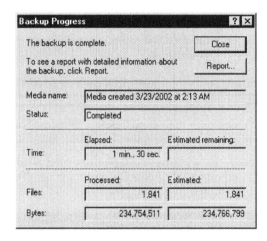

Backup Security Issues

You must address some important security issues related to backups in your security policy and management practices if you want to delegate backup tasks to other individuals. Because backups must be performed in a user context that has access to all files on the server, you need to make sure your security policy and practices will prevent abuses.

Management Controls for Backups

The issues related to the access control, permissions, and restrictions for backup operators are as follows:

- Backup responsibilities and privileges should not be assigned to regular user accounts. They should be performed by administrators or by a specially privileged group of users. Windows 2000 includes a preconfigured group called Backup Operators for this purpose. Remember the Enable Auditing For Backups setting you activated in Chapter 5? That setting audits the activity of Backup Operators, so it's important to use the group if you delegate the task.

- Members of the Backup Operators group should have special logon accounts. No single user account should be given backup privileges in addition to regular account privileges. Individuals who will be Backup Operators should be given new accounts for their backup responsibilities, even if it means that these individuals will have two accounts on the server—a user account name and an account name that makes the user a Backup Operator.

- It's a good practice to set restrictions on the backup account, such as forcing the user to log on from a particular system and allowing backups only during appropriate hours.

The vulnerability created by backup delegation is that, even though they cannot directly read the files they back up, users with backup rights might try to restore these files on another system. The preceding three measures will work together to introduce some management control to the backup process. Using the Backup Operators group allows you to audit operators. Auditing creates an audit trail. Location restrictions lets you implement other measures to augment the system security, such as media check-in and check-out, for a truly secured process.

Setting Backup Access Control and Restrictions

Creating new user accounts for backup operators is a simple process. If your Web server is a stand-alone server, you will use the Microsoft Management Console (MMC) Computer Management tool to create the accounts locally. If your server is in an intranet Windows domain, you will use the Active Directory Users and Computers tool.

The procedure follows:

1. Select the appropriate MMC tool from the Windows Start menu or the Administrative Tools folder of the Control Panel. You will see a console that looks something like this:

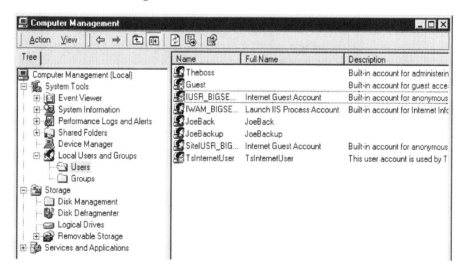

2. Expand the items in the tree and find the Users folder under Local Users and Groups. Right-click the Users folder and select New User from the pop-up menu to open the New User dialog box shown here:

3. Type in the new account user name, a description, and a password (according to the policy controlled by your Local or Group Security Policy settings); then click Create. When you close the window, your new user account will appear in the Local Users and Groups folder of the MMC.

4. Right-click the account and select Properties to open the Properties window, where you can place the account in the Backup Operators group. Select the Member Of tab in the Properties window.

5. It's a good idea to remove the account from the Users group, because you want to explicitly track everything the Backup Operator does.

6. Then click the Add button and select the group to add the account to the list (Backup Operators), shown next. When you complete the task, you will see that your new account is now a member of the group.

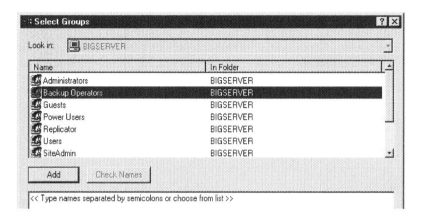

After members are assigned to the Backup Operators group, all you have to do to finish the previously discussed management controls is to set location restrictions on the group. This is done in Windows 2000 by defining a "permitted logon workstation" policy.

NETWORK LAYOUT AND FILTERING ON AN INTRANET

All the work you have done so far to secure your site physically, harden your server, set up local security policy, implement authentication, configure access controls, and audit user activity has created a set of barriers that have to be defeated before anyone can gain access to your system. On your intranet, you can create yet another barrier through the use of *filtering*.

TIP   If you are going to use filtering on your intranet Web server and you have physically located the server in a secure location, you might not want to use the filtering on the network interface used for managing the server. You shouldn't need to do so if your physical security measures are done properly.

Filtering Features in Windows 2000

Windows 2000 has a filtering feature in the TCP/IP stack. The feature uses a simple set of rules that will allow you to block all but a specific port (or to use inverse syntax to allow access to all but a specific port) or to block (or allow) an entire protocol.

TIP The Windows 2000 features could theoretically be useful on the Internet just as well as an intranet. However, organizations that connect their sites to the Internet usually deploy firewalls for blocking and filtering. Firewalls have more blocking capability and use a more sophisticated variety of techniques to stop various kinds of Internet traffic. While useful on an intranet, the Windows 2000 filters are no substitute for a good Internet firewall.

Here's how to use Windows 2000 TCP/IP filtering:

1. Choose Start I Settings I Control Panel, or right-click My Network Places on the desktop and open the Control Panel from there.

2. Click the Network And Dialup Connections icon, right-click the appropriate Local Area Connection icon, and select Properties from the pop-up menu to open the Local Area Connection Properties window, shown here:

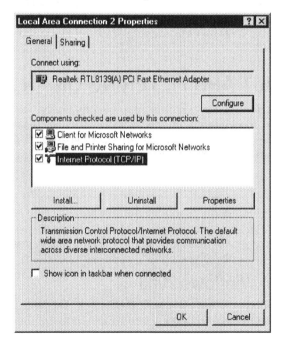

3. Select the Internet Protocol (TCP/IP) component, and click the Properties button to see the Internet Protocol (TCP/IP) Properties window.

4. Click the Advanced button in the lower-left corner of the Internet Protocol Properties window to open the Advanced TCP/IP Settings window, and then click the Options tab. The options for TCP/IP settings are shown next.

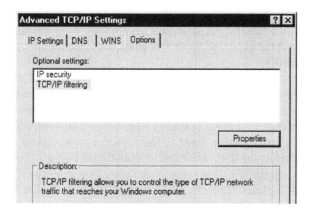

5. Choose TCP/IP Filtering from the list of options, and then click the Properties button to open the TCP/IP Filtering dialog box, shown here:

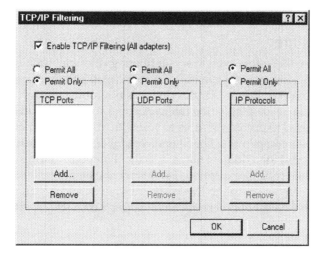

6. The filtering rules you use will depend on the purpose of your site and the applications you run on it. If your Web site will serve only static Web pages, you can block everything except TCP port 80 for HTTP. To build this rule click the Permit Only radio button in the TCP column and then click Add, which will bring up a dialog box enabling you to specify the port number. If your site will use Secure Sockets Layer (SSL), you'll need to add port 443 as well. Before you click OK to save your changes, you should remove the check mark next to "Enable TCP/IP Filtering (all adapters)" if you know you don't want that filtering rule to apply to the network interface you're using to manage the server.

SECURITY ALERT Be careful if you experiment with the rules. If you choose Permit Only and then don't add any port numbers, it will be interpreted as "don't permit anything," and you will shut everybody out of your site.

The process is essentially the same to build rules that filter for User Datagram Protocol (UDP). You need to know the port number on which you want to build a rule. The third column in TCP/IP Filtering dialog box, labeled IP Protocol, is used to filter on a specific protocol. You need to refer to the protocol by a number from a reference table of protocols maintained by an Internet standards body called the Internet Engineering Task Force (IETF). This table is included in Appendix C in case you need to use it or if you are curious. You can add new protocols to the list as needed.

TIP You can look up information regarding the IP Protocol options on the Microsoft Technet Web site (www.Microsoft.com/technet) under the topic "IP Protocol Filtering" or by document number Q309798.

IIS Filtering Feature

IIS includes a feature that allows you to set up filtering rules that prohibit access to your site from specific IP addresses or Domain Name Service (DNS) domains. While the last section suggested that Windows 2000 filtering was not robust enough for the Internet, this IIS filtering feature is perfect for the Internet. For example, IP address domains and restrictions can be used to prohibit visitors to your site from the Internet from the domains of your organization's competitors. The filters work by creating a blanket rule that denies access (or grants access) for a domain name, specific IP network addresses, or a range of IP addresses, and then making exceptions to override the blanket filters.

The feature is managed through the MMC Internet Services Manager. A filter can be applied to all sites on the server or it can be applied on a site-by-site basis.

CHALLENGE

Filtering is a broadly used technique in security. Windows 2000 uses it, firewalls use it, Web servers use it, and a number of other products use it. Even you have used the feature. When you turned off the NetBIOS protocol as you hardened your server in Chapter 3, you were filtering on a protocol. In that case, so you didn't have to build your own rule, Microsoft made it easy by giving you a box you could check.

Frankly, it's not common to use the protocol number method of TCP/IP filtering on a specific protocol. However, it could probably be needed when you build custom applications on a Windows 2000 server or IIS Web site that use special protocols and port numbers. In those cases, you could use this feature to block everything but the custom applications' protocol.

The procedure to set up IIS filtering follows:

1. Open the MMC Internet Services Manager under Start | Administrative Tools. You'll see the Internet Information Services console view shown here:

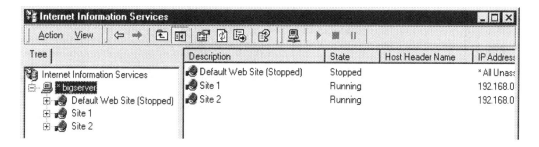

2. Right-click the server name in the left pane if you want to set the properties globally for all Web sites, or right-click a specific Web site under the server name. Select Properties from the pop-up menu.

   - If you are setting the properties globally for all Web sites, you will see the Server Properties window, shown next. Make sure WWW Service option is selected in the Master Properties box and click Edit to go to the Properties window.

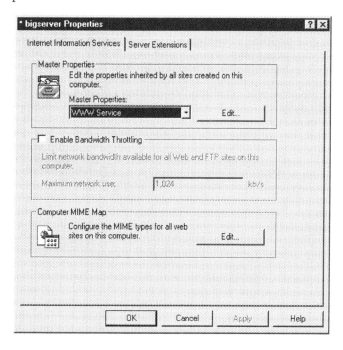

- For individual sites, when you right-click Properties, you'll go straight to the following window, which includes all the site's properties tabs. Select the Directory Security tab.

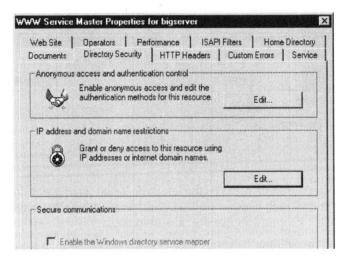

3. In the IP Address And Domain Name Restrictions section of the Directory Security tab, click the Edit button to bring up the following dialog box:

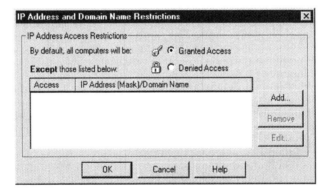

The IP Address and Domain Name Restrictions dialog box is used to build access rules. Begin by choosing Granted Access or Denied Access to set rules for the particular policy you are implementing. Your choice will depend on your goal. If you want to allow broad access to your site but block a small number of domains or addresses, you should choose Granted Access and then create your list of denied sites in the next dialog box. If you want to deny access broadly, but grant access to a similarly small group, you would base your rule on Denied Access and build a small list of granted sites.

Here's how to build a rule to block specific IP addresses or domain names:

1. Click the Granted Access radio button for this procedure to set the general case of the rule.
2. Now define the rule's exception (i.e. the addresses you want to deny) by clicking the Add button to open the Deny Access On dialog box, where you'll build your list of denied addresses or domains (if any).

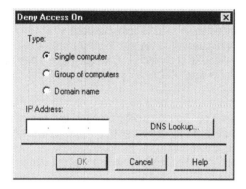

3. In the Deny Access On dialog box, do one of the following:

   - Deny access to a single computer on your local subnet or in a specific domain, in which case you will click the radio button next to "Single computer" and type the IP address of the computer into the IP Address field and the name of the domain if the computer is not on your local subnet. Click the DNS Lookup button to specify the domain.

   - Deny access to a group of computers on the same subnet, in which case you will click on the radio button next to "Group of computers" and type the network ID and subnet mask into the new input fields that will appear at the bottom of the dialog box. The network ID will be the first IP address in the range you want to block. The subnet mask is a value that, in this context, will indicate the size of the range. It will vary from organization to organization, based on the type of addresses the organization is using (Class A, Class B, or Class C). For example, if the organization is using Class C addresses, and you wanted to block all the addresses from the start of your range up to address 128, the value for the subnet mask that you used would be 255.255.255.128, because in Class C addresses the first three fields indicate the network number and the last field is the node number.

TIP   You can do a search on the Internet under the topic of "TCP/IP Addressing" if you want to learn more about the address types and subnet masks described here. You can find a nice tutorial at http://www.techtutorials.com/tutorials/tcpguide.shtml.

- Deny access to an Internet domain, in which case you click the radio button next to "Domain name" and type the name of the domain into the new input field at the bottom of the dialog box.

Repeat the add process for any other addresses, groups of addresses, or domains that you want to filter. When you finish your deny access rules, they will appear in the exception list of the IP Address and Domain Name Restriction window.

TIP   A warning message will tell you that the first option will be costly in terms of performance if you deny access to specific computers in specific domains, because the server will have to do a reverse DNS lookup every time a new guest visits the site. In other words, it will have to compare the address or each visitor to the subnet masks of domains in DNS each time a new visitor accesses the site. So think about whether the filter is worth the price if you block a lot of individual computers.

 SECURITY ALERT   Filtering by IP address will work effectively only when the systems you are trying to filter out use fixed IP addresses. On an intranet subnet using Dynamic Host Configuration Protocol (DHCP), where many of the system addresses are subject to change, filtering by address is problematic. So IIS IP address filtering might not be helpful on an intranet but Domain filtering would still work on the Internet.

SECURING THE NETWORK PERIMETER

All the barriers you have set up so far have been created on the server itself, and that's not enough to give your site all the protection it needs. When your Web server will be publicly available on the Internet, your network must also play a role in protecting your Web site and your other IT assets.

The outermost barrier in your Web site defense is a *secure network perimeter*. If your ISP provides the facilities to locate your server, the outer reaches of your network perimeter will extend to the hosting facility of your ISP. If you choose to locate the server on your own premises, your network perimeter is much closer to home. Whatever the case, that network perimeter is where security for your Web site starts, and your goal is to make sure that nothing gets inside the perimeter that can harm your site or any other system that belongs to your organization.

Filtering with Firewalls and Routers

A network perimeter defense requires that some type of secure device or set of devices protects each access point into the network. The devices block and filter network traffic to allow activity to or from only certain network addresses, over certain ports, to pass through the perimeter, as shown here:

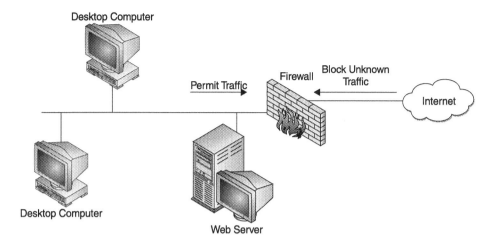

These perimeter security devices are called *firewalls*. Firewalls stop attempts to scan an organization's internal network, stop activity that tries to footprint the network, discard floods of packets sent in Denial of Service (DoS) attacks, and prohibit a range of other behavior from the Internet that might be used by a hacker to penetrate your internal network. Blocking and filtering rules are determined by your organization's security policy.

TIP   The examples mentioned so far discuss the use of firewalls to protect an internal network from hacks from the Internet. But they can also be used to protect resources from attacks within an intranet. Firewalls separate and protect one segment of a network from another, regardless of what type of network (public or private) or systems are on the network segments.

The best firewalls provide a range of security services, including packet filtering, Network Address Translation (NAT), and stateful packet inspection. *Packet filtering* in the firewall can block traffic such as Internet Control Message Protocol (ICMP) Pings. *Network Address Translation* will hide the true network address of the Web server. *Stateful inspection* actually looks inside the data packets of network traffic and stops any packets that try to come in from the Internet that aren't part of a network session currently open on an internal system. When used together, these capabilities provide a significant amount of system protection.

The services of a firewall are always provided in conjunction with a network router that bridges the two networks that surround the firewall. Many times, depending on the sophistication of the router, the router will be configured to perform packet filtering and NAT and allow the firewall to specialize in port blocking and packet inspection.

This kind of setup will help improve overall network performance. The illustration below depicts a hypothetical network configuration that works in this way.

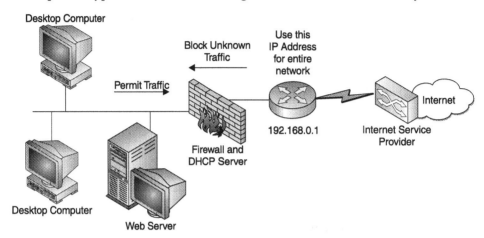

The safest and easiest way to configure a firewall for this scenario is first to have it block all ports and inspect all packets. Then, ports can be selectively opened for desired services. Generally, to make a Web server usable on the Internet, only information arriving through port 80 (http) and port 443 (https—the SSL protocol) must be allowed to pass.

Using a Network DMZ

Unfortunately, when ports are opened through a perimeter guarded by a single firewall, the perimeter security is unavoidably weakened. It's better than it would be if no firewall were present, but it's not optimal. If your ISP provides it, or you have the resources to support it, you should implement a network configuration called a *DMZ* to establish a "best practice" level of protection. The DMZ allows you to place your Web server on a separate network segment outside your intranet, as shown in the following illustration:

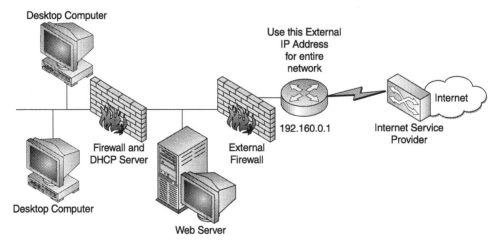

The acronym DMZ comes from what was originally a military term, Demilitarized Zone, which describes a neutral zone of land between two opposing military forces. A well-known example of a military DMZ that is still in use today sits between North Korea and South Korea. The DMZ isolates the two sides from each other. The military concept is a good analogy for a network DMZ, because a network DMZ separates and isolates two networks from each other. Most of the time, the DMZ is set up between the Internet and an organization's internal network. Thus, should a hacker succeed in penetrating the first firewall, he/she can attack only the servers in the DMZ.

The reason a DMZ works is that network traffic cannot travel between two network subnets without being routed. By putting the Web server in the DMZ, you put it on a different subnet than your intranet, so your internally facing router and firewall can be used to filter and inspect the traffic as it's being routed. Because the DMZ is a proven security practice, in addition to your Web site, you should consider putting other Internet services such as a Simple Mail Transfer Protocol/Post Office Protocol (SMTP/POP) e-mail server in the DMZ.

By design, the firewall in between the DMZ and the internal network should have different rules than the firewall in front of the DMZ. This firewall should allow only inbound application-specific service calls to reach specified systems and should not let unsolicited inbound port 80 Web traffic into the internal network. In other words, the firewall should pass only inbound traffic from a server in the DMZ that needs to communicate with one of your internal systems, be it a browser session from a desktop or an application to which the Web server is connected. For example, if your Web server needs to collect or display data from a customer database, the Web server might communicate with the database via SQL, in which case you'd have to open TCP ports in the firewall to pass the SQL queries and responses and block everything else. With Microsoft SQL Server, those ports are 1433 incoming and ports 1024 to 65535 outgoing, but the port assignments vary from application to application.

It would further enhance security for you to have different makes of firewalls on each side of your DMZ. Each type of firewall has its own set of strengths and weaknesses. With different types of firewalls guarding the entrances, a hacker is less likely to be able to use the same exploit to defeat both systems. Furthermore, a bug on one of your firewalls probably does not exist on the other. So, like all the other security measures you've taken so far, using two different firewalls puts up another barrier to make your network that much more difficult to hack and to make it more likely your defense will hold.

SECURING REMOTE MANAGEMENT

When you locate your Web site at your ISP, or locate it locally in a DMZ that separates it from your intranet, you create a necessary and beneficial security barrier. The firewall separating the DMZ from the intranet blocks traffic that could otherwise pose a threat to your internal systems. Unfortunately, the MMC Internet Information Services Manager does not work through a firewall by default, so you can't manage a remote Web site from your desktop without modifying your environment. Microsoft says IIS Manager was intentionally designed this way for security reasons, because if it was a pure TCP application, it could potentially expose sensitive configuration information to the Internet.

Of course, this is not a workable situation if you are not physically near your server, particularly if your site is located at your ISP. To resolve this issue, you have a choice of any of the following:

- *Use the MMC Internet Information Services Manager over a VPN.* Using Microsoft's Point to Point Tunneling Protocol (PPTP) or the Secure Internet Protocol (IPSec) encapsulated in the Internet-standard Layer 2 Tunneling Protocol (L2TP), you can set up an encrypted VPN through a firewall to a remote location where your Web site is hosted.

- *Use HTMLA over SSL.* The HTML version of the Internet Information Services Manager (also known as the HTML Administration, or HTMLA) can be run over an encrypted SSL session.

- *Use Windows 2000 Terminal Services.* Terminal Services allows you to run the MMC on a remote workstation, using encryption, to administer the IIS server from your desktop.

TIP   We don't recommend using the HTMLA Web-based interface, even with SSL, because we don't believe that it has enough field history to indicate how safe it is. Using Terminal Services for remote administration is a good alternative when not using a VPN or encrypted tunnel.

Virtual Private Networking

A Virtual Private Network (VPN) will secure connections to a remotely managed Web site by providing an authenticated and encrypted communications channel between two locations. Using MMC over a VPN is a good solution for secure remote management but it can be difficult to set up.

If you are hosting your Web site at your ISP, it's likely they offer a VPN service to which you can subscribe. If you choose not to use it or if the option is not available to you, you can self-manage your own VPN.

There are several options available for Virtual Private Networks:

- Use Microsoft Windows 2000–based VPN services. You will probably have to dedicate a server at the Web site location to be the VPN server in order not to impact the performance of the Web site.

- Use VPN services available on many firewall products like CheckPoint or Raptor, or routers from vendors like Cisco, 3Com, and others.

- Use a dedicated VPN server hardware/software platform.

There are tradeoffs to consider with each of these choices. If you go with the Windows 2000 VPN solution, you have the option to use PPTP and not IPSec. The other options are almost certain to use IPSec and will thus require the use of Digital Certificates and PKI. Encryption is covered in Chapter 8, and an overview of PKI is part of that discussion if you want to learn more about the topic. Chapter 9 contains a discussion about using Windows 2000 ISA services for VPNs and will also cover third-party VPN products.

Windows 2000 Terminal Services

To install Terminal Services in Remote Administration mode on an IIS server, log on to server as an Administrator and do the following:

1. Select Add/Remove Programs from the Control Panel folder on the Windows desktop, or access the Control Panel from the Windows Start menu and select the Add/Remove Programs icon. You'll see the window shown here:

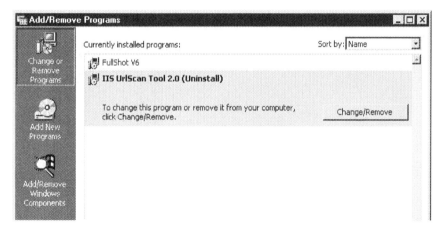

2. Start the Add/Remove Windows Components Wizard by clicking the icon in the left frame, which will help you install the Terminal Services component, as shown next.

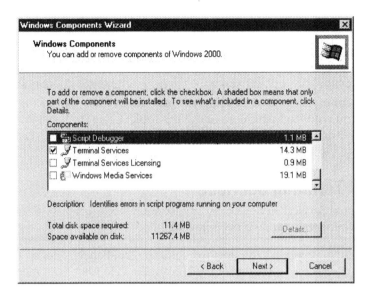

3. Select the Terminal Services check box, and click the Next button. You'll see the wizard's settings page, as shown here:

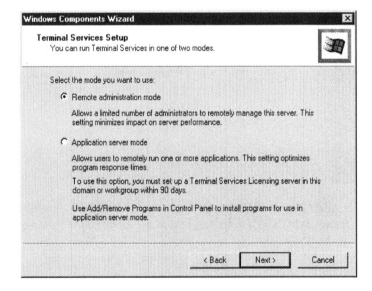

4. Select the Remote Administration Mode option and then click Next to begin the installation.

After the Terminal Services server component is installed, select Terminal Services Configuration from the Administrative Tools group in the Windows Start menu. Under Connections in the MMC Terminal Services Configuration console, double-click the connection for which you want to change the encryption level. Choose the high encryption level in the Encryption Level box.

To install Terminal client files on a remote workstation from where you will manage your server, choose Terminal Services Client Creator from the Administrative Tools group in the Windows Start menu to create installation disks for Terminal Services client computers.

TIP   You do not need a Terminal Server Client Access License to run Terminal Services in Remote Administration mode. A maximum of two concurrent connections are automatically allowed on a Terminal server in Remote Administration mode.

DEPLOYMENT PREPARATION CHECKLIST

- ☐ Make a set of recovery tools before putting your Web server online
  - ☐ Create bootable setup disks
  - ☐ Create Emergency Repair Disk
  - ☐ Make a Registry and system state backup
- ☐ Perform a complete system backup that you store offsite
- ☐ Use Windows 2000 filtering for additional security where appropriate on an intranet
- ☐ Make sure you have a secure network perimeter behind your Web server on the Internet
  - ☐ Use a DMZ
  - ☐ Use firewall filtering to block outside traffic
  - ☐ Consider using VPNs
- ☐ Use an encrypted session for remote management

CHAPTER 7

The Security Management Lifecycle

Your knowledge of hacking methods and the steps you take to mitigate the vulnerabilities on your IIS Web site are critical to keeping your site running reliably and continuously. It's good to be paranoid when it comes to security—you can't be too careful. A vigilant attitude will help you detect and report security incidents and take corrective measures at an early stage.

Staying on top of a site's security is a lot of work. If you encounter security problems, you are thrown into a reactive posture, and it's easy to get so immersed that you lose track of the forest for the trees. You must take a long-term view to be successful and implement proactive as well as reactive policies. By following a structured approach—a lifecycle process—you will make your security management tasks much easier and increase your chances for success. Some of the best lifecycle management practices are discussed in this chapter.

LIFECYCLE METHODOLOGY

A lifecycle management process uses a standardized, repeatable set of procedures to upgrade, reassess, and defend a site in a continuous way. Standardization will ensure proper control over configurations of software and will ensure that tasks are executed in an orderly and predictable manner. With well-defined policy guidelines in hand, an organization can also ensure that responses are sufficiently covered. The workflow of a lifecycle management process is illustrated in Figure 7-1.

The lifecycle approach is an important approach because the Internet world is a dynamic and variable environment, constantly changing, and it takes a constantly evolving management process to stay on top of the situation. Your initial hardening and configuration process was based solely on facts that were known at the time they were performed. Reassessing your approach throughout a site's lifecycle ensures that you keep up with changes in technology that can affect your site.

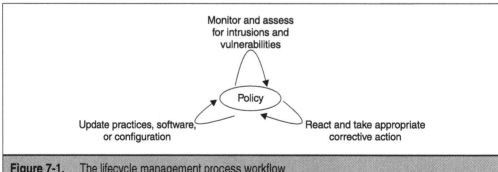

Figure 7-1. The lifecycle management process workflow

VULNERABILITY ASSESSMENTS AND PROACTIVE MONITORING

On the proactive side of monitoring, you should attempt to limit intrusions by performing periodic vulnerability assessments to ensure that you remain secure. On the reactive side of security management, system monitoring and vulnerability assessments should be performed on your Web site so that intrusion attempts are detected in a timely manner, thus enabling you to respond quickly to threats. System monitoring includes regularly scheduled log reviews but can also include more dynamic forms of monitoring that use alerts to notify you of potential problems.

Assessing Vulnerabilities

Assessment is a critical process that determines the security bill of health for any system and should be planned as a regular part of your security maintenance procedures, because vulnerabilities in products are discovered continually. New and existing installations should be checked for new vulnerabilities that may have been discovered and reported by security resources such as the SANS Institute since the last Microsoft updates.

Every system that has already been deployed, or that has just been installed, should be examined through a structured process that verifies or measures the current state of security. Your periodic assessment should include adhering to the information found in the checklists in this book, along with new information you gather from the security resources, and you should run Microsoft's current security tools to verify that you have addressed all the issues that these tools fix. Indeed, the tools that you originally used to secure and harden your system in Chapter 3 are subject to updates as Microsoft learns of new vulnerabilities.

A structured approach is the key to successful site security. It's easy to forget a step or leave a task incomplete if you get busy. However, you will decrease the chance for mistakes if you follow an organized process. A brief overview of your assessment workflow follows:

- Apply latest security fixes and hardening procedures found in the security section of Microsoft's TechNet Web site (www.microsoft.com/technet/security). Because these fixes change frequently, no specific URL is listed here.

- Double-check you security baseline by running a new tool called the Microsoft Security Baseline Analyzer (MSBA) to look for Windows 2000 policy and configuration vulnerabilities that security updates do not address. You can get more information about the tool and find out how to download it in document Q320454 on TechNet.

- Rerun Microsoft hardening tools, such as IIS Lockdown, that address the configuration and policy issues of IIS. (See Chapter 3 for IIS Lockdown download information.)

- Perform some real-world testing, adjusting the new security baseline as appropriate and implementing security best practices as a proactive defense.

- Repeat this cycle according to your organization's security policy.

Double-Checking Your Baseline

The Microsoft Baseline Security Analyzer (MBSA) is a tool designed to scan machines that are running Windows 2000 to identify whether security updates and secure policy and settings have been properly applied to a system. MBSA is a superset of HFNetChk—a well-known tool used by many Windows 2000 and system administrators. MBSA scans your server to determine the operating system, service packs, and programs you are running, and then it looks to the Microsoft database and identifies security patches that are available for your combination of installed software.

MBSA, like HFNetChk, can determine whether a specific patch is installed on a given server by the checking for the Registry key that is installed by the patch, the file version, and the checksum for each file that is installed by the patch. But MBSA also incorporates capabilities that check for common security best practices, such as strong passwords, Guest account status, file-system type, available file shares, members of the Administrators group, and a long list of common security misconfigurations. It then produces a report. The IIS-related tests, which read like a good hardening checklist, are as follows:

- **Simple passwords** MBSA checks machines for blank, simple, and misused passwords during a scan, including the following:

  - Password is blank

  - Password = username (account name)

  - Password = machine name

  - Password = "password"

  - Password = "admin"

  - Password = "Administrator"

- **Administrators Group Membership** Identifies and lists the individual user accounts that belong to the Local Administrators group. If more than two individual administrative accounts are detected, the tool will list the account names and flag the check as a potential vulnerability. In general, it is recommended that you keep the number of administrators to a minimum as administrators essentially have complete control over the system.

- **Auditing** Determines whether auditing is enabled on the scanned computer. Microsoft Windows' auditing feature tracks and logs specific events on your system, such as successful and failed logon attempts. You should always use logging and monitor your system's event log to help you identify potential security issues and malicious activity.

- **Auto Logon** Determines whether the Auto Logon feature is enabled on the scanned computer and whether the logon password is encrypted in the Registry or stored in plaintext. If Auto Logon is enabled and the logon password is stored as plaintext, the security report reflects this as a high-level vulnerability. If Auto Logon is enabled and the password is encrypted in the Registry, the security report flags this as a potential vulnerability.

- **Check for Unnecessary Services**   Determines whether any services contained in the services.txt file are enabled on the scanned computer. It can help you identify whether a service you intended to turn off was not disabled or has been restarted.

- **Guest Account**   Determines whether the built-in Guest account is enabled on the scanned computer. The Guest account is used to log onto a computer running Windows 2000, and it should be disabled.

- **MSADC and Scripts Virtual Directories on IIS**   Determines whether the MSADC (sample data access scripts) and Scripts virtual directories are installed on a scanned Internet Information Services (IIS) computer. These directories typically contain scripts that, if not required, should be removed to help reduce the attack surface of the computer.

- **IISADMPWD Virtual Directory**   Determines whether the IISADMPWD directory is installed on the scanned computer. IIS 4.0 enables users to change their Windows passwords through the IISADMPWD virtual directory, but this can create a vulnerability that exposes passwords to attacks and should be deleted if your server is upgraded to IIS 5.

- **IIS Lockdown Tool**   Determines whether version 2.1 of the IIS Lockdown tool (IIS Lock) has been run on the scanned computer. IIS Lockdown works by turning off unnecessary features and setting security policy in IIS to reduce security vulnerabilities.

- **IIS Logging**   Determines whether IIS logging is enabled and whether the W3C Extended Log File Format is used. IIS logging goes beyond the scope of the event-logging or performance-monitoring features of Windows and can be important in helping you detect areas of your server or your sites that may be subject to attacks or other security problems. You should always enable it.

- **IIS Parent Paths**   Determines whether the ASPEnableParentPaths setting is enabled on the scanned computer. By enabling parent paths on IIS, Active Server Pages (ASP) pages can use relative paths to the parent directory of the current directory—that is, paths that use the . . syntax.

- **IIS Sample Applications**   Determines whether the following IIS samples file directories are installed on the computer:

  \Inetpub\iissamples
  \Winnt\help\iishelp
  \Program Files\common files\system\msadc

These directories and all virtual directories should be removed.

- **Members of the Sysadmin Role**   Determines the number of members of the Sysadmin role and displays the results in the security report. As a rule, as few individuals as possible should be enabled as Sysadmins.

- **Password Expiration**   Determines whether any local user accounts have non-expiring passwords. Passwords should be changed regularly to mitigate password attacks. Each local user account with a nonexpiring password will be listed.

- **Restrict Anonymous Users**   Determines whether the RestrictAnonymous Registry key is used to restrict anonymous connections on the scanned computer to basic Read permission or Read and Execute in scripts directories if the site uses them.

- **Shares**   Deter mines whether any shared folders exist on the computer that is being scanned. The scan report will list all shares found on the computer, including administrative shares, along with their share-level and NTFS-level permissions. Folders should never be shared on a Web server.

You should be aware of two things before you run MBSA: First, the logon checks will produce event log entries in the Security log if auditing is enabled on the machine for logon/logoff events. Second, the Unnecessary Services check uses a services.txt file as its control list. You have to configure this file to include those specific services to be checked on each scanned machine. The services.txt file that is installed by default with the tool contains the following services:

MSFTPSVC (FTP)
TlntSvr (Telnet)
RasMan (Remote Access Service Manager)
W3SVC (WWW)
SMTPSVC (SMTP)

You can find the list of other services that should be disabled in Chapter 3.

Real-World Vulnerability Testing

Security professionals recommend that you perform real-world testing so that you can try the same attacks that hackers are likely to mount on your Web site to determine whether your site security holds up. The goal is summarized perfectly in an article titled "Vulnerability Assessments: The Pro-active Steps to Secure Your Organization," originally published on the SANS Web site by an author named Robert Boyce, who states "when conducting a vulnerability assessment the tool set being used should be very similar to that of the identified adversary. This will ensure that the systems are secure from attacks that are currently being employed out in the wild."

The following list contains a sample of some useful tools that can be found on the Internet for free. Commercial scanning software is also available from Symantec. Network Associates, BindView, eDigital Security, and Internet Security Systems.

- **Nmap** A utility for network discovery and/or security auditing, it can be used to scan large networks or single hosts quickly and accurately, determining which hosts are available, what services each host is running, and the operating system that is being used. Available at http://www.insecure.org/nmap.

- **Nessus** A remote security scanner that can audit a given network and determine whether any weaknesses are present that may allow attackers to penetrate the defenses. It launches predefined exploits and reports on the degree of success of each exploit. Available at http://www.nessus.org/.

- **Whisker** A Common Gateway Interface (CGI) Web scanner that scans for known vulnerabilities found in Web servers, providing the URL that triggered the event. It can also determine the type of Web server being run. It is easy to update and has many useful features. Available at http://www.wiretrip.net/rfp/p/doc.asp?id=21&iface=2.

- **Enum** A console-based Win32 information enumeration utility. Using null sessions, enum can retrieve user lists, machine lists, share lists, name lists, group and member lists, and password and policy information. Enum can also perform a rudimentary brute-force dictionary attack on individual accounts. Available at http://razor.bindview.com/tools/index.shtml.

Some of these tools are Windows programs and some are available only for UNIX or Linux. If you know a little bit about hacking, have access to the non-Windows platforms, and have the time to spend testing, you can perform a reasonable set of assurance tests. However, because most of us do not meet all those requirements, it's good to know that other alternatives are available.

One alternative is to use a consultant. Another option is to use a new breed of service that is available on the Internet that does automated test scanning of your site. A quick search on Google under the topic of "Online Vulnerability Testing Service" will net several companies that offer such services. Several of these services have free demos, and they seem well worth your while to research.

More on Log File Monitoring

Chapter 5 discussed how you can use the Windows 2000 Event Viewer to track operating system logs and how you can browse the W3Cformat log files in IIS to look for signs that your site may have come under attack.

Although searching for a security breach might seem like searching for a needle in a haystack, you can look at a few items that can point to a security problem. Microsoft recommends that you watch in particular for the events listed in Table 7-1. The table includes the identifier of the events and the questions you should ask yourself as you peruse the information.

Event Identifier	Comments
517	The Audit Log was cleared. Did you do this, or is it an attempt by an intruder to cover his tracks?
529	An attempt was made to logon by using an unknown user account or a valid account with a password that is not valid. An unexpected increase in the frequency of this event could indicate an attempt to guess passwords.
531	An attempt was made to logon by using a disabled account. Who would attempt this and why?
539	A logon attempt was made and rejected because the account was locked out. Who would attempt this and why?
612	The audit policy has changed. Verify who changed it and why.
624	A user account was created. Did you or a trusted person create it?
628	A user account's password was set. Did you or a trusted person do this?
640	A change was made to the SAM database. Did you make this change?

Table 7-1.   Suspicious Security Log Entries

Lack of information is not much of a problem if you track a large number of events. Making sense of the information can be quite a challenge, however. Windows 2000 provides several tools that can help you do a better job of sorting through and making sense of the information. Commercial solutions are also available for what you are about to learn (these are covered in Chapter 9), but here we will focus on the Microsoft tools.

Exporting Logs to Text Files

There is no shortage of the amount of information that you can collect in log files—in fact, the huge amount of information can be overwhelming. A technique that sometimes makes it easier to review the information is to export the information in the form of a text file to another program such as a spreadsheet or database for further investigation. There you can sort the list by event numbers or search for specific messages. The IIS logs are automatically stored as text, so they are ready for use, but the Windows 2000 logs need to be converted.

You can convert Windows 2000 logs to text files in two ways: You can use the Save As command in the Windows 2000 Event Viewer to save the file as either tab-delimited text or comma separated value (CSV) formats. You can also dump the Event Log using dumpel.exe, a command-line tool that is available for download on the Microsoft Windows 2000 Web site at http://www.microsoft.com/windows2000/techinfo/reskit/tools/existing/dumpel-o.asp.

If you are going back through historic logs for information, the command line conversion method can make the task much easier. Dumpel.exe will convert an event log for a local or remote system into a tab-separated text file and can filter the file for information you seek at the same time based on the command-line parameters used. The following syntax is used by the dumpel.exe tool:

dumpel -f *file* [-s *server*] [-l *log* [-m *source*]] [-e *n1 n2 n3...*] [-r] [-t] [-d *x*]

- **-f *file***   Specifies the file name for the output file. There is no default for "-f," so you must specify the file.

- **-s *server***   Specifies the server for which you want to dump the event log. Leading backslashes on the server name are optional.

- **-l *log***   Specifies which log (system, application, security) to dump. If an invalid log name is specified, the application log is dumped.

- **-m *source***   Specifies in which source (such as redirector (rdr), serial, and so on) to dump records. Only one source can be supplied. If this switch is not used, all events are dumped. If a source is used that is not registered in the Registry, the application log is searched for records of this type.

- **-e *n1 n2 n3...***   Filters for event id *nn* (up to 10 can be specified). If the "-r" switch is not used, only records of these types are dumped; if "-r" is used, all records except records of these types are dumped. If this switch is not used, all events from the specified *source* are selected. You cannot use this switch without the "-m" switch.

- **-r**   Specifies whether to filter for specific sources or records or to filter them out.

- **-t**   Specifies that individual strings are separated by tabs. If "-t" is not used, strings are separated by spaces.

- **-d *x***   Dumps events for the past *x* days.

Setting Windows 2000 and IIS Alerts

In addition to examining log files, an after-the-fact technique, you can use real-time monitoring and detection by setting alerts. The Windows 2000 Performance Monitor has a feature called *counters* that can flag possible hacking attempts and automatically let you know if something might be wrong.

The Performance Monitor is generally used, as its name implies, for tracking system performance issues. But you can use it for security, too, by creating custom rules to monitor operating system events or Web service events. The rules trigger a predefined action when a predefined condition is met. For example, by using counters to establish an event threshold, you can trigger an alert that will send you a message over the network when the threshold is exceeded. The following actions may be taken by the server when an alert is triggered:

- Send a network message

- Log an entry in the application event log

- Start a performance data log

- Run a specified program

Setting an Operating System Alert

One good scenario for using performance counters and alerts on a Web server not using anonymous authentication is to have a notification sent to you on the occurrence of a high number of logon failures. A high concentration of logon failures often indicates an attack. So, for example, if you set a threshold of 25 failed logons, when that threshold is exceeded the system will send you a message.

The procedure for setting this kind of alert follows.

1. Open the MMC Performance Monitor, shown in Figure 7-2. Right-click the Alerts icon and select New Alert Settings from the pop-up menu. Choose a name, when asked, that describes the setting, such as Logon Failures.

2. After you name the rule, a Logon Failures dialog box appears, in which you begin to define the rule for the alert you are creating; it looks something like Figure 7-3, although all the fields will initially be blank. Note that you begin your process on the General tab. Add a comment at the top field and then click the Add button to begin the rule creation process.

3. Counters are the first rule parameter you need to define. The Select Counters dialog box is shown in Figure 7-4. When you are counting events on the local machine, as in this example, click the Use Local Computer Counters radio button in the upper-left corner. If you were counting events on another server in a Windows domain, you could name the computer by clicking Select Counters From Computer.

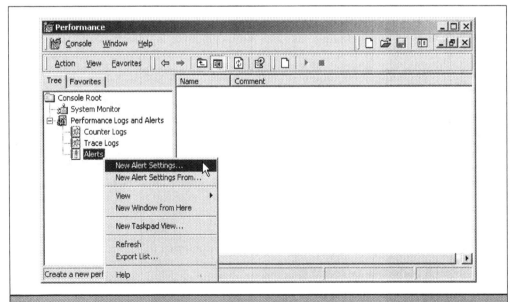

Figure 7-2.   Use the Performance Monitor to create an alert.

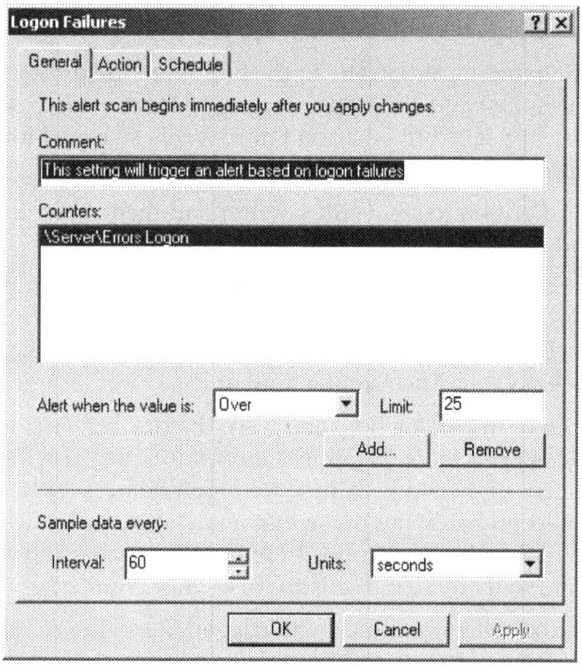

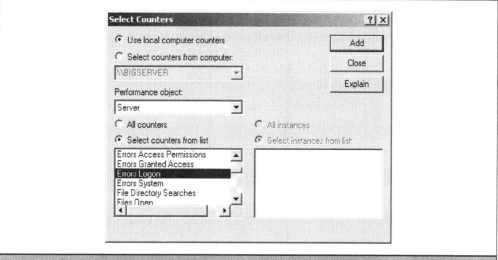

Figure 7-3.   The first step in creating an alert is to add the rule.

Figure 7-4.   The Select Counters dialog box defines the counter details.

4. Select the type of performance object that your counter is tracking in the Performance Object drop-down box. For this example, select Server Object.

5. Finally, define the counter itself. At the bottom of the dialog box, click Select Counters From List and choose Errors Logon from the list. Another choice, All Counters, appears, but you don't need a rule so broad for the purposes of this example.

6. Click the Add button to create the counter and then click Close to exit the window and return to the previous screen.

7. Back at the Logon Failures dialog box where you began to create the rule (Figure 7-2), define how your counter will be applied. In the middle of the dialog box, click the drop-down menu next to the Alert When The Value Is field, and select Over. Then set the limit at 25.

8. At the bottom of the dialog box, you'll see that the rule is set to sample the counter data every 5 seconds—this is the default. Because that is probably more often than you need to sample for logon failures (even an automated program could probably not make that many attempts in 5 seconds), change it to a more reasonable 60 seconds to reduce the processing requirements of your alert and to increase the sensitivity of your counter.

9. Now define the action your alert will trigger. Select the Action tab at the top of the dialog box, as shown in Figure 7-5. At the top of this dialog box, select the options for the actions you would like to take. In particular, it might be desirable to have a pop-up network message sent to the management console of the server (so the server sends a message to itself to pop up a notification and instantly alert you). Further, if you are doing remote management, you might want a message sent to your workstation by using its Windows computer name.

10. When you finish defining your action, the rule is ready to go. You can set a schedule for when the rule will go into effect if you want, via the Schedule tab, but Windows 2000 will default to start the rule immediately if you don't do anything with the schedule.

11. Click Apply to put your rule into effect and click OK to exit the window.

Obviously, it's not feasible to define alert rules to monitor *all* the objects in the operating system. The objects that are probably the most important to monitor and be alerted to in real time when events exceed your thresholds are related to failed attempts to access a resource because you might be able to stop the attack or observe it as it happens.

Table 7-2 lists the parameters you would use in defining the alert rules.

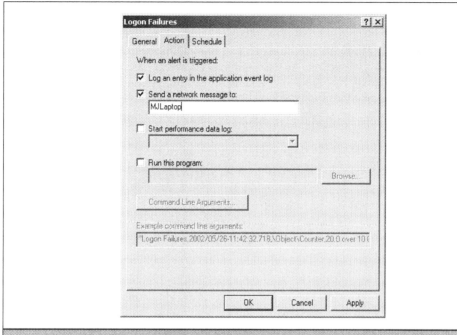

Figure 7-5.   Use the Action tab to define how the server handles the alert.

TIP   The alerts and alert messages built into Windows 2000 are pretty basic. Third-party tools such as intrusion detection systems (IDSs) have much more sophisticated alerting capabilities and can send messages to pagers or other locations and devices to make you aware of a problem.

Operating System Counter	Description
Errors Access Permissions	Indicates whether somebody is randomly attempting to gain access to files in the hopes of finding an improperly protected file
Errors Granted Access	Logs attempts to gain access to files without proper access authorization
Errors Logon	Displays failed logon attempts, which could mean that password-guessing programs are being used to crack security on the server

Table 7-2.   Windows 2000 Events to Monitor with Alerts

Setting a Web Service Alert

Similar to operating system alerts, you can set alerts on events in IIS Web services. You can use a broad range of Web service thresholds to create your rule, related to the number of occurrences of events per second, current count for connections, total rejected events, and other criteria that cover hundreds of alerts. A few examples of some useful alerts are shown in Table 7-3; many others are not listed here.

To set a Web service alert, you begin with the same procedures discussed in "Setting an Operating System Alert," but you will make different choices in the Select Counters dialog box.

1. Open the MMC Performance Monitor, shown in Figure 7-2, and right-click the Alerts icon. Select New Alert Settings from the pop-up menu. Choose a name, when asked, that describes the setting.

2. After you name the rule, you can begin to define the rule for the alert you are creating in the Logon Failures dialog box shown in Figure 7-3. Add a comment at the top of the screen and click the Add button to begin the rule creation process.

3. In the Select Counters dialog box, shown in Figure 7-6, once again click Use Local Computer Counters and also Select Counters From List. This time, choose Web Services in the Performance Object field.

4. The right side of the screen will become activated. Click All Instances if you want the counter to be active on all of the server's Web sites, or select the specific sites for which you want to use the counter.

Web Services Counter	Description
Not found errors per second	If this value spikes, it could indicate someone is trying to guess or decode your server's URLs on your virtual directories.
Total connection attempts	If this value spikes, it may indicate that your site is under a Denial of Service (DoS) attack that is trying to overwhelm your server with connections.
Current anonymous users	If this value spikes, someone may have penetrated your Web site and used it to store something that is being linked to from another site on the Internet. It's a less ominous problem than the DoS attack because it might not bring down your server, but your resources are still being stolen. A number of similar counters relating to the current or total number of simultaneous events can also help you gauge usage anomalies.

Table 7-3. IIS Alerts and Their Potential Causes

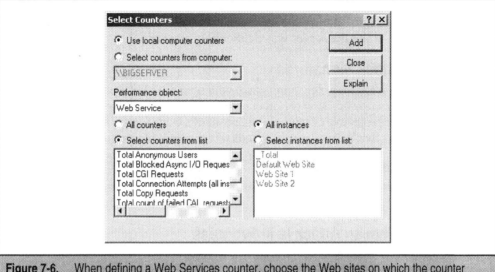

Figure 7-6.   When defining a Web Services counter, choose the Web sites on which the counter will be used.

5. Click the Action tab and select the action you want your rule to trigger, as shown in Figure 7-4. When you finish, click Add to add your rule and then close the window.

6. Back in the Logon Failures dialog box, click Apply to activate your rule, and then click OK to exit.

Using Crash Logging and Notification as a Security Tool

Because hackers will attempt to crash a server to gain access to it, it's useful for you to receive and retain crash information. In addition to the crash log file, you can enable two other methods of crash notification and logging by changing several variables in the Windows 2000 Registry so that you are alerted in the event of a server crash.

To set up crash alert notification:

1. Select Start | Run, and load the Regedit program.

2. In the program, you can enable an administrative alert by setting HKEY_LOCAL_ MACHINE/SYSTEM/CurrentControlSet/Control/ CrashControl/SendAlert to 1. The next time the server crashes, an administrative alert will be sent.

3. Then you can make the operating system log the crash in the event log by changing HKEY_LOCAL_MACHINE/SYSTEM/CurrentControlSet/ Control/CrashControlLogEvent to 1. Now the exact time of the crash will be permanently recorded.

The crash notification you enabled through these instructions will alert you to the problem. You can use the information recorded in the log during a security audit to determine whether or not the server was deliberately crashed.

Watching for Attack Signatures

Often, attacks that don't immediately bring down your server can leave programs that infect and affect your site over a long period of time. You should keep an eye on your log files for signs of these programs. Like viruses, many attacks using worms or Trojan horses are automated attacks that leave signatures (predictable patterns of events or deposited files) in the log files that become a sign of their presence. For example, many organizations learned that they had been hit by the Code Red worm after they found the distinctive GET request for default.ida in their log files. If you subscribe to security mailing lists or pay attention to the CERT Web site, you'll learn about these signatures and can check for them in your own logs.

Other Signals That an Attack Is in Progress

Some kinds of attacks are easy to identify, such as a buffer overflows that immediately crash your server, but other attacks may have more subtle symptoms. Your Windows 2000 and IIS log monitoring and alerts will help catch some attack attempts, but other signs, independent of your Web server, can help you spot a potential problem. Some of the common attack identifiers to look for are listed here:

- *A sudden increase in outbound traffic.* While this could just mean that your marketing campaigns are finally paying off, it could also mean that someone is up to no good, particularly if the traffic is outbound, as was another symptom of Code Red. You will also see the same effect if a machine on your network has been commandeered to participate in a distributed DoS attack. Your routers or firewalls should be able to measure both inbound and outbound packet counts. The best ones have tools that will provide reports that you can compare on a weekly, daily, or ad-hoc basis.

- *Large numbers of packets caught by your router's or firewall's egress filters. Egress filters* refer to a set of router policies that inspect outgoing packets and look at their source addresses. Because most organizations know what network addresses are behind their firewall, they can filter out packets whose source addresses do not match those networks. This system filters potentially forged traffic, typically seen when attackers seize an unsuspecting host and generate packets from it that are meant to flood a well-known target elsewhere on the Internet. Egress filters prevent spoofed packets from *leaving* your network, so if your filter is catching them, you need to identify their source, because that's a clear sign that machines on your network have been compromised.

- *Sudden jump in the number of malformed packets at your firewall.* Most firewalls and routers collect packet-level statistics. You can also use commercial software network scanners to do this. You should monitor the packet-level statistics on the edge of your network. If you notice spikes in malformed packets, it's likely that you are experiencing a DoS attack.

INCIDENT RESPONSE

If your system is on the Internet, it is going to get attacked—it is only a matter of time. The same may be true for your intranet. Therefore, for a number of reasons, it's important that you have a response plan in place when your monitoring processes detect suspicious activity.

Remember that successful attacks often follow a series of unsuccessful attacks. If your monitoring shows you have experienced a likely attack, even if unsuccessful, you must react. If a successful attack does occur, the earlier you find out and respond, the easier it will be to contain the damage.

Responding to an Attack

When you know your server has been compromised, you need to be decisive and act quickly. The first thing you should do is try to identify the attacker. Use your server logs and firewall logs to attempt to identify where the attack came from so you can tell whether it's coming from another compromised machine on your network or from the Internet. Don't make assumptions—*get the facts.*

When you know where the attack is coming from, you've got to try to stop it. You can filter the address or domain to block the source. Pull machines from the network if you know they have had files planted or have been infected with a worm or virus. If you've experienced a Distributed DoS (DDoS) attack, you may have to get help from your communications service provider.

CHALLENGE

When you think your system is under attack, it can be difficult to stay calm and keep your head, but it's critical that you do so, and it's important that you make good decisions. Not all perceived security incidents are real. A *false positive* refers to a situation in which your indicators tell you a security incident has occurred when in fact it was something else.

It helps to have a detailed guide during those stressful moments. It's annoying to customers if you take you site offline, and it's embarrassing to you if it turns out you didn't really have a security problem. Thus, the following list of procedures is included to help you analyze your problem and follow a methodical process to identify the scope and the cause of a suspected incident.

Perform these steps first on your Web site:

1. Identify all systems involved in the perceived incident.

2. Avoid restarting the computer, logging on and off, or otherwise inadvertently starting malicious code.

3. Examine audit logs for signs of unauthorized behavior. Look for absence of logs or gaps in the logs that are sure signs of tampering.

CHALLENGE *(continued)*

4. Examine key accounts and groups. Look for attempts to log onto default accounts. Perform a check of Administrators, Backup Operators, and Web Site Operators groups for unauthorized entries or group members. Examine accounts for increased privileges. Watch for activity during nonworking hours.

5. Look for files in your Web server's directories that you did not put there. Search the system for hacker tools (Trojan horses, like Subseven, and so on.)

6. Check the Windows 2000 Task Manager (summoned by pressing CTRL-ALT-DEL) for unrecognizable applications or processes. Check your services configuration for services configured to start automatically that were not part of you initial hardening configuration.

If none of these steps provides any signs of intrusion, don't make any conclusions, affirmative or negative, just yet. Broaden your search by performing the following steps:

7. Validate functionality and match system performance against historical baselines.

8. Perform all the procedures of your regularly scheduled log review.

9. Check the logs in your IDS, if you use one, to determine whether it has detected any suspicious activity.

10. Change all of your Web server's passwords as a precaution.

Every situation is different, and it is difficult to provide specific advice that will work in all cases. As a rule, it's probably better to be safe than sorry. So when in doubt, take appropriate measures to ensure that if you have had a problem it does not spread. But sometimes, if your investigation is inconclusive, it's best to monitor for a repeat of the incident before you take the extreme measure of shutting down your system.

As the expression goes, "Don't recycle trouble." Until you've performed an audit on the affected site, you can't be sure what happened to it. Rather than try to put the attacked site back online quickly, apply a short-term solution until you have more information. If you can, reinstall the operating system on another server and then restore your backup on it as well (assuming you've done them as you should have). CERT maintains a list of steps for restoring a compromised server at the following URL: http://www.cert.org/tech_tips/root_compromise.html.

Take advantage of CERT's experience and follow its advice. Sometimes, even though you think everything is fine, it's not, and you won't know for sure until you investigate further.

Finally, perform a security audit and protect the evidence. Keep backup copies of any logs you generate, and take detailed notes so that you have a good record of your findings.

Perform a Security Audit

So what do you look for as you audit a site after a security incident? The answer to that question is either overly simple—you look for anything that indicates suspicious or unusual activity—or else the answer is that there is no simple answer to that question. A better question would be "Where do I start?" You start with a structured methodology whereby you comb through your logs looking for clues in a number of different areas.

You first need to identify the damage you have experienced. Are files missing? Was your server intentionally crashed? Have you found the signature of a well-known attack in your logs? Is there a virus on your system? This information will give you a starting point.

Then you should begin by investigating each of the event categories that will help you trace the steps of the attack. If you have enabled auditing, as was recommended in Chapter 5, you should have log information for each of the following event categories:

- Logon events
- Account management
- Object access
- Privilege use
- Policy change
- System events

In general, by working back from the file or other object(s) that was affected, you can look for the series of events that lead backward from the time the problem was discovered.

A detailed auditing guide is available in Chapter 6 of the Microsoft *Security Operations Guide Windows 2000 Server*. This guide provides details about all of the specific events for which you should watch. The URL for the guide is extremely long and is probably subject to change, so it's not listed here, but you should be able to find it if you do a search on the Microsoft TechNet Web site (www.microsoft.com/technet) for "Security Operations Guide for Windows 2000 Server."

Eliminate the Problem

In response to a specific intrusion, you need to ensure that your site is protected against the same type of attack in the future. Intruders widely advertise compromised systems and regularly trade system addresses and access information in exchange for attack tools or similar information. Many victims of intrusions indicate that intruders try to access their system addresses long after the original intrusion has occurred.

Before redeploying, you must be sure that your site is no longer vulnerable. After you have determined the cause of an attack, visit the Microsoft Web site to see if a patch is available for the vulnerability. If the vulnerability was in your perimeter, check the vendor sites of your firewalls and routers and update your filtering rules.

As part of a successful intrusion, intruders typically install back doors or other means that help them re-attain access later on. Unless you are sure this has not happened on your system, you should completely reinstall all the software on your system. Because its often difficult to tell what, exactly, has been compromised in an attack, many administrators choose to reinstall the systems as a matter of policy. You should also change all the user account names and passwords on the server.

MANAGEMENT LIFECYCLE CHECKLIST

- ☐ Double-check and test your security baseline
  - ☐ Apply latest security updates and patches
  - ☐ Run Microsoft Basic Security Analyzer
  - ☐ Rerun IIS Lockdown
  - ☐ Perform Real-world vulnerability testing
- ☐ Practice proactive security monitoring
  - ☐ Perform regularly scheduled reviews of your logs
  - ☐ Audit server shutdowns and watch logs closely after a crash
  - ☐ Watch logs for common attack signatures
  - ☐ Set Windows 2000 and IIS alerts
  - ☐ Watch for external signs of attacks in firewall and router logs
- ☐ Respond appropriately to security incidents
  - ☐ Trace the source of an attack
  - ☐ Stop the attack ASAP by filtering source addresses and taking servers offline when necessary
  - ☐ Apply a short-term solution to keep your site in operation. Consult security policy for guidance.
  - ☐ Perform a security audit to determine extent of damage and the source of the attack. Keep good records of evidence.
  - ☐ Identify and implement security lessons learned. Eliminate all means of intruder access.
  - ☐ Return systems to normal operation

CHAPTER 8

Using Encryption

E ncryption is used to protect the privacy of data. It is a fundamental part of the security features of most computer operating systems and software (at least the secure kind). Windows 2000 and IIS will support encryption in a number of ways:

- Authentication via Kerberos or other supported methods (as covered in Appendix D)

- File encryption on an NTFS hard disk or volume

- Virtual Private Networks (VPNs) using Point-to-Point Tunneling Protocol (PPTP), Secure IP (IPSec), or Layer Two Tunneling Protocol (L2TP)

- Secure communications from an IIS Web site using Secure Socket Layer (SSL) encryption or the next generation of the standard, Transport Layer Security (TLS)

The encryption used in Windows 2000 authentication is something you have little control of as an administrator. Windows 2000 authentication is a self-contained system; and, beyond configuring the authentication settings on your server, there is nothing else you are required to do—although you can change the encryption strength in the Windows 2000 Registry. However, by default, Microsoft now uses a 128-bit encryption strength, which is quite adequate for most Web environments; only special-purpose security applications need anything much stronger.

On the other hand, NTFS file encryption—a data protection method for NTFS volumes—lets you configure and tailor it to meet your needs. Many organizations use NTFS encryption on intranet file servers to augment the server's access control for highly sensitive documents. However, it is not practical to use on a high-volume Web site because broadly encrypting the site's data would bog down even the most powerful server. When file encryption is used with a Web site, it's generally done to encrypt specific elements of data for application-specific purposes, such as protecting credit card numbers in a customer database. Many times, the data is actually stored and managed on a different server than the Web server, and the database server contains its own encryption logic to protect the file.

A Windows 2000 server can be configured as a VPN server. However, in order to enable VPN support, you must configure the server for Routing and Remote Access. You may recall that Chapter 3 adamantly recommended that you disable the Routing and Remote Access service on your Web server because of the way it might expose other systems that you manage to Web-based attacks. The VPN that you use to remotely manage your server should be hosted by a separate server if you want to run it from Windows 2000, or you should use dedicated firewall or hardware-based VPN equipment. (These options were discussed in Chapters 6 and 9, respectively.)

The most common and practical use for encryption on an IIS Web site is to secure the Web site by encrypting information with SSL/TLS as it is being sent to browsers over a network. SSL is widely used both on the Internet and on intranets where information privacy and confidentiality is important. This chapter will discuss the implementation and configuration of IIS SSL/TLS encryption features for secure Web sites.

THE BASICS OF ENCRYPTION

Before discussing SSL/TLS configuration, let's cover a few essential encryption concepts that you will need to understand. Encryption involves the encoding of data so that it can be understood by the intended recipient only. It is an old science—reportedly traced as far back as 1900 B.C. in Egypt. The Romans routinely used encryption to encode messages for military communications. Today, encryption systems are widely used to transmit sensitive digital data across computer networks.

Keys and Ciphers

Encryption systems change data from readable form to unreadable form and back again using algorithms known as *ciphers*. A cipher provides a defined method for encoding and decoding the data. In the time of Julius Caesar, the Romans used a simple cipher that shifted the letters of the alphabet (much like the encoder rings you used to get in cereal boxes and Cracker Jacks®). To decrypt a Roman message, a recipient needed the *key*—in other words, the recipient needed to know how far the letters of the alphabet were shifted, and in which direction. Today, encryption systems use sophisticated mathematical formulas in ciphers and large binary numbers as keys, but the basic science is still the same.

Computerized encryption systems are designed so that data to be encrypted, with the input of the key, is processed through a program most often referred to as an *encryption engine.* As always, before an engine can decrypt computer-encrypted data, it needs to know two things: the cipher and the key. In the case of Windows 2000 and IIS, that encryption engine is an integral part of the Windows 2000 operating system. This allows Windows operating system services and applications to perform encryption in real time. For example, when a Windows 2000 server is configured to encrypt files in a folder, the encryption happens as the file is being saved. Likewise, when a server is configured for a VPN, or a Web server is using SSL/TLS, the data can be encrypted at the moment it is sent out over the network and decrypted when it is received.

Symmetric-Key (Secret-Key) Encryption

Historically, encryption systems were *symmetric-key* or *secret-key* systems. A symmetric-key encryption system uses the same key for both the encoding and decoding of data. When the Romans were sending messages encoded by shifting the alphabet, the key that a message recipient needed to know consisted of the amount and the direction of the shift. With this information, the recipient could decode the message by shifting the letters of the message back to their original positions. In this system, the key was a single number (less than the number of letters in the Roman alphabet) plus a direction (left or right). The problem with the Roman system was that someone who knew the cipher could guess the key and decode the message with relative ease.

Today, because computerized encryption programs enable the use of very long keys, it makes little difference if an untrusted third party knows the encryption cipher. A long key of 128 bits will still take a significantly long time to guess even if computerized methods are used to assist in the discovery, since there are 3.4×10^{38} possible keys. Therefore, the encryption ciphers used in industry and government security standards are publicly published and well known. This might seem counterintuitive, but the open distribution of ciphers has actually served to make them more secure because it has given more encryption experts the opportunity to evaluate, contribute to, and improve the ciphers. The Digital Encryption Standard (DES), Triple DES, and the more recently developed Advanced Encryption Standard (AES) are all examples of well-tested standards where the details of the ciphers are public knowledge. Even some commercial symmetric algorithms, such as RC4, have been made public in order to gain credibility through public inspection. A few modern symmetric ciphers are listed here:

- **DES**   Data Encryption Standard is an encryption algorithm used by the U.S. Government.

- **Skipjack**   This is a classified symmetric-key algorithm implemented in FORTEZZA-compliant hardware (which is used by the U.S. government).

- **Triple-DES**   DES applied three times (to make it harder to crack).

- **RC2, RC4, RC5, and RC6**   These are commercial ciphers created and licensed by a company called RSA Security, Inc. Microsoft uses RC4 by default in its PPTP and L2TP, SSL/TLS, and IPSec protocol support, but this can be changed through the system registry.

- **AES**   Advanced Encryption Standard is a new federal information-processing standard that will specify a cryptographic algorithm for use by U.S. government organizations to protect sensitive (unclassified) information.

SECURITY ALERT   The DES standard was published in the early 1970s. It became the standard method for encrypting financial transactions between banks and financial institutions; for decades, virtually all such transactions were encrypted with DES. However, it is now becoming obsolete because it's limited to 56-bit key lengths; other, more recent standards do not have that limitation. With the power of modern microprocessors, a 56-bit DES key can now be broken in a number of hours, whereas a 128-bit key would take months and months even with the most powerful computers. The moral is this: don't use anything less than 128-bit encryption keys.

The advantage of symmetric-key encryption algorithms is that they are fast and efficient, which makes them very good for applications that require real-time encryption, as opposed to other methods that have bigger impacts on performance.

The disadvantage of symmetric-key encryption is that the keys must be decided on between the sender and recipient in advance, and so there is a key sharing or exchange process that must happen. Special care must be taken to ensure that the key exchange is secure because, if the keys are compromised, the encryption can be broken. That is not an exceptionally difficult thing to manage when your encrypted data is sent to a small number of recipients, but it becomes progressively more difficult as the number of recipients increases. Thus, unless the sharing process can be automated, symmetric-key sharing becomes a liability on Internet Web sites that are used by large numbers of customers.

Asymmetric (Public-Key) Encryption

In the 1970's, a new sort of encryption system was invented called the *asymmetric-key* or *public-key* system. This system is called asymmetric because it does not require the use of identical keys on both the sender and the recipient side of an encrypted message or data stream. Alternatively, they are called public-key systems because one of the keys does not need to be kept a secret.

Let's rewind for a second to make these definitions more clear. Public-key encryption is characterized by the use of two different keys that make a pair, but which are not identical because they are in symmetric-key encryption; instead, each key is unique. The public/private key pair works together: what one key encrypts, the other will decrypt, and vice versa. One of the keys, the *private key*, must be kept secret in order to maintain security, but the *public key* can be sent over an insecure network without risk of compromising the system (hence the name, public-key encryption). Thus, public-key encryption gets around one of the main problems of the older-style symmetric-key encryption systems: how to securely exchange the encryption key with the party to whom you are sending the encrypted data.

As a rule, because they are not secret, public keys are used only to encrypt data. Once the data is encrypted, only the person whose PC holds the corresponding private key can decrypt the data. All of this works because the mathematics used in public-key ciphers ensures that there is one and only one unique private key that can ever be matched to a unique public key. Therefore, if you encrypt data with a person's public key, you can be sure that only the person who possesses the other half of the pair—the private key—can decrypt that data.

The first commercial public-key encryption algorithm was called the RSA algorithm (after the first initials of the surnames of the three men who invented it and then formed their own company using the name RSA Security, Inc.). This algorithm was used by Netscape as part of the first revision of SSL (although it was not the only cipher that Netscape used), and eventually became a de facto part of the standard when Netscape released SSL into the public domain. Microsoft first used RSA cryptography in their Windows NT operating system and has continued to use it in Windows 2000. RSA keys are a fundamental part of the encryption features of Windows 2000/IIS.

Combining Encryption Methods

Although public-key encryption has the advantage over private-key encryption of solving the problem of secure key exchange, it also has a disadvantage when it comes to speed. Generally, asymmetric-key systems are much slower than symmetric-key systems. While they may be suitable for encrypting small amounts of data, they are not practical for encrypting large amounts of data in real time, as is required over a secure communications session.

Therefore, standards such as SSL/TLS or IPSec, which are used for real-time data encryption over the Internet, use a combination of asymmetric and symmetric encryption algorithms to take advantage of each method's strengths. For example, in practice, public-key encryption isn't actually used to encrypt the data in a secure communication session because it is slow when compared to private-key encryption with the same key length.

Instead, public-key encryption is used to authenticate, encrypt, and send the key for a symmetric cipher such as RC4 or AES (which is a relatively small amount of data). Then the symmetric cipher is used to encrypt the session data (which can be many megabits long). At the receiving end, the decryption software first decrypts the symmetric key, and then uses that key to decrypt the data payload that follows.

Combining encryption methods also enhances the overall security of the encryption system. By using asymmetric encryption to deliver symmetric encryption session keys, the system can use a different symmetric key for each session. Indeed, that's the way it's done with both SSL and IPSec. The software picks the symmetric key at random. So, if one communication session key is somehow compromised (which is highly unlikely), it won't matter the next time a communication session is established.

Digital Certificates and Public-Key Infrastructure

Public-key cryptography has led to the invention of digital certificates, which are used for Web site authentication with both the SSL/TLS and IPSec protocols. A *digital certificate* is a digital document (a small file) that vouches for the identity and key ownership of an individual or a computer system. For example, a businesses certificate verifies that the business owns a particular public key. Digital certificates also help to automate the distribution of public keys within a public-key encryption protocol. When another computer wants to exchange information with your computer, it accesses your digital certificate, which contains your public key.

The set of products and processes required in order to securely issue, maintain, and manage digital certificates is called the *public-key infrastructure (PKI).* One of the components of PKI is a computer system called a *certificate server.* An entity that has a certificate server and that issues certificates is called a *certificate authority (CA).* A CA is responsible for verifying the identity and key ownership of an individual or organization before issuing the certificate.

There are companies such as Verisign and SSL.com that are commercial CAs. They will issue certificates to individuals or businesses for a fee. If an organization chooses to act as it's own certificate authority and issue their own digital certificates, they can use a product such as the Microsoft Certificate Server, but they need to install and maintain it on a dedicated server to ensure it's security. Many organizations prefer to pay a service to issue their certificates instead of purchasing their own equipment and allocating the resources necessary to do it themselves.

A standard for digital certificates called X.509 v3 is required for compatibility with the SSL/TLS and IPSec protocols used with Microsoft Windows 2000 and IIS. According to this standard, in order for an X.509 v3 digital certificate to be accepted as valid identification by the SSL/TLS or IPSec protocols, the certificate must contain four things:

- The Distinguished Name (DN) of the entity to whom the certificate was issued (that is, the name entered into the Name field of the certificate)

- The public key of the individual or organization that the certificate identifies

- A digital signature derived from the private key of the certificate authority as rendered by its certificate server
- Date stamps indicating the issue and expiration dates of the certificate

With this information, two nodes on a VPN, or a Web server and a properly configured browser, can send and receive encrypted streams of data that only they can decrypt.

Whether or not the certificate authority is trusted is a personal or business decision that individuals and organizations must make for themselves, but the norm on the Internet is that a Verisign certificate is acceptable. Once the trust decision is made, the root certificate of the certificate authority must be installed on the servers and clients that will be authenticating to each other. The *root certificate* is a certificate containing the CA's public key, to which the individually issued and signed certificates will be compared via public-key techniques in order to verify their authenticity. For example, a browser will authenticate a digital certificate installed on a Web site by comparing the certificate's signature to the public key of the CA's root certificate that is installed on the browser. By making this check, the browser can verify that the site actually belongs to the business or organization it claims to represent—as long as the issuing certificate authority can be trusted.

Authentication with Public-Key Protocols

Public-key protocols allow authenticated, encrypted communications to be established between hosts within intranets and over the Internet. There are three models of authentication within these protocols; they can be used individually or in combination:

- **Client authentication**   Allows a Windows 2000 VPN server or an IIS Web server to confirm a user's identity, using standard public-key cryptography techniques, by checking that a client's certificate and public ID are valid and have been issued by a certificate authority (CA) whose root certificate has been installed in the server's list of trusted CAs. This confirmation might be important if the server, for example, is a bank sending confidential financial information to a customer and wants to check the recipient's identity. Figure 8-1 illustrates the authentication process.

- **Server authentication**   Allows a VPN client or SSL/TLS client browser to confirm a server's identity by checking that a server's certificate and public ID are valid and have been issued by a certificate authority (CA) whose root certificate has been installed in the client's list of trusted CAs. This confirmation might be important to a Web site user, for example, if the user is sending a credit card number over the network and wants to be sure of the server's identity.

- **Mutual authentication**   Allows a client and server to authenticate each other simultaneously. Mutual authentication requires that both the client and the server have certificates and have had the appropriate CA root certificates installed on their list of trusted CAs.

Most commercial CAs, such as Verisign, work with Netscape and Microsoft to have their root certificates installed on the browsers by default. This way, users (and network managers) do not have to go through the trouble of installing the certificates, and server authentication works automatically. When your organization acts as its own certificate authority, you have to go through the extra step of installing the root certificate on all of your intranet client browsers; you must also provide instructions so that any Internet browser clients can have the root installed as well.

Figure 8-1 shows you how SSL/TLS authentication works. In practice, most Internet Web sites only use server authentication by digital certificate, since the process of distributing client certificates to all of their customers is a formidable management undertaking (although distribution is a little more easy when it's done over an intranet).

The downside to not using certificates on your clients is that you open up your system to potential dictionary attacks. A client with a browser authenticates the server with public-key methods, but the server just uses passwords to authenticate its clients, so a hacker has the opportunity to try attacking the server by guessing a password. Businesses that choose not to use client certificates believe that the cost of deployment outweighs the risks; like most business decisions, it's driven by economics.

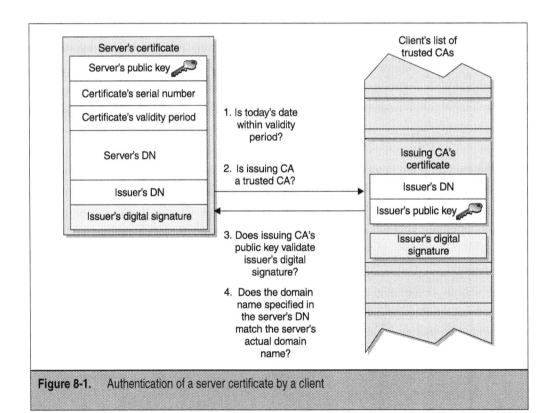

Figure 8-1.   Authentication of a server certificate by a client

USING IIS SECURE COMMUNICATIONS

From a security point of view, an unencrypted link between your IIS Web site and a browser is essentially wide open. In general, this might not be a problem if your site is used only on an intranet and nothing on your site is confidential, or if you use your site for marketing and you want to spread the word as widely as possible about your organization and its products. However, if you also use your site to take orders or to distribute proprietary information, then you need to protect some of that data.

The SSL/TLS protocols protect virtually all Web-based online banking, purchases, and monetary transactions. For example, financial institutions use SSL to secure the transmission of each customer's PIN number and other confidential account data. When a customer uses a credit card to purchase products online, the order form information is usually sent through an SSL-secured "tunnel" so that only the folks in the vendor's order department can see it.

TIP   The SSL protocol was originally developed and named by Netscape corporation in the mid-1990s. Since then, the Internet Engineering Task Force (IETF) has begun work on a new specification for encryption between clients and servers, called Transport Layer Security (TLS) that is based on the Netscape SSL v3.0 specification but is not interoperable. Microsoft IIS supports TLS 1.0 (the new specification); but to ensure compatibility with versions of browsers that predate TLS, it also supports SSL v3.0.

SSL and TLS provide very strong encryption. There have been some well-publicized cases of credit card numbers being stolen from Web sites that use SSL/TLS—but this happens when a Web site has insecurely stored the information in its database, not because a hacker has cracked the SSL/TLS encryption.

How Secure Web Communication Works

TLS and SSL constitute an integral part of most Web browsers (clients) and Web servers. SSL/TLS uses a program layer located between the Internet's HTTP and TCP layers that is included as part of both the Microsoft and Netscape browsers and also is built into IIS. The *sockets* part of the Secure Socket Layer protocol name refers to a capability of all operating systems that applications use to transmit and receive data over the network.

An encrypted SSL/TLS connection allows all information sent between a client and a server to be encrypted by the server and decrypted by the client, and vice versa. The encryption is done by a symmetric cipher after one-time session keys are securely exchanged via public-key encryption (as described in the earlier section "Combining Encryption Methods"). The public-key algorithm is RSA, and the default symmetric cipher is RC-4. In addition, all data sent over encrypted connections is protected with a mechanism for detecting tampering by determining whether the data has been altered in transit.

An SSL session is established between a client and a server in a series of events as follows:

1. A client opens a socket and requests a connection to the server.
2. The server authenticates the client (either by password or with a certificate sent by the client).
3. After a connection is established, the server gives the browser its public key by sending the browser the server certificate as issued by a trusted CA.
4. The client authenticates the certificate.
5. The client and server exchange their configuration information in order to negotiate the type and strength of encryption that will be used in the session.
6. The client creates a session key that will be used to encrypt the data.
7. The client encrypts the session key with the server's public key (which it got from the server's certificate) and sends it to the server. Only the server possesses the private key that can decrypt the session key.
8. The server decrypts the session key and uses it to establish the secure session over which it will exchange data with the client.

A prerequisite to the success of these events is that the client has preinstalled the root certificate of the trusted CA. This is a foregone conclusion if you are using a certificate from a commercial CA, such as Verisign, that has had its root embedded in Microsoft Internet Explorer or Netscape Communicator. If client certificates are used, then the server also needs to install the client's root certificate from the client's CA.

Configuring IIS for SSL/TLS

As you follow this discussion and configure your IIS site for SSL/TLS encryption, you will perform four required processes:

- Creating a public-key pair in IIS that will be submitted to a CA when you request a certificate
- Requesting a server certificate from the CA
- Installing the certificate
- Configuring the directories and pages that you want to secure

---

TIP   If you purchase a certificate from a commercial CA, it will take a substantial amount of time—not so much in front of the computer, but rather waiting for the CA to complete its approval process. This will take several days, so you won't be able to finish all four steps in a single setting. You will have to supply the CA with a certain amount of business identification that they will first verify before sending you your certificate. However, some commercial CAs will send you a trial certificate over the Web that will expire in a very short period of time but will at least let you proceed with the configuration on an experimental basis.

Performing a Certificate Signing Request

If this is the first time you are installing a secure protocol on your server, odds are that you don't have a public key yet, so there is a preliminary step required to create a key pair and prepare your site to request a certificate from a CA. Creating the key pair for your IIS server is done through the process called a *certificate signing request (CSR)*. To ensure the proper matching of public and private keys, you should perform the CSR from the computer for which the certificate will be requested. The steps are as follows:

1. Open the MMC Internet Services Manager, and navigate the resource tree to the Web site on which you want to use SSL/TLS to secure Web pages. Right-click on the site and choose Properties from the pop-up menu.

2. In the Web Site Properties window, choose the Directory Security tab. In the Secure Communications section at the bottom of the tab, click the Server Certificate button, as shown in Figure 8-2. This will bring up a wizard that will generate your public-key pair and create a CSR. (Notice that the View Certificate button and the Edit button are not operable yet, since you have not previously installed a certificate.)

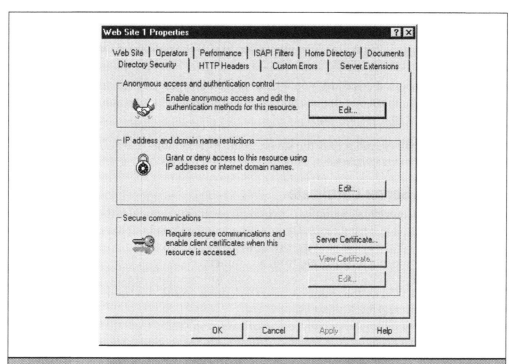

Figure 8-2.   Use the Web Site Properties Directory Security tab to create a CSR.

3. Follow the wizard's instructions, and answer the questions as you step through its screens. The choices you should make as you generate your request are the following:

- Select Create A New Certificate as the assignment method.

- Select Prepare The Request Now, But Send It Later as the request method.

- For Name and Security Settings, enter any name that you want, and then choose a length of at least 1024 bits in the Bit Length selection box (assuming it is available to you). If you are operating your site in the United States, you should not choose Server Gated Cryptography.

TIP   If you go beyond 1024 bits in your key length, it will take a fairly long time to calculate—probably several minutes, and much more if you make it longer. 1024 provides good protection for most applications.

---

4. Provide your organization's name and supply your organizational unit in the Organization Information screen. The organizational unit is not significant if you are a small company, but you still need to supply a name.

5. For Geographic Information, choose your country from the selection box, type in your state, and then type in your city. Do not abbreviate any of your entries because doing so would cause your certificate request to be rejected.

6. For Certificate Request File Name, choose a convenient name and location that you can get to from your browser when you are eventually filling out the Web form for your certificate request.

7. As you finish the wizard, you will be presented with a summary screen that looks something like the one shown in Figure 8-3. If everything looks accurate, click Next to exit the wizard.

The wizard will output a CSR file saved in the location with the name you've just chosen during the wizard process. This file contains a public key for your site.

Requesting a Server Certificate

The first step in acquiring a certificate is to make a certificate request to the CA that will be the issuer. When you make the request, you will be required to submit the information that identifies your business along with the public key you have created.

If you are requesting a certificate from a commercial CA, you'll be making your request at the CA's Web site (www.verisign.com, for example). If you are requesting a certificate from a CA within your organization, then your CA administrator will set up a Web page and a URL that you can use.

Generally, you will not receive your certificate at the same time that you apply. An exception might be a situation in which certificates are being used internally. In this case, your organization might have a policy that does not require a review of certificate requests if it trusts the requestor (that is, if it recognizes your name from the Windows Domain user list) and if its internally managed certificate server has been set for automated

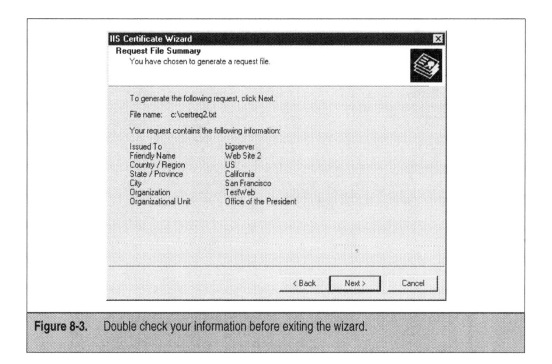

Figure 8-3. Double check your information before exiting the wizard.

approval under that condition. However, most of the time when you submit a certificate request to a CA, it will be considered Pending until the administrator of the certification authority approves or rejects the request.

When you reach the CA's certificate request page, you will be led through a series of forms that ask you to input various items of information. These will vary depending on the CA, although all of them will ask for the minimum information required by the x509 v3 standard, if that is the type of certificate you will be using. During this process, you will also be asked to choose a password and to enter your public key. Figure 8-4 shows the form you would use to provide your public key in Verisign's certificate request process.

The public key is a large binary number that was saved in the file you created during the CSR process. You can look at the contents of the public-key file by opening it up in the Windows 2000 Notepad, as shown in Figure 8-5. At the appropriate time in the certificate registration process, you are going to submit this key to the CA. In the case of Verisign, you would supply the key by opening the file, and then cutting and pasting its contents from Notepad into a box on the form. Again, however, this process will vary among CAs. Just follow the instructions provided by the CA you are using.

When you have completely filled out the CA's forms and submitted your information, your request will be put into the CA's Pending queue. Upon approving your certificate request, the CA will prepare the certificate and sign it. Most CAs will put your information through a verification process and notify you of your application's rejection or approval in an e-mail message.

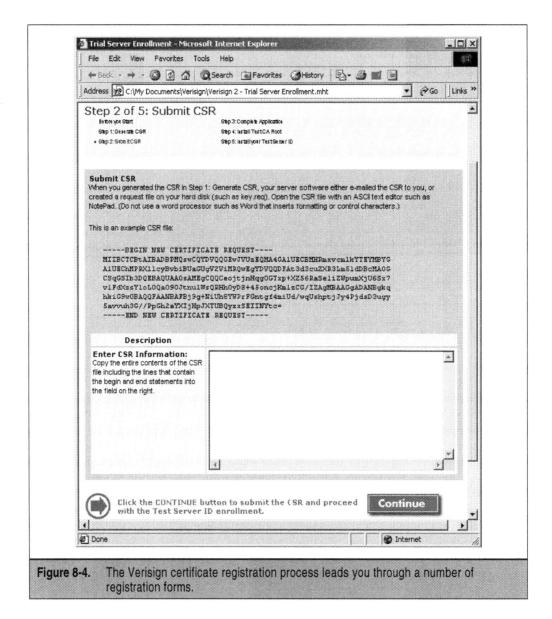

Figure 8-4. The Verisign certificate registration process leads you through a number of registration forms.

If you are approved, depending on the CA's policy, the message may contain the certificate itself or a link (URL) to a page on a site secured by SSL; this page will guarantee that your certificate can be securely delivered. When you visit the page, you will enter the password you created when you submitted your application, and then you will be allowed to download the certificate to your server's local disk.

Figure 8-5. Usually, the certificate authority will ask that you cut and paste your public key into their Certificate Request form.

TIP The example in this discussion uses a Verisign test certificate. When Verisign sends an e-mail message to approve a test certificate request, the test certificate will be embedded at the bottom of the message. It will look very similar to the public key that you cut and pasted into their certificate request form. You will need to cut and paste that certificate into a new Notepad document and save it with a filename that ends in .cer; this extension lets the wizard know that the file is a certificate.

Installing Your Digital Certificate

Once you receive notice of approval for your certificate request and you have downloaded your certificate, you can install the certificate on your Web server. To begin the installation, you'll go back to the MMC Internet Services Manager and perform the following steps:

1. Open the Internet Services Manager, and navigate the resource tree to the Web site on which you will be installing the certificate. Right-click on the site, and then select Properties from the pop-up menu to bring up the Web Site Properties window.

2. Select the Directory Security tab and click the Server Certificate button at the bottom of the window, just as you did when creating a Certificate Signing Request (CSR) in Figure 8-2. This will start the Web Server Certificate Wizard.

As you run the wizard, it will recognize that you have a pending certificate request, as shown in Figure 8-6. Make sure the option for processing a pending request is selected, and click Next to continue the installation.

TIP   If something should fail at any point in the certificate registration process, you can click Back to return to the previous step, or click Cancel if you simply want to close the wizard and start over.

---

3. Next, you will be asked for the location and filename of the certificate you've received from the CA. Use the Browse button to navigate to that file, or type in its filename, and click Next to proceed. The final procedural screen of the wizard will be a summary screen, as in Figure 8-7, showing you the details of your certificate.

4. Check all the details to make sure that everything is correct. If your certificate looks OK, click Next

5. On the screen that appears, click Finish to complete the installation.

Securing a Site or Directory

Once your certificate is installed, you can complete the rest of the SSL/TLS configuration for your site. In order to do this properly, you need to think through your site's organization.

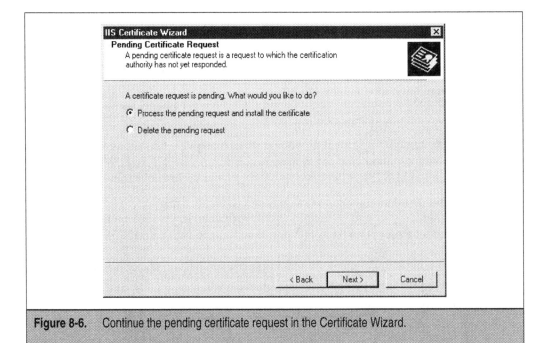

Figure 8-6.   Continue the pending certificate request in the Certificate Wizard.

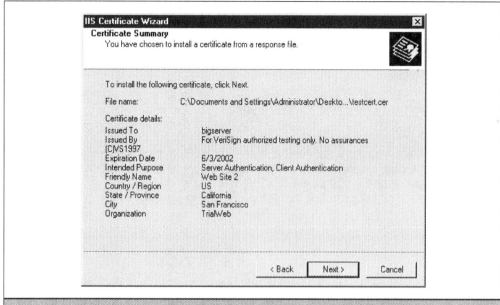

Figure 8-7.   When you receive your actual certificate, make sure the information is correct before completing the installation.

Most Web sites, even when they use encryption, also have a nonencrypted section. It's very costly, from a performance point of view, to encrypt all of your pages. Every time the server has to encode a page, it requires CPU cycles. If you encrypt everything on your site, you can quickly overwhelm and bog down a high-volume server. You can help the situation by using an encryption coprocessing card, which will be discussed in Chapter 9, but it's also wise to manage your server load through good planning.

Your home page does not have to be encrypted. Most companies leave the section of the site that has their marketing material, contact information, and anything else they want the public to have easy access to in separate, unencrypted directories. The designer will create a separate section—or sometimes even a different site—with content that is only for their customers' confidential access, and encrypt only that information. If your site will be similarly organized, it makes sense to structure it something like what you see in Figure 8-8.

When you have your information organized the way you want it, you can start your setup. Now that the site is SSL/TLS capable, you can indicate whether you will have encrypted pages on the entire site or only in certain directories. The procedure for configuring SSL/TLS encryption is as follows:

1. Open the MMC Internet Services Manager, and navigate the resource tree to find your server. Right-click on the server, or open the server to navigate to the directory containing the pages that you want to secure, and select

Properties from the pop-up menu to bring up the appropriate Properties window.

2. Set the port that IIS will use for SSL/TLS. You can do this on the Web Site tab, as shown in Figure 8-9. Port 443 is the standard port for secure communications on the Web.

3. Click Apply to save your configuration.

TIP IIS directory encryption works differently than Windows 2000 directory encryption. If you set a directory with encrypted properties in Windows Explorer or from the Windows Desktop, the information will be encrypted on disk. In contrast, the IIS SSL/TLS encryption properties on a directory will encrypt the information as it is being sent over the network to a browser client.

---

4. Click on the Directory Security tab. In the Secure Communications section at the bottom of the window, you will see that the View Certificate and the Edit button are now selectable, as shown in Figure 8-10. If it is a directory that you are securing, you will also see that the button to configure your certificate is inoperable because that is an operation you perform at the Web site level, not at the directory level. Click the Edit button to configure SSL/TLS settings.

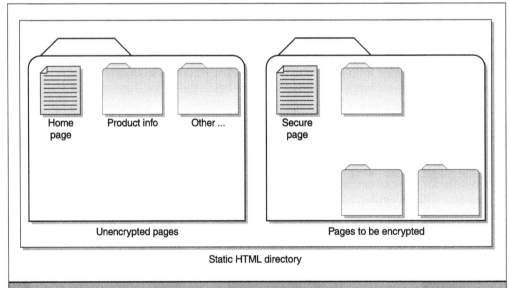

Figure 8-8. It's usually not necessary—or efficient—to encrypt every page on your Web site.

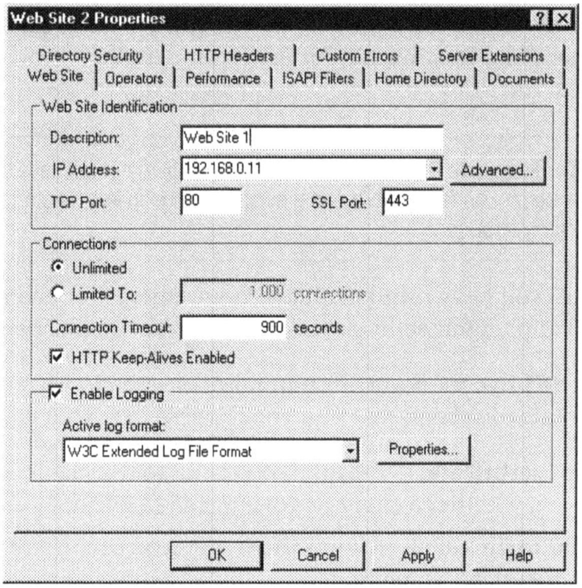

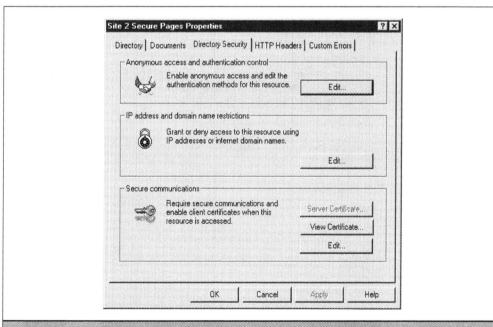

Figure 8-9. Use the Web Site tab to set the SSL port.

Figure 8-10. At the bottom of the Directory Security tab, Click Edit to configure Secure Communications on a certificate-enabled site.

5. In the Secure Communications window, shown in Figure 8-11, select the checkbox at the top of the screen labeled Require Secure Channel (SSL). The next checkbox, Require 128-Bit Encryption, will become selectable; click this box, too.

 SECURITY ALERT   To ensure that your site is safe, you should not use less than 128-bit encryption. 56-bit DES can now be broken fairly easily, but a simple change in key length to 128 bits makes encryption exponentially stronger.

6. At this point, you have fulfilled all the requirements for enabling SSL/TLS. Click OK to apply your settings and exit the Web Site Properties window.

Notice in Figure 8-11 that the Secure Communications window also lets you choose how to handle certificates on clients that visit your Web server. Your choices are as follows:

- **Ignore client certificates**   Tells the server not to use client certificates for authentication, whether a client has one installed or not

- **Accept client certificates**   Allows the server to accept client certificates as one of its authentication methods

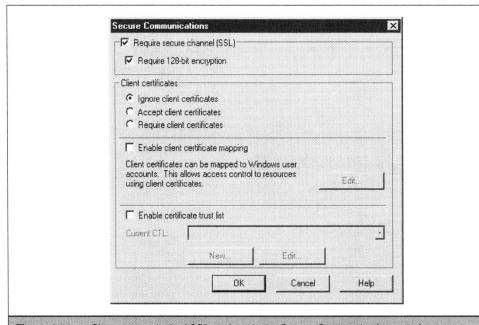

Figure 8-11.   Choose your desired SSL settings in the Secure Communications window.

- **Require client certificates** Prevents any users who do not have client certificates installed on their systems from accessing the secure content of your site

You can also map client certificates to Windows user accounts on your Web server. Once you enable this mapping, each time a user logs on with a client certificate, your Web server will automatically associate that user with the appropriate Windows user account. Using this feature, you can automatically authenticate users who log on with client certificates, without requiring the use of Basic, Messaging Digest, or Integrated Windows authentication.

CHALLENGE

The IIS Secure Socket Layer (SSL) and Transport Layer Security (TLS) features both provide the ability to use different ciphers by changing values in the Windows 2000 Registry. Note that changing the key length or cipher value will affect ciphers on the entire computer so that all other applications, such as Internet Explorer (which uses the same Registry entries to determine the ciphers that are available for use) will also use the new ciphers. While this is not a feature that everybody needs, it can be useful under certain circumstances on a Web site, where IIS is the primary application. To change the IIS SSL/TLS cipher settings, follow these steps:

1. Run Regedit and locate the following registry key:

   HKEY_LOCAL_MACHINE\SYSTEM\CurrentControlSet\Control\
   SecurityProviders\SCHANNEL\Ciphers

2. From the list of available ciphers, select one that you do *not* want to use. In the right-hand pane, view the Enabled Value for this entry. The value can be either one of the following:

   0xffffffff (enabled)

   0x0 (disabled)

3. Click Enabled, choose Edit, and then choose Modify.
   - In the Edit DWORD Value window, make sure that the Value option is set to Enabled and the Base Value option is set to Hexadecimal.
   - In the Value Data box, delete the previous value, and either enable it by entering **0** or disable it by entering **ffffffff**.

4. Click OK. Restart Internet Information Services so that the changes will take effect.

CHECKLIST FOR CONFIGURING SSL

- ☐ Decide upon your trust policy and authentication method for Digital Certificates and pick a commercial CA or install a self-managed certificate server.

- ☐ Create a public-key pair in IIS Internet Services Manager by creating a certificate signing request that will be submitted to a CA when you request a certificate.

- ☐ Request a server certificate from your CA by visiting the certificate request URL and filling out the certificate request application.

- ☐ Install the certificate on your Web server by following the instructions included in the response you get from the CA.

- ☐ Configure the directories and pages that you want to secure. Follow these steps:
  - ☐ Set the Web Site Properties to use port 443 (or another port of your choice) for SSL/TLS.
  - ☐ From the Directory Security tab, access the Secure Communications window and configure the settings so that 128-bit SSL is required.
  - ☐ Decide whether you want to require client authentication by digital certificates, and make the appropriate selections in the Secure Communications window.

CHAPTER 9

Third-Party Security Enhancements

So far, we've looked at how to configure the security of IIS itself, but unfortunately this alone is not going to be enough to ensure your Web server is safe. To minimize the chances of a successful attack, you can deploy third-party security enhancements to establish an acceptable level of overall protection for your IIS server and the network. Some of these enhancements are considered essential for any Web server, while others may be viable or appropriate only for large enterprise Web servers. You'll find that many products deliver several security services in one package, as the trend is toward providing integrated security tools. This often means that you have only one interface to learn and one support desk to call. This may be suitable for a small organization with limited IT resources, but larger organizations should probably look at integrating best of breed or the most appropriate tools to reach a desired level of security.

Before you rush out to spend your security budget on enticing shrink-wrapped security products, check to see whether Microsoft hasn't already provided what you need for free. For example, the Microsoft Windows 2000 Internet Server Security Configuration Tool conducts an interview to determine which services you want to provide and the general way that you'd like the server to operate, and then it generates and deploys a policy to configure the server appropriately. Other standard Windows tools, although basic, can help you identify possible vulnerabilities. Here are some examples:

- **Netstat.exe**   Displays protocol statistics, current TCP/IP network connections, all connections, and listening ports.

- **Nbtstat.exe**   Displays protocol statistics and current TCP/IP connections using NetBIOS over TCP/IP (NBT).

- **Net Share**   Creates, deletes, or displays directories being shared on a server.

These programs are all originally found in the WINNT\system32 folder, but you may have moved them to a utility disk instructed in Chapter 3. The "Windows 2000 Utilities" topic in Windows 2000 Help explains how to use them. For example, an easy way to check that you have only the necessary ports open on your server is to type **Netstat -a** at the command line. This will list all the open connections and listening ports on your machine. If you find that a port listed at www.doshelp.com/trojanports.htm has been opened, you probably have a Trojan Horse.

TIP   The Windows 2000 Server Resource Kit ships with System Scanner from Internet Security Systems (ISS), which includes 300 vulnerability checks for Windows. It isn't installed automatically, so look for Sysscansetup.exe in the Apps\Systemscanner folder on the kit's CD.

Unfortunately, despite the many capabilities included in these freebies, you will need to augment them with additional security products to protect your IIS server.

Beware of Examples and Samples

Before you consider which products to put on your shopping list, a quick word of warning about installing any new security product is in order. To understand how a product works, it's obviously important that you read the help documentation that comes with it. This documentation often includes examples and sample source code to help you get the most out of your new purchase. However, these examples are just that, examples, and should never be installed on a production server, even those that can be accessed only from http://localhost.

Stay Up-to-Date

It is critical that you stay up-to-date with IIS and any security products that you purchase to protect your server. Security software, in particular, is subject to constant change as a result of newly discovered vulnerabilities, and you need to be aware of any updates affecting your system.

Most major hardware and software manufacturers have support areas on their sites that deal specifically with security issues, although they're not always easy to find. You need to bookmark the relevant sites and subscribe to any newsletters or discussion forums that cover your particular products.

NTBugTraq at www.ntbugtraq.com is also essential reading for anyone running Microsoft-based products. Whenever a patch or upgrade is released, you will need to evaluate it before installing it on your production server, as even patches and new releases include a risk of bugs and downtime. You will need to determine the risk of immediate deployment against the costs of keeping services down or unprotected while you make sure the new software does not adversely affect your server.

Patch management is a subset of the change management process, so it requires an audit trail, a clear announcement and review period, testing procedures, and a well understood back-out plan. Another problem you face is keeping abreast of which product versions are still being supported, as you're unlikely to be able to obtain patches for new vulnerabilities for unsupported versions of your software. This effectively forces you to upgrade, so always find out a company's product support and upgrade policies before you commit yourself. Microsoft, for example, posts a six-month notice regarding expiration of support for a product or product version at support.microsoft.com/directory/discontinue.asp.

FIREWALLS

The first essential security enhancement that you need to think about for your IIS Web server is the protection offered by a firewall. Chapter 6 discussed the role your network must play in protecting your Web site and your other IT assets and the importance of a firewall as a perimeter security device. A firewall is typically defined as a system that enforces an access control policy between two networks, protecting a trusted network from an untrusted network by controlling the flow of data between the two. The Internet is always assumed to be untrusted, but areas of an internal network can also need protection—you don't necessarily want to give all your staff access to the accounts department's files, for example. Firewalls are often referred to as *gateways*, because they are the gateways leading to and from an internal and external network. Because a firewall is a choke point, it can be used to enforce and enable your security policy and can provide additional security services such as encryption and decryption of traffic that passes through.

Many security administrators believe that to protect their Web server and the resources that reside on it, all they need to do is deploy a firewall, which is often purchased and deployed without any proper consideration of a particular server's requirements. As we've seen with IIS, a firewall is effective only if the implementation is completed correctly and proper maintenance and auditing are carried out according to a security policy. The correct choice of a firewall will usually make other security strategies, such as Virtual Private Networks (VPNs) and IDSs, much easier to integrate. When deciding on the right firewall for your network, it is important that you read the functional specification to understand how a particular firewall is designed, and you should understand the technologies used.

Firewall Technologies

The following criteria must be met for a firewall to work:

- All traffic from inside to outside and vice versa must pass through the firewall.
- Only authorized traffic as defined by the security policy is allowed to pass through.
- The system itself must be immune to penetration.

Firewalls are classified into three types, based on whether they take connection history into account and the level of protocol that they handle:

- **Packet-level firewalls**   Analyze incoming and outgoing packets at the network and transport layers and filter them based on the source and destination IP addresses.
- **Proxy firewalls**   Establish the connection with the remote host, hiding and protecting individual computers on the network behind the firewall by acting on their behalf and making all packet-forwarding decisions.

- **Stateful inspection firewalls**   Work at the network layer, tracking each connection traversing the firewall to make sure it is valid. By examining not just the header information but also the contents of a packet up through the application layer, the firewall can make filtering decisions based on context that has been established by prior packets.

Today's firewalls, known as *hybrids*, tend to combine various techniques for providing security services. Let's have a look at each of these methods to understand how it can contribute to your defenses.

Packet Filtering

All firewalls perform some sort of packet filtering, usually by means of a packet-filtering router. The router looks at packets at the IP level and filters them as they pass between the router's interfaces, based on a set of rules that you establish. Filtering can be based on protocol type, source and destination IP addresses, and source and destination ports. This allows certain types of messages, such as HTTP requests, to pass through but not others. Because packet filters do not inspect the payload of a packet, they cannot filter it based on its contents, which means that potentially dangerous traffic can be allowed through undetected.

Packet filtering is also vulnerable to fragmented packet attacks. Packets are not remembered after they've been filtered, so there is no way to determine whether a connection attempt is malicious or not. As a single line of defense, packet filtering is fairly weak, which is why firewalls also use proxy services to increase their capacity to control access to your system. Another advantage of combining the two is that you do not need such complex filtering rules, as the packet filter needs to allow only application traffic destined for the proxy and can reject the rest. Simpler rules are easy to implement and, therefore, are more likely to be correctly configured.

Proxy Services

The major difference between proxy services and packet filters is that packet filters operate on individual packets, whereas the proxy service is aware of the entire session with the server, so it can forward or filter connections for requested services such as HTTP, FTP, and Telnet. Proxy services are hosted on a proxy server, often called an *application gateway*, and act on behalf of a network, as a *proxy*. All requests for access to a service are captured at the application gateway, which starts another session with the requested service so that all packets are sent to and from the gateway, rather than from the hosts behind the firewall. The outside host thinks it is communicating with the firewall, and it knows nothing about the hosts inside the firewall. This hides the configuration of the internal network behind the firewall.

The application gateway understands for which application it is performing the proxy service, and it inspects the data passing through. This allows various access-control rules to be enforced so traffic can be preauthenticated before it reaches the internal hosts, and logged more effectively. There are five main types of application gateway: circuit-level, traffic-aware, command-aware, content type-aware, and policy-aware. The command and content-type aware give you the best degree of control and protection. A command-aware proxy segments data streams into separate commands and responses, and can, for example, distinguish between FTP GETs and FTP PUTs commands. This proxy can also log the filenames of files being transferred through the gateway. A content-type aware proxy extends these capabilities by including checks on the content format, allowing traffic to be filtered for malicious code. It can block all HTTP transfers of Word and Excel documents that include macros, for example. You do need proxy software for each application type that you want to support, having to provide only nonstandard types yourself.

Stateful Inspection or Smart Session Filtering

While application gateways have access only to the application layer and routers have access only to the lower layers, stateful inspection integrates the information gathered from all layers to control the network session rather than the individual packets. Using a detailed knowledge of the rules of communication for each protocol, stateful inspection remembers which outgoing requests have been sent and allows responses only to those requests through the firewall. The firewall scans for problems in each packet that might be a symptom of an attack, such as IP Spoofing, Ping of Death, and other Denial of Service (DoS) attacks. Any attempt to access the internal network that has not been requested by the internal network will be denied. This type of filtering requires more processing power than packet filtering, but it actually requires less work than application processing and doesn't require that a new proxy be written every time a new service is required.

What Packet Filters Look At

To understand firewalls, it's useful for you to have at least a basic idea of how data is sent over the Internet via TCP/IP and how a basic packet-filtering firewall functions.

The term TCP/IP (Transmission Control Protocol/Internet Protocol) refers to a family of protocols, of which TCP and IP are just two. A *protocol* is a pre-established means of communication. Each different facet of communicating or sending data via TCP/IP is handled by a corresponding layer of the TCP/IP protocol. The network layer, for example, is responsible for figuring out how to get data to its destination.

When data is transmitted over TCP/IP, it is sent in a *packet*, the basic unit of transmission. Packets contain both data and header information, which consists of a combination of checksums, protocol identifiers, destination and source addresses, and state information. Each layer takes the previous layer's packet and adds its own header information.

Packet filters operate at the network layer and transport layer of the TCP/IP protocol stack. Every packet is examined, and the network and transport headers are examined closely for the following information:

- Protocol
- Source address
- Destination address
- Source port
- Destination port
- Connection status

The filtering device compares the values of these fields to rules that have been defined, and then it either passes or discards the packet. Many filters can also allow additional criteria from the link layer to be defined, such as the network interface where the filtering is to occur.

Deciding What You Need

Before buying a firewall, you need to develop a network service access policy that defines the services that will be allowed, or explicitly denied, from an untrusted network, and the conditions for any exceptions to this policy. This policy will allow you to define the features that your firewall must have to implement the policy, such as encryption and VPN support. It's important that the firewall supports your security policy and doesn't undermine it due to any limitations it may have. Once you've selected a firewall, your firewall design policy will describe and define the rules used to implement your network services access policy.

 SECURITY ALERT   Your secure access policy should be based on the "Deny any service unless it is expressly permitted" principle, which follows the classic access model used in information security.

Speed of implementation may well be one of the factors in your selection criteria, particularly if you've just suffered a security incident. If this is the case, firewall appliances have a big advantage over software-based firewalls in that they come with the software embedded or bundled with the hardware platform, usually making them faster to deploy and configure. They also offer ancillary features such as high availability and load balancing, but they are not necessarily more inherently secure. Both types will need to be configured correctly!

Built-in high availability, offered by appliances like the Nokia IP600 Security series, means that if your firewall loses its operational capabilities, it can make a transparent cut-over to a second firewall. This is probably not a critical feature unless you're operating in a large managed service provider or similar environment. To create high availability with a software-based firewall, you need to purchase two sets of hardware and software packages, and then install a high-availability package like Stonesoft's Stonebeat (www.stonesoft.com) on top of them.

Software-based firewalls come into their own when flexibility and scalability are at the top of your requirements list. However, the often richer feature set can make the correct configuration of these firewalls a longer and therefore more costly undertaking.

If you need to support site-to-site encryption, go for a firewall with built-in VPN capabilities with support for Internet Protocol Security (IPSec) and a secure remote access VPN client. Applications like VPN and streaming media will affect your server's performance, so you'll need to specify a firewall configured with adequate RAM that can handle a large number of simultaneous connections. Top-end enterprise firewalls, such as the Cisco PIX Firewall Series for example, provide more than 1 Gbps of firewall throughput with the ability to handle up to 500,000 concurrent connections.

Leading Firewall Products

By now you should have a list of essential and desirable requirements for your firewall. It's impossible to say which is the best firewall due to the many different environments in which they may be deployed, so this section will cover only a few of the leading brands to give you a flavor of what is available.

TIP One resource that can help you review your firewall requirements is the ICSA Labs' free annual "Firewall Buyer's Guide," available at http://www.icsalabs.com/html/communities/firewalls/index.shtml. (ICSA Labs is part of TruSecure Corporation, which also publishes NT Bugtraq.)

Check Point Next Generation FireWall-1

Probably the best-known firewall, FireWall-1 (www.checkpoint.com) has always benefited from an intuitive user interface that enables administrators to define, manage, and view their security policy rules with ease.

FireWall-1 offers firewall security, VPN, network address translation, Quality of Service (QoS), software distribution management, and VPN client security, and it runs on the latest versions of Windows, Solaris, and RedHat Linux. For anyone daunted by the task of managing a firewall, check out FireWall-1. Its easy management—and for the enterprise administrator, its centralized policy management—will dramatically increase your efficiency.

Figure 9-1 shows the FireWall-1 Policy Editor, where you can access object definitions and security settings.

Cisco PIX Firewall Family

The Cisco PIX Firewalls (www.cisco.com) are purpose-built firewall appliances that utilize a proprietary hardened operating system, which eliminates the security risks associated

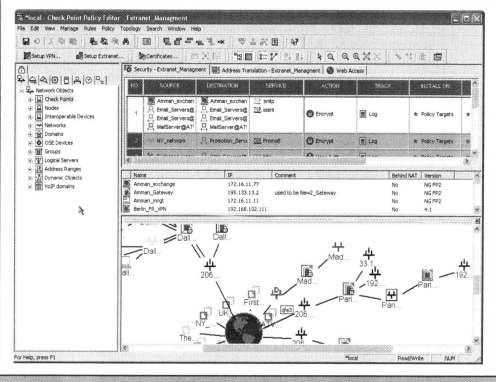

Figure 9-1.   The detailed graphical map of the Policy Editor offers easy access to object definitions and security settings.

with general-purpose operating systems. They range from desktop firewalls for small offices to top-end appliances for enterprise and service provider environments, and they utilize technologies ranging from stateful inspection firewalling to content filtering, integrated intrusion detection, plus VPN support via IPSec and Layer Two Tunneling Protocol (L2TP). They are managed using a Web-based interface, which can create real-time and historical reports. Installation and configuration are relatively straightforward if you are familiar with other Cisco products.

Network-1 Security Solutions CyberwallPLUS-SV

If you are running a small number of Windows NT or Windows 2000 servers and have a small budget, consider the CyberwallPLUS-SV firewall from Network-1 Security Solutions, Inc. (www.network-1.com). This firewall is implemented as an extension of the Windows OS kernel, surrounding it with security that hardens it from network attacks. At the heart of CyberwallPLUS-SV is a multilevel, stateful-inspection engine. The documentation isn't great, and be aware that the default installation allows all protocols to pass! However, it's a cost-effective solution, with easy installation, administration, and maintenance.

Microsoft Internet Security and Acceleration Server 2000

Internet Security and Acceleration (ISA) Server 2000 (www.microsoft.com/ISAServer/) is a combined enterprise firewall and Web cache server that integrates with Windows 2000 to provide policy-based security. The firewall provides filtering at the packet, circuit, and application layer; stateful inspection; control of access policy; and routing of traffic. The cache server helps improve network performance. The firewall and cache can be deployed separately on dedicated servers or integrated on the same computer. The familiar Microsoft Management Console is used to configure your ISA server, as shown in Figure 9-2.

If you run a Windows-based network, this is an obvious choice to consider. ISA makes it easy to manage your policy definitions, traffic routing, and server publishing, and it will also help you manage employee Internet activity.

TIP Although your firewall plays a critical role in protecting your server, your network, and the resources that reside on it, it shouldn't be your only solution. With any form of perimeter defense, if an attack is launched from inside, firewalls are not effective, and they cannot control insiders abusing authorized access, for example. Some firewalls can be configured to check incoming data for signs of viruses and Trojan Horses, but a proper anti-virus policy and scanner is the way to tackle this problem. These systems are discussed later in the chapter in the section "Virus Scanners."

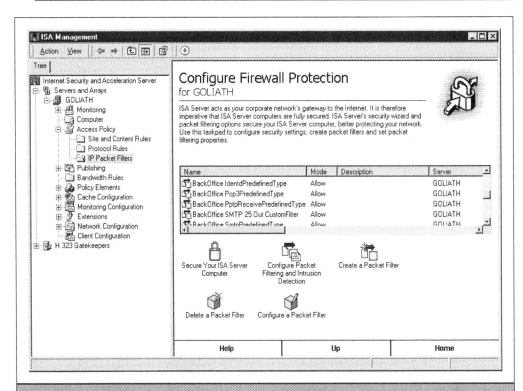

Figure 9-2. You'll use a familiar Microsoft GUI to work with ISA Server.

INTRUSION DETECTION SYSTEMS

Multiple layers of defense are needed to ensure that your Web server is well protected. While a firewall provides a controlled point of access to your IIS server, the goal of an IDS is to identify or detect unauthorized activity correctly. IDSs automate the process of detecting anomalies in network usage by collecting information from a variety of vantage points within a computer or network and analyzing it for warning signs of security breaches. They are passive devices, and most cannot block network traffic or control network access.

How Intrusion Detection Works

An IDS examines packets in the network traffic to identify threats from both authorized as well as unauthorized users who thwart your perimeter defenses. It does this by using string matching and context analysis, working from a set of rules that determine what it is looking for. These rules can vary depending on the role of a user and are based on a variety of metrics and parameters:

- **Threshold barriers**   Specific events, such as failed log-ins.

- **Profiling**   Analysis of actual usage versus a baseline profile.

- **Known Attack Signatures**   Network activity is screened for such actions as invalid TCP headers or sudden, mass e-mailings.

String matching looks for a series of characters to identify a possible threat, while context analysis, also known as *signature* analysis, builds on string matching by allowing a scripted analysis of the string's context. While string matching is fast, it is prone to false positives. Context analysis reduces false positives but it takes longer to detect attacks in context.

Top-of-the-range IDS fully decode protocols to expose packets and their contents completely to the scrutiny of large attack-signature databases. You can tune an IDS to balance performance against accuracy and extend its signature base so that it can identify any unique network characteristics. Tuning your IDS to reduce false alerts is essential to avoid an inordinate number of false positives, which would soon swamp you with unnecessary work and annoyed users. It's important that you clearly define a method for addressing all IDS alerts to ensure that you have an appropriate response to the possibility of an actual attack. Do this before you activate your IDS.

TIP   An IDS relies on rules to recognize and respond to a seemingly infinite number of possible attacks, so it can completely miss an attack, which is called a *false negative*. You can reduce this risk by ensuring that your rules are current with respect to known attacks and by keeping a constant eye on network activity. A *false positive* is an alert generated by an IDS for something that is not actually an attack. An example could be a user backing up an entire project folder on some type of removable media for legitimate purposes.

Many IDS applications provide specific automated responses for rule infractions, such as e-mailing an administrator or suspending a user's privileges. They also record network usage, which can be used for detailed analysis. Due to the enormous amount of data logged, many IDSs incorporate log analyzers, which are discussed later on in the chapter in the section "Log Analyzers."

Two distinct IDS implementations can be used: *host-based intrusion detection systems (HIDS)* and *network-based intrusion detection systems (NIDS)*. On a large network, both should be used, while on a small network a NIDS should be your first choice.

Host-Based Intrusion Detection

An HIDS is an application installed on any critical DMZ host devices, such as a Web server, and monitors activity on that device only. Typically, HIDSs monitor and record user authentication, application processes, connections, and file changes, which are critical in detecting attacks such as a Back Orifice or time-bomb attack. To preserve processing power, they need to be configurable to track specific program activity, such as automatic macro execution and worm virus signature activity.

Centralized host-based IDSs (CHIDSs) are derived from HIDSs but conduct their analysis centrally by sending monitored files, logs, and registry settings to a central console for analysis. This makes them more secure, because they send all required information off the host so analysis can carry on even if the host is compromised. *Hybrid IDSs* complement HIDS technology by monitoring network traffic coming in or out of a specific host. NIDS technology, on the other hand, monitors all network traffic for attacks that exploit the connections between the computers on your network.

CAUTION   Remember to take into account the costs in terms of human resources needed to install and maintain complex security products. Many of the products discussed in this chapter will place additional demands on your system. An intrusion detection system (IDS), for example, has the potential to generate gigabytes of log data and will consume plenty of processing power comparing network usage to programmed rules. You may need to add in the expense of upgrading hardware to the cost of the IDS itself. You must balance the total cost with your requirements and your budget.

Network-Based Intrusion Detection

An NIDS provides an umbrella for your network by monitoring inbound and outbound traffic to flag an attack before it can access network resources. Of all IDS technologies, the NIDS provides the broadest coverage and detects the broadest range of attacks, including DoS attacks.

NIDS should be deployed on the network segment external to the DMZ and then on the DMZ segment. This will allow you to monitor all external and DMZ activity. An NIDS consists of a collection of agent applications strategically placed within the network to monitor network-based activity, and it can be hardware or software based.

TIP   Intrusion detection doesn't just provide security. Internal network misuse is one of the most costly problems in business today. An IDS can address this by providing information about how employees are using the network—such as for searching for jobs or wasting or abusing company resources.

Choosing an IDS

Industry standards mandate the use of both NIDS and HIDS. If you can't afford both, an HIDS should be deployed after an NIDS to ensure that the network is protected. An NIDS will provide far greater detail on network traffic than an HIDS, as the HIDS provides information only for a specific PC or server, and it provides no traffic information at all. Many NIDSs can block an attack and stop a hacker from gaining access.

Although these blocking tactics vary in efficiency, they occur in real time and thus potentially limit the damage of an attack. Because HIDSs are based on log file analysis, they can provide attack information only after the fact. Hybrid IDSs can respond in real time but can protect only the individual host. Finally, NIDSs can often interact with other perimeter defense systems by dynamically updating their policies to respond to threats in real time.

It is important that the IDS you select fits both your current and future requirements. Its level of customization is important, as it lets you adapt an IDS to your unique environment and will increase the value of the data produced. Because an IDS functions as a burglar alarm, you will need to be able to respond if it sounds the alarm. This requires an incident response policy, which includes written and fully tested procedures to ensure that a proven procedure is in place if a malicious attack is detected.

For easy deployment of a NIDS, you should buy an appliance rather than a software-based system that can take longer to deploy—although an IDS does not have to come in a shrink-wrapped or off-the-shelf package. You can design an IDS using combinations of personal and enterprise firewalls with logging capabilities, automated log analysis tools, and packet sniffers. For smaller networks, a homegrown solution can often be cost-effectively implemented if you have the in-house expertise.

Suggested Products

The following products cover the range of IDSs discussed previously. Choosing the right product for your needs depends on your own network environment and budget. The following products all support automatic updating of attack signatures, remote management, and prevention methods in addition to detection.

 SECURITY ALERT Change any default passwords, which are often blank, that come with programs that you install, especially those that create a predefined account. Failing to do so can quickly result in hackers exploiting these well-known passwords.

The NETGEAR Firewall Router is a good entry-level combined firewall and NIDS for a small network, while RealSecure for Nokia is a feature-rich hardware and software appliance. LANguard Security Event Log Monitor & Reporter (S.E.L.M.), shown in Figure 9-3, uses Windows NT/2000 event logs in real time to alert you to any important security events, so it is not impaired by IP traffic encryption or high-speed data transfer. For networks consisting of one server and five hosts, you get the whole thing for free!

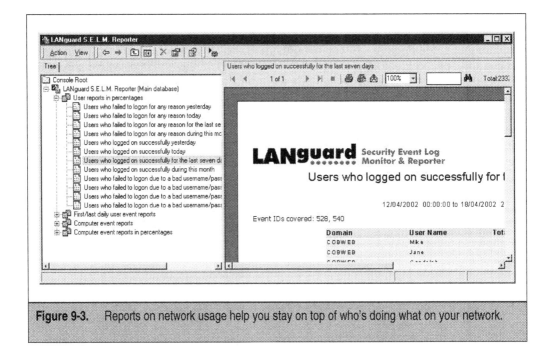

Figure 9-3. Reports on network usage help you stay on top of who's doing what on your network.

Table 9-1 shows a comparison of several manufacturers' IDS products.

IDS	Manufacturer	Type
FR314 Cable/DSL Firewall Router	NETGEAR, Inc. www.netgear.com	Combined hardware firewall and NIDS
Intruder Alert	Symantec Corporation www.symantec.com	Software HIDS
LANguard Security Event Log Monitor	GFI www.gfi.com/languard/	Software NIDS
RealSecure	Internet Security Systems www.iss.net	Software NIDS
RealSecure for Nokia	Nokia www.nokia.com/securitysolutions/ network/iss.html	Stand-alone appliance; hardware and software NIDS

Table 9-1. Comparison of IDS Products

TIP If you have a limited budget, plenty of free or "build-your-own" IDS programs are available on the Internet, but remember that support may be limited or nonexistent. Snort is a well-known free, basic NIDS, and you can find plenty more IDS tools and information sources at Google's Intrusion Detection Systems page at http://directory.google.com/Top/ Computers/Security/Intrusion_Detection_ Systems/.

Monitoring your system with an IDS provides security against both new and old vulnerabilities, and against any flaws that may exist in the software that you are running. IDSs are seen by many security experts as a realistic way of providing resilient security, because they make network security less dependent on keeping patches up to date.

Many surveys show that the majority of attacks are carried out via known vulnerabilities for which patches have been available for months or, in some cases, years. Vigilant monitoring of your system won't give you complete security, but you're more likely to catch and stop a hacker regardless of the vulnerability they exploited to break in.

LOG ANALYZERS

Log files are useful only if you read them, but many system administrators only glance at the logs generated by their firewalls, routers, IDS, mail servers, and Web servers when trying to troubleshoot a problem. Truth is, they are great sources of information about the traffic and activity on your network.

Log analyzers are often a key component of an IDS, but for large networks a heavy-duty analyzer may be required. As discussed in Chapter 5, IIS goes beyond the scope of the event-logging or performance-monitoring features of Windows 2000. Even a small site can generate too much information for anyone to be able to analyze it all manually. Who really has the time to notice that the log files recording user activity show the user account for the head of the sales department is being used to try to access customer records while she is currently away on vacation? In an environment with tens, hundreds, or thousands of nodes, users, and other resources, even a dedicated staff of network administrators and security personnel would not be able to wade through the gigabytes of data generated by network usage. Log analyzers are the best way to track this type of analysis.

Gathering Clues

Log analyzers automate the auditing and analysis of your network logs and can often tell you what has happened or is happening by revealing unauthorized activity or anomalous behavior. This feedback can be used to enhance current IDS signatures or firewall rule sets. It can also provide a basis for focused security awareness training, reduced network misuse, and stronger policy enforcement. Some of the features that you will come across in log analyzers to analyze this data include interactive database warehousing, data mining algorithms, graphic visualization, and artificial intelligence–based attack prediction.

Recommendations and Resources

If you are responsible for a large network, your log analyzer should be able to collect and summarize log events from diverse network devices, collating them in one secure centralized place. It must also have the ability to protect the integrity of log data in case it is needed in any litigation.

The three products in the following table enable you to integrate multivendor applications and security devices to achieve comprehensive analysis and generate reports required to understand any risks and take appropriate action.

Product	Manufacturer
e-Sentinel	e-Security www.esecurityinc.com
netForensics	netForensics www.netforensics.com
SilentRunner	SilentRunner, Inc. www.silentrunner.com

VIRUS SCANNERS

On July 19, 2001, more than 350,000 computers were infected with the Code-Red worm in 13 hours. At the peak of the outbreak, more than 2000 new hosts were infected each minute. Viruses—or in this case, a worm—can cause crippling damage to any organization due to a loss of productivity, client confidence, and staff morale. Virus scanners can be instrumental in helping you detect dangerous worms and viruses.

 SECURITY ALERT   The vast majority of worms and viruses in the past few years have been targeted at Web browsers and e-mail clients. It is vital that you keep these two applications updated with the appropriate patches in your fight against viruses.

How They Work

Virus scanners can use several different methods to try to correctly detect viruses. All scanners use pattern matching, whereby the scanner looks inside files for a string of bytes, or a *signature*, that matches one in its database of known viruses. This finds the majority of known viruses, but to detect viruses that use techniques such as polymorphism to change their code, scanners have to use more sophisticated inspection techniques. This can entail processing files in a real-time emulation mode to watch for the polymorphic engine to decrypt the virus.

Heuristic or behavior-based scanning analyzes files for suspicious or irregular virus-like code, such as time-triggered events or routines that search for .com and .exe files, which enables scanners to catch unknown viruses before they can infect a computer. Virus scanners must be continually improved to keep up with the ever-expanding range of infectable objects that they need to be able to inspect, and they must be constantly updated with the latest virus definitions.

The Lock-Down Alternative

Some AV tools try a different approach to catching viruses and other malicious code by watching application behavior. StormWatch from Okena, Inc., (www.okena.com), for example, sits alongside the operating-system kernel and intercepts requests for resources to make a real-time allow/deny decision according to defined access control rules. This prevents both users and viruses from running unauthorized programs and is an effective way of preventing unknown attacks. Unlike traditional signature scanning software, StormWatch does not inspect content, and therefore it has negligible impact on system performance. This product also comes with default policies for IIS, providing out-of-the-box protection against SYN floods, distributed port scans, network worms, and Trojan Horses. The lock-down approach has a lot to offer if you are running IIS on a dedicated machine and know exactly what programs you want running on it.

Centralization and Cooperation

A trend to watch for is a merging of AV tools with network security. Many vendors are introducing products that offer better centralized control of security tools, even if they are protecting different parts of the network infrastructure, such as e-mail gateways and servers. More and more threats, such as the Nimda zombie, can attack networks in multiple ways, infiltrating the system as an e-mail attachment or via a Web browser. By sharing information with different security tools, it is easier to catch these latest threats.

A typical move toward unified tools is Symantec's Web Security, which scans e-mail for inappropriate content, such as obscenities, as well as viruses. Another is ePolicy Orchestrator from McAfee, which allows you to manage and enforce AV protection and policies centrally for McAfee and Symantec products. Hackers look at the big picture of your system when they plan their attack, so having antiviral tools that do the same is a step in the right direction.

The Model Solution

Although the key factor in evaluating an AV product is its accuracy at finding viruses while discriminating between viruses and non-viruses, you definitely want a single point of management control to protect your network and your IIS server effectively. Most scanners consistently score within a couple of percentage points of each other in terms of scanning ability, so it's their scalability, maintainability, and overall ease of use that differentiates them. Speed of scanning, disinfection, automatic updates, and 24-hour technical support are also important features to look for.

A good network AV package should be able to handle compressed files and macro viruses, and it should be able to detect a virus wherever it enters the system and stop it spreading from workstations to servers, and vice versa. For minimum disruption, the software should scan without having a significant impact on file operations, and it should be able to disinfect most files on the fly.

Popular Virus Scanners

McAfee's WebShield SMTP (www.mcafee.com) is a firewall-independent gateway virus scanner that stops viruses and blocks specific SPAM e-mail before it can enter your network. It automatically monitors network e-mail looking for activities representative of new virus outbreaks. Other features include content filtering, automatic updates, remote manageability, alert notification, and reporting capabilities. Being able to block files from entering or leaving your network according to their size or name will give you control over your internal users as well.

Sophos Anti-Virus (www.sophos.com) incorporates centralized management that provides controlled installation across the network and automated update of all machines from a single point. All virus incidents anywhere on the network are centrally logged, and Sophos Anti-Virus allows centralized reporting and messaging. It also monitors e-mails, Internet downloads, groupware, and archive files, complementing the gateway protection offered by Sophos MailMonitor, which is similar to the McAfee WebShield.

Norton AntiVirus Corporate Edition from Symantec (www.symantec.com) also offers centralized policy management for desktops and servers, allowing you to lock down policies that will keep systems up to date and properly configured. This is a good choice as it is cost effective for smaller organizations and simple and easy to use. Figure 9-4 shows the Symantec System Center, from which servers and network clients can be centrally managed. Client installations can be configured with preset parameters, such as realtime scanning options, which can be locked by the administrator. Clients can be prevented from stopping centrally configured scheduled scans. Control over the version of the virus definitions file used on all servers and clients ensures that each machine is protected with approved files that are updated automatically.

SECURITY ALERT   Double-check that your AV software is working correctly. Use the EICAR test file, a harmless file that AV products detect as if it were a virus. Use it to test the proper operation of your AV product and policy. Download it from any AV vendor's site.

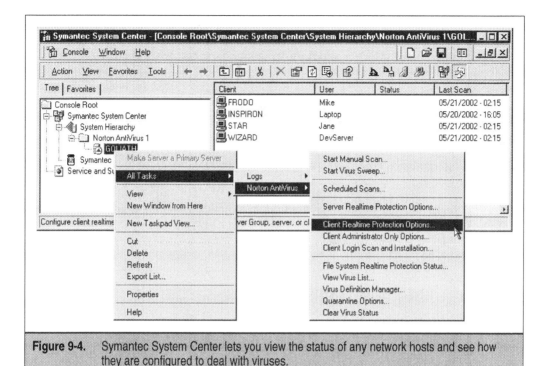

Figure 9-4.   Symantec System Center lets you view the status of any network hosts and see how they are configured to deal with viruses.

SECURITY AWARENESS TRAINING

In addition to the technical aspects, you need to manage the human side of the security of your IIS server. Capital expenditure and the latest technology, however well implemented, cannot accomplish security alone. Unless you get your organization to invest in user security awareness training and compliance, security technology investments can be a waste of money. For example, your Web site developers may be dedicated employees, but they may not have a "security mentality" when it comes to building Web sites. Code and scripts written without security in mind can create holes in an otherwise carefully planned security policy. While most staff will probably be aware of the dangers of opening e-mail attachments, do they really appreciate the importance of not divulging passwords, or do they understand why they must wear their security badges at all times? Without a culture of security, which often entails changing current behaviour, you will be facing an uphill struggle to maintain the security of your network.

All employees should be given security awareness training to make them fully appreciate the importance of an organization's data and the security processes that protect that data. All employees should fully understand the specific security-related requirements relative to their particular duties and should be held accountable for specific security tasks as part of their jobs. Employees should come away from a security awareness session believing that security is everyone's job, as indeed it is. This way, security is not superimposed but carefully fitted into your organizational structure, as people understand security as a business issue, and not just an IT issue.

Security awareness not only applies to operational staff; it is for senior management too. In fact, commitment from senior management is essential to any security program of this kind.

TIP   The Human Firewall Council at www.humanfirewall.org provides resources that will help you to stress the importance of security training to your senior management, as well as providing a free survey contributed by PentaSafe Security Technologies to test the security awareness level in your company.

In-House vs. Third-Party Training

The answer to how you provide your staff with security training depends on your organization's resources. If you have in-house training services and the knowledge base to develop your own training material, you can easily incorporate your specific security policies into any training material. However, this route is probably an option only for very large organizations, and most will have to turn to third parties to provide training.

Third-party training providers should be able to offer courses customized to match your organization's security profile and policy. It is important that they record exactly who has taken and completed specific courses, as this may well be important in proving due care in court. They will need to deliver courses aimed at general staff and at employees more directly involved in sensitive areas of the business. Depending on the industry you are in, you may need to consider training third-party employees who have access to your premises—such as cleaning services or business partners that use your extranet. This may be more easily achieved by using a third party trainer, as they will be better placed to deliver training at different locations.

CHANGE CONTROL

Many IIS administrators make the mistake of implementing changes to the settings of a live IIS server without a review-and-release cycle and advance maintenance announcements.

Beating Web Defacements

What happens if, despite your best efforts, someone breaks into your IIS Web server and changes the content and defaces your site? If the attack goes unnoticed by you or your staff, the first you'll know about it will be via a customer or the press who will more than likely have been tipped off by the perpetrators. At this point you'd need a quick and easy way to restore your site. Obviously you can restore the site from your backup tapes, but it's certainly not an automatic process.

Web site defacements are different from other types of attacks because their high visibility can attract media attention and are more common than full-scale invasions into company networks. If you are running a small Web site with static content, you could look at serving pages from a CD or other read-only media, but this isn't really a practical answer for most sites. The ultimate solution would be to use a military-grade, compartmentalized OS with incoming and outgoing HTTP filtering, public key signing, and dynamic on-the-fly restore in conjunction with a firewall that blocks all ports apart from HTTP port 80. This is not an option for all but the largest organizations that have a large security budget.

Formalized testing, impact analysis, and separation of duties are key items to implementing changes successfully in your system. If you carefully control and document changes to your server, you will be better placed to recover from attacks and locate security problems.

Change control products can be loosely categorized by the countermeasures they provide—prevention, fast repair, and detection—and by how they are deployed—directly on the server, on a dedicated hardware platform, or on a separate machine.

Restore and Backup Products

In serving dynamic Web content, you should opt for a remote-checking system with an automated restore capability or local cryptographic verification.

Various available software packages can help you restore a site quickly; these products also simplify backup procedures. Lockstep Systems, Inc., (www.lockstep.com) produces WebAgain, shown in Figure 9-5, which automatically detects Web site hacks and restores the correct content. The company's sister product, SiteRecorder, protects your Web site content against accidental changes made by internal staff by maintaining a complete audit trail and archive of all content changes. This allows for an easy rollback or restoration of Web content.

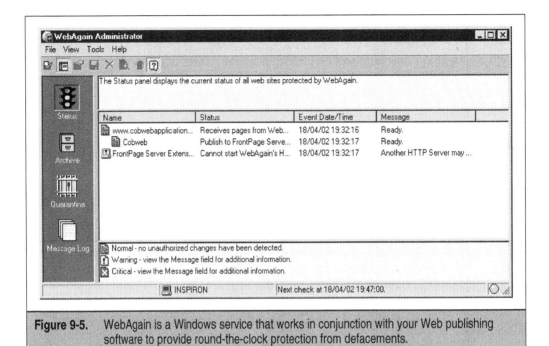

Figure 9-5. WebAgain is a Windows service that works in conjunction with your Web publishing software to provide round-the-clock protection from defacements.

CimTrak Web Security by CIMCOR (www.cimcor.com) is similar to WebAgain in that it provides quarantining of any modified files for forensic purposes.

PERFORMANCE AND ACCESS-CONTROL HARDWARE

Hopefully your Web site is going to be a big success, but heavy traffic on the site can create its own security problems. Will your site crash when it tries to handle heavy peak loads? The best way to find out if your server is up to the job is to use a stress test tool.

You can download the free Web Application Stress (WAS) tool from Microsoft at http://webtool.rte.microsoft.com/download.asp. You may want to consider the Webserver Stress Tool from Paessler (www.paessler.com/WebStress/webstress.htm), which is shown in Figure 9-6. Both products simulate the traffic and usage generated by a large number of simultaneous Web users, enabling you to gather performance and stability information about your Web application and test the ability of your IIS server to handle various loads and capacities.

By creating an environment that is as close to production as possible, you can find and eliminate problems with your site and IIS server prior to deployment. If you're running an e-commerce site, for example, these tests might reveal that managing the

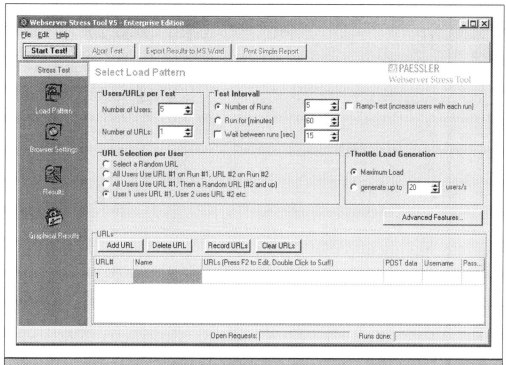

Figure 9-6. Stressing out your server before it goes live will reduce your stress levels when it does.

heavy processing burden of the Secure Sockets Layer (SSL) protocol becomes a serious challenge. Heavy SSL traffic can cause processing bottlenecks that overwhelm even the most powerful servers, impacting the overall performance of your server.

Hardware Performance Solutions

Apart from increasing RAM and processing power, you can dramatically increase your server's SSL processing capacity by adding an SSL accelerator as the security processing is transferred to the accelerator, leaving the server to do the important job of processing your orders and transactions. An accelerator avoids the expense of adding either general-purpose processors or further servers, which can be a welcome benefit if space is at a premium. Most accelerators are available as either PCI cards or external units and are built to be modular, allowing you to add capacity when and where you need it. Some, like the Rainbow CryptoSwift (www.rainbow.com), can be integrated into specific projects by using the cryptographic developer tool kits.

SSL Acceleration Products

The number of *transactions per second (TPS)* is often used to identify the performance of SSL acceleration products, but be aware that no standard exists for defining a TPS. Most vendors use TPS to measure the number of RSA private key operations that can be performed with 1024-bit keys. Another measure, *requests per second (RPS)*, defines a request as a single HTTP GET command with a full SSL handshake. However, neither of these metrics measures true performance, as most HTTP requests will not incur the overhead of a full RSA handshake. Throughput and response time are probably better metrics to look for when assessing accelerators.

Leading manufacturers of SSL accelerators include the following:

- **nCipher**   nForce Secure SSL Accelerators (www.ncipher.com)
- **Rainbow**   CryptoSwift and NetSwift SSL Accelerators (www.rainbow.com)

Hardware Authentication Solutions

You may want to restrict areas of your Web site to specific users or ensure that you know exactly who a user is before serving up sensitive information, such as account details. This is usually accomplished by the user entering a username and password that is matched to a list of users in a database, or possibly Active Directory if your server is part of a Windows domain. These types of security measures might suffice if the content that the authenticated user can access is of little value, but what if the user wants to display a stock portfolio or medical information? Password-based authentication is known to be weak, due to users sharing and disclosing their passwords. Trying to authenticate remote users with passwords provides little assurance that you can accurately identify them and be able to grant the appropriate access. If you need to be more certain of who is requesting information from your Web server, authentication must be strong—that is, at least *two-factor*.

Two-factor authentication means you must combine any two of the following to be identified and authenticated:

- Something you know, such as a username, password, or PIN
- Something you have in possession, such as a token, card, or key
- Something that identifies you personally, such as a fingerprint or signature

Adding two-factor authentication for staff that have direct access to sensitive resources on your Web server, such as developers, is another security measure that you should consider. While biometrics—using fingerprints or retinal scans for identification—is still a relatively expensive means of authenticating a user, issuing smart devices such as smart cards or USB devices is now a cost-effective solution to implementing strong user authentication. A user must not only know the PIN to access the authentication credentials stored on the device but also have the device in his or her possession to authenticate him/herself. Most devices can store digital certificates and public/private keys for use in a PKI infrastructure, or like Rainbow's iKey, they can also be used for shared secret authentication, a less expensive but effective form of user authentication. Normally, user's keys are stored on their computer's hard drive, immediately making the whole system less secure; by storing them directly on a smart device, you improve your overall security and authentication process.

Security Token Products

USB security devices plug into any standard USB port, making them both a smart card and a reader, and they are small and light enough to fit on a key chain, as you can see in Figure 9-7. They are technologically identical to smart cards, with the exception of their form factor and interface. The leading manufacturers of smart devices include the following:

- Alladin (www.ealaddin.com)
- Eutron, Itema Group (www.eutron.com)
- Rainbow Technologies, Inc. (www.rainbow.com)
- SchlumbergerSema (www1.slb.com/smartcards/)

Biometric authentication shouldn't be dismissed out of hand as the costs of implementation are becoming more affordable. Biometrics can help make security less onerous for users—an added benefit as users are renowned for trying to circumvent any security methods that are difficult to use. If you are interested in biometric authentication for staff who have special privileges on your server, the MagicSecure fingerprint ID optical mouse from Eutron provides easy-to-use three-factor authentication. It is shown in Figure 9-8.

Figure 9-7.   Two-factor authentication can actually make your authentication process more user friendly, and most smart devices are easy to carry around.

Figure 9-8. The MagicSecure optical mouse provides simple authentication with something that can't be stolen or forgotten, a personal fingerprint.

ADDITIONAL RECOMMENDED SECURITY ENHANCEMENTS

You've looked at the main technologies necessary for creating a robust and secure environment for your IIS server. Here's a quick look at a few other tools and services that will make maintaining the security of your server that much easier, and therefore more effective.

Web Security Scanners

Trying to maintain a secure IIS site can be a daunting prospect when new threats evolve so quickly. One useful tool that can substantially ease your burden is a security, or vulnerability, scanner, which will put you on an even footing with potential intruders, as the scanner can reveal the same vulnerabilities that intruders are looking to exploit. A vulnerability scanner will help you stay up to date on security threats and countermeasures. You can discover what the threat is, where it's located, and how to fix it. Good vulnerability scanners provide documentation about the nature of a vulnerability and links to further information and fixes.

The scanner typically resides on one host, from which it launches probes, collects results, and compares the results with a database of vulnerability fingerprints. In this sense, a security scanner is similar in function to a virus scanner but more introspective, determining whether devices comply with established security policy. Like a virus scanner, a good security scanner package will include regular updated vulnerability checks.

The System Scanner (Figure 9-9) from Internet Security Systems (ISS) is the best-known product in this category. System Scanner can validate your security configuration and run simulated attacks against a target server to validate the enforcement of the security lockdown procedure. ISS also provides a real-time monitoring product (RealSecure) that can detect any security breaches and alert administration staff to the type of incursion and steps to take to close the breach. For more information on ISS or Database Scanner, which assesses the security settings for your databases, go to www.iss.net.

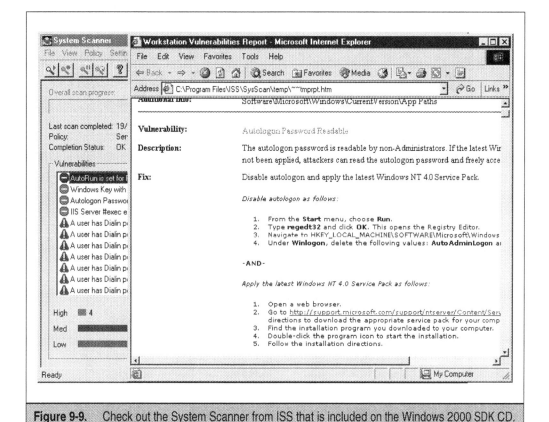

Figure 9-9.   Check out the System Scanner from ISS that is included on the Windows 2000 SDK CD.

If you're interested in other security scanners, Network Associates produces CyberCop Scanner (www.pgp.com/products/cybercop-scanner/); Intrusion, Inc., produces SecurityAnalyst (www.intrusion.com); and WebTrends, better known for their Web analysis software, also offers WebTrends Security Analyzer (www.webtrends.com). The cost of most commercial vulnerability scanners is substantial, but you can find some effective public-domain vulnerability scanners on the Web, such as ShieldsUP! at www.grc.com, or nmapNT at www.eeye.com/html/Research/Tools/nmapNT.html.

You can't rely on patches as an approach to keeping your system secure, which is why IDSs are so important, but a good security scanner will definitely help you find the holes in your security that hackers are looking for. Even if systems are initially set up in a perfectly secure and pristine state, they degrade over time. The more people who have access to a system, the faster this degradation occurs. Therefore, the more administrators you have, the more often you should audit. Security scanning helps you audit the system to verify that the intended configuration hasn't changed.

TIP   The NIST Computer Security Division's ICAT (Internet Categorization and Analysis of Threats) project team (http://icat.nist.gov/icat.cfm) has made the ICAT vulnerability database available for public use. The most important data in ICAT is the mapping of Common Vulnerabilities and Exposures (CVE) to hyperlinks leading to various vendor and security company advisories. CVE is a list of standardized names for vulnerabilities and other information security exposures. For more information, visit http://cve.mitre.org. Another useful data set in ICAT is the list of vendor names, product names, and version numbers associated with each vulnerability.

Benchmarking Tools

Wouldn't it be great if you could see how other security experts have configured their IIS Web servers, and then check to see whether your setup matches the industry best practice? The Center for Internet Security (CIS) at www.cisecurity.org/ is defining consensus best-practice security configurations for computers connected to the Internet, and their free Benchmark and Scoring Tool for Windows 2000 (Figure 9-10) provides a quick and easy way to evaluate your system and compare its level of security against the CIS minimum due care security Benchmark.

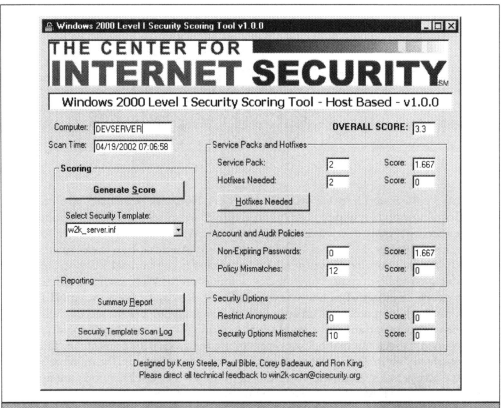

Figure 9-10.   With a score of only 3.3, the administrator for this server needs to read this book to figure out how to achieve better security!

Various reports guide you in how to harden both new and active systems while monitoring them to ensure that security settings continuously conform to the configuration specified in the Benchmark. You can show management how your system security measures up, and by being able to demonstrate compliance with an accepted security standard, you can protect yourself from prosecution or regulatory sanction. You could even insist that your business partners report compliance with an agreed-upon Benchmark.

CIS Benchmarks

CIS Benchmarks enumerate security configuration settings and actions that harden your system. Many organizations running the CIS scoring tools report that compliance even with a CIS Level 1 Benchmark has produced a substantial improvement in security for their systems. CIS Level 2 Benchmarks define prudent security beyond the minimum level, but they require that an administrator have a greater knowledge of security to apply them in the context of a particular environment. A Level 2 Benchmark for Windows IIS 5 Web Server is also available.

The Benchmarks are developed through a global consensus process, which pools the security knowledge and recommendations of IT security specialists around the world. It is a similar approach to that used by the National Insurance Crime Bureau, where key stakeholders have come together to combat a common risk. The Benchmarks are kept up to date as new vulnerabilities are discovered through various security incident tracking sources, such as the Internet Storm Center (www.incidents.org) and the CERT Coordination Center (www.cert.org).

CIS Scoring Tool

The CIS Benchmark and Scoring Tool for Windows 2000 is a host-based, noninvasive, "Analyze and Scan Only" program available free from the CIS Web site at www.cisecurity .org/, along with an implementation guide with step-by-step instructions for utilizing, scoring, analyzing, configuring, and customizing the Scoring Tool. The scoring criteria also include an assessment of the status of hot fixes in place on your system using HfNetChk to obtain the most current database of hot fixes available from Microsoft. You and your IIS server can benefit from this knowledge, expertise, and experience for free, so don't waste the opportunity.

Web Site Monitoring Services

Many companies are outsourcing the job of either monitoring their Web sites for possible attack or analyzing security data to managed security service providers such as Counterpane Internet Security (www.counterpane.com). The advantage of outsourcing these services is immediate access to experienced security specialists. This can solve problems of staff costs or shortages as it reduces the number of skill sets necessary in your security department personnel. Other players in this field include Loudcloud (www.loudcloud.com) and Cyber Attack Management Services (www.exodus.co.jp/managed_services/index_e.shtml), which offer network and host-based IDS and incident response services.

The service level agreement will be an important part of the contract between you and your service provider, so look for firm commitments rather than vague assurances. The agreement should specify the following:

- 24/7 service
- Response times
- Customer reports
- Lapse times for policy changes
- Financial penalties for poor performance

Many high-visibility Web sites are also employing "Red Teams" that are invited to attack a system to uncover system weaknesses. This ethical hacking is a controlled simulation of an attack against a network to achieve a predetermined goal. The goal might be to find specific information on the client's servers, to determine whether an outsider could disrupt client operations for a significant period of time, or to modify the client's Web site. The holes in security can then be fixed before a real intrusion occurs. Another benefit of the simulated attack is realistic training for your security team in trying to deal with the attack.

Network Documenters

The task of documenting your Web server is an important but often neglected one. A well-documented system can save valuable time when it comes to tracking down

---

Validating Third-Party Programs

If you contract outside developers to help build or monitor your intranet or Web site, or you use off-the-shelf Internet Server Application Programming Interface (ISAPI) DLLs on your server, how can you tell whether third-party executable content is safe? For example, it's possible for an ISAPI DLL to elevate its privileges, and therefore access rights, to the level of the built-in SYSTEM account by calling an API function called `RevertToSelf()`. You must inspect each executable running on your site using an analysis tool capable of dumping out any included function calls. One such program is Microsoft's Binary File Dumper (DumpBin.exe) tool, which is included with many Windows developer tools such as Visual C++. If you want to check whether a file called UntrustedISAPI.DLL calls RevertToSelf(), you'd use the following syntax:

```
dumpbin /imports UntrustedISAPI.DLL | find "RevertToSelf"
```

If no result appears on screen, you know that UntrustedISAPI.DLL doesn't call `RevertToSelf()` directly. It may call the API through `LoadLibrary()`, in which case you can search for this, too.

a problem, a possible security hole, or recovering from an attack. It also helps when you're deciding what needs upgrading or replacing, which all contributes to the overall health of your server. Every IIS administrator would love to have a well-documented system, with all relevant information consolidated in one well-laid-out document, but the chore of collecting, organizing, and documenting a server that is part of a large network is a drain on valuable resources and time as well as being a daunting undertaking.

If you are setting up a new IIS server, cataloging it as it is brought online makes the documentation process less painful and allows you to create a tailored and detailed report that is cost effective. However, if you're tasked with documenting an existing server or network, possibly the only way to ensure that you create a worthwhile document is to pay for a network documenter.

Discovery, Documentation, and Diagrams

You need to weigh the time and money that it will take you to produce meaningful reports against the cost of installing and running a dedicated program. If you have a small network that doesn't change often, it will be better to bite the bullet and make time to do it yourself; however on a large, constantly changing network, this isn't going to be an option.

Configuration Reporter, available from Ecora at www.ecora.com, offers a solution to the problem of making time to document your networks. A fast, browser-based program, it gathers information about your network, such as hardware configuration, TCP/IP settings, and file shares. In addition, Configuration Reporter sorts, stores, and delivers the information in HTML, Microsoft Word, or Portable Document File (PDF) formats. It displays the reports in two formats—short and long. The short format includes summary information about network devices, such as IP addresses and number of networked CPUs, while the long format covers the consequences of server settings, explaining how a setting could be a breach in security. The reports may not be as detailed as you'd ideally like and the cost quickly mounts for multiple servers; however, it will document Windows NT and Windows 2000 systems far more efficiently than an overworked administrator.

Determining a Cost-Effective Solution

This chapter has covered a lot of ground, and you may be wondering where best to spend your money. The ultimate goal when deciding on third-party security enhancements is to protect the resources on your network. Don't try to tackle every aspect of security at once, but try a phased approach, starting with your critical assets first. Look to see how well a product or service solves a problem and whether it creates any problems of its own, such as requiring additional staff to implement and maintain it. If you're not sure how to allocate your security budget, you might want to take a look at RiskWatch at www.riskwatch.com. This is a risk analysis software package that conducts automated risk analysis and vulnerability assessments to highlight, which security measures are most effective for your organization, and which ones give you the "best bang for your buck." By performing "what if" scenarios, you can decide which potential security measures meet acceptable levels of protection and should, therefore, be considered during your budgeting process. Insecure.org, the producers of nmap—a utility for port scanning large networks—has compiled a list of the top 50 security tools based on a survey of 1200 nmap users' favorite security tools. The list is available at www.insecure.org/tools.html.

CHALLENGE

You've just recovered from a virus outbreak on your network, and management has finally given you a decent budget to upgrade your AV protection. You need to act quickly to avoid another incident, so what do you do first?

Before you spend your entire budget on a new AV product, you need to review your anti-virus policy to see whether it needs updating in light of recent events. If your AV policy is sound, and the cause of the outbreak was a member of staff not following it, then you need to ensure all network users fully understand the consequences of not abiding by the AV policy. Arrange security awareness training sessions that senior management requires everyone to attend. Although this will eat into your budget, it will make your new AV protection more effective as everyone will understand its role and importance.

Next, review where additional AV protection is required. Is it the firewall, the Web server, the mail server, or the workstations? Ideally you should install protection for all types of servers and workstations. Content Vectoring Protocol (CVP) software sits on the firewall scanning data as it enters your network, while groupware protection is software that sits on your mail server and scans the message store. Trend Micro's InterScan VirusWall, and ScanMail at www.antivirus .com provide firewall and groupware protection respectively. Review the section "Popular Virus Scanners" for products to provide server and workstation protection.

CHECKLIST

- ☐ Try out the many free tools available from Microsoft before deciding which additional security products your IIS server needs.

- ☐ Subscribe to the newsgroups and forums that cover any products you purchase in order to stay up to date.

☐ Don't install any of the samples and examples that come with a new product on your production server.

☐ Change any default passwords for installed products to strong passwords.

☐ Look to secure your most important resources first, and check that your choice of product does indeed protect them.

☐ Develop a Network Service Access Policy to help define the features that your firewall must have.

☐ Deploy an IDS to provide security against imperfect products and new and old vulnerabilities. Monitoring your system will help you to catch a hacker regardless of what vulnerability they exploit to gain access.

☐ Log files are useful only if you read them, so get a log analyzer or a product that includes one to automate the auditing and analysis of your network logs.

☐ Choose an AV tool that centralizes control and can interact with other security products.

☐ Implement a change control and backup policy and supplement them with restoration software to recover from Web defacements.

☐ Get senior management on board as part of your security awareness training program to educate your staff about the need for security and their security-related duties.

☐ Stress test your site to see whether it can handle peak loads, and think about adding SSL accelerator hardware if you're planning an e-commerce site.

☐ Decide whether you need strong authentication for those clients or users that need access to sensitive information on your server and issue them with security tokens.

☐ Look to find holes in your security before the hackers do by using a vulnerability scanner.

☐ Download the CIS Scoring Tool and check whether your IIS configuration matches industry best practice.

☐ If you don't have enough qualified security staff in-house consider outsourcing some duties such as site monitoring.

☐ Keep your documentation up to date. Use a network documenter if you're managing a big enterprise network.

PART III

Advanced Topics

CHAPTER 10

Securing FTP, NNTP,
and Other IIS Services

IS is a feature-rich Web server providing a range of useful services in addition to its Web services, such as FTP, NNTP, and SMTP. As with the WWW Publishing Service, these subcomponents of IIS are based on Transfer Control Protocol/Internet Protocol (TCP/IP) and, therefore, are open to abuse or misuse. If you provide any of these additional services, you will have to configure your firewall to control access to the required protocols, ports, and addresses. Your particular firewall's user guide will explain how to do this. In this chapter, we will concentrate on how to secure the IIS subcomponents within the IIS server environment and reduce the actual level of service offered to the minimum required. There is no need to allow 10,000 FTP connections for your employees if you have only 50.

INSTALLING IIS SUBCOMPONENTS

IIS subcomponents can be installed during IIS installation or at a later date using the Add/Remove Windows Components option of the Add/Remove Programs control panel. Select the Internet Information Services component, click the Details button, and select any additional IIS services that you wish to install, as shown here:

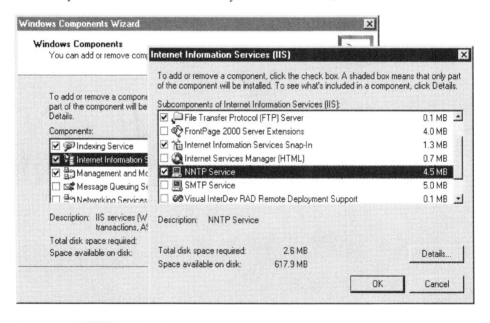

TIP   When you set up your IIS server, install only those components that provide the services you need to make available.

Every service you install is a potential entry point to your server since it processes client requests. The more services you run on your IIS server, the more entry points are available to attack. The role of your Web site, and its related security policy, will determine which additional services need to be installed and enabled—if any. In order to reduce the entry points for a possible attack, you should not install, or enable, any unnecessary services. Your Network Service Access Policy should define the rules controlling when and to whom IIS services are allowed or denied. Chapter 3 covered the minimum services that are required to run IIS, as well as those that are not required. The only essential IIS services are the World Wide Web (WWW) Publishing Service and the IIS Admin Service.

All volumes used by IIS-related services must be formatted with NTFS to enable access control and benefit from NTFS security. Put the content for each supported service, such as WWW or FTP, on its own partition—or preferably on its own volume. Make certain that your server has the resources required to deliver an acceptable service while running additional services under your security settings, since they will impact overall performance. As you will see, some security configurations to consider are resource hungry. Let's start by looking at the *FTP (File Transfer Protocol) service*, which is the service you most likely will provide—after the Web Publishing service itself.

FTP (FILE TRANSFER PROTOCOL) SERVICE

FTP is the simplest way to exchange files between remote computers and is used to download or upload files to another computer. It's a standard Internet protocol, optimized for transferring data over TCP/IP networks like the Internet. To reliably transfer data, FTP establishes a client/server relationship using two TCP ports on both the client and server for communications between the two. The first port is called *FTP Control* because it handles session establishment and error control operations; the second port is called *FTP Data* because it handles the actual data transfer between the client and server. The FTP service uses the well-known port 21 for control operations and port 20 for data transfer. The client TCP ports are assigned dynamically when the session is created.

Well-known port numbers are reserved for assignment by ICANN (Internet Corporation for Assigned Names and Numbers) for use by an application's end points, which communicate using the Internet's TCP (Transmission Control Protocol) or the UDP (User Datagram Protocol). Each kind of application has a designated and thus "well-known" port number. When an application from one client communicates with another, it specifies that application in each data transmission by using its port number. Well-known ports cover the range of possible port numbers from 0 through 1023, with registered ports numbered from 1,024 through to 49,151, and the remaining ports, up to 65,535, used as dynamic or private ports. You can change the port number used by any IIS service, including SMTP and NNTP. This may be appropriate for security purposes on a small-sized private network; however, most hackers use port scanners to find open ports.

You may want to provide FTP services so that users can download files, such as product manuals, from your site. Your FTP service also can enable your sales staff to file orders or reports while out on the road. However, these benefits come at a cost. The FTP protocol transmits all data, including user names and passwords, over the network in the clear, which can make your local file system available to everyone on the network unless it is secured correctly (the right to log on locally is required by anyone connecting to your FTP server).

> **TIP** If you change the FTP Control port to a number other than 21, you will hide your server from most FTP clients on the Internet. You can then give the new port number to all the users that you want to be able to use your FTP service, such as ftp://www.yourserver.com:1025

Securing Your FTP Site

FTP servers are managed and configured the same way as IIS by using the Internet Services Manager (ISM), which allows you to control individual FTP sites, although you can control the FTP service using the Services Management Console or the Net command, discussed later in the chapter in the section "Starting and Stopping Services."

You can configure FTP site properties at three levels: master, site, and virtual directory. Settings at the master-site level are inherited by all new FTP sites. You can open the IIS Master Properties sheet, shown in Figure 10-1, by right-clicking the Internet server node in the Internet Services Manager (ISM).

Specific properties configured at the individual-site and virtual-directory level will override the parent settings. You can add multiple FTP sites to your server to give your single FTP server the appearance of being multiple FTP servers.

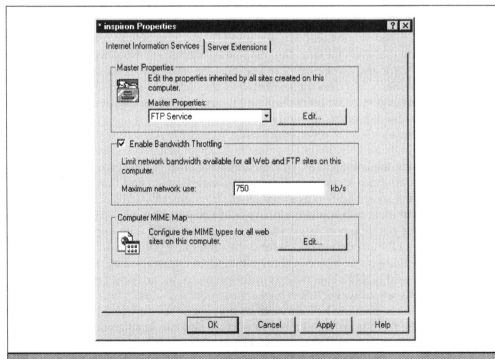

Figure 10-1. The IIS Master Properties sheet sets the default values inherited by all sites.

Bandwidth throttling, which is set from the Internet Server Properties sheet, applies to all Internet services running on your IIS server; however, unlike Web sites, it's not possible to control the bandwidth throttle placed on an individual FTP site. If your IIS server uses the same Internet connection as your internal users, employ the Maximum Network Use setting to prevent your entire Internet connection from being consumed by the FTP and Web services during periods of heavy activity or a denial of service attack. Select he Enable Bandwidth Throttling option, and type the maximum number of kilobytes per second you want to be used by IIS, as shown in Figure 10-1.

We will look at each of the properties of a service that has a security impact on your server. These include some of the performance settings that help prevent denial of service attacks. To ensure that all FTP sites are added with the correct security configuration, you need to edit the FTP Master Properties of the Internet server object. Right-click the Internet server object in ISM and select Properties. Next select FTP Service in the Master Properties drop-down box and click the Edit button to open the FTP Service Master Properties sheet shown in Figure 10-2.

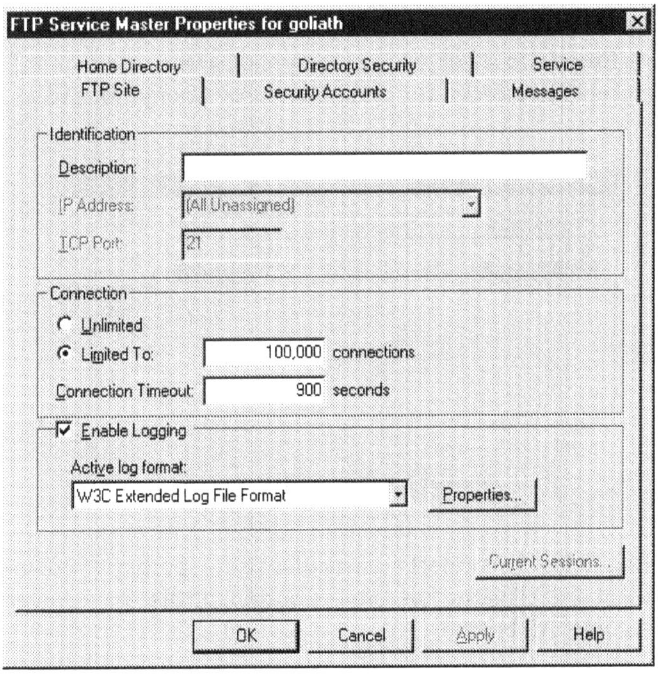

Figure 10-2.   Reduce the FTP Service Master Properties sheet's default connection setting of 100,000 unless you need such a high number of connections.

Limiting Connections

If you're running the FTP service for a few select clients or staff, there is no point allowing unlimited simultaneous connections to your server, since this only makes denial of service attacks easier. On the FTP Site tab under Connection, enter an appropriate limit that reflects the role of your server in the Limited To box. If you place a connection limit on your site, you can display a message to users trying to connect when the maximum number of connections is exceeded from the Message tab. In the Connection Timeout box, type the length of time before the server disconnects an inactive user. This ensures that all connections are closed if the FTP protocol cannot close a connection.

Logging FTP Activity

To comply with your security audit policies, you need to record FTP activity, so select the Enable Logging check box. To record user activity, enable the Log Visits option on the Home Directory tab of each FTP site. Your IDS system may be able to monitor these logs but confirm the log formats they can read. The log options and settings are the same as for the WWW service.

Disconnecting Users

From an FTP site's Properties sheet, you can view the users currently connected to the site by clicking the Current Sessions button, as shown next. Anonymous users appear with question marks.

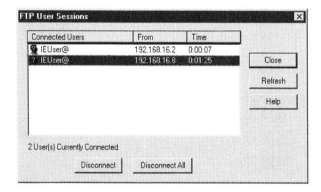

If you need to quickly disconnect a particular user—perhaps you suspect server misuse—select them and click the Disconnect button, or disconnect everyone by clicking the Disconnect All button.

> **TIP**   Use the Internet Services Manager to control individual FTP sites. For example, if you have two FTP sites on your server, you can stop the FTP service on one site, while leaving the other site running. What actually happens is that the FTP service continues to run, but the stopped FTP site is taken offline.

Security Accounts

To gain access to your FTP server, users must log on. The Security Accounts tab controls who can access your FTP server and who can administer it. If you want to provide general Internet access to the files on your FTP server you need to select the Allow Anonymous Connections option and select an account that will be used for anonymous access. In Figure 10-3, the default account is IUSR_*computername*, which is the same account that is used for anonymous Web access to your IIS server. (If your FTP service is configured to

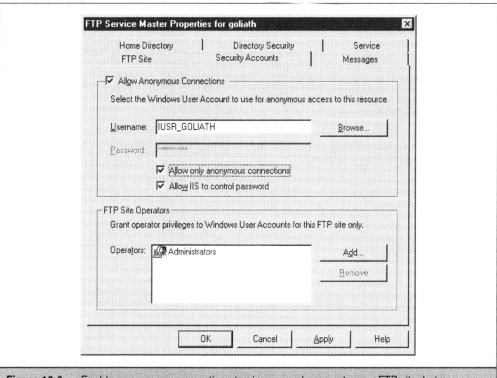

Figure 10-3.   Enable anonymous connections to give general access to your FTP site, but use a different account.

allow anonymous access, clients can log on with the user name "anonymous." Traditionally, anonymous FTP users provide their e-mail address as the password. Internet Explorer will automatically log on anonymously to any FTP server that permits anonymous logon.)

If you use the same account for both services, any vulnerability in your FTP service will allow your IIS server to be compromised as well. Unless your FTP and Web servers need to access the same folders, which is not recommended, you should create a new account for anonymous FTP users. By using separate accounts, NTFS permissions can control access rights, and problems are limited solely to the FTP folders. By selecting the Allow Only Anonymous Connections option, you can force anonymous access, which deters users from using real user names and passwords over a nonsecure FTP connection or attackers trying to gain access with an administrator account. If you clear the Allow Anonymous Connections check box, every initial request from a user causes an authentication dialog box to prompt for a user name and password.

SECURITY ALERT   The Allow Only Anonymous Connections option will not stop uninformed staff from trying to use their domain user name and password to log onto your FTP server. Make certain that relevant users understand how to log onto your FTP server so as not to compromise passwords.

Grant specific users or groups operator privileges at the master and individual site levels by adding them to the list of FTP Site Operators. *FTP Site Operators* are a special group of users who have limited administrative privileges on individual FTP sites. Operators can administer properties that affect only their respective sites. They do not have access to properties that affect IIS, the computer hosting IIS, or the network. For example, you can assign a member of staff from each department in an organization as the operator for that department's FTP site. The operator can set FTP site access permissions, enable logging, and set messages, but cannot change the identification of FTP sites, configure the anonymous user name or password, create virtual directories, or change their paths. Operator accounts need not necessarily be members of a Windows Administrators group. Site operators are a feature common to the other IIS services, such as WWW, NNTP, and SMTP.

SECURITY ALERT   If you need to use nonanonymous connections, enforce strong passwords via your Windows Security Policy.

Messages

IIS FTP Services allows you to display a welcome message, which is set from the Messages tab shown next. Use this feature to display a warning message explaining the terms and conditions users must agree to before using the site. For example, "This is a private computer system and is provided only for authorized use. Unauthorized use may subject you to criminal prosecution. Evidence of unauthorized use collected during monitoring may be used for administrative, criminal, or other adverse action. Use of this system constitutes consent to monitoring for these purposes." Check the wording that would be suitable for your particular site with a legal advisor.

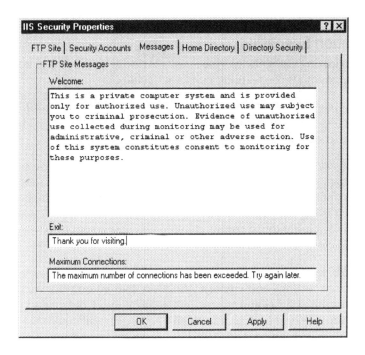

Home Directory

So far, we've configured how many users can access your site, how they are authenticated, and what message they'll see when they log on. Now we need to configure what they can do once they've connected to your server. Set the directory that will be used by the FTP site, or a virtual directory from the Home Directory tab shown in Figure 10-4. Never use a network share because the remote share is controlled by the share's account access privileges. This makes a secure access configuration for a share difficult than maintain and is not worth the risk. If your budget allows, run the FTP server on a different server than your main IIS server. Failing that, place the root folders on a different volume than the IIS server. Not only does this help isolate the FTP service, but it also makes managing Windows 2000 disk quotas and Write permission easier.

Once you've chosen the directory location, enable either Read or Write permission on the directory. If you grant Read access to your FTP site, a user will see the physical directories and files that exist under your Home Directory, as well as any virtual directories you have configured, and can read and download any files listed. Write permission allows users to upload files to the FTP site. If you need to grant Write permission to a directory so that users can upload files to the site, grant it on a separate virtual directory that doesn't also have Read permission. The reason for this is that giving anonymous users the ability to read and write to the same directory creates a *warez* site. Hackers use these sites to upload pirated software or music files for everyone to download, which leaves you with a lot of legal problems. Only internal users with appropriate permission should be given Read permission to the uploaded files.

Authentication Scenarios

Review the following authentication scenarios to decide whether you need to allow or disallow anonymous connections to your FTP site.

All users access your FTP site from the Internet.   In this scenario, you should only allow anonymous connections, which averts real user names and passwords from being sent in clear text across the Internet.

All users access your FTP site from the local network.   In this situation, you would want everyone to log onto their own account and use the security features of NTFS to control access permissions. However, unless you are sure that the network is trusted (which is not realistic in anything other than a very small intranet), you should use anonymous-only connections to prevent passwords from being transmitted in clear text.

Users in a trusted network log onto their own FTP subfolder by default.   Disable Allow Anonymous Connections and create a Windows user account for each of your users. Give Administrators and the System account Full Control and remove the Everyone Group. Create a subfolder for each user, which will inherit the root folder's security settings; add the user who will use that folder, and give that user Full Control access.

Users access your FTP site from both the Internet and the local network.   Again, because of the limitations of FTP, you must opt for anonymous connections to prevent your local users from sending passwords in the clear.

FTP site must allow users to exchange confidential files.   You will have to install a server certificate and provide your users with a program, such as SecureFX from Van Dyke Software at www.vandyke.com/products/securefx/. SecureFX provides SFTP (Secure FTP) over an encrypted SSH2 connection that ensures all traffic is protected from network sniffers. Alternatively, some firewalls, such as Microsoft's ISA Server, allow you to use IPSec to encrypt FTP traffic and authenticate users with their regular Windows account credentials.

 SECURITY ALERT   Only use the NTFS file system for your FTP directories. A FAT (File Allocation Table) file system only supports share-level security.

Folder and File Permissions

Setting the Read and Write permissions from the FTP Site or Virtual Directory tab does not override the NTFS security attributes of that directory or the files it contains. If the NTFS permissions for a directory only allow Read access for a user, even if you grant Read and Write access from the Directory tab, the user will only have Read access. Currently the

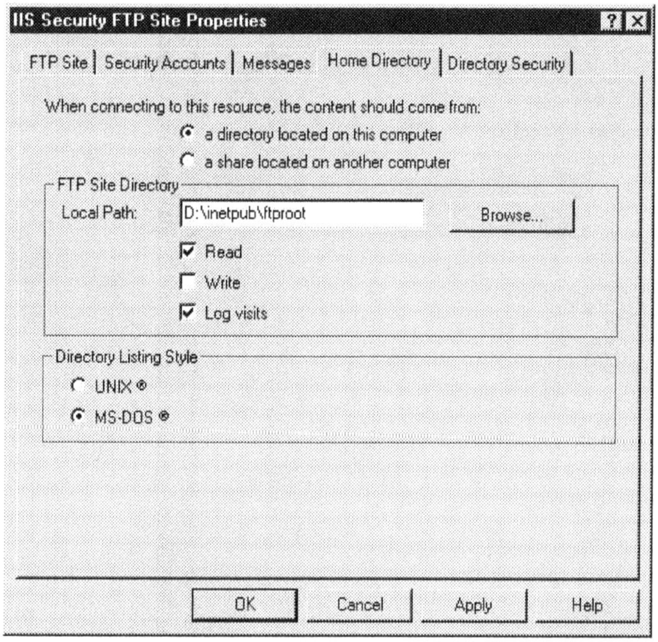

Figure 10-4.   Never use a share as the directory for an FTP site.

user receives the most restrictive set of rights. Only add the users who need to access the FTP directory and assign them minimum permissions. Users must have the privilege to "Logon Locally" and either Read or Write permission. Do not grant any users the right to "Access this Computer from the Network." Doing so will allow him or her to bypass the Web, FTP, or Gopher services.

> **SECURITY ALERT**   Granting the right to "Access this Computer from the Network" allows a user to bypass FTP services to connect to your server. This defeats one of the significant security provisions of IIS. When a client logs onto your server, the user is limited to the FTP home directory and its subdirectories. This is a significant control on the areas that the user is able to access.

Directory Security

Using this slightly misleading named tab you can restrict access based on a user's IP address. The default setting for your FTP server grants access to all IP addresses, but you might want to restrict access to users from a specific IP range or address, such as a trusted client or subnet of your intranet. This is easily done by denying access to all computers and then configuring your trusted user's IP address as an exception, as shown in Figure 10-5.

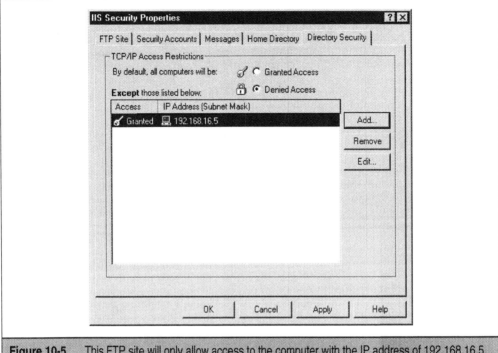

Figure 10-5. This FTP site will only allow access to the computer with the IP address of 192.168.16.5.

You can also do the reverse and let every computer access your site except those you specify. This is useful if results from your log analysis show suspicious activity from a particular IP address and you want to deny them further access. You can deny access based on a domain name, for example, to prevent your competitors at rival.com from accessing your FTP site.

TIP If you deny access to your FTP site based on domain name, all users will find your FTP service slower because your FTP server will go through the Reverse Lookup process to determine whether each client attempting to access your site has an IP address associated with the denied domain.

FTP can add to the overall effectiveness of your Internet-based services, but the default installation settings have to be changed to secure the service based on how and by whom it will be used.

NNTP (NETWORK NEWS TRANSPORT PROTOCOL) SERVICE

IIS includes support for the *NNTP (Network News Transport Protocol)*, an Internet standard for reading and posting articles to newsgroups—a kind of e-mail mailbox that is accessible to everyone. Articles are posted in much the same way that e-mail messages are sent to a person's mailbox. Public newsgroups are a great way to share and exchange information; and since they can be secured using SSL encryption and NTFS permissions, they are an ideal way of communicating with specific groups of users, such as employees, suppliers, and customers, with each being able to have their own private newsgroup. Use the Internet Services Manager to manage your newsgroups and NNTP service, as shown here:

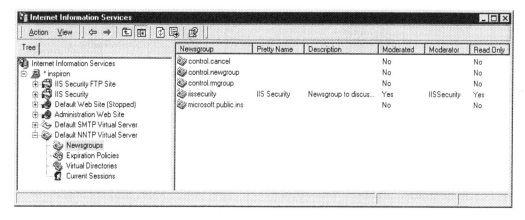

NNTP should only be installed once you have secured the actual IIS service itself. If you need to provide SSL client authentication, you will need to install a server certificate for your IIS server. Installing NNTP creates the nntpfile folder beneath the Inetpub folder, which contains subdirectories and files used in the maintenance of the NNTP service and the newsgroups hosted on the server. As with FTP, place these root folders on a different NTFS volume than the IIS server to aid access control and space allocation. Active newsgroups can generate a lot of storage requirements. To change the location of your root folders, expand the NNTP object in the Internet Services Manager and click Virtual Directories. The Newsgroup Subtree, which lists the directories used by NNTP, will be displayed in the right-hand pane, as shown here:

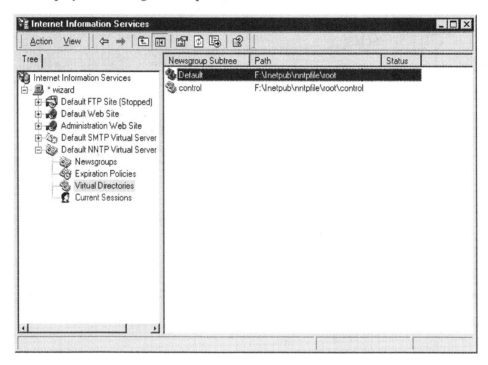

Double-click the Default directory to open the Properties sheet shown in Figure 10-6, and click the Contents button. You can now select the volume and directory that you want the NNTP service to use. See the section "Virtual Directories," later in the chapter to learn how to set access restrictions to these directories.

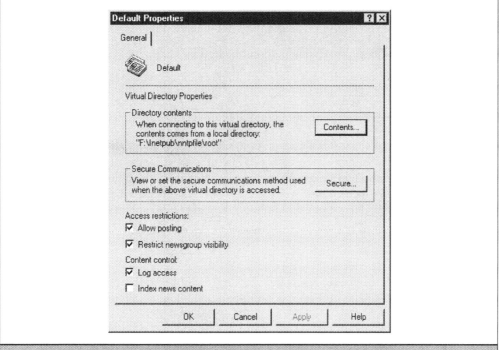

Figure 10-6.   Use the Properties sheet of the Default directory to select which directory you want your NNTP service to use.

Securing Your NNTP Site

You must be a member of the local Administrators group on the IIS server to manage the NNTP service, which is done via the Internet Services Manager. Right-click the NNTP server object to view its Properties sheet, which has four tabs. This Properties sheet, the General tab selected, is shown in Figure 10-7.

As with FTP, you need to enable logging of NNTP activity for all newsgroups at the NNTP virtual server level and the individual Virtual Directory level. All events that the NNTP service generates are recorded in the System Log, and counters for the NNTP service are added to Performance Monitor.

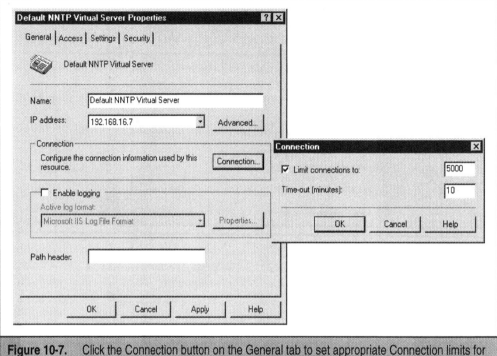

Figure 10-7. Click the Connection button on the General tab to set appropriate Connection limits for your NNTP server.

Controlling Access

The Access tab, shown in Figure 10-8, provides options for configuring client access to the NNTP virtual server and establishing transmission security, including authentication, encryption, restricting the ability to read or post articles, and whether remote NNTP servers can download newsgroups. To configure the authentication methods that the NNTP server will support, click the Authentication button.

If your newsgroup is going to be open to the public, you need to enable the Allow Anonymous Connections option. You must change the account used by anonymous users from the default IUSR_*computername* by clicking the Anonymous button. Set it to an account created solely for anonymous NNTP connections. Do not enable Basic Authentication, since this will allow user names and passwords to be transmitted in the clear.

If your users have a news client, such as Microsoft Outlook Express, that supports Windows Security Package authentication, you can select Windows security package, which provides secure logon services as a way of authenticating newsgroup users.

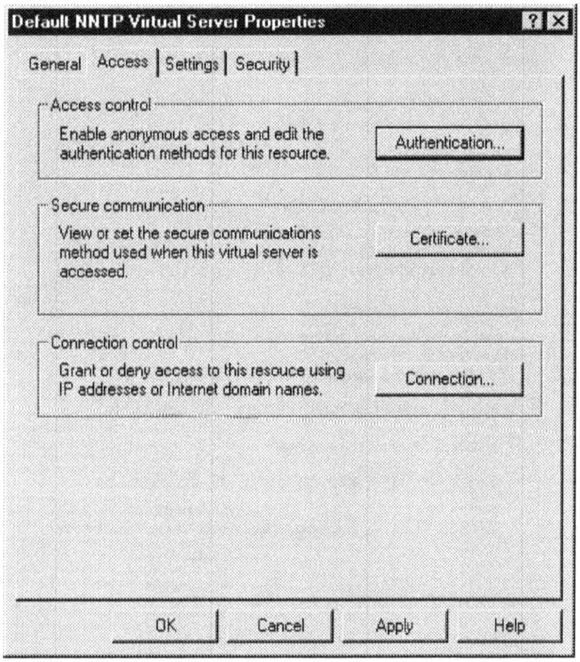

Figure 10-8. Use the Access tab to configure the main security settings for NNTP.

Alternatively, you can require SSL client authentication to force users to provide SSL-encrypted user names and passwords. If your users have their own digital certificates installed, you can map these certificates to Windows accounts by enabling client certificate mappings, which will help prevent spoofing or impersonation. This is the best approach if newsgroup articles are highly confidential because NTFS file permissions and auditing can be enforced for each individual user. Figure 10-9 shows the settings for an NNTP server that requires users to present a digital certificate that is mapped to a Windows account.

To prevent a user or group from accessing a newsgroup, assign Deny permission to the folders containing the newsgroup articles. By default, these are in Inetpub\nntpfile\root*newsgroupname*. Make sure that you give the local system account full access to all newsgroup folders so that Microsoft NNTP service has access to its files. The connection control settings operate in the same way as the FTP Directory Security tab, granting or denying access based on IP addresses or domain names. You can use this to limit access to users from a particular domain, such as a trusted third party. Use the

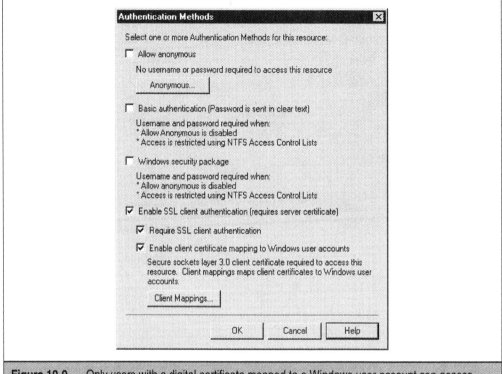

Figure 10-9.   Only users with a digital certificate mapped to a Windows user account can access newsgroups on this NNTP server.

Security tab to add Windows accounts and groups to the list of NNTP virtual server operators, in the same way as you do for FTP sites.

Settings Tab

From the Settings tab you can configure a maximum limit for the size of news articles and news feeds, and whether to allow other news servers to pull news articles from your NNTP server. Figure 10-10 shows the Settings tab and the posting limit options. The difference between the post size and the connection size is that the post size limits the size of an article that can be posted, while the connection size limits the total size for all the articles that a user can post within a single connection. Set limits that are appropriate for the type of newsgroups you are running. If you have moderated newsgroups that do not have a specified moderator, enter the default moderator domain so that postings can be sent to *news_group_name@default_moderator_domain*.

Allow News Servers to Pull Articles from This News Server   Remote NNTP servers can download local newsgroups and their articles and then make them publicly available.

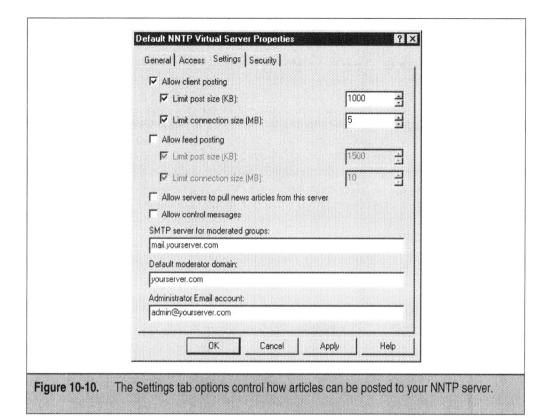

Figure 10-10.   The Settings tab options control how articles can be posted to your NNTP server.

This may be acceptable if your newsgroups are for public use anyway, but disable this option if you want to retain control of where and when your newsgroup articles are published.

Allow Control Messages   Newsreader clients and other NNTP servers can send commands to create and delete newsgroups on your NNTP server or to cancel previously posted articles. Clear this check box so that any control messages your server receives are only logged and not processed. This puts you back in control of what happens on your NNTP server.

Managing Your Newsgroups

The default NNTP site has four container objects beneath it in the Scope pane.

- **Newsgroups**   Lists the newsgroups hosted by the NNTP server.
- **Expiration Policies**   Lists the policies that control when newsgroup articles are automatically deleted.

- **Virtual Directories**   Lists the virtual directories used by the NNTP service for storing newsgroup articles.

- **Current Sessions**   Lists remote NNTP clients and servers that are engaged in uploading or downloading articles.

Once you have created a newsgroup, double-click it to set its properties. Selecting the Read Only option prevents anyone except the NNTP administrator or moderator—an editor who must approve all articles before they can appear—from posting to the newsgroup. If you need to tightly control articles that appear in a newsgroup—for example, if it is used to post company press releases—then select Read only, or Moderated. In a moderated newsgroup, users cannot post directly to the newsgroup. Articles are sent to the Moderator's e-mail address for approval before they are posted, as in Figure 10-11.

Expiration Policies

Your NNTP server can host thousands of different newsgroups, and popular newsgroups can receive hundreds of articles a day. If you don't limit the number of stored newsgroup

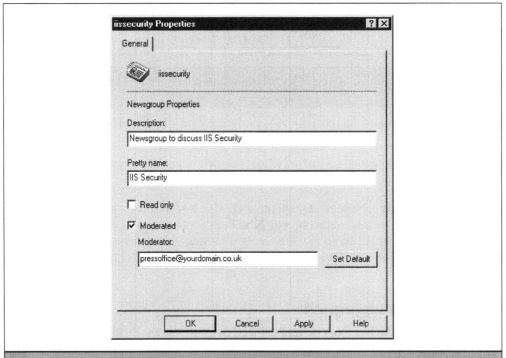

Figure 10-11.   Use to specify an e-mail address where moderated messages are sent, or to configure a server-level default domain level for moderated groups without a specified moderator.

articles, your NNTP server can run out of hard drive space; and if you've configured your server with a single partition for the operating system and NNTP data, it can crash. This is another reason why you should always move the location of your NNTP files to a separate hard drive. You can help limit the amount of hard-drive space used by newsgroup articles by implementing Expiration Policies, which will automatically delete articles once they have reached a specified age. To create an Expiration Policy, right-click the Expiration Policies node and select New, and then Expiration Policy. This will start the Expiration Policy Wizard, which will guide you through creating a new policy.

Virtual Directories

An NNTP virtual directory is an alternative physical location for a newsgroup's articles to the default C:\Inetpub\nntpfile\root*newsgroupname*. You can use shared folders; however, never use them for the same reasons as we stated in the section on FTP earlier in the chapter. The benefit of using virtual directories is that the articles for newsgroups can be spread across multiple drives, making permissions assignment easier and improving I/O performance. A virtual directory can contain the articles for a single newsgroup or for an entire category of newsgroups. For example, using the Virtual Directories node you could create a virtual directory for storing all newsgroups related to internal announcements on one disk drive, and another for storing all public related newsgroups on another.

Secure Communications   Figure 10-3, earlier in the chapter, shows the Properties sheet for a virtual directory, with options for setting user access, communications, and content control. If newsgroup articles need to be secured against network sniffers, you need to enable secure communications to require clients to use SSL for connections to the NNTP service. This ensures that outgoing data is encrypted. Again, you'll need a Web server certificate to do this.

Access Restrictions   With the Allow Posting option, you can specify whether to let users post new articles to a newsgroup, while the Restrict newsgroup visibility option ensures that only users with access permission for a newsgroup will see it listed. We recommend that any nonpublic newsgroups you host make use of this option.

Index News Content   A useful service to offer your newsgroup users is the ability to search for specific text in the news articles. NNTP uses Microsoft Indexing Services to regularly scan newsgroup articles and create a searchable database. However, the Indexing Service can lead to the incorrect publication of sensitive information if it's not configured properly. Before you enable this option, read the next section, "Microsoft Index Server and the Content Index Service."

NNTP is one of the great successes of the Internet, allowing the quick and easy exchange of information, and it doesn't carry the same security risks as FTP. Even so, it is important to set NTFS permissions and restrict and secure access to any of the newsgroups you run that are not for the general public.

MICROSOFT INDEX SERVER AND THE CONTENT INDEX SERVICE

As your Web site grows, there will be a lot of content for users to navigate through, and you will probably need to install a search engine to help them find the information they're after. Microsoft Index Server is an add-on service to the Internet Information Server that makes text-based documents—such as HTML, MS Word, Excel, and PowerPoint—stored on your Web server searchable. Index Server operations are performed by the Content Index service, which operates as an NT service configurable from the Services Management Console. The Index Server builds a master list of the contents and properties of documents contained within a defined set of directories, termed the *scope,* that are collectively grouped within a catalog. As we've mentioned, it can also index Network News Transfer Protocol messages on a news server.

Before you use Index Server, consider the additional hard-disk space and memory requirements that it may require. It can consume up to 40 percent of the size of the Corpus, which is the entire collection of indexed directories and documents. "No problem," I hear you say, "it provides a feature-rich search engine and my site needs it." Unfortunately, Index Server has been the root cause of several security breaches in IIS Web sites due to flaws and poorly configured servers. For example, a form-based search query can send up to 4 kilobytes of data, but if a query larger than this is sent, Index Server can become unstable. All submitted queries should be checked to ensure that this maximum size is not exceeded. We will cover how to do this in Chapter 11.

TIP If the free disk space on the index disk starts running low (less than 3MB), filtering will be temporarily paused and a disk-full event will be written to the event log.

Configuring Index Server

Because Index Server lets users search your Web site, you must carefully control which files and folders it indexes; otherwise, users may be able to find and read sensitive information not intended for publication. You can enable indexing at the server, Web site, or folder levels. Server-level settings apply to indexable content on all Web sites on the server, site-level settings apply to all indexable content within that site, and folder-level settings apply to all indexable content within that folder and subfolders. Index Server is managed from the Index Server Manager MMC snap-in or from the Computer Management MMC. To open Computer Management, click Start, point to Settings, and click Control Panel. Double-click Administrative Tools, and then double-click Computer Management. In the console tree, expand Services and Applications, and click Indexing Service.

When you expand the Indexing Service object, you will see the two default catalogs, System and Web. The System catalog includes your C drive and should be deleted immediately. The Web catalog includes the inetpub\wwwroot folder and various other

folders that you do not want to have indexed on a secure server, such as the
iisadmin folder shown here:

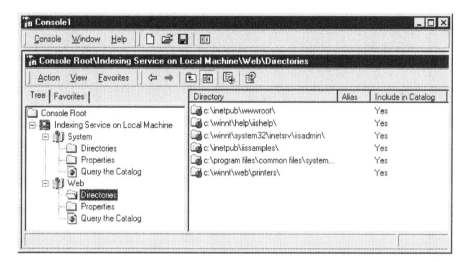

Delete this catalog as well, and create a new catalog, adding only the specific folders that
you want users of your Web site to be able to search. This reduces the risk of sensitive
documents or system passwords embedded in scripts being indexed and made accessible.

 SECURITY ALERT   Index Server can index and provide access to documents in a virtual directory
that points to a remote share. Disable the Add Network Share Alias Automatically option on the Index
Server Properties Sheet Tracking tab to prevent shared network drives inadvertently being added to
a catalog. As we've stated several times, never use remote shares in your Web site architecture.

Protecting Index Server Files with NTFS File Security

Index Server is completely integrated with IIS and Windows 2000 Server security, so access
to indexed documents can be controlled, allowing users to view only the documents that
they have permission to access. It is critical to your system's overall security, therefore,
that Index Server is located on an NTFS partition, as are all the folders that you wish to
index. The key Index Server files that need strict access control protection are

- **Internet Data Query files (.idq)**   Define several query parameters, such as the
  scope of a search, and any restrictions on a search that Index Server will run.
- **Index Data Administration scripts (.ida)**   Similar to Internet Data Query files,
  but store Administrative requests.

- **Hypertext Markup Language Extension template (.htx)**   A template that formats how results are returned to the user by taking the query information and converting it into an HTML file.

- **Query Form files (.htm)**   Form to submit a search query.

- **Catalog folders (.wci)**   Consist of the content and property indexes and other files that contain the indexed information.

Limiting Content Access with Catalogs

An *Index Server catalog* is a folder of files containing indexing information. Index Server populates the catalog with generated content and property information. User access permission for indexed documents is also maintained in this catalog. Every time a user submits a query, Index Server checks the file security information. Only permitted documents are included in the query's result set so that a user never sees a document reference in a result set if the access permissions on that file prohibit their reading it. This is unlike other search engines that show users hits to all documents that meet their search, even if the user can't read the document.

Indexing in Microsoft Index Server is based on virtual roots, and there is no explicit way of excluding certain physical directories from being indexed. However, in your

Internet Data Query File Parameters

In an Internet Data Query file, the line "CiRestriction=" represents the query that will be issued to the Index Server, and the "CiTemplate=" line specifies the file that is set to receive the information from the .idq file. This line usually references an .htx file. Avoid substituting parameters for the CiTemplate parameter because you could unintentionally allow files in execute-only script directories to be sent over the network. For example, if an .idq file contained these lines,

```
[Query]
CiTemplate=%CiTemplate%
```

a client could send a URL that contained this line in the query string,

```
CiTemplate=/scripts/payrollaccess.pl
```

which would allow an unauthorized user to read the contents of the Perl script file. To avoid this, it is better to switch among different .htx files by using just the file's base name and adding the script directory and file name extension in the parameter substitution, for example,

```
[Query]
CiRestriction=%q%
CiTemplate=/scripts/%t%.htx
```

.idq file you can specify files that should not appear in search results. For example, if the virtual root /reports points to D:\reports, but you do not want results from D:\reports\private to appear in the result set, you can modify the CiRestriction parameter in your .idq file as follows:

```
CiRestriction=%CiRestriction% AND NOT #path D:\reports\private*
```

 SECURITY ALERT   Index Server will index a subfolder that does not have Read permission if it is located within a folder that has Read permission. To prevent this, you can mask unreadable roots by setting the CiRestriction in the .idq query file. For example, you can mask a directory named /_readforbidden by setting the CiRestriction in the .idq file to CiRestriction=(%UserRestriction%) &! #vpath *_readforbidden*.

Limiting Remote Administration

Some Index Server management functions are, by default, available from a remote Web site. This is a security risk, since someone else could make unauthorized changes. If you need to place additional controls on administrative operations, put access permission controls on the .ida, .idq, and .htx files, which control how Index Server returns results.

> **TIP**   All administrative operations for Index Server are controlled by the access control list on the following registry key: HKEY_LOCAL_MACHINE\System\CurrentControlSet\Control\ ContentIndex.

CHALLENGE

You have set up the intranet for a university using IIS. All members of the staff are allowed to access the intranet, but only those from the research departments are allowed to search it. Since the university runs an all Windows 2000 network with Internet Explorer as the default browser, you have disabled Anonymous Access so that each user logs onto the site automatically using their domain account, thus forcing authentication prior to any queries being submitted. At the start of the next semester, there are several new members of staff joining, and the previous year's research material is also being added to the site. How can you simplify managing access to the site's search functionality? To ensure that only research staff can access the search form, create a Windows group called Research and add all the research staff to this Group. Next, only allow the Research Group read access to the search form, and limit access to the .idq or .htx file used in the query to the Research Group as well.

On a large Web site, users will appreciate the search functionality that Index Server provides; however, to ensure the security of your Web content, it requires the careful assignment of access permissions. Do not enable Index Server until you are completely familiar with its query process and the query parameters that control the results returned. For more information about changing Internet Data Query files, see the Index Server documentation. Finally, IIS logging will pick up query information, such as the querying IP address and the queries posted to the server. Watch for queries that are unusually long or specifically targeting script files, since they may point to hacker activity.

SMTP (SIMPLE MAIL TRANSPORT PROTOCOL) SERVICE

STMP (Simple Mail Transfer Protocol) is the predominant protocol used to transport e-mail throughout the Internet. IIS includes support for SMTP via the SMTP service, which can be installed as an optional subcomponent if required. Before you get too excited, though, this is not a full-featured mail system like Microsoft Exchange. The SMTP service does not include Post Office Protocol version 3 (POP3) or Internet Message Access Protocol (IMAP), which let users have separate private message storage areas. Since SMTP only sends e-mail between mail servers, neither SMTP nor IIS can sort incoming e-mail into mailboxes and let users check their e-mail! So why would you install the SMTP service if it doesn't provide mailbox functionality? It provides an easy way for applications to access an e-mail service, and, if you need just a simple SMTP-based mail server, this will certainly do.

 SECURITY ALERT Windows 2000 installs SMTP by default when you promote a server to Domain Controller (DC) status, since SMTP is an optional transport method used for replicating information between domain controllers. Unless you explicitly configure the DC for SMTP replication, you can disable the SMTP service if it is not required for any other purpose.

If your site requires the use of SMTP, a secure configuration is essential. Running SMTP on your IIS server exposes it to DoS attacks, arbitrary code attacks, spammers who use your server as a waypoint for spoofed e-mail or spam, or network sniffers intercepting messages as they are routed from SMTP server to SMTP server. As you did with your FTP server, you need to configure your SMTP server to provide only the minimum level of service required.

Securing Your SMTP Site

Like the other IIS subcomponents, SMTP server is managed from the ISM Management Console, so you need to be a member of the local Administrators group in order to change any settings. To open the Properties dialog box, shown in Figure 10-12, right-click the SMTP server and select Properties from the pop-up menu. The first thing to do is to configure the connection information and enable logging for the same reasons as we discussed in the section on FTP earlier in the chapter. You can also use the same log settings here as you have for IIS.

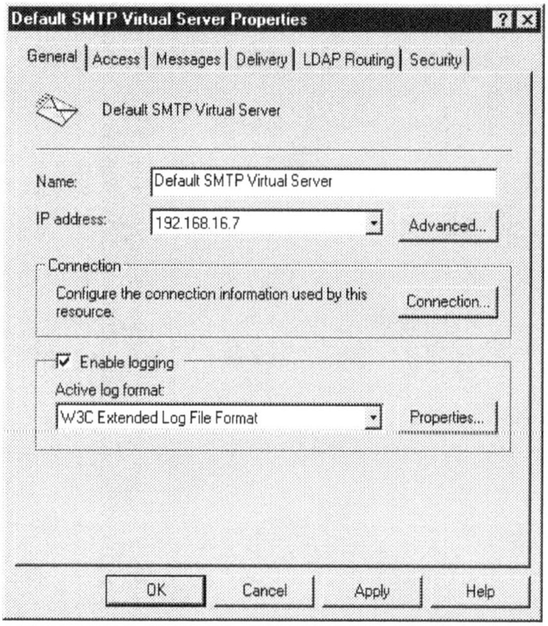

Figure 10-12.   The SMTP Server Properties sheet has its own set of tabs with names that don't necessarily relate to those of other IIS Properties sheets.

In the same way we limited the number of connections to the FTP server, you need to limit the maximum number of connections to the SMTP server so that no single domain can monopolize the SMTP service's incoming and outgoing connections. Click the Connection button on the General tab and set the number of connections and time-outs to the level required by your particular site.

Access Control

The Access tab lets you set the four main security features used to prevent unauthorized use of your SMTP server and to secure incoming communications, as shown in Figure 10-13.

- Access Control
- Secure Communication
- Connection Control
- Relay Restrictions

Authentication   You can require that remote clients and servers authenticate themselves before being granted access to your SMTP services. There are three options for

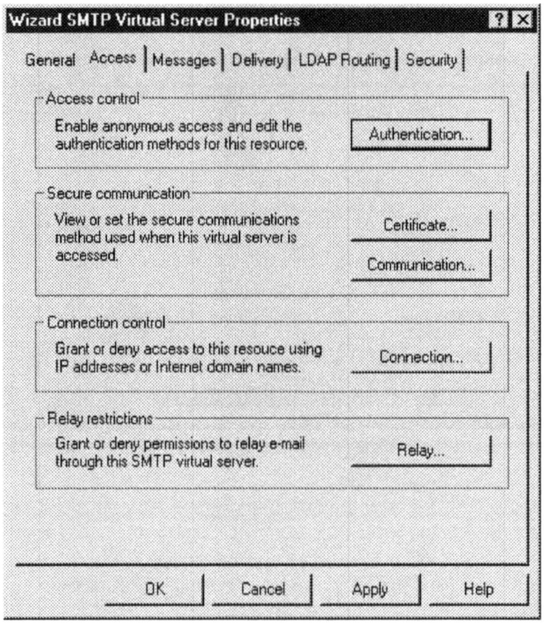

Figure 10-13. You can control incoming mail using the Access tab and outgoing mail using the Delivery tab.

authenticating incoming connections to your SMTP service: Anonymous, Basic, and Windows security services. The default is Anonymous Access used by Internet clients and doesn't require a user name or password. This option is required if you need an Internet-based server that acts as a general mail server. Basic Authentication requires the client to send a valid user name and password, which will be authenticated against the domain entered in the Default Domain field. Like basic authentication in IIS, this password is sent in clear text, but you do have the option of requiring TLS (Transport Layer Security) encryption. TLS requires a valid server certificate in the same way SSL does in IIS. The Windows Security Package option doesn't require actual passwords to be sent because it uses the Windows 2000 Security Support Provider Interface (SSPI) to perform Win2K authentication of the passed credentials, such as Kerberos or NTLM. The mail client, such as Microsoft Outlook Express, does need to support this authentication method.

Secure Communication   You can ensure that incoming data is encrypted by requiring the use of TLS between servers. Client computers can use TLS to submit encrypted messages, which the SMTP service can then decrypt. You can also opt to enforce the use of 128-bit encryption, the default being 40-bit, if you know that the servers needing to connect to you also support 128-bit encryption.

Connection Control   You can restrict access to your SMTP server based on the remote computer's IP address or DNS domain name. Configure these options exactly as you do for the FTP Service described earlier. Refer to the upcoming "Challenge" to see how Connection control can protect a Microsoft Exchange Server.

Relay Restrictions   If an SMTP service receives a message destined for another remote domain, it can forward, or relay, it on to the destination domain. SMTP servers that accept and forward messages to mail domains for which they are not responsible are often referred to as "open mail relays." Spammers can take advantage of open mail relays to send thousands of unsolicited e-mail messages, clogging the server and recipients with unwanted mail. Hackers can also use mail relay to attack another site by sending it thousands of e-mail messages. All this mail appears to come from the relaying mail server, which can result in accusations of spamming or DoS attacks. It can also lead to a loss of reputation and possible loss of connectivity to large parts of the Internet, since many organizations block sites from which spamming is allowed to originate. It is critical that your SMTP server is configured to control and block third-party mail relay; otherwise, anyone on the Internet can send e-mail messages to your server and it will process and deliver the messages. By default, the SMTP service is configured to accept only incoming messages destined for local domains hosted on the server itself.

TIP   You can test whether your mail server is configured to relay external e-mail messages at the http://mail-abuse.org/tsi/ar-test.html Web site, or you can download the rlytest utility at www.unicom.com/sw/#rlytest.

If you have a business requirement for mail relay capability, you can make an exception in two ways. One is by granting an exception based on the IP address or DNS domain name of the computer that wants to have a message relayed. The other is by specifying which remote destination domains should always have their e-mail relayed to them, regardless of the IP address or DNS domain name of the originator. This permits the relaying of messages based on final destination not originating source.

Messages

The settings you specify on the Messages tab can prevent abuse of your system by both internal and external users; however, be aware that some of the settings are not actually enforced.

Limiting Message and Session Size   The message size limit is the SMTP service's advertised message size limit for incoming messages, but it does not actually enforce it. When an SMTP client or server connects to IIS, the message size limit is advertised to the remote computer via the Size command. However, IIS will still accept and process a message if the remote system sends a message larger than this advertised limit.

The maximum session size is an enforced limit; and if a remote SMTP system sends a message that exceeds this value, IIS terminates the connection and cuts the message off mid-transfer. You need to be careful when setting this limit because the remote

---

CHALLENGE

You have installed SMTP services on your IIS server so that your Web master can add pages to the site that let customers file feedback information about a beta program that they are testing via a form that is mailed to betasupport@mail.yourcorp.com. These pages are accessed over an SSL connection; and by having customers use a form for sending their feedback, you can ensure that all the relevant information about their operating system is completed before the feedback is sent. The form creates a text file with the proper SMTP headers, and it's placed in the Mailroot\Pickup folder. The SMTP service continually scans this folder for text files and moves them to the Mailroot\Queue folder until they can be delivered. The IIS and SMTP servers are situated in Houston, but the messages are sent to your Dallas office where the technical support team is based. You suspect that your competitor has set up packet sniffers to capture e-mail sent between the two offices. You have set the SMTP servers in Houston and Dallas to require Windows NT Challenge/Response Authentication and are using IP address restrictions to limit connections to just the Dallas and Houston offices. Since this is the only application using the SMTP service you have also changed the default port number from 25 to 1700 on both SMTP servers. However, you still think that your competitor is managing to capture vital information from the feedback e-mail.

Although authentication, port number changes, and IP address restrictions would exclude other SMTP servers from interoperating with your two SMTP servers, your competitor is waiting for the two SMTP servers to successfully authenticate and connect to each other. They can then capture all the traffic between the two servers when they start forwarding messages to each other. You need to Require TLS on each server (see the upcoming section, "Outbound Security") and use a 128-bit key to encrypt the text of the messages, so even if the packets are captured, the message contents will not be readable.

---

system is likely to resubmit the entire message with the next connection, which causes a loop that continues until the remote system reaches its retry limit.

Limiting Messages and Recipients   Although the Limit Number of Messages Per Connection and Limit Number of Recipients per Message settings sound like they might help you control misuse of your SMTP server, they just control how it handles message delivery. The maximum number of recipients per message value does not prevent an SMTP client from submitting a message with more recipients than set in this box. Instead, the SMTP service sends the message with as many recipients as permitted, and then sends another copy of the message to the remaining recipients, repeating this process until all recipients get a copy of the message. If the number of queued messages exceeds the messages-per-connection value, concurrent connections are established with the target SMTP server to improve performance.

Outbound Security

You can set outgoing encryption as a default for all connections to remote domains, or particular remote domains can have their own custom encryption settings from the Delivery tab. To require encryption on all outgoing messages to remote domains, click the Outbound Security button at the bottom of the Properties sheet, and select the TLS Encryption check box, shown next. Outbound Security controls how your SMTP server authenticates to other SMTP servers and whether outgoing messages are encrypted. To configure the default encryption settings for a particular remote domain, create a new domain in the Domains container. Open the Properties sheet for the remote domain object and click the Outbound Security button. Next, select check box for TLS Encryption to set this option; remember that properties set here apply only to the domain referenced by this object. To require that incoming messages be encrypted, you must have a Server Certificate installed. Sending encrypted messages does not require a certificate on the local server.

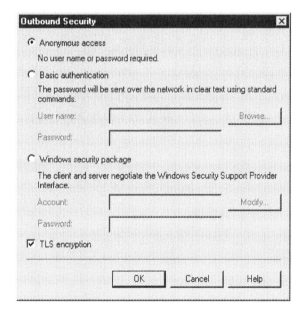

Operators

The Security tab lets you delegate limited authority to the users or groups listed for the SMTP server, but not any other aspect of IIS, as with the other types of Operators we've discussed.

Although SMTP is a useful service with interesting features, they fall well short of a full-featured mail server. Nevertheless, it can be a useful service if safely configured.

CHALLENGE

You can use the IIS SMTP mail relay service to prevent spammers from directly interacting with your Microsoft Exchange Server! Your Exchange Server is probably set up on your internal network to receive all mail for users in your domain for onward delivery. If you publish your Exchange Server's SMTP service, Internet users can send messages directly to your Exchange Server. Allowing the Internet to have direct contact with your Exchange Server is never a good idea. To stop this direct contact, set up an IIS SMTP relay, and instead of publishing the Exchange Server's SMTP service, publish the IIS SMTP Service. Now when mail destined for yourdomain.com hits the external interface of your firewall, it will be forwarded to the SMTP relay, which, in turn, forwards it to your Exchange Server. Now set your Exchange Server to send outgoing SMTP mail messages to the IIS SMTP relay server so it forwards them on to the Internet. With this configuration, your Exchange Server's SMTP service never has to interact with an Internet SMTP server.

To secure this set up, for incoming mail, you should allow your IIS SMTP server to relay only to your own domains; while for outgoing mail, it needs to relay to all domains. If you allow incoming mail to be relayed to all domains, you'll be processing thousands of spam e-mails within a few days, since spammers will take advantage of your open mail relay. A default configuration allows all computers that can authenticate to relay through the server; however, authentication requires more overhead, so it's better to allow relay based on IP address. Since you only want to allow your Exchange Server to use the IIS SMTP server as an open relay, add the IP address of your Exchange Server to allow Only The List Below. You need to allow the IIS SMTP service to act as an open relay for your Exchange Server because the Exchange Server needs to send SMTP mail to all Internet mail domains, so the open relay for outbound mail is required. You also need to prevent relay for incoming messages. You do this by configuring your server to relay only messages destined to your own domain.

In the Internet Services Manager console, expand the Default SMTP Virtual Server node. Right-click the Domains node, point to New, and click Domain. Select the Remote option and click Next. Type in your mail domain name and click Finish. Double-click your new Remote Domain name. Put a check mark in the check box to Allow Incoming Mail to Be Relayed to This Domain so that inbound mail destined for other domains is dropped by the SMTP relay. Then, in the Route domain frame, select Forward All Mail to Smart Host. Enter the IP address of your Exchange Server in the text box under this selection in brackets, like [**192.168.1.254**].

Another advantage of using this type of setup is that you can take down the Exchange Server for maintenance without losing any incoming mail. You can also improve fault tolerance by setting up multiple IIS SMTP servers. Another possibility would be to add an additional mail relay server to filter e-mail for spam or viruses before relaying it on to the Exchange Server.

Action	Net Command	Connection Status
Start	net start	Starts the service and allows new connections.
Stop	net stop	The service immediately terminates all connections.
Pause	net pause	The FTP service prevents new connections from being made but does not disconnect existing users. The SMTP service prevents new connections from being made but continues to deliver and receive messages over existing connections. The NNTP service prevents new connections from being made but continues to transmit news articles over existing connections .
Resume	net continue	Disengages the pause and allows new connections.

Table 10-1. Networking Commands That Control IIS-Based Services

STARTING AND STOPPING SERVICES

You can start, stop, pause, and resume the FTP, SMTP, and NNTP Services using the Internet Services Manager or the Services Management Console, or from the command line using the networking commands in Table 10-1.

Be aware that there is a difference between Stop and Pause. While both commands stop new connections from being established, Pause does not terminate any existing connections. Stop does. The actual program names for FTP, NNTP, and SMTP are msftpsvc, nntpsvc, and smtpsvc, respectively; so to stop the FTP service, for example, you would type the following at a command prompt:

```
net stop msftpsvc
```

WINDOWS MEDIA SERVICES

Windows Media Services is not an IIS service as such, but because streaming media is becoming such a popular Web service, we wanted to highlight the security features it provides you to protect your media files. If your site only includes a few audio clips, Web server streaming may suffice; however, once you offer content, such as Web shows or conferences, the best way to deliver them is by using a Windows Media server. The Windows Media components provide many additional features not available purely by streaming from IIS. Not only does Windows Media server more efficiently handle system resources such as processor usage and network bandwidth than a Web server, it also provides two important security features: Windows Media Security and Logging.

Windows Media Security

Windows Media Security features can limit access to media on a Windows Media server and implement pay-per-view content. Using the latest Windows Media Rights Manager SDK, you can create applications that encrypt or package digital media files and issue licenses for them. A *packaged* Windows Media file contains a version of the file that has been encrypted with a key so that only the person who has obtained a license for that file can open it. The license is separate from the packaged Windows Media file, which means that the content and license for that content can be acquired at different times. Encrypted files can be either streamed or downloaded to the consumer's computer.

Administering and Logging

With Windows Media Administrator, you can control how a Windows Media server manages live content and files, and monitor overall system activity in real time. It can create detailed logs that include individual client connection information and server events, which are useful for tracking down undesirable activity.

TIP   Media Services is a relatively new technology, and security holes are being exposed; so stay up-to-date with the latest security news at www.microsoft.com/windows/windowsmedia.

Windows Media and Firewalls

Windows Media normally streams via UDP/IP on a range of ports. To avoid the security problem of having so many ports open, it can stream via TCP/IP through a single port (1755). If your security policy does not allow opening a non-well-known port, Windows Media can also stream via HTTP on port 80.

The following firewall configuration will allow users from the Internet to access a Windows Media server sitting behind your firewall:

Streaming Windows Media Technologies Files (ASF) with UDP:
In: TCP on port 1755
In: UDP on port 1755
Out: UDP between port 1024-5000—port assignment is random between 1024 and 5000, but only open the necessary number of ports.

Streaming Windows Media Technologies Files (ASF) with TCP:
In/Out: TCP on port 1755
Streaming ASF with HTTP
In/Out: TCP on port 80

The Out port is the port that Microsoft Windows Media Player or other clients use to communicate with the server.

SIMPLE TCP/IP SERVICES

The Simple TCP/IP services are not a subcomponent of IIS but of Networking Services, and they provide services such as Character Generator, Daytime, Discard, Echo, and Quote of the Day. This component is not required by IIS or any of its subcomponents, but many administrators install it, mistakenly believing it is required by services using the TCP/IP protocol. We strongly recommend that you do not install this subcomponent, since DoS attacks already exist that target Simple TCP/IP services in Windows 2000. For example, there are programs that spoof systems running the Echo service, making them echo a message back and forth continuously. To check whether Simple TCP/IP Services are enabled or installed on your server, double-click each LAN-type network connection listed in the Network and Dial-up Connections tool, and click the Properties button, as shown in Figure 10-14. If Simple TCP/IP Services is listed or enabled in the list of Components used by the connection, select it and click the Uninstall button to remove the service.

The IIS services that we've covered in this chapter can play an important role in making your Web site a success, but carefully evaluate which you really need. Each service you enable is one more access point for attackers, and one more component that you must configure, manage, and update with security patches.

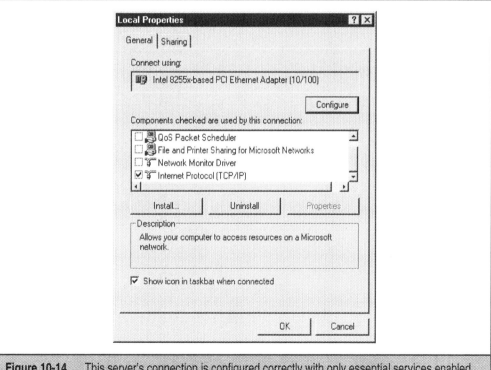

Figure 10-14. This server's connection is configured correctly with only essential services enabled.

CHECKLIST

- ☐ Review the services you do and don't need on your IIS server.
- ☐ Only install and enable services that are essential for your site.
- ☐ Do not install, or enable, any unnecessary services.
- ☐ Record which services are installed in your Services Log along with any relevant notes using Table 10-2.
- ☐ All drives used by IIS-related services must be formatted with NTFS.
- ☐ Do not use the default setting of any service, but configure each one individually.
- ☐ Create new accounts for FTP and NNTP anonymous users.
- ☐ Check that you haven't created an FTP warez site.
- ☐ Use Secure FTP connection to protect sensitive FTP traffic.
- ☐ Consider issuing users digital certificates to enable client certificate mapping if newsgroup articles are highly confidential.

Service	Installed	Enabled	Secured	Notes
FTP publishing				
NNTP service				
SMTP service				
Content index				
Certification authority				
RPC locator				
Server service				
Telephony service				
Remote access				
Alerter				
Network DDE and DSDM				
Network monitor agent				
Simple TCP/IP services				
WWW service				

Table 10-2.   A Sample Services Log

☐ Only install Index Server if you need it. Restrict the folders it indexes to those storing nonsensitive files.

☐ Watch for security alerts relating to Index Server, as it has been the cause of several security breaches.

☐ Edit your server search scripts (.idq files) to make sure Index Server only searches specific folders and files, such as plain HTML files.

☐ Make sure that your SMTP server is not providing open mail relay for the Internet.

☐ Use SMTP relay to protect your Exchange Server.

☐ Use Windows Media Services to protect copyright material that you want to control access to, but stay up-to-date regarding new security holes.

☐ Don't install simple TCP/IP services.

CHAPTER 11

Active Content Security

B y this point, you have set up and secured your IIS server and you are probably
eager to publish your Web site on your intranet or the Internet. If your Web site
consists purely of static content—that is, content that can only be changed by
manually editing the file, such as plain HTML pages or image files—you are pretty
much ready to go. When a visitor requests your Web page by entering its URL in a
browser or clicking a hyperlink, your server will simply send the files that make up
the requested page. Unfortunately, however, one of the drawbacks of static content
is that it can appear out of date or dull.

Most sites, particularly commercial and e-commerce sites, need to update their content
regularly, adding information such as product prices or special offers, or building
customized pages on-the-fly based on the type of request the Web server receives. Dynamic
or active content allows pages to be customized based on individual requests, such as
the results of a search or the display of information pulled from a database or other source.
Complex objects, such as movie clips or Java applets, can also be embedded into HTML
pages. Dynamic content makes an Internet or intranet site come alive, and it can make
one site more appealing and successful than another. Active content presents an enhanced
and more personal experience to the user than simple, static HTML pages. However,
your site may not require active content; and certainly from a security perspective, a
static site is the more secure option, because active content is yet another service IIS
has to handle that brings potential vulnerabilities into the picture.

Dynamic content is crucial to the success of an e-commerce site, where shoppers
can search for and buy goods online, with the store's pages displaying the latest prices
and stock information. Another example of dynamic content could be used on an
organization's intranet that publishes an internal telephone directory. If the directory
listings are created from the HR database, any personnel changes can be immediately
reflected in the online directory as soon as the HR database is updated, without anyone
having to edit the directory pages manually.

For IIS to create Web pages on-the-fly, it typically passes the data to another
application program for processing and then builds and returns a Web page based on
the information received from the application—such as an order confirmation number.
This method of passing data back and forth between the server and an application is
called a *Common Gateway Interface (CGI)*, and HTTP is the underlying mechanism on
which CGI operates. Unfortunately, this power and functionality comes at the cost of
weakening overall security, since it can literally create a gateway into your server. CGIs
operate as independent entities, and they are not within the realm of security provided
by IIS.

As an IIS administrator, it is more than likely that you will need to deliver active
content, so you'll want to ensure that you can do so without compromising the security
of your IIS server; this is what this chapter is all about.

ACTIVE CONTENT TECHNOLOGIES

CGI, ASP, and Perl are the most common technologies used on IIS for providing
active content, and they are discussed in the following sections. Active Server Pages

is a server-side technology from Microsoft that enables you to combine HTML, scripts, and reusable ActiveX or COM server components to create dynamic Web pages. As it is the Web developer's choice for creating server-generated content on IIS, we will mainly concentrate on ASP, but first let's look at the original approach to creating dynamic content, CGI.

COMMON GATEWAY INTERFACE

CGI is a powerful concept; and on UNIX machines, it has typically been the approach for creating real-time active content on the Web. However, since each application is a compiled program, it requires recompiling the executable each time a change is required to the output that it creates. To overcome this burden, server-side scripting languages were developed, which are interpreted and executed by a *scripting engine* and the output sent to the Web server application via CGI.

CGI scripts are widely used for extending a Web server's capabilities, with one of the most ubiquitous uses being form processing. The script acts as a bridge between a resource and the server—a resource being any program or object that provides a service, such as e-mail or a database. The script formats the information provided by the resource into HTML to make it understandable to the requesting browser. This allows a Web server to be extended to serve information from different resources, including those residing on different hosts.

Information is passed to a CGI application by specifying the name of the application in the *uniform resource locator (URL)*. Here's an example:

```
<FORM ACTION=http://www.yourserver.com/scripts/processorder.pl METHOD=POST>
```

Here, the URL is specified as part of the FORM tag. On receiving the form data, the yourserver.com server will pass control to the CGI application—in this case, the Perl interpreter indicated by the .pl file extension—which will parse the processorder.pl script, process the request, and then return a page based on the form data it received.

IIS continues to support CGI scripts and programs but offers a much more tightly integrated means of providing dynamic content. IIS supports the *Internet Server Application Programming Interface (ISAPI)*, which allows executables to operate more efficiently than a standard CGI application. ISAPI provides access to IIS memory space, giving broader access to the Web server than the simple stdin and stdout functions on which many technologies such as Perl engines rely. This is how *ASP*, or *Active Server Pages*, communicates with IIS via ISAPI. ASP scripts can be added directly to your HTML pages and can do virtually anything CGI scripts can do—and more. We will look at ASP, and how to ensure that your active content is implemented securely.

Active Server Pages

An ASP page is an HTML page that includes one or more scripts that are processed by IIS before the page is sent to the user. ASP interfaces with IIS via ISAPI and the asp.dll (the

ASP dynamic-link library), running as an in-process application within the same memory space as IIS. This provides fast access and response times, as asp.dll has direct access to values in IIS memory. Asp.dll runs with the privileges of the IWAM_*computername* account. IIS is configured to use ASP by default, so no additional software must be installed if you need to use ASP to create dynamic content.

> **TIP** The acronym for Application Service Providers is also ASP. These kind of ASPs deliver and manage computer services and applications from remote data centers to multiple users via the Internet or a private network.

ASP can call Component Object Model (COM) components to provide increased functionality by instantiating server-side resources, but this capability presents a security risk. You should disable or remove any unneeded COM components—such as the File System Object component, which provides Web applications with access to hard drives—if your site does not need them. To disable the File System Object, execute the following at the Run command line:

```
regsvr32 scrrun.dll /u
```

To learn more about managing COM applications, use the Component Services applet in the Administrative Tools folder of the Control Panel.

> **TIP** COM is also known on the Web as ActiveX, a software architecture that allows applications to be built from reusable software components. This framework for creating and using components forms the foundation for higher-level software services like OLE (for object linking and embedding), which provide system functionality such as inter-application scripting and data transfer.

Server-Side Include (SSI) Directives

Server-side is a limited form of CGI application. In fact, ASP recognizes SSIs as just an instruction as it parses the file. Within an ASP page you can use the `#include` instruction to replace the `#include` instruction with the contents of another file. The following line will insert the entire postalrates.inc file in its place:

```
<!-- #include file="/includes/postalrates.inc" -->
```

Ssinc.dll is used to process the SSI `#include` directive, with asp.dll then interpreting the complete page. This is very handy when you want to reuse several lines of code on different pages. Microsoft recommends the use of include files to make code maintenance easier, as only one page has to be changed to alter code used by many others. However, if an attacker opens an include file directly in a browser, the source code can be visible, since include files themselves are not interpreted by ASP. To prevent this from happening, you should either map .inc files, the common file extension for include files, to ASP or rename them .asp files to ensure that any script code is executed with only the *results* returned to the browser rather than your code. (See the section "Application Mappings," later in this chapter, to learn how to do this.)

IIS supports five other SSI directives:

```
#config
#echo
#fsize
#flastmod
#exec
```

You cannot use any of these directives in an ASP page. Instead, you need to use one of three special HTML extensions, which are set to use SSI directives by default in IIS: .stm .shtm, and .shtml.

The #exec directive should be disabled on a secure server because it allows command-line or CGI programs to be executed in the context of the Web server in a separate memory space. IIS disables this directive by default, but you should double-check by making sure the following value is set to zero or is missing in the Registry: HKEY_LOCAL_MACHINE\SYSTEM\CurrentControlSet\Services\W3SVC\Parameters\SSIEnableCmdDirective.

ActivePerl

ActivePerl is maintained and distributed by ActiveState and is available free at http://www.activeperl.com. It is included in this discussion of scripting languages because Perl is a popular scripting language, particularly with developers from a UNIX background. The Windows version of ActivePerl provides additional components that take advantage of the IIS platform: PerlScript and Perl for ISAPI. ActivePerl is a good choice if you are moving your Web site from a UNIX server and your Web developers are more familiar with the Perl language than Microsoft's VBScript.

Whereas ASP interfaces with IIS via ISAPI and the ASP DLL, Perl uses the Perl interpreter, a compiled executable called Perl.exe. As Perl.exe runs as an independent application, it uses additional server resources each time the Web server calls it to process a request, which is inefficient. If an error occurs within the script, the Web server will continue to wait until the request times out, since it has no control over the Perl program. However, the CGI script can continue to consume system resources and could eventually bring down your server—although if the actual Perl program itself fails, it will not affect the Web server.

Unlike most versions of Perl, PerlScript allows you to embed script tags directly into a Web page, making it similar to how VBScript is used in ASP pages. During ActivePerl installation, you should select the option to install the Perl for ISAPI, so that ActivePerl will run as an ISAPI application in the same way as ASP.

TIP   Review some of the freely available secure Perl scripts that provide the functionality that you need, and analyze how they avoid creating security weaknesses. A good Web site for examples on how to write Perl scripts with security in mind is http://superscripts.com/resources/.

FOLDER STRUCTURES FOR ACTIVE CONTENT

As discussed in Chapter 4, you can configure both Web server permissions and Windows NTFS permissions for specific Web sites, folders, and individual files to control how users access your Web content. Instead of setting permissions on each file, it is easier and safer to create folders to hold specific file types, such as static content or scripts. A good Web site structure makes it easier for you to manage permissions to the Web's content, since the appropriate security permissions can be set at the folder level rather than on a file-by-file basis. For a typical Web site, you need to create the following folders, as covered in Chapter 3:

Folder	Content	File Types	Web Folder Structure
static	static content, client side scripts	.htm, .html, .js	D:\my_website\static
include	include files	.inc	D:\my_website\include
content	script files	.asp	D:\my_website\content
live	executables	.exe, .dll, .cgi, .pl	D:\my_website\live
images	image files	.gif, .jpg	D:\my_website\images

This type of site structure is not going to be a favorite with your Web designers, since it can lead to awkward references for images and scripts; but from a security standpoint, it is by far the best approach.

 SECURITY ALERT   On a production server, you should use non-obvious names for the folders containing scripts or executable content.

Script File Permissions

After you have created the folders that will hold your Web content, set the permissions on each folder. Following are the recommended baseline NTFS permission settings for the folder structure shown in the preceding table:

Folder	Internet Guest Account Access (IUSR_*computername*)	Administrators Access	System Access
static	Read	Full	Full
include	Read	Full	Full
content	Read	Full	Full
live	None	Full	Full
images	Read	Full	Full

Application Settings

To allow scripts to run on your server, you must configure IIS Application Settings at the master, site, or virtual directory level. An IIS application is any file, or set of files, that performs some coherent function and is executed within a defined set of folders in your Web site, using the folder boundaries to define the scope of an application. Every file and folder under a "starting-point" folder in your Web site is considered part of the application until another starting-point folder is found. More than one application can exist per Web site. An application can share information among the files in the application. For example, ASP applications share context flow, session state, and variable settings across the pages of the application.

Application Starting Points

In Internet Services Manager, a package icon (Figure 11-1) indicates an application starting point, with its subfolders considered part of the application.

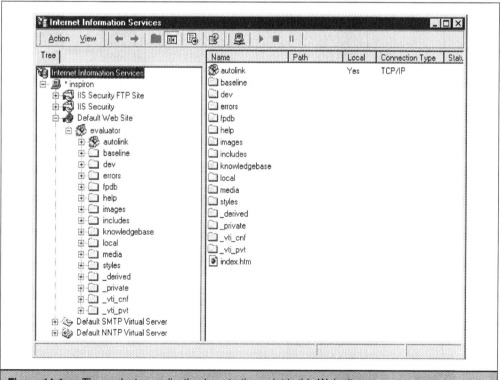

Figure 11-1.   The evaluator application is a starting point in this Web site.

The default Web site that is created when you install IIS is the application starting point, or application root, as shown in the Properties dialog box in Figure 11-2. Use Internet Services Manager to designate an application's starting-point directory by opening the master, Web, or virtual directory Properties sheet, which is accessed by right-clicking the relevant object in ISM, and then selecting Properties from the pop-up menu and clicking the Home Directory tab. IIS supports ASP, ISAPI, CGI, IDC (Internet Database Connector), and SSI applications.

Execute Permissions

If your site consists purely of static content, you must ensure that the None option is selected in the Execute Permissions drop-down box of the Default Web Site Properties sheet. To allow a script-mapped application to run, such as ASP, select the Scripts Only option. Do not select the Scripts And Executables option unless it is essential that executable programs can be run on your server.

It is important that you understand the distinction between these Web server permissions and NTFS permissions. Web server permissions apply to all users

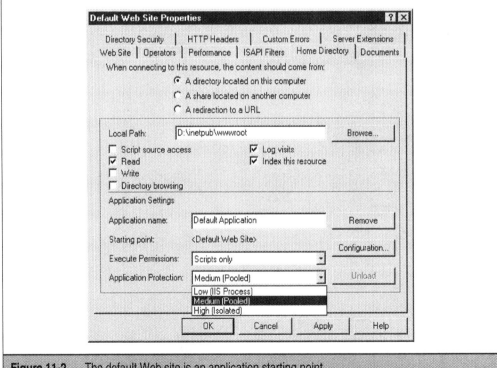

Figure 11-2. The default Web site is an application starting point.

accessing your Web site. NTFS permissions apply only to a specific user or group of users with valid Windows accounts, and they precisely define access to physical directories on your server; Web permissions control access to virtual directories on your Web site. These permissions apply to all users regardless of their specific access rights. For example, setting Read permission on a virtual directory allows all users to view that directory, unless NTFS permissions restrict which users can view it

By default, the anonymous user account (IUSR_computername) is given NTFS permissions by IIS for the actual folders that make up the Web site. If Web permissions and NTFS permissions differ for a directory or file, the more restrictive settings are used.

Application Protection

IIS offers three options regarding the process in which an application is run:

- The same process as Web services (Inetinfo.exe)
- A pooled process, a separate instance of DLLHost.exe
- A process separate from Web services (DLLHost.exe)

These options provide varying levels of protection when an application fails and causes the process in which it is running to stop responding. By default, inetinfo.exe runs in its own process, and the other applications run in a single, pooled process. There is a trade-off between performance and level of application protection. Applications that run in the Web services process result in higher performance with a greater risk that a misbehaving application can make the Web services become unavailable. Therefore, you should run inetinfo.exe in its own process; run mission-critical applications in their own processes (High); and run remaining applications in a shared, pooled process (Medium).

APPLICATION MAPPINGS

So that IIS knows which ISAPI or CGI program to call to process a particular type of file, the file name extension needs to be associated or mapped to the correct ISAPI or CGI program. When your server receives a URL identifying a file with a mapped extension, it calls the associated program to process the request. IIS is preconfigured to support common application mappings. For your scripts to work correctly, you will need to add or modify the mappings between the script's file name extension and the program or interpreter that processes it. (The importance of removing any unwanted mappings was discussed in Chapters 3 and 10.)

Application mappings are set at the application starting point from the App Mappings tab on the Application Configuration sheet. To map a file type to an application:

1. Open the Internet Services Manager and select the Web site or the starting-point directory of an application.

2. Open the Properties sheet by right-clicking the object and selecting Properties.

3. Click the Home Directory, Virtual Directory, or Directory tab.

4. Click the Configuration button to open the Application Configuration sheet, and select the App Mappings tab, which is shown in Figure 11-3.

   IIS uses these mapped file name extensions to determine which ISAPI or CGI program to run to process the request. In Figure 11-3, you can see that IIS will call the Perl.exe program to process any requests for files ending with a .pl extension.

5. To add an application mapping, click the Add button to open the Add/Edit Application Extension Mapping dialog box shown in Figure 11-4.

6. In the Executable box, type the path to the ISAPI or CGI program (.exe or .dll) that will process the file. This executable must be located in a local directory on the Web server.

7. In the Extension box, type the file name extension you want to be associated with the program entered in the Executable box. In Figure 11-4, .inc file types have been added.

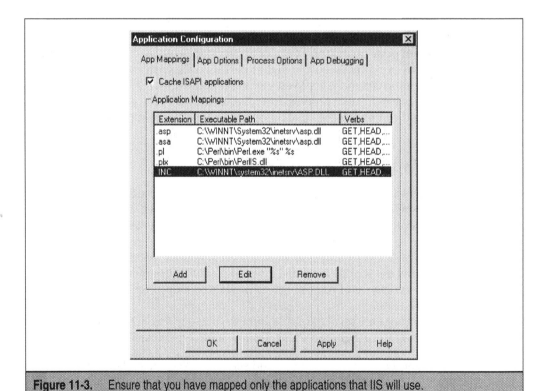

Figure 11-3.   Ensure that you have mapped only the applications that IIS will use.

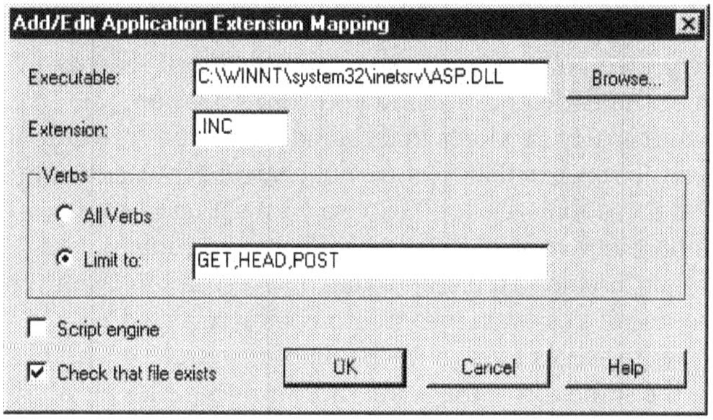

Figure 11-4. Ensure that any code in include files is executed before being sent to the client by mapping .INC files to ASP.

8. Now set the verbs that can be passed to the application. You should not select All Verbs but add only the allowed verbs to the Limit To box. This is certainly true of ASP, which should be limited to the HTTP verbs GET, HEAD, and POST. Separate each verb with a comma. If you have placed all scripts in one folder, you do not need to select the Script Engine option. This is applicable only when you want the application to run in a directory without Execute permissions, which weakens your ability to control permissions.

TIP Check the sidebar "URLScan Security Tool," later in the chapter for more information on which verbs you may need to allow for particular applications.

---

9. Select the Check That File Exists option so that IIS will verify the existence of the requested script file and ensure that the requesting user has access permission for that script file. If the script does not exist or the user does not have the correct permission, an appropriate warning message is returned to the browser and the script engine is not invoked. This option can be useful for scripts mapped to non-CGI executables such as the Perl interpreter that do not send a CGI response if the script file is not accessible. Because the script will be opened twice, once by the server and once by the script engine, some performance cost is incurred to enable this option—but it's worth it.

Finally, to remove an application mapping, select the file name extension on the App Mappings tab and click the Remove button. Requests for files with the deleted file name extension will no longer be processed by IIS.

SOURCE CONTROL

So far, we've concentrated on securing and protecting your IIS server and its resources from attacks from both inside and outside your organization, and in Chapter 9 we discussed various third-party products that can help restore Web content should it be defaced or destroyed. To ensure that files are not changed by accident by your Web developers, and that these changes don't expose your server in some way, you need to engage some form of source control. For example, if an include file is deleted or moved without the pages that "include" it being updated, an error will occur when they are accessed, which can result in system information being revealed.

By controlling write access to your Web content, source control ensures that no two people are editing the same file at the same time and that files aren't deleted or moved without other related files being updated. This is important, for example, when a team of developers is working on a single application, because it ensures that only the latest version of the file is being used at any one time. A change-control program simplifies the management of file updates, and the tiresome requirement to change a file's attributes manually to and from read-only is automated.

Source-Control Software

Typical source-control programs use a system of checking files in and out, somewhat akin to a library system. If a file is checked out by one user, no one else is able to use or edit that file until it is checked back in. Similarly, if no one has checked out the file, no one is able to edit the file. In a Web application setting, you should store all files on a development server. Each user then downloads the file to his or her local computer, edits and tests it, and uploads it back to the development server. Once any changes have been approved by the appropriate people, the edited file can be uploaded to the production server.

Source-control software can be integrated with IIS if FrontPage Server Extensions (FPSE) are installed. FPSE is a set of programs and scripts that support authoring in FrontPage (Microsoft's popular Web editor) and extend the functionality of IIS. If you need to install FPSE, read the section "FrontPage Server Extensions," later in this chapter. We recommended that FPSE not be installed on production servers.

If FPSE is installed, you can enable version control.

1. Open the Internet Services Manager, and, in the console tree, right-click the Web object for which you want to enable source control.

2. Choose Properties from the shortcut menu, and then click the Server Extensions tab in the Properties window, as shown in Figure 11-5.

3. Select the Enable Authoring option, and in the Version Control box, select either Use External if you have a source-control program such as Visual SourceSafe, or select Use Built-In to use the basic FrontPage source control.

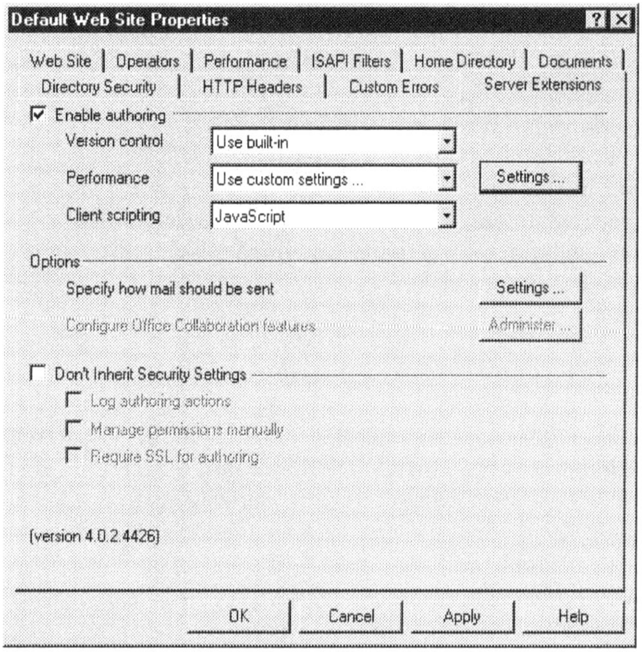

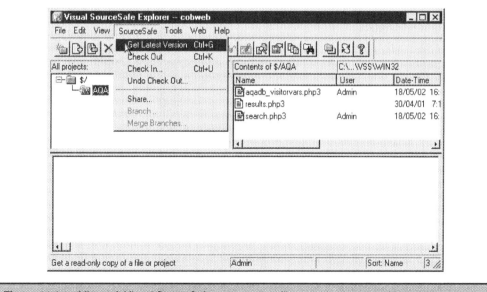

Figure 11-5.   Control the editing of Web content by your developers by enabling version control.

Figure 11-6.   Microsoft Visual SourceSafe saves project files to a database so old versions can be retrieved.

Visual SourceSafe, shown in Figure 11-6, is an enterprise-level source-control program that provides advanced versioning capabilities, such as version tracking and rollback features. For information about how to integrate Visual SourceSafe with FrontPage, see the section "Overview of Server Extensions Source Control" in the Microsoft FrontPage Server Extensions Resource Kit.

FrontPage provides two methods of source control: the built-in FrontPage lightweight source control, and integration with an external source control program that supports FrontPage, such as Visual SourceSafe. Lightweight source control provides a measure of control over users who maintain pages on your Web site, providing check-in and check-out functionality. Before you can use this FrontPage component, IIS must have the FPSE installed.

Backups

Depending on which Web authoring tool your developers use, you may need to check whether your machines are littered with .bak files. Many Web authoring tools, such as Microsoft Visual InterDev and Allaire HomeSite, allow users to create a backup copy of their work automatically. If any developers are allowed to save their work directly to the server—something we strongly advise against—these backup files are saved to the server as well, usually with the extension .bak. Anyone who points their browser at one of these .bak files can easily view all the script code by viewing the source returned by the server, since IIS won't process the page and the script tags will remain intact. To avoid this problem, ensure that all .bak files are deleted every time your developers finish updating the site, and associate .bak files to the scripting engine to ensure that the pages are executed and that only the results are sent to the client.

Copyright Protection

You can occasionally come across a site that goes to great lengths to try and stop anyone from copying the site's content. Hiding the browser's toolbar and navigation bar and using JavaScript to disable the pop-up menu are techniques often used. However, not only are these techniques irritating for the genuine user, but they also are pretty futile in protecting copyrighted content, because many ways can be used to circumvent them.

TIP If you add a copyright statement to your code, it will be easier to show in any litigation that your work was illegally copied. See the section "Script Encoder," later in the chapter, for more information.

You should always include a copyright line at the bottom of each Web page. (For example, "The contents of this site are copyright © 2002, *your name/company*. All Rights Reserved.") This can easily be implemented by selecting the Enable Document Footer option on the Documents tab of the Web site's Properties sheet, as shown in Figure 11-7. IIS automatically appends the contents of the footer file to every document it sends out, although this does reduce performance slightly.

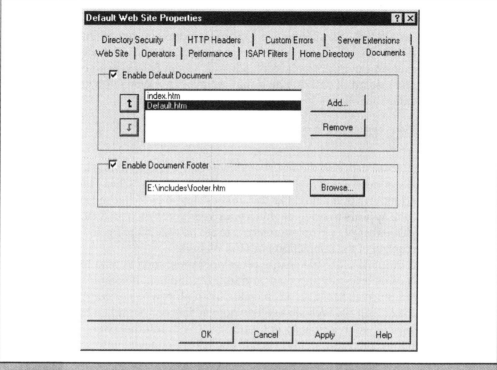

Figure 11-7. Type the full local path to the footer file, or use the Browse button to navigate to it.

TIP You should register copyrights for domain names associated with your site, and you might want to look at registering your entire site with the U.S. copyright office at http://lcweb.loc.gov/copyright/.

VALIDATING USER INPUT

The most common flaw in scripts used to generate dynamic content on a Web site is processing user input, such as the contents of a form, without checking the validity of the input. If this input is treated as valid and nonmalicious and is not checked, a number of possible attacks open up for hackers to exploit. Any site that accepts user input introduces a security risk if the data being collected is not validated before being processed either on receipt or on publication.

In HTML, to distinguish text from markup tags, some characters are treated in a specific way. For example, the less-than sign (<) typically indicates the beginning of an HTML tag. When a browser reads the < character, it looks for a valid HTML tag to follow. If an HTML page needs to display the actual < character, the developer needs to replace < with <.

Tags can either affect the formatting of a page or introduce a program that the browser executes, such as the <SCRIPT> tag, which introduces code from a variety of scripting languages. An attacker can insert malicious code into a form field instead of the expected data. For example, instead of entering an e-mail address in a Web site's guest book, an attacker could enter the following code:

```
<A HREF=http://www.badserver.com/scripts/malicious.asp>Click Here - Special
Offer</A>
```

If this input is not validated, and the script sends this data back to anyone looking through the previous visitors' comments in the guest book, they will see "Click Here — Special Offer" as a hyperlink. Anyone who clicks this link will be taken to the badserver.com site. This malicious code appears to originate from your Web site. When an attacker submits and views a malicious script, a problem referred to as *cross-site scripting*, the attacker can potentially take control of the interaction with the Web site.

Unvalidated input data can also cause other problems, such as data integrity being compromised, cookies being set and read, and user input being intercepted. Considering the numerous holes unvalidated data can create in an otherwise secure Web server, it is surprising that the majority of Web sites still do not validate data supplied by a third party before processing it. If your scripts accept input data from Internet users, you must run sanity checks on the data received, and encode and filter characters with special meaning so that they're not interpreted as HTML code.

Filtering Input Data

Input data is data that is sent to your scripts for processing, and it usually comes via a Web form, but it can also be data from a database or another resource. Filtering input works by removing some or all special characters from the input. Special characters are characters that enable script to be generated within an HTML stream. Special characters include the following:

```
< > " ' % ; ) ( & + -
```

Your specific situation may warrant the filtering of additional characters or strings beyond these special characters.

Client-Side Validation

IIS passes data sent by a Web form to your scripts for processing, and the first opportunity you have to validate and filter this data is before it is even sent to your server, at the user's browser. This is called *client-side validation*. This type of validation is usually accomplished using JavaScript, since it can execute on both Internet Explorer and Netscape browsers. This first check is to ensure that the data your script requires has actually been entered in the form fields. The following JavaScript function checks that a telephone number has been entered in the form field called Telephone:

```
function ValidateFormData(form) {
   var theNumber = form.Telpehone.Value;
   var valid = true
   var GoodChars = "0123456789()-+ "
   var i = 0
   if (theNumber =="") {
      // Return false if there is no number
      valid = false
   }
   for (i =0; i <= theNumber.length -1; i++) {
      if (GoodChars.indexOf(theNumber.charAt(i)) == -1) {
         alert(theNumber.charAt(i) + " is an invalid character.")
         form.Telephone.focus();
         valid = false
      }
   }
   return valid
}
```

The data entered in the Telephone form field is checked before being submitted to your server by calling the `ValidateFormData` function in the `onSubmit` method of the form, as follows:

```
<FORM ACTION="scripts/process.asp" METHOD="POST" onSubmit="return
ValidateFormData(this);">
```

This function not only checks that data has been entered, but also that it is the correct type of data. The following filter, written in JavaScript, demonstrates how to remove special characters and can be used in a similar way as the first script:

```
function RemoveBadChars(strTemp) {
    strTemp = strTemp.replace(/\<|\>|\"|\'|\%|\;|\(|\)|\&|\+|\-/g,"");
    return strTemp;
}
```

Another way to help control user input is to place data-length limits on your form input fields by adding the `MAXLENGTH` attribute into your text input tags. For example, if you're expecting an eight-character reference number in a particular field, you should restrict the user to an eight-character input with

```
<input type="text" name="ordernumber" MAXLENGTH="8">
```

The advantage is that it makes it more difficult for an attacker to include rogue code. The `<applet></applet>` or `<script></script>` tags alone take 17 characters.

Client-side checking of user input also prevents the needless processing of form data due to a genuine mistake by a user. Client-side validation is not as sophisticated as server-side validation, though; and for scenarios in which you are receiving `<TEXT>` input from an HTML form, you may not know what type of data is to be entered, and some normally filtered characters may be acceptable.

If your script has to process data from a database or another resource, you cannot automatically assume that it is valid data. If you have control over how data is entered into the database, you must implement validity checks at the point of data entry. This is part of good database design.

ASP.NET Validation Controls   Because validation of user input is so important from a security standpoint, ASP.NET, Microsoft's latest version of ASP for the .NET platform, provides validation server controls that validate user input and display an error message whenever invalid data is encountered in a validation control. The validation controls always perform validation checking in server code. However, if the user is working with a browser that supports DHTML, the validation controls also perform validation at the client.

The following snippet of code in an ASP.NET Web application ensures that the user enters a correctly formatted e-mail address by using a `RegularExpressionValidator` control. When the user submits the form, the contents of the e-mail field are tested against the regular expression; and if no match to the expression is made, the user receives an error message.

```
E-mail Address:
<BR>
<input id=txtEmail type=text size=35 MAXLENGTH=35 runat=server/>

<asp:RegularExpressionValidator ID=valEmailAddress
ControlToValidate=txtEmail ValidationExpression=".*@.*\..*"
ErrorMessage="The email address you entered is invalid."
Display=None EnableClientScript=true Runat=server/>
```

If the user submits an e-mail address that does not conform to the correct format, the ErrorMessage content is displayed. ASP.NET introduces a variety of such security-related controls; and if you port your Web site to ASP.NET, you should ensure that all your developers understand how to incorporate these additional safety features into their code.

Server-Side Validation

When data is passed to your script, it must validate and clean the data before processing it. This will ensure that any erroneous data is removed and the code can run correctly. Server-side validation is important because some data might be passed within the URL itself, which can't be validated client-side. Also, more powerful algorithms can be used to check the data. If you are using VBScript as your scripting language, since the release of version 5.0, you can use its regular expression capabilities to filter and clean incoming data. By creating patterns to match specific strings, you can search and replace user input to ensure that it's nonmalicious. The VBScript pattern syntax derives its pattern set from Perl.

The following example code will remove any characters that are not 0–9, a–z, A–Z, or a space from the string `strTatinted`:

```
<%
Set reg = New RegExp
reg.Pattern = "\W+"
strUnTainted = reg.Replace(strTainted, "")
%>
```

TIP For further help on how to write common regular expression patterns using VBScript, see http://msdn.microsoft.com/workshop/languages/clinic/scripting051099.asp, while there's further general information about Windows scripting at http://msdn.microsoft.com/scripting/.

SECURITY ALERT If your script requests data from a database, it will probably do so using a query or stored procedure. Ensure that the total amount of data passed to the stored procedure does not exceed the database's allowed maximum. Even though your data has been checked and cleaned, this could still crash the database server. All submitted queries should be checked to ensure that the maximum size is not exceeded. Keep up to date on security alerts for your database.

All data passed to your database must be filtered. A malicious user can pass in SQL wildcard characters (% and _), which are permitted in certain SQL expressions and retrieve all the records from the SQL table. Filter these wildcard characters from any user input destined for a database query.

HTML Encoding

IIS sends an HTML document to a browser as a stream of bytes, and the browser interprets them as a sequence of characters. So that a browser knows how to display this stream of characters correctly, all your HTML and active content pages should include explicit information about the document's character encoding. If your pages do not specify which character set they are using, a browser may incorrectly format your pages, possibly allowing malicious code to be run from the page. Since character sets have more than one representation for special characters that are used as HTML tags, such as < or >, your filter may not remove all the representations of the character you're expecting it to exclude, possibly leaving malicious code intact.

When you filter user input, specify a character set for your Web pages to ensure that your filter is checking for the appropriate special characters. The recommended approach to filtering dynamic page content is to set character encoding for every page and to allow only characters that are known to be safe, rather than excluding those that might be unsafe. As browsers and scripting languages are continually developing, you can never be sure that you've covered every character combination that may expose a vulnerability.

To set character encoding on a Web page, you need to include the following META tag, which should appear as soon as possible in the page, preferably immediately after the <HEAD> tag. This example forces the page to use the ISO-8859-1 character-set encoding:

```
<html>
<head>
<META http-equiv="Content-Type" content="text/html; CHARSET=ISO-8859-1">
<title>Safer HTML</title>
</head>
```

Commonly used character encodings on the Web include ISO-8859-1, also referred to as Latin-1, which is suitable for most Western European languages; and ISO-8859-5, which supports Cyrillic, SHIFT_JIS, or EUC-JP, which are both Japanese encoding. Many HTML editors automatically set this tag, so don't delete it thinking it's yet another unwanted insertion by your editor. You must take into account localization issues when you change these parameters.

Encoding Output for Special Characters

Any input data should be encoded when it is written out as HTML. This technique is particularly effective for data that cannot easily be validated during input. Consider, for example, a database in which you do not have control over the input process. A disgruntled member of the organization's staff could add malicious code into a database field, knowing that it will be displayed when called from a script. Most scripting languages include an encoding function, such as the ASP server object's HTMLEncode and URLEncode methods. Your Web developers should be aware of this form of server-side encoding and incorporate it where appropriate. This technique is similar to filtering input, except that you encode characters that are written out to the client. Further information about handling input data can be found on the CERT Web site at www.cert.org/tech_tips/malicious_code_mitigation.html.

Nine-Point Developer Security Checklist

Ensure that your Web developers follow these nine rules when creating dynamic content for your IIS server:

1. Specify a character set at the start of each page.
2. Filter and encode all form data.

Developers should read the CERT advisory on Malicious HTML tags at www.cert.org/advisories/CA-2000-02.html, and then review the following Microsoft Knowledge Base articles:

- **Q252985**   HOWTO: Prevent Cross-Site Scripting Security Issues
- **Q253119**   HOWTO: Review ASP Code for CSSI Vulnerability

3.   Filter and encode all cookie data.

Values read from cookies should be treated as untrusted input data and filtered and encoded as in step 2. Never store sensitive data in persistent cookies.

4.   Use SSL for sending and receiving any sensitive data.

Passwords, credit card details, and any personally identifiable information should be transmitted only over an SSL connection.

5.   Disable IE's Autocomplete feature for password fields.

Add the AUTOCOMPLETE=OFF attribute to either the <FORM> or <INPUT> tag of any forms that are used for requesting passwords. For example, <INPUT TYPE=password NAME=Password SIZE=16 MAXLENGTH= 16 AUTOCOMPLETE=OFF>

6.   Disconnect sessions when inactive for 5 minutes.

By default, the Connection Timeout value for IIS is set to 900 seconds. Change this value to 300 seconds using the Internet Services Manager. Alternatively, if users have logged onto your site, add the following code to the top of each page:

```
<SCRIPT Language="JavaScript">
<!--
window.setTimeout("window.navigate('Logoff.asp')", 300000);
//--></SCRIPT>
```

Users will be sent to the Logoff.asp page after 5 minutes if they just sit on a page.

7.   Remove all comments from code.

Good developers will always provide well-commented code, but these comments should be removed on pages that are loaded on the production server because they can provide possible clues to an attacker in the event of a security breach.

8.   Use a COM+ component to store database connection information.

Many developers store database connection information in the global.asa file. This information contains the server name, database name, database login, and password, so it must be protected. See the section "Parsing the

COM+ Constructor String" at http://msdn.microsoft.com/library/
default.asp?url=/library/en-us/dnduwon/html/d5bizdev.asp for
further information on how to use a COM+ component to do this.

9. Use stored procedures to access a database.

    Stored procedures provide better access control over data and
    a performance advantage over SQL statements.

ISAPI FILTERS

ISAPI filters are different from applications in that they are driven by Web server events
rather than by a client request. An ISAPI filter hooks into the IIS system and monitors
certain events that occur while the client tries to read a page from your server. The filter
application sits between the network connection to the client and the HTTP server, allowing
you to control the data exchange between IIS and the client, and augmenting the server's
functionality by creating custom features, such as advanced HTTP logging or encryption.
The ISAPI filters are based on notifications of different stages that each request has to pass,
which IIS sends to an ISAPI filter. Each notification handles a different type of data, which
is relevant to the particular stage of the request process. When the ISAPI filter receives a
notification from IIS, the filter can manipulate the notification's data and how IIS continues
to process the request. The URLScan tool covered in the upcoming sidebar "URLScan
Security Tool" is an example of how ISAPI filters can be used to improve IIS security.

 SECURITY ALERT   If you contract outside developers to help with building your intranet or Web site,
or you use off-the-shelf ISAPI DLLs on your server, refer to the sidebar, "Validating Third-Party Programs,"
in Chapter 9.

URLScan Security Tool

URLScan is a security tool that works in conjunction with the IIS Lockdown Tool,
which we covered in Chapter 3, and gives you the ability to turn off unneeded
features and restrict the kind of HTTP requests that IIS will process. As an ISAPI
filter, URLScan is able to screen all incoming requests to the server and filter them
based on rules set by you. By filtering out all unusual requests, it prevents potentially
harmful requests from reaching IIS, ensuring that only valid requests are processed.
How URLScan is configured, and which HTTP verbs you may need to allow for
particular applications, is explained in depth at www.microsoft.com/technet/
security/URLScan.asp.

Configuring ISAPI Filters

The ISAPI Filters Properties sheet enables you to select which filters are installed on IIS, as shown in Figure 11-8. These ISAPI filters will be active for all Web sites as they are set at the master level, and they will be executed in the order listed in the dialog box. You can install global filters for all sites on a server or just for individual Web sites. When several filters have registered for the same event, they are called sequentially, with filters with a higher priority running before filters with a lower priority. To add a filter to a Web server or Web site, select the Web server or Web site in ISM, open its Properties sheet, and click the ISAPI Filters tab.

TIP   If you are adding filters to a Web site, you will see only the filters installed for that Web site in the Properties sheet, even though global filters inherited from the Web server's master may exist.

Click the Add button, and type in the name of the filter in the Filter Name box. Browse for the ISAPI DLL file in the Executable box, and then click OK. To change the load order of a filter, use the arrow buttons. If you add or change a global filter, you

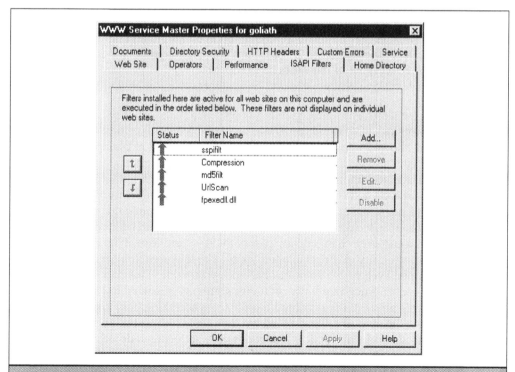

Figure 11-8.   These ISAPI filters are run on all Web sites hosted by this server.

must stop and restart the Web server to load the new filters into memory. A filter added at the Web-site level is automatically loaded when you add it.

Protecting Proprietary Code with an ISAPI Filter

Most JavaScripts are embedded in a Web page or included in a JavaScript (.js) file, and the code is visible to anyone who views the file's source code. This is generally not a problem, but what if you have developed various JavaScripts that you do not want to be viewed by all and sundry? This is where an ISAPI filter could be used.

By monitoring the OnUrlMap notification, an ISAPI filter can ensure that only IIS can read your server-side JavaScript file. When IIS maps the file's logical path to the physical path, it will fire the OnURLMap notification, allowing the ISAPI filter to check who is attempting to read the JavaScript file. If anyone tries to access the file directly, the filter can block the request, whereas a request to view an HTML page linked to the JavaScript file will display as usual because the request to read the file will be made by IIS. An example of how to write this type of filter is available at http://www.15seconds.com/issue/010104.htm. This method can also be used to ensure that only IIS can access files that contain system passwords needed to access other resources, such as databases. Hard-coding system passwords into general scripts should be avoided.

SECURITY ALERT   Never embed system passwords in a script. Any developer can see these passwords, and a compromise of your site could expose them.

Script Encoder

One of the shortcomings of using scripts is that any proprietary algorithms and code are visible to anyone allowed to edit the file because they are stored as plaintext. This lack of protection of your intellectual property is of particular concern if you provide Web development services for others or use third parties to help maintain your site, since they have access to your code and can copy it. Script Encoder is a simple command-line tool that can be downloaded free at http://msdn.microsoft.com/scripting/. It enables you to encode your server-side scripts so that the source cannot be viewed or modified.

After a script is encoded, changing any part of the resulting file will leave it inoperable, thus ensuring the integrity of your encoded script. This ensures that clients for whom you have developed Web pages do not tinker with your code. This makes solving error problems a lot easier, since you know whether someone has tried to change any of your code. It won't prevent a determined hacker from accessing your code, but it will certainly frustrate the majority. Once you have debugged and tested your script, use this utility to encode your final script. It encodes only scripting code, leaving the rest of the file content to appear as plaintext. Script Encoder uses markers within your source code to identify where encoding should begin.

The following example in VBScript illustrates how the encoding marker is used to encode all of your code apart from the copyright message:

```
<SCRIPT LANGUAGE="VBScript">
'Copyright© 2002. Your Company. All rights reserved.
'**Start Encode**
   Your proprietary code goes here
</SCRIPT>
```

When the Script Encoder is invoked, anything in the script block before the start marker is left unencoded, while everything else in the script block is encoded. After the encoding takes place, the language designator in the <SCRIPT> tag changes to

```
<SCRIPT LANGUAGE="VBScript.Encode">
```

ADDITIONAL METHODS FOR SECURING ACCESS TO WEB CONTENT

Some of your dynamic Web content may be sensitive or should be accessible only to users who have registered to use a service you provide. You can control access to these pages by setting up access control lists (ACLs) and Windows accounts for every user who is allowed access to them, but this is not practical on sites such as e-commerce sites, where you hopefully will have thousands of users. By using scripts, you can easily control access to pages without having to create Windows user accounts.

Securing Pages Using ASP

This type of access control is easily implemented using ASP. The following code shows how to create a logon page to authenticate registered customers to your site, who will then be able to access a special offers page. Anyone who hasn't successfully logged on will be redirected to a different page.

First, create a form to collect the customer's user name and password to check that they exist in your customer database:

```
<HTML>
<HEAD>
<TITLE>Customer Log On</TITLE>
</HEAD>
<BODY>

<FORM METHOD="POST" ACTION="../scripts/logon.asp">
   <TABLE WIDTH="100%">
     <TR>
       <TD>User name:</TD>
       <TD><INPUT TYPE="text" NAME="Username" SIZE="30" MAXLENGTH="30"></TD>
     </TR>
     <TR>
       <TD>Password:</TD>
```

```
      <TD><INPUT TYPE="password" NAME="Password" size="16" MAXLENGTH ="16"></TD>
   <TR>
      <TD COLSPAN="2" align="CENTER"><INPUT TYPE ="submit" VALUE="Log On"></TD>
   </TR>
</TABLE>
</FORM>

</BODY>
</HTML>
```

The form input is sent to the logon.asp page in the scripts folder using the POST action. If the content to be accessed is particularly sensitive, such as account and credit card details, the logon information and any sensitive content, such as passwords, should be sent over an SSL connection. The logon.asp script checks the user name and password against a database of valid users. If a match is found, the logon.asp script sets a session variable and transfers the customer to the special offers page. If a match is not found, the user hasn't yet registered and is sent to the registration page.

```
If NoMatch = TRUE Then
   Session("Authorized") = FALSE
   strURL = "registrationpage.asp"
Else
   Session("Authorized") = TRUE
   strURL = "specialoffers.asp"
End If
Server.Transfer strURL
```

Now we have a session variable that we can use to check whether a user has successfully logged onto the site. By performing this check at the start of each page to which you need to control access, you can ensure that only logged on users can access them.

```
<%@ LANGUAGE="VBSCRIPT" %>
<% Option Explicit %>
<%
If Session("Authorized") = FALSE Then
   Response.Redirect "accessdenied.asp"
End If
%>
```

Anyone who tries to access a page with this script at the top that has not successfully logged on will be redirected to the accessdenied.asp page. This page can explain that the person is not authorized to view the page requested and can invite the person to register.

SECURITY ALERT   Always use the POST method for a form when sending sensitive information. The GET method will display the form's data in the URL, which is visible to everyone.

The Encrypting File System

The Encrypting File System (EFS) provides the core file encryption technology used by the Windows 2000 file system and enables you to encrypt files and folders on NTFS volumes. EFS is enabled for documents in Windows 2000 through an advanced file attribute. To encrypt the contents of a folder, navigate to the folder in Windows Explorer, right-click the folder, and click Properties to open the Properties sheet, as shown in Figure 11-9.

Click the Advanced button and select the Encrypt Contents To Secure Data option, as shown in Figure 11-10. Finally, click OK to return to Windows Explorer.

After you encrypt a folder, you can work with it and the files it contains just as you do with any other files and folders because the encryption process is transparent to the user who encrypted the folder. However, any intruder who tries to open, copy, move, or rename your encrypted files will receive an access denied message.

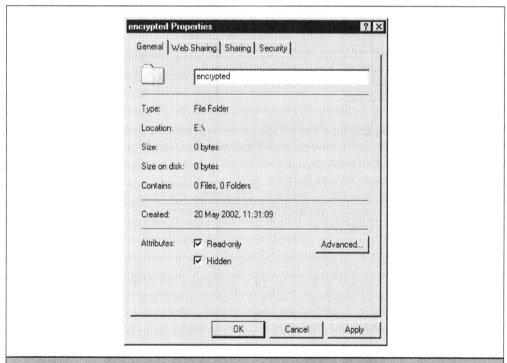

Figure 11-9.   You can encrypt a folder's contents using the Properties sheet.

Figure 11-10. The Advanced Attributes dialog box allows you to encrypt a file or folder.

CAUTION EFS will fail encryption attempts on files with the `System` attribute. You should not attempt to defeat this safeguard to encrypt files in the system directory. The private keys needed for decryption are not available during the boot process. Therefore, a system will be rendered unusable if its system files are encrypted.

So, how can you use EFS on a Web site to protect sensitive content? The most common use is on a company intranet where each user has his or her own Web folder for publishing documents. By creating an encrypted subfolder, each user can access private documents over the intranet, but other users will not be able to access them even if anonymous authentication is enabled for the entire site. This is because files that are encrypted with EFS are private files, and only the user that encrypted the files can access them. The authentication method used can be Windows Integrated or Digest, depending on how the Web site is configured.

SECURITY ALERT If you use EFS, you should encrypt folders rather than individual files, as applications can create temporary files in the same folder as the original file, particularly during editing. By encrypting at the folder level, you ensure that these temporary files are not saved as plaintext. You should also encrypt the Temp folder, usually found at %SystemRoot%\TEMP, for the same reason.

DEBUGGING ACTIVE CONTENT

When searching the Internet, you may have come across links to pages returned by Web search engines that produce a runtime scripting error. The cause of the error is explained in some detail, often revealing system information that the script uses, such as details of business logic or the location of a database. This is the result of a scripted page that has not been properly tested before being published on the Internet. If scripts that generate errors are published on the Internet before being fully debugged, the major search engines will index them.

For example, if you search in the altavista search engine at www.altavista.com for "Microsoft VBScript runtime error + .inc," you will get hundreds of results, many of which will reveal the full path and file name for an include file (.inc). If you append this to the host name and call up the page in a Web browser, you can often see the unparsed content of the include file.

This leaking of system information will help a hacker enormously in planning an attack on your server. We've already highlighted the importance of mapping include files to ASP, but you should also ensure that your Web site developers thoroughly debug any scripted pages offline, before publishing them on the production server. You should also run a Web search for your own pages to determine whether any of them have been incorrectly indexed, and then remove or rename them if they have been.

Error Trapping

Most Web developers are under time pressure to develop content and usually prioritize look, feel, and functionality ahead of security. This approach needs to be changed, however, as discussed in Chapter 9. Development and testing must be accomplished offline so the security implications of new scripts can be fully assessed, since it is only when the scripts are run in context that *semantic* coding errors manifest themselves.

Syntax errors are easily found, because the program compiler or interpreter stops running the code and indicates the line in which the syntax is incorrect. A poorly trained developer will correct his or her syntax errors and then upload the new code, happy in the fact that the compiler or interpreter parsed and accepted this latest work. However, semantic, or runtime, errors can still occur when the code is executed, which can result in the source code being revealed to anyone running the script. For example, a semantic error would occur if someone tries to add a sixth item to an online shopping basket when the code has been written to accommodate a maximum of five items. Although the code is syntactically correct, a semantic error would occur if the attempted addition of a sixth item cannot be handled by the code.

It is important that developers code defensively. Examples of defensive coding include checking that a file exists before trying to open it and ensuring that input values are of the correct type. Code should be tested with a range of values that include expected values, boundary condition values, and out-of-bounds values. These pre-release checks will help prevent most errors caused by user input.

Since there is no such thing as perfect code, it is important that your active content can handle unexpected errors when they occur and alert you to the fact that an error has occurred. By default, the 500-100.asp file processes any errors that occur during compilation or running of .asp files. When an ASP error occurs, IIS returns the 500-100.asp file with information about the error, such as the line number in which the error occurred and a description of the error.

The following VBScript code will write any asp errors that occur to a log file while displaying a message to the user. This ensures that no source code from the page that caused the error is displayed. It can be modified to send the error information by e-mail to your Webmaster.

```
<% @ LANGUAGE="VBSCRIPT" %>
<% Option Explicit %>
<%
' Stop any further errors from halting execution of this page
On Error Resume Next

Dim objASPError                         ' Error Object
Dim strErrNumber, strASPCode
Dim strErrDes, strASPDes
Dim strCategory, strFileName
Dim strLineNumber, strColNumber
Dim strSourceCode, strErrorMsg
Dim strErrorLog, strReferrer            ' Strings
Dim lngColNum                           ' Long
Dim objFSO                              ' File Object
Dim objTStream

Dim blnLogFail                          ' Boolean

' Set a reference to the ASPError object
Set objASPError = Server.GetLastError()

' Store the ASPError object's property values
strErrNumber = CStr(objASPError.Number)      ' Normal error code
strASPCode = objASPError.ASPCode             ' ASP error code
If Len(strASPCode) Then
    strASPCode = "'" & strASPCode & "' "
Else
    strASPCode = ""
End If
strErrDes = objASPError.Description
strAspDes = objASPError.ASPDescription
strCategory = objASPError.Category           ' Type of error
strFileName = objASPError.File               ' File causing error
strLineNumber = objASPError.Line             ' Line number in file
strColNumber = objASPError.Column            ' Column number in line
If IsNumeric(strColNumber) Then              ' Convert it to an integer
```

```
    lngColNumber = CLng(strColNumber)
Else
    lngColNumber = 0
End If
strSourceCode = objASPError.Source          ' Source code of error line

' Create an error message
strErrorMsg = "ASP Error " & strASPCode & "occurred on " & Now
If Len(strCategory) Then
    strErrorMsg = strErrorMsg & " in " & strCategory
End If
strErrorMsg = strErrorMsg & vbCrlf & "Error number: " & strErrNumber _
 & " (0x" & Hex(strErrNumber) & ")" & vbCrlf
If Len(strFileName) Then
    strErrorMsg = strErrorMsg & "File: " & strFileName
    If strLineNumber > "0" Then
        strErrorMsg = strErrorMsg & ", Line " & strLineNumber
        If lngColNumber > 0 Then
            strErrorMsg = strErrorMsg & ", Column " & lngColNumber
            If Len(strSourceCode) Then
                strErrorMsg = strErrorMsg & vbCrlf & strSourceCode & vbCrlf _
                & String(lngColNumber - 1, "-") & "^"
            End If
        End If
    End If
    strErrorMsg = strErrorMsg & vbCrlf
End If
strErrorMsg = strErrorMsg & strErrDes & vbCrlf
If Len(strAspDes) Then
    strErrorMsg = strErrorMsg & "ASP reports: " & strAspDes & vbCrlf
End If


' Log the error to a log file.
' Edit the log file path to suit your own system.
' You will need to give the IUSR_machinename account permission to
' write and modify this file.
strErrorLog = "D:\temp\custom_error.log"
Set objFSO = Server.CreateObject("Scripting.FileSystemObject")
Set objTStream = objFSO.OpenTextFile(strErrorLog, 8, True)  '8 = ForAppending
If Err.Number = 0 Then
    objTStream.WriteLine strErrorMsg & vbCrlf
End If
If Err.Number = 0 Then
    objTStream.Close
    blnLogFail = False
Else
    blnLogFail = True
End If
' Output a message to the browser.
```

```
%>
<meta http-equiv="Content-Type" content="text/html; charset=ISO-8859-1">
<HTML>
<HEAD>
<TITLE>Error</TITLE>
</HEAD>
<BODY>
<P>Sorry, there is a problem with the page you requested, and it cannot be
displayed.</P>
<%
' Add links to return to the previous or home page
strReferrer = Request.ServerVariables("HTTP_REFERER")
If Len(strReferrer) Then
    Response.Write "<P><A HREF=""javascript:history.go(-1)"">Return to the
previous page</A></P>"
End If
Response.Write "<P>Return to the <A HREF=""http://www.yourdomain.com"">Home
page</A></P>"
%>
</P>
<P>Please contact
<A HREF="mailto:webmaster@yourdomain.com">Webmaster</A> about this problem</P>
</BODY>
</HTML>
```

Custom errors can be set at the master, Web, and directory levels by changing the properties of the HTTP error messages that are sent to clients when errors occur.

To configure IIS to use your own custom error page, such as the one in the preceding listing, open the Internet Services Manager, and right-click the server or Web site that you want to configure. Then select Properties. Select the Custom Errors tab and scroll down the list of custom error messages to HTTP Error 500;100, as shown in Figure 11-11.

Click the Edit Properties button to change the Error Mapping Properties to point to your customized error page, as shown in Figure 11-12.

TIP Make sure your error-processing file does not contain syntax or runtime errors; otherwise, these errors will be displayed in the browser. Line 5 of the preceding example code

```
On Error Resume Next
```

ensures that our file will execute without causing an error.

ASP Errors and the Windows Event Log

ASP errors can be sent to the Windows event log by configuring the Process Options Properties sheet. To set these options, open the WWW Service Master Properties sheet for your server by right-clicking the server object in Internet Services Manager. Select the Home Directory tab, and then click the Configuration button, which opens the

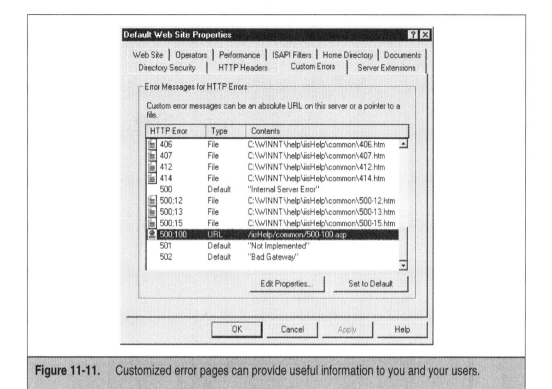

Figure 11-11. Customized error pages can provide useful information to you and your users.

Application Configuration Properties sheet. Select the Process Options tab, as shown in Figure 11-13.

Selecting the Write Unsuccessful Client Requests To Event Log option sends the most serious ASP errors to the Windows event log. The Enable Debug Exception Catching

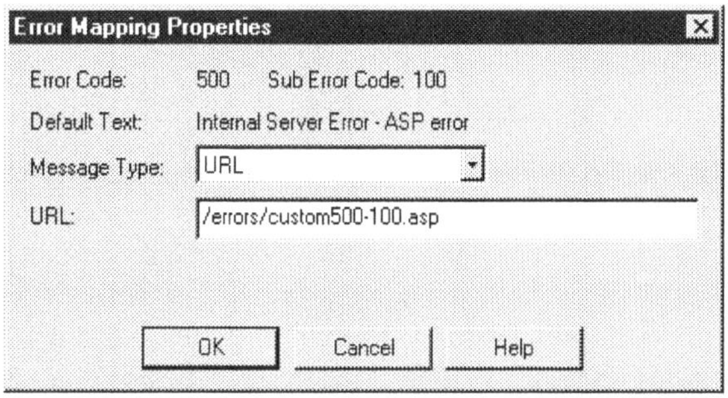

Figure 11-12. If the output type is a URL, it must exist on the local server.

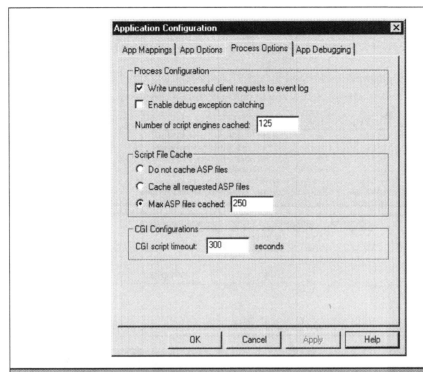

Figure 11-13. Although other application configuration settings can be made at the Web site and virtual-directory level, process options can be set only at the master level.

option should be selected only when you are debugging a component as it logs any specific error messages from the component. As debugging should be performed only on a development server, ensure that this option is not selected.

CHALLENGE

Sam, a young developer working on your new e-commerce site, has been writing the ASPs that connect the Web site to your Microsoft SQL Server database that will hold all your customer details, such as names, addresses, orders, and so on. On Monday morning, he announces that he is leaving the company immediately to pursue a different career. As the deadline for the launch of the site is fast approaching, you assign his work to another staff member. You've been happy with the work Sam has been doing, but you need to check that his work in progress is OK to use.

CHALLENGE (continued)

Your first priority should be to prevent Sam from having access to the ASP files and the rest of the company network. The network administrator should be informed so that Sam's Windows account can be disabled. This will prevent him from being able to log onto the network. In addition, ask the administrator to ensure that all members of the development team have to change their passwords the next time they log on. This is a precautionary step in case Sam knows the passwords of the other developers.

Since he has had access to the SQL Server database, Sam will know the user name and password being used by the ASP pages to open a connection. He may also have his own SQL Server account with elevated privileges to allow development work. Inform the database administrator so that Sam's database account can be disabled and the password is changed for the account used by the ASP pages. Any other system passwords that Sam may have knowledge of will need to be changed as well.

Your next task is to review all of Sam's work. Even though his code is well commented, you need to review each line of it, checking for the following:

- Each page sets the character set at the start of the page.
- All input data received from forms or cookies are filtered for illegal characters.
- All data received from the database that is to be displayed on a Web page is encoded.
- No malicious code is embedded within his code, such as an unnecessary call to the mail server.
- No system passwords have been used in the code, but are instead accessed using a COM+ component.
- All calls to the database are made using stored procedures.

After his code has passed these checks, test it on your development server for any syntax or semantic errors. Testing should involve passing data to the scripts—not just of the correct type, but also with values that exceed the expected values, such as incorrect dates and values that match boundary conditions. An example would be checking how the code handles an order for exactly $500 if the maximum order value allowed is $500.

Although Sam may have had no malicious intentions at all, these checks are necessary because he has had extensive access to your network and its resources.

CODE SIGNING

You may want to add ActiveX or Java applets to your site to add functionality, such as drop-down menus or scrolling text. Since the possible security threats posed by malicious applets are well known among Internet users, once you have developed and tested these applets, how can you let visitors to your site know that the site can be trusted and is safe to use? Many firewalls are configured not to let untrusted applets through, and security policies may state that untrusted third-party applets cannot be installed or run on network machines. The easiest way of assuring clients that an applet or macro has been written safely by you and has not been tampered with is to sign it with a code-signing digital certificate.

A certificate identifies your organization and is issued by a certificate authority only after that authority has verified your organization's identity. VeriSign is an example of a certificate authority. Code-signing certificates (called digital IDs by VeriSign) will enable your developers to digitally sign software and macros for secure delivery over the Internet. Anyone who downloads your digitally signed ActiveX controls, Java applets, dynamic-link libraries, and cab (cabinet file) and JAR (Java Archive) files from your site can be confident that the code really comes from you and hasn't been altered or corrupted since it was created and signed. Code signing acts as a virtual "shrink wrap" for your software because, if the software is tampered with in any way, the digital signature will break in a way similar to the shrink wrap on prepackaged products if they have been tampered with, alerting the user to the fact that something is wrong.

Unfortunately, you need to use different code-signing certificates to sign code from the two main proponents of mobile code—Microsoft and Netscape. Microsoft's Authenticode technology enables you to digitally sign .exe, .cab, .dll, and .ocx files; Netscape's Object Signing tools enable you to digitally sign Java applets, JavaScript scripts, plug-ins, or any JAR files. Authenticode certificates only work for Microsoft Internet Explorer browsers, and Object Signing certificates work only for Netscape browsers. You will also need additional certificates to sign macros for Office 2000/XP and VBA objects and for content created with Macromedia Director Shockwave Studio or Macromedia Flash.

Multipurpose code-signing certificates can be obtained from Certificate Authorities such as Thawte at http://www.thawte.com. These can be used by more than one code-signing application, so you do not have to buy a certificate for each application you want to sign.

FRONTPAGE SERVER EXTENSIONS

FrontPage Server Extensions (FPSE) is a set of programs that can be installed on an IIS server to support authoring and administering FrontPage-extended Webs, allowing remote users to perform certain authoring tasks directly on the server. The phrase "directly on the server" is the reason we advised not to install FPSE on a production server in Chapter 3, and that advice still stands because FPSE has been the subject of attacks. However, you may want to take advantage of the administrative and authoring functionality FPSE provides on a development IIS Web server, or you may need to offer FPSE to clients if you are planning to offer Web-hosting services. If for some reason you need to install FPSE, read the following sections to understand the security implications and how to tighten FPSE security.

Managing FPSE

Always use the latest version of FPSE, currently version 2002, shown in an example server Properties sheet in Figure 11-14. The extensions can be downloaded at the FrontPage section of MSDN at http://msdn.microsoft.com/library/default.asp?url=/library/en-us/ dnservext/html/fpse02win.asp. The FrontPage Server Extensions Resource Kit is available at http://office.microsoft.com/Assistance/2000/FPserk.aspx, and it provides useful advice on managing FPSE.

After you have installed FPSE 2002 by running the install program, you can use either HTML Administration pages or a command line to administer your Web sites and server. FrontPage 2000 Server Extensions were administered using a Microsoft Management Console (MMC), but this is no longer the case. As the HTML forms allow administration by remote access, these forms should be removed. They are installed by default in the C:\Program Files\Common Files\Microsoft Shared\Web Server Extensions\50\ admisapi\1033 folder, along with the command-line tools used to administer FPSE.

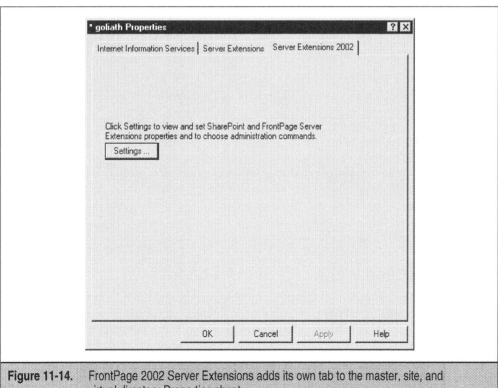

Figure 11-14.   FrontPage 2002 Server Extensions adds its own tab to the master, site, and virtual directory Properties sheet.

If you require remote administration, take the following precautions:

- Require an SSL connection.
- Grant access to fpadmdll.dll and the HTML forms only to trusted administrators.
- Require the use of a nonstandard HTTP port.
- Use IP address mask restrictions to prevent unauthorized computers from accessing the HTML Administration Forms.

Two command-line administration tools are also installed: owsadm.exe and owsrmadm.exe. Owsrmadm.exe allows administration from a remote computer and should be removed if remote administration is not required. The command-line tools have slightly more functionality than the HTML Administration pages. You can use the command-line tools to perform the following tasks:

- Manage users and roles.
- Detect potential problems with the server extensions installation and repair it.
- Add, delete, or merge subwebs.
- Recalculate a Web site to generate up-to-date reports on Web content.
- Upgrade to the new version of the server extensions.
- Uninstall the server extensions for a particular Web site.
- Set properties for a subweb, root Web, or all Web sites on a server.

Two useful commands are `Disable` and `DatabaseConnection`. Use `Disable` to disable authoring and administering from the FrontPage client after any changes have been made, and re-enable them only when making further changes to content is required. The `DatabaseConnection` command verifies database connection information and also encrypts the account name and password before storing it. Further help on command-line administration can be found in the Administrator's Guide at http://www.microsoft.com/technet/treeview/default.asp?url=/technet/prodtechno/sharepnt/proddocs/admindoc/ows000.asp.

FrontPage-Extended Webs

A FrontPage-extended Web contains all the Web pages, graphics, and other files and documents that make up a Web site. Users can be assigned roles to manage or update a FrontPage-extended Web. Previously, user roles for FPSE were managed from within the FrontPage client, using the Security option on the Tools menu. With 2002 Extensions, you can manage roles with either the command-line administration tool or HTML Administration pages. The following roles are included by default:

- **Browser** Rights to view pages, view Web document discussions, and read lists
- **Author** Browser rights, plus rights to edit pages and directories and edit lists

- **Advanced Author**   Author rights, plus rights to define and apply themes and borders, link style sheets, and recalculate a Web site
- **Administrator**   All rights from other roles, plus rights to configure roles, create local machine user accounts, manage source control, create subwebs, manage Web document discussions and subscriptions, manage server health, and manage usage analysis.

The FPSE DLLs

FrontPage can take full advantage of FPSE. When an author or administrator performs an operation using FrontPage, it communicates with the server extensions using a Remote Procedure Call (RPC) protocol that is layered on top of HTTP and HTML. A POST request is sent from the FrontPage client to one of three FPSE's DLLs:

- Requests for administrative actions go to Admin.dll.
- Requests for authoring actions go to Author.dll.
- Requests for browsing actions go to Shtml.dll.

When a browser to a FrontPage-extended Web site requests a page that requires FPSE, such as submitting a search form, it sends a POST request to the browse-time FPSE program, Shtml.dll. When IIS receives a request for the FPSE, it first logs on and impersonates the user and then passes the request directly to Admin.dll, Author.dll, or Shtml.dll. The FPSE DLL then checks the permissions of the impersonated administrator, author, or site visitor against the ACL in the root folder of the FrontPage-extended Web or subweb. If the check is successful, the request is processed; otherwise, a "Permission Denied" message is sent to the FrontPage client or the Web browser.

Permissions

Permissions on a FrontPage-extended Web's content initially apply to the entire FrontPage-extended Web, so all Web authors have access to all the Web's pages and visitors can browse to all pages. Divide content on your server so that different groups of users have permissions to administer, author, or browse to different areas of the content by dividing the content into subwebs.

 SECURITY ALERT   Do not enable account lockout on the Internet Guest account because it can lead to a Denial of Service (DoS) attack. Instead, you must rely on a strong password for the account as a means of preventing password cracking.

FrontPage grants full control to all files for members of the Windows Administrators group and the SYSTEM account. Execute permissions for site visitors, authors, and administrators are added to any folders that are marked with an executable virtual root. The Execute permission is allowed only if the Allow Authors To Upload

Executables check box is selected in the Properties dialog box for the FrontPage-extended Web.

The ACLs for a FrontPage-extended Web are listed in Table 11-1.

Web Folder or Content	ACL Setting on Folders or Content	Setting on New Content Created Within Folder
Top-level folder of root Web or subweb site	Visitors: read, execute Authors: read, execute, write, and delete Administrators: read, execute, write, delete, and change permissions	Site visitors: read Authors: read, write, and delete Administrators: read, write, delete, and change permissions
A folder of a Web below the top-level folder	Site visitors: read Authors: read, execute, write, and delete Administrators: read, execute, write, delete, and change permissions	Site visitors: read Authors: read, write, and delete Administrators: read, write, delete, and change permissions
Executable folder	Making a folder executable does not change the current ACL.	Making a folder executable adds execute permissions for site visitors, authors, and administrators to the current ACL.
Folder containing form results	If a folder contains discussion group or database form handler results, FrontPage adds write permissions for site visitors to the current ACL.	If a folder contains discussion group or database form handler results, FrontPage adds write permissions for site visitors to the current ACL.
FrontPage _vti_pvt folder	Site visitors: read, execute, write, delete Authors: read, execute, write, delete Administrators: read, execute, write, delete, change permissions	Site visitors: read, write, delete Authors: read, write, delete Administrators: read, write, delete, change permissions
FrontPage _vti_log folder	Site visitors: read, execute, write, delete Authors: read, execute, write, delete Administrators: read, execute, write, delete, change permissions	Site visitors: read, write, delete Authors: read, write, delete Administrators: read, write, delete, change permissions
FrontPage _vti_txt folder	Site visitors: read, execute, write, delete Authors: read, execute, write, delete Administrators: read, execute, write, delete, change permissions	Site visitors: read, write, delete Authors: read, write, delete Administrators: read, write, delete, change permissions
Content files	Site visitors: read Authors: read, write, delete Administrators: read, write, delete, change permissions	
Files in folder containing form results	Adds write permissions for site visitors to the current ACL	

Table 11-1. Permissions for the Content of a FrontPage-Extended Web on IIS

TIP   If you add a database such as Microsoft Access to a FrontPage-based Web, store it in the folder that FrontPage creates, _fpdb. FrontPage automatically marks this folder as not browsable, scriptable, or executable. Also ensure that you make use of the security mechanisms that are built into the database or database server to restrict who can update the database content. Generally, Web authors' accounts do not need privileges beyond SELECT. Web authors should not be allowed to update, insert, or delete records on a database. These tasks should be performed via the database front end.

Subwebs

FPSE allows the creation of separate subwebs. A subweb is a complete FrontPage-extended Web that can be created at any level of your content structure, including below another subweb. Although they appear as normal subdirectories when accessed via a Web browser, subwebs can have administrators and authors completely separate from the parent Web. If your site has distinct areas of content that are managed by different people and you do not want to allow authors access to all the site's content, you can use separate subwebs to segregate their duties and ensure they can author only their own pages. This enables a Web site's content structure to match the structure of your organization—for example, allowing different departments to maintain just their own areas within the site. As each subweb maintains its own security settings, finer security granularity can be achieved. For example, an author of a FrontPage-extended Web would not automatically have permission to edit any of its subwebs.

Because a virtual server has its own security settings and its own user list, creating a virtual server is also a way for an administrator to limit access to certain Web content. An additional benefit of virtual Webs and subwebs is potentially better performance, because the time required to recalculate hyperlinks is directly proportional to the number and size of the documents stored in a single Web.

TIP   When an administrator sets the ACLs for a FrontPage-extended Web using the FrontPage client's `Permissions` command, FrontPage displays the server's computer account list by default. You can set up a restricted list of users and groups for each FrontPage-extended Web. This prevents the full Windows account list being displayed. See the FPSE documentation for a full explanation of how to do this.

Removing FPSE

You can temporarily or permanently remove FrontPage 2002 Server Extensions from your IIS server. To remove the extensions temporarily, use the `uninstall` command. In this mode, the data about your site is preserved, so you can extend the virtual server again and return to your original configuration. To remove the extensions permanently, use the `fulluninstall` command, which removes all related files apart from the actual site content. Here's an example command:

```
owsadm.exe -o fulluninstall -p <port>
```

To temporarily uninstall FrontPage 2002 Server Extensions, you would type the following at a command prompt, replacing `<port>` with the port number of the specified virtual server:

```
owsadm.exe -o uninstall -p <port>
```

FPSE Configuration Variables

Sometimes feedback from command-line tools can be fairly minimal. To check or configure the values of server extension configuration variables, you can check them in the Registry or in the Service.cnf file. Variables are set at one of three levels:

- **Global variables**   Applied to all virtual servers and subwebs on the server computer, and are set in the Registry at HKEY_LOCAL_MACHINE\ SOFTWARE\Microsoft\Shared Tools\Web server Extensions\All Ports.

- **Virtual server variables**   Applied to a single virtual server and set in the Registry at HKEY_LOCAL_MACHINE\SOFTWARE\Microsoft\ Shared Tools\Web server Extensions\Ports\<Port instance number>.

- **Web and subweb variables**   Set by editing the text file _vti_pvt/ Service.cnf in the root Web or subweb.

If a particular variable has never been set, it may not have a Registry entry. Setting conflicts are resolved in order: subweb configuration variables have the highest priority, virtual server configuration variables have the second priority, and global configuration variables have the third priority. The most important variables are listed in the following sections.

One advantage of using FPSEs is that no file-sharing access on the Web server machine is needed, and neither FTP nor telnet access is required for users to be able to maintain their Web pages, since they execute via HTTP. However, you will need to monitor Microsoft security alerts carefully to stay abreast of any new vulnerabilities. FrontPage 2002 Server Extensions are a big improvement over earlier versions, but you must read the extensive online help to ensure that you understand how to manage them correctly.

AccessControl

Set AccessControl to 1; otherwise, whenever a subweb is created, any user can author it until the access control is manually set.

Default	Set Globally	Set per Virtual Server	Set per Subweb
1	Yes	Yes	No

AllowExecutableScripts

This variable should be set to 0 if you do not want to allow any files to be marked as executable.

Default	Set Globally	Set per Virtual Server	Set per Subweb
0	Yes	Yes	No

NoExecutableCGIUpload

When NoExecutableCgiUpload is set to a nonzero value, the FPSE will not set the execute bit on any CGI scripts that an author uploads to a Web using FrontPage. This allows the Webmaster to set the Execute permission manually after inspecting the script. If NoExecutableCgiUpload is set to 0 and AllowExecutableScripts is set to 0, authors will be able to upload and use ASP and IDC files, but not CGI or ISAPI files.

Default	Set Globally	Set per Virtual Server	Set per Subweb
1	Yes	Yes	No

ClientVerCutoff

Sets the earliest version of FrontPage client that can connect to the server.

Default	Set Globally	Set per Virtual Server	Set per Subweb
Any version	No	No	Yes

NoMarkScriptable

When NoMarkScriptable is set to a nonzero value, FrontPage users cannot modify the scriptable bit on any folders in a Web, ensuring that only your Webmaster can set the scriptable bit on folders.

Default	Set Globally	Set per Virtual Server	Set per Subweb
0	Yes	Yes	Yes

NoSaveResultsPipeTo

Earlier releases of FrontPage allow the default (Save Results) form handler to pipe form results to any arbitrarily chosen program. For backward compatibility, NoSaveResultsPipeTo disables this capability when it is set to a nonzero value.

Default	Set Globally	Set per Virtual Server	Set per Subweb
1	Yes	Yes	No

NoSaveResultsToAbsoluteFile

When NoSaveResultsToAbsoluteFile is set to 1, the default (Save Results), Registration, and Discussion form handlers cannot write to an absolute file path even if the browsing account has the NTFS rights to write to that path: the form handlers can write only to a file within the Web's content area.

Default	Set Globally	Set per Virtual Server	Set per Subweb
1	Yes	Yes	No

PrivateBrowsable

To prevent site visitors from browsing the _private directory, set PrivateBrowsable to 0. Once you have added this setting, it will apply to new Web pages you create. It does not affect Web pages that were created before making the setting.

Default	Set Globally	Set per Virtual Server	Set per Subweb
0	Yes	Yes	No

RequireSSL

When RequireSSL is set to 1, the server extensions require a Secure Sockets Layer (SSL) connection between the FrontPage client and the server.

Default	Set Globally	Set per Virtual Server	Set per Subweb
0	Yes	Yes	No

RestrictIISUsersAndGroups

If this option is set to a nonzero value for a given FrontPage-extended Web, the server extensions look for a predefined Windows group. RestrictIISUsersAndGroups cannot be set at the subweb level.

Default	Set Globally	Set per Virtual Server	Set per Subweb
0	Yes	Yes	No

ROBOTS AND SPIDERS

WWW *robots*, which are also called spiders, Web crawlers, or wanderers, are programs that automatically traverse the World Wide Web by recursively retrieving hyperlinked pages. A robot simply visits sites by requesting documents from them and creates a database of documents that can be used by a search engine to find documents relevant to a search. If your Web site is available to the public, you will want people to be able to find the content it contains by using a search engine. However, you may not want these robots to visit every page on your site, particularly areas that contain sensitive information, because they can attract the attention of hackers if they appear in results returned by a search engine. Most Web robots offer two mechanisms to limit what areas of a site they will visit—the Robots Exclusion Protocol and the Robots META tags, although some robots ignore both of these directives.

The Robots Exclusion Protocol

You can indicate which parts of your site a robot should not visit by providing a specially formatted file called robots.txt on your site. This file needs to be placed in the top level of your Web space, for example, at http://www.*yourdomain*.com/robots.txt. If a robot finds this document, it will analyze its contents, which specify a basic access policy for visiting robots. Unfortunately, everything not explicitly disallowed is considered accessible by a robot. Since only a single robots.txt file can exist on a site, there is no point in putting robots.txt files in different folders because robots will never read them. If your Web developers create their own robots.txt files, you will need to merge them all into a single file. If this isn't practical, you may want to use the Robots META tags instead (which are discussed in the next section).

The robots.txt file contains a record similar to this:

```
User-agent: *
Disallow: /scripts/
Disallow: /includes/
Disallow: /mike/
```

In this example, all robots can visit all parts of the site, but they are excluded from three subfolders: scripts, includes, and mike. Regular expressions are not supported in either the User-agent or Disallow lines, but the asterisk (*) in the User-agent field has a special value: it means "any robot." Therefore, you cannot include such lines as `Disallow: /tmp/*` or `Disallow: *.gif`. You need a separate Disallow line for every folder you want to exclude. Also, you cannot include blank lines in a record, since they are used to delimit multiple records.

Following are a few examples that show how you can exclude robots from all or part of your Web site.

To exclude all robots from the entire site:

```
User-agent: *
Disallow: /
```

To exclude all robots from certain folders on the site:

```
User-agent: *
Disallow: /scripts /
Disallow: /includes/
Disallow: /private/
```

To exclude a single robot:

```
User-agent: BadBot
Disallow: /
```

To allow a specific robot:

```
User-agent: WebCrawler
Disallow:
```

Since there is no "Allow" field, if you need to exclude all files except one, you must put all files to be disallowed into a separate subfolder—for example, *private*—and leave the one file in the level above this folder, like so:

```
User-agent: *
Disallow: /corporate/private/
```

Alternatively, you can explicitly disallow each page:

```
User-agent: *
Disallow: /corporate/private.html
Disallow: /corporate/sensitive.html
Disallow: /corporate/hr.html
```

You should ensure that your robots.txt file excludes all folders apart from those that you really want to be indexed and reachable via a Web search engine.

The Robot META Tags

If several Web developers or several different departments are all maintaining a different section of a Web site, trying to keep the robots.txt file up to date may be a difficult task. If this is a problem, you can use the special HTML Robot META tags to indicate whether a page may be indexed or analyzed for links by visiting robots—although not all robots currently implement Robot META tags. Microsoft Index Server does support the Robot META tags and will exclude Web pages that include them. Robot META tags are case insensitive and are placed in the <HEAD> section of an HTML page—the same as other META tags. Here's an example:

```
<HTML>
<HEAD>
<META NAME="robots" CONTENT="noindex,nofollow">
<META NAME="description" CONTENT="This paper is about ....">
<TITLE>Internal Security</TITLE >
</HEAD>
<BODY>
```

The content of a Robots META tag contains directives separated by commas. The currently defined directives are INDEX, NOINDEX, FOLLOW, and NOFOLLOW. The INDEX directive specifies whether an indexing robot should index the page. The FOLLOW directive specifies whether a robot is to follow links on the page to reach other pages. The defaults are INDEX and FOLLOW. The values ALL and NONE set the directives on or off: ALL=INDEX, FOLLOW and NONE=NOINDEX, NOFOLLOW.

To allow a robot to index and analyze a page for links, you would add the following META tag.

```
<META NAME="robots" CONTENT="index,follow">
```

or

```
<META NAME="robots" CONTENT="all=index,follow">
```

Other combinations are shown here:

```
<META NAME="robots" CONTENT="noindex,follow">
<META NAME="robots" CONTENT="index,nofollow">
<META NAME="robots" CONTENT="noindex,nofollow">
```

You obviously should not specify conflicting or repeating directives such as

```
<META NAME="robots" CONTENT="index,noindex,nofollow,follow">
```

TIP   You can find out more information about how robots work at http://www.robotstxt.org/.

CHECKLIST

- ☐ Create a folder structure to simplify managing Execute permissions on active content.
- ☐ Check that the minimum NTFS permissions are assigned to Web folders that allow the content to be viewed by specific accounts.
- ☐ Map active content to the program that will process it, including include files.
- ☐ Use source-control software to manage changes to active content and remove unnecessary editor-generated backups.
- ☐ Add copyright notices to your code.
- ☐ Validate user input before using it for processing or displaying.
- ☐ Encode all content that originates from third-party sources, such as databases and user input.
- ☐ Check that all code passes the nine-point checklist.
- ☐ Configure and use ISAPI filters on your site to protect proprietary code.
- ☐ Use Script Encoder to obscure script in Web pages
- ☐ Control access to sensitive content using ASP, HTTP 401, and even EFS.

☐ Thoroughly debug all scripts and executables before installing them on the production server.

☐ Add error trapping to all scripts so system information is not leaked via the browser but recorded in log files.

☐ Sign code for applets or macros that visitors will need when accessing your site.

☐ Do not use FrontPage Server Extensions unless you have to.

☐ Configure FPSE variables to tighten security from the default installation.

☐ Use the Robot Exclusion Protocol or Robot META tags to prevent sensitive content from being indexed by visiting robots.

CHAPTER 12

Web Privacy

When you are charged with protecting an IIS Web site, or any other information system, it is natural to think in terms of *you* versus *them*—where *them* is anyone who tries to compromise the confidentiality, integrity, or availability of *your* data. In fact, it is unlikely that all the data handled by your Web site actually belongs to you. The people who visit your site will generate or supply data, some of which can be said to belong to them and not you. This might be data that you actively request—for example, information needed to complete an online order form—but it could also be passive data, such as logs showing who visited the site and what pages they viewed. Some of the people to whom this data relates may consider it private information—that is, they may think that they have a right to determine how it is used and by whom. You may have a legal obligation, under applicable privacy laws, to allow people to review and make changes to data pertaining to them that your Web site collects, stores, or processes. While common sense says you should use reasonable security measures to protect the confidentiality of any information relating to individuals that your Web site handles, some privacy legislation makes such security mandatory.

This chapter reviews privacy principles and laws that may impact your IIS Web site and its security, and it provides practical advice on how best to handle this aspect of Web site management.

WHAT IS WEB PRIVACY?

The Electronic Privacy Information Center (EPIC, at http://www.epic.org/) defines *privacy* as the right of individuals to control the collection, use, and dissemination of personal information that is held by others. Web privacy is about ensuring that your Web site's handling of *personally identifiable information* (*PII*) complies with a wide range of applicable laws, industry standards, and business best practices. In short, if it is PII, you need to "Handle With Care." Failure to do so could result in problems ranging from angry customers and lost business to fines and imprisonment.

The potential for negative consequences from what is commonly referred to as a *privacy breach* is the first of two reasons why no book on Web site security would be complete without addressing Web privacy. The second reason is that the tools and techniques of security play a vital role in enabling your Web site to meet the privacy standards you establish for it.

TIP PII can be defined as information that can be traced back to an individual user, such as name, postal address, or e-mail address. According to the electronic privacy organization TRUSTe (http://www.truste.org/), "Personal user preferences tracked by a Web site via a 'cookie' are… considered personally identifiable information when linked to other personally identifiable information provided by you online." In its Data Protection Directive, discussed later in the section "The EU Data Protection Directive," the European Union highlights several other aspects of PII, including an identification number assigned to a person, or one or more factors specific to "physical, physiological, mental, economic, cultural or social identity."

Most societies have determined that the privacy of PII is important enough to merit legal protection. In some countries, that legal protection is broad and applies to almost all personal data in almost every situation. In other countries, notably the United States, the legal protection is piecemeal and applies only to certain information in certain circumstances (for example, there is a Federal law protecting the privacy of your video rental records, passed in 1988, very shortly after newspapers published records of this type belonging to Supreme Court nominee Robert Bork).

Adding to the privacy challenge faced by Web site operators is the global nature of the World Wide Web. Consequently, this chapter maps the legal landscape of privacy requirements both at home and abroad. However, for many commercial Web site operators, the legal requirements with respect to data privacy will often be nothing more than a baseline, a minimum standard that they will want to exceed in the interests of good business. For example, here you can see an example of a Web site displaying a "privacy seal," a form of self-regulation among Web site operators—the seal can be displayed only by sites that meet or exceed a voluntary, self-imposed set of privacy standards.

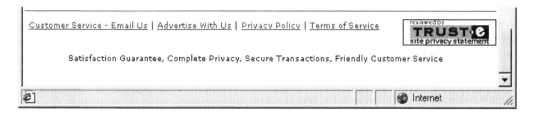

One powerful indicator of privacy's importance to Web users is the fact that within three years of its launch, the TRUSTe seal shown here was the most clicked symbol on the Web, way ahead of second-place Microsoft and registering more impressions than Yahoo!, Amazon, and eBay combined. All major Web portals display the seal, and it can be found on 15 of the 20 most popular Web sites and on more than half of the top 100 sites. Obviously, costs are associated with using such programs, but the risk of negative legal and business impacts arising from a privacy breach makes risk mitigation a worthwhile investment for many companies. Privacy tools and technologies are being developed to aid in this process, and these are discussed later.

Privacy Paradoxes

Of all the tasks involved in making sure that your Web site is an asset to your organization and not a liability, privacy is probably the most mentally challenging. When you start to come to grips with privacy issues, you can quickly find yourself wondering why it seems to be such difficult work. Hopefully, this section will help you understand why securing Web privacy is so difficult, and it will give you a framework for dealing with some of the tough decisions you, or someone in your organization, will have to make about privacy.

Privacy is a formidable challenge because nobody yet understands exactly what privacy means in today's highly interconnected, heavily computerized, data-dependent world. Privacy in the information age is a work in progress. In the same way that environmental risks continue to emerge as the dark side of the industrial/technological age, emerging privacy risks have been cast as the dark side of the information age. Whether or not you agree with that assessment, it is indisputable that many people see databases and computer networks as a threat to their personal privacy. Thus, to the extent that your business depends on access to, or makes use of, personal information, you will want to provide reassurances to those who need them regarding the handling and protection of their personal information.

On the other hand, a lot of people enjoy considerable commercial benefits from information technology, many of which depend upon the sharing of personal information. A widely cited example is consumer credit, rapid and widespread access to which has been made possible by the sharing of information about people's accounts and payment histories. Personalized service, special offers, and loyalty programs are other examples. When I stay at my preferred hotel chain, for example, I automatically receive expedited check-in, a free room upgrade, and a bottle of wine. So I choose to stay at this hotel chain whenever I can. The same principles can be seen at work in frequent traveler mileage programs operated by airlines. Such personalized brand loyalty programs are possible only when customers are willing to trust companies with private information, such as travel plans and personal preferences (typically through use of an assigned customer number). If my preferred company were to betray my trust—for example, by selling my preferences without my permission to a marketing company, which then used them to pester me with sales calls—chances are it would cease to be my preferred company.

Wherever consumers see their trust abused, or perceive a lack of trustworthiness in those to whom they entrust personal information, they usually show reluctance in sharing personal information. In the context of the Web, this is reflected in consumers' reluctance to provide credit card information to Web sites, which surveys have consistently linked to doubts about the ability of Web sites to keep such personal data secure. The first privacy paradox can thus be stated as *a reluctance to divulge personal information, despite a desire for personalized products and services.*

SECURITY ALERT   Do not underestimate how upset some visitors to your Web site can become if they think you have done, or have even thought about doing, anything that might amount to an invasion of their privacy. Many Web site defacement and Denial of Service (DoS) attacks are motivated by an attacker's feelings of righteous indignation. While such attacks can never be justified, taking steps to avoid becoming a target makes sense, particularly when those steps, such as posting and abiding by a comprehensive privacy statement, already make sense from a business perspective.

The second privacy paradox concerns the *ownership* of information. Consider your company's customer list, the names and addresses of people who have purchased your products or services. Traditionally, businesses consider such information to be the property of the business. Indeed, customer data can be a valuable business asset, particularly if it includes purchase histories, buying habits, personal preferences, and similar information. You can imagine what a competitor could do with such data to understand that it merits the protection of strong security measures, such as access control and encryption. However, your company's ownership of this data is, in many ways, shared with the people to whom it relates—and some of this sharing is prescribed by law.

Consider your bank: it has both a right and a duty to know how much money you have in your account, but a number of laws limit how, and with whom, the bank can share this information. On the one hand, your bank is prohibited from sharing the information with you, unless it takes reasonable steps to assure that you are, in fact, you (a fact that is of direct relevance to Web sites operated by banks). On the other hand, the bank can tell anyone it likes how much money you have in your account, if that data is either aggregated or "de-identified" (stripped of identifying data). Your bank can share detailed and fully identified information about you with another company, such as a stock brokerage or insurance affiliate, but only if it has your permission to do so. Yet your permission is not required for the bank to reveal certain information about your account to the government (such as certain deposits and withdrawals, which banks must report under various laws relating to money laundering, tax evasion, and terrorism). The bank is also required to tell you what information it maintains about you and give you an opportunity to correct any errors within that information.

So the second privacy paradox is this: *a company's ownership of information about people, such as its customers, may not preclude their ownership of certain aspects or pieces of that information.* And the third privacy paradox is that *ownership of information about people may create an obligation to share some of that information, for example with government agencies or individuals identified by the data.*

TIP   The Europeans use the term *data subject* to avoid the clumsy phrase "the individual identified by the data" or "the person to whom the data refers." You will see *data subject* used in this sense in this chapter.

The Privacy Landscape

To oversimplify, the *privacy landscape*, at least in the United States, is shaped by two forces: marketers and privacy advocates. The marketers want to use information about data subjects to sell more products—for example, to target data subjects with a specific message: "Dear Jane: We know you prefer to stay in finer hotels, so you'll be happy to know that rates at our luxury resorts are now 50-percent off." It can also mean analyzing large amounts of information to discover trends (urban couples with new babies tend to eat in, so send them offers from restaurants that deliver). Privacy advocates want greater legal restrictions on what companies (and governments for that matter) can do with information about individuals. Privacy advocates in the United States would like to establish a clear legal right of data privacy where none currently exists, so that individuals would know they had some control over how information about them was used, regardless of the new ways of using such information that may be developed.

Marketers and privacy advocates disagree a lot. You need to know this because privacy advocates act as unofficial privacy watchdogs. In a landmark case cited later in this chapter (in the section, "Privacy Statements and the FTC"), a major corporation was faced with serious regulatory action involving the privacy statement on its Web site, due in no small part to the American Civil Liberties Union. If marketers are a driving force behind your Web site, take note: you may need to balance their perspective with the near certainty that any flagrant violation of what privacy advocates consider to be "fair information practices" will come to their attention, with potentially costly consequences. In recent years, every major business and computer publication has run at least one cover story about privacy. This means you will not be able deflect privacy-related criticism of your Web site simply by saying, "I didn't know it was that important."

Privacy Policies and Statements

The widespread media coverage of privacy helps explains why, when you visit any Web site belonging to a well-known company, the chances are good that you will see a link on the home page that contains the word *privacy*, as illustrated in Figure 12-1.

Such links invariably lead to a page stating the company's Web site privacy policy. If you want your site to be seen as part of the Web's "upper-crust," so to speak, you need to make sure that all your main pages have a similar link to a similar page. In other words, a privacy statement should be an integral part of your site's design. (This is true even if your Web site does not collect or maintain any PII—the privacy statement for such a site can be short, but should still be posted.)

Figure 12-1.   A prominent privacy link on a commercial Web site.

TIP   Several sites on the Web offer help in building a site privacy statement. The Better Business Bureau Online and TRUSTe have model statements you can adapt, and the Direct Marketing Association has a free Privacy Policy Generator you can use, as does the Organization for Economic Cooperation and Development (online links to these can be found at http://eprivacygroup.com/sources). The most difficult part of the process will be determining what personal data your site handles so that it can be addressed in the statement. Another difficult part may be getting the company lawyer to review and approve the statement.

Posting a privacy statement on your Web site is not simply a matter of looking professional. There is considerable evidence from consumer surveys that people look for such statements when browsing to new sites, and people pay particular attention to them when shopping on the Web. You may have seen some surveys that suggest that few consumers read privacy statements. This may well be true, but it does not mean they don't notice when a site doesn't have one. If the experience of sites that display a privacy seal is any indication, this extra attention to privacy is well rewarded. Surveys indicate that nine out of ten Web users actually mistrust privacy statements unless the site uses a third-party oversight program such as TRUSTe. (See the section "Web Privacy Seals" for more on how you go about getting one for your Web site.)

What's the difference between a privacy policy and a privacy statement? For some companies, these amount to the same thing—although this is probably not the best approach. Ideally, a privacy statement on a Web site will say how the site implements the company's overall privacy policy, particularly with respect to Web-related data such as cookies, visitor tracking, e-mail addresses, and so on. If you want to refer to this as "the Web site privacy policy," meaning a subset of the company's overall privacy policy, that is fine. However, at many companies the need to place a privacy statement on the Web site was the company's first encounter with privacy in the sense of something about which it was necessary to have a policy. (Many Web sites have had a corresponding effect with respect to security.) As a result, the Web site privacy statement became the de facto privacy policy for the company. This can lead to problems, however, because the company may well need—for both business and regulatory reasons—policies covering other aspects of privacy. When relating the company's overall privacy posture to privacy statements on your Web site, you need to bear in mind that the Federal Trade Commission (FTC) considers privacy policies posted on a company's Web site to represent its offline data collection, use, and disclosure practices—unless the company clearly states that the privacy policy applies only to its online activities. In other words, what you say on your Web site could have serious implications for data handling throughout the rest of the company. (The FTC's role in enforcing privacy policies is discussed in more detail in the section, "Privacy Statements and the FTC," later in the chapter.)

PRIVACY PRINCIPLES AND PRACTICE

Although attitudes about the sharing of personal information, particularly computerized information, can vary significantly, some general principles have evolved over the years and are outlined in this section. If you want to read up on these principles in greater depth, you will find links to them at http://eprivacygroup.com/sources.

Basic Principles

You need to be aware of these principles for several practical reasons. First, they are the basis for a lot of the privacy legislation in the United States today, some of which imposes specific security requirements on Web sites. Second, these principles have guided the privacy legislation of many countries outside the U.S. In fact, some countries have elevated basic privacy principles to the level of privacy *rights*, which means that, in many cases, personal data enjoys legal protection by default.

This is not currently the case in the U.S., which has taken a piecemeal approach to privacy legislation, passing more than 30 federal laws that address data privacy topics as specific as video rental records, school records, and the use of driver's license data (an even more complex patchwork of laws exists at the state level). Because even more U.S. privacy laws will be enacted in the future, and more American companies are engaging in international business via the Web, a third reason for acquainting oneself with these privacy principles is their ability to provide a default approach to privacy that will meet standards for best practices anywhere your business takes you.

You might be surprised to learn that the first U.S. legislation to consider privacy in the context of computers appeared in the early 1970s. Elliot Richardson, who was Richard Nixon's Secretary for Health, Education, and Welfare, commissioned a study of record-keeping practices in the computer age. The resulting report, commonly known as the "HEW Report," formed the basis of the Privacy Act of 1974, which established protections for data held by the federal government. The HEW Report recommended the enactment of a federal "Code of Fair Information Practice" for all automated personal data systems. The code envisioned by HEW contained five principles that would be given legal effect as "safeguard requirements" for automated personal data systems:

1. There must be no personal data record keeping systems whose existence is secret.

2. There must be a way for an individual to find out what information about him is in a record and how it is used.

3. There must be a way for an individual to prevent information about him that was obtained for one purpose from being used or made available for other purposes without his consent.

4. There must be a way for an individual to correct or amend a record of identifiable information about him.

5. Any organization creating, maintaining, using, or disseminating records of identifiable personal data must assure the reliability of the data for their intended use and must take precautions to prevent misuse of the data.

The OECD Protection of Privacy Guidelines

Another important set of data privacy principles was published in 1980 by the Organization for Economic Cooperation and Development (OECD). Rather than summarize the OECD guidelines here, you can consult the following online link to the full document: http://eprivacygroup.com/sources. You can use this site as a reference point for your organization's data privacy practices, because this information forms the basis of data privacy laws and practices in many countries around the world. The full title of the document is "Guidelines on the Protection of Privacy and Transborder Flows of Personal Data."

One of the main motives for the OECD in developing these guidelines was the need to ensure the free flow of economically necessary personal information. For example, in 1991 an airline under Swedish law was not allowed to deliver personal data to U.S. Customs without first warning passengers of the inadequacies of U.S. data-protection laws, and therefore obtaining informed consent. In another case, a German data processing bureau was prevented from carrying out its processing in the United Kingdom, due to inadequacies in U.K. law. France even required contractual guarantees of adherence to French law before Mormon genealogical records could be transferred to Utah. Later in this chapter, the section "U.S./EU Safe Harbor" describes a means by which companies can avoid some of problems that can arise when data needs to flow into the U.S.

Fair Information Practice Principles

While basic data privacy principles were put forth long before the commercialization of the Internet, they clearly shaped the 1998 FTC document "Privacy Online: A Report to Congress." The report began by observing the following:

> Over the past quarter century, government agencies in the United States, Canada, and Europe have studied the manner in which entities collect and use personal information—their "information practices"—and the safeguards required to assure those practices are fair and provide adequate privacy protection. The result has been a series of reports, guidelines, and model codes that represent widely-accepted principles concerning fair information practices. Since its publication, this report has become quite significant because it helped shape the current "privacy-enforcement" role of the FTC (there is a link to this document at http://eprivacygroup.com/sources).

You'll read more about this role, and what it might mean for your Web site, later in this chapter in the section, "Privacy Statements and the FTC." For now, let's examine the five core principles of privacy protection that the FTC determined were common to all of these documents and outline their practical implications: Notice/Awareness, Choice/Consent, Access/Participation, Integrity/Security, and Enforcement/Redress.

Notice/Awareness

Notice is a concept that should be familiar to security professionals. Many systems, including many Web sites, put users on notice with respect to security. Such notice might be a banner that appears during network logon, warning that access to the network is restricted to authorized users. It might be a splash page for a Web site that informs visitors that clicking to enter constitutes agreement to the terms of use. In the context of Web privacy, notice means that you advise visitors to your Web site of your policies with respect to the personal data you collect. As the FTC puts it in Privacy Online: A Report to Congress:

> Consumers should be given notice of an entity's information practices before any personal information is collected from them. Without notice, a consumer cannot make an informed decision as to whether and to what extent to disclose personal information. Moreover, three of the other principles (Choice/Consent, Access/Participation, and Enforcement/Redress) are only meaningful when a consumer has notice of an entity's policies, and his or her rights with respect thereto.

In practical terms, the primary means of providing privacy notice to Web site visitors is the privacy statement, described earlier in the chapter. For simple sites that set no cookies or receive no user input, such a statement is easy to draft. The more complex and interactive the site, the more work it will take to craft a statement that covers all the bases. Here are the main points that need to be covered:.

- Identification of the entity collecting the data

- Identification of the intended use of the data

- Identification of any potential recipients of the data

- The nature of the data collected and the means by which it is collected, if not obvious (passively, by means of electronic monitoring, or actively, by asking the consumer to provide the information)

- Whether the provision of the requested data is voluntary or required and the consequences of a refusal to provide the requested information

- The steps taken by the data collector to ensure the confidentiality, integrity, and quality of the data

Of course, it might not be your job to pull together this information and come up with a privacy statement—in recent years, many large organizations have been appointing chief privacy officers to oversee the creation of privacy policies for the organization and its Web sites. Nevertheless, if you are responsible for the Web site, you may be asked to do some of the work, notably documenting logging activity, the use of cookies, and the mapping of data flows. The following sections briefly discuss these issues.

Logging Activity   You need to let visitors to your site know whether you use automated tools to log information about their visits. Many sites say something like this:

We process this information in the aggregate to determine site performance issues, such as popular pages, most frequently downloaded forms, and other site performance characteristics. This information does not identify you personally. We do not track or record information about individuals and their visits. This aggregated log data is processed by a software tool. The raw log data is retained for three months and is then destroyed.

You might want to state specific data you collect, such as the following:

1. The Internet domain (for example, www.earthlink.net) and the Internet protocol (IP) address (the number that is assigned to your computer when you are surfing the Web)

2. The type of browser and operating system used to access our site

3. The date and time you access our site

4. The pages that are viewed, and paths that are taken through the Web site

Use of Cookies   If your IIS Web site uses cookies to enhance and improve visitor experience, this should be stated. A distinction can be made between *session* cookies, which expire when the user closes the Web browser, and *persistent* cookies, which are downloaded to the user's machine for future use on the site. You need to document,

Positive Privacy Reminders

The privacy statement on your site will be the main form of privacy notice you provide, but other forms of notice may be needed as well. You may want to provide additional notice at the point at which users of your site supply information—for example on any forms they submit. This can sometimes be accomplished by stating, in an appropriate place on the form, "Information supplied on this form will be treated in accordance with our privacy statement." This reassures the user that you do have a privacy policy in effect, and it may lead to more people completing the form. Even more specific assurances are sometimes advisable when requesting such information as a user's e-mail address, such as, "We will not share your e-mail address with anyone, and any messages we send to you will have a clear link to a simple unsubscribe process that will to enable you to stop further mailings." Of course, if you make statements like this, you must be prepared to abide by them.

and may want to disclose, either in the site privacy statement or on specific pages that use them, what information is being collected by persistent cookies, why it is being collected, and how it is being used.

Mapping Data Flows   Many companies find that when they try to get a handle on privacy, no definitive documentation is available as to what data is being collected, on whom data is being collected, how data is being collected, or where data is being stored or sent. The person running the Web site can hardly be expected to answer these questions for the company as a whole, but he or she can be expected to answer them with respect to the Web site. Those answers will shape the part of the privacy statement that notifies users of the site as to the type of data collected and any "downstream" implications, such as a data-sharing agreement or cross-marketing with another organization.

Choice/Consent

Like Notice/Awareness, this second principle should be addressed with honesty and sensitivity. *Choice* means giving consumers options as to how any personal information collected from them may be used. This relates to secondary uses of information, which the FTC describes as "uses beyond those necessary to complete the contemplated transaction." The FTC notes that "such secondary uses can be internal, such as placing the consumer on the collecting company's mailing list in order to market additional products or promotions, or external, such as the transfer of information to third parties."

Whether or not you are involved in deciding what use is made of personal information that comes from your Web site, you need to know whether you are going to give users of the site any choice in the matter, even if it is something as simple as a check box that says "You may e-mail us about special offers on related products." As you might expect, privacy advocates prefer the opt-in form of consent, in which people specifically request that a certain use be made of their information. To continue the example, you would present the user with the "keep me informed" check box, which provides the user with the choice, but the box is not checked by default. This makes the user positively affirm a decision by opting in.

Some privacy advocates would like to go further and require what is known as confirmed opt-in or double opt-in, at least with respect to e-mail permission. In this example, *conformed opt-in* means that when someone checked the box and gave permission to be contacted, the company would have to confirm this—for example, the person would receive an e-mail from the company saying "You indicated that we may e-mail you about special offers on related products—please confirm this by replying to this message." While this might seem like overkill, there are practical benefits to this approach since a surprising number of people enter their e-mail addresses incorrectly. The confirmed opt-in assures that you are using a valid e-mail address for that person.

Marketers have tended to favor the *opt-out* approach to choice, which has several levels, the most basic being to use a person's information without any permission, until such time as he or she objects. (You may have encountered this approach in an e-mail message from a company you have never heard of, and it includes a link to opt-out from future mailings.) When collecting information on your Web site, to follow the example above, opt-out can mean a box labeled "You may not contact me about special offers on related products." If this is unchecked by default, the person filling out the form must specifically request that his or her information not be used. This is more honest than what is called *pseudo-opt-in*, where "Yes" is preselected in a "Use my data" check box (which is particularly annoying to privacy-sensitive individuals).

Access/Participation

The point of *access* and *participation* is to let people about whom you have information find out what that information is and contest its accuracy and completeness if they believe it is wrong. Many online systems currently lack the means to implement such processes securely. However, access is considered an essential element of fair information practices and privacy protection. The main obstacle is reliable and secure authentication of users. Currently, compliance with U.S. laws that mandate access, such as the Fair Credit Reporting Act, uses more traditional communication, such as letters and faxes. Unless you have a high level of online assurance that you are giving access to the appropriate person, such as multiple factor authentication, there is a serious risk that providing access in support of privacy will actually lead to privacy breaches through unauthorized disclosure to someone posing as the data subject.

 SECURITY ALERT Because the cost of communicating with customers via the Web and e-mail is so much lower than communicating via voice or paper, management may want you to implement data subject access to company databases through the Web site and/or e-mail. However, this is fraught with risks, such as unauthorized disclosure through spoofing, pretexting, or the interception of unencrypted e-mail; it should not be attempted unless management is fully aware of the risks and prepared to fund appropriate levels of security.

Integrity/Security

The fourth widely accepted principle is that data be *accurate* and *secure*. To assure data *integrity*, collectors must take reasonable steps, such as using only reputable sources of data and cross-referencing data against multiple sources, providing consumer access to data, and destroying untimely data or converting it to anonymous form. Security involves both managerial and technical measures to protect against loss and the unauthorized access, destruction, use, or disclosure of the data. Managerial measures include internal organizational measures that limit access to data and ensure that those individuals with access do not utilize the data for unauthorized purposes. Technical security measures to prevent unauthorized access include the following:

- Limiting access through access control lists (ACLs), network passwords, database security, and other methods

- Storing data on secure servers that cannot be access via the Internet or modem

- Encryption of data during transmission and storage (Secure Sockets Layer, or SSL, is considered acceptable when submitting information via a Web site)

Enforcement/Redress

The FTC has observed that "the core principles of privacy protection can only be effective if there is a mechanism in place to enforce them." What that mechanism is for your Web site will depend on several factors. As you will see in the next section, "Privacy Laws," your Web site may have to comply with specific privacy laws. Your organization may subscribe to an industry code of practice or *privacy seal program*, both of which may include dispute-resolution mechanisms and consequences for failure to comply with program requirements. A private action against your organization is also a possibility if the organization is found to be responsible for a breach of privacy that caused harm to an individual. Class-action lawsuits have also been brought, alleging privacy invasion. Later in this chapter, in the section "Privacy Statements and the FTC," the general oversight role of the government will be discussed, specifically the willingness of the FTC to find that failure to live up to privacy policies constitutes deceptive business practice.

PRIVACY LAWS

Regardless of your personal opinions about privacy principles or privacy laws, there may be some laws with which your Web site is required to comply, including specific security requirements that need to be met. This section should give you a good indication as to whether or not your site has specific legal obligations with respect to privacy and security.

Depending on your position within your organization, your responsibilities may or may not include determining which laws apply to your site. (Consultation with corporate counsel is probably a good idea in any event, particularly if any of the following descriptions suggest to you that specific laws may be applicable to your site. This book is not a legal treatise, and this section should not be construed as legal advice.) Of course, even if your responsibilities are simply Web site security, you will probably want to know which laws apply and what are their security implications. If you want to read up on them in greater depth, you will find links to these laws at http:// eprivacygroup.com/sources.

Children's Online Privacy Protection Act

Of the federal statutes relating to privacy, the one that contains the most explicit reference to Web sites is the Children's Online Privacy Protection Act, or COPPA. This law was passed by Congress in October 1998 and required that the FTC issue and enforce rules concerning children's online privacy. The primary goal of the act and associated rule is to give parents control over information collected from their children online. The COPPA Rule applies to operators of commercial Web sites and online services that are directed to children under 13 and that collect personal information from children, plus operators of general audience sites with actual knowledge that they are collecting information from children under 13. If you are such an operator, COPPA says you must complete six requirements:

- Post clear and comprehensive privacy policies on the Web site describing your information practices for children's personal information.

- Provide notice to parents, and with limited exceptions, obtain verifiable parental consent before collecting personal information from children.

- Give parents the choice to consent to your collection and use of a child's information while at the same time allow them to forbid disclosure of that information, by you, to third parties.

- Provide parents access to their child's personal information to review it or have it deleted.

- Give parents the opportunity to prevent further collection or use of the information.

- Maintain the confidentiality, security, and integrity of information you collect from children.

Note this last point. In essence, the law says your Web site must be secure. While this law does not apply to all Web sites, it might help you persuade management to take Web site security more seriously.

Another provision of the rule embodies the "minimum necessary" principle. Children's Web sites are prohibited from conditioning a child's participation in an online activity to require that the child provide more information than is reasonably necessary to participate in that activity. This provision, along with several of the others, has more impact on site design than on site security, but it highlights a set of issues common to many Web sites: the role of security versus compliance. For example, suppose you are responsible for the security of a Web site that falls within COPPA. Clearly, COPPA requires you to ensure that the information collected by the site is protected, but is it your job to make sure that the data collected by the forms on the site conform to the restrictions of COPPA? The answer will vary depending on your organizational structure and the allocation of responsibilities.

Regardless of who is tasked with COPPA compliance, it might help to know that the FTC has approved several Safe Harbor programs for COPPA. Safe Harbor programs are industry self-regulatory guidelines that, if adhered to, are deemed to implement or comply with government regulation. COPPA Safe Harbor is available by participating in the TRUSTe seal program, from the Entertainment Software Rating Board (ESRB), or the Children's Advertising Review Unit of the Council of Better Business Bureaus (CARU), an arm of the advertising industry's self-regulatory program.

Gramm-Leach-Bliley

Beginning in the summer of 2001, many Americans received stacks of letters about privacy, sent to them by banks, credit card companies, and other financial institutions. These are results of the Financial Services Modernization Act of 1999, more commonly referred to as Gramm-Leach-Bliley or G-L-B, after the three congressmen who drafted the legislation. The main purpose of G-L-B was to dismantle the regulation of financial services imposed after the Depression by the Glass-Steagall Act of 1933. Under G-L-B, financial services providers, including banks, securities firms, and insurance companies, can affiliate with each other and enter each other's markets—the goal being open and free competition in the financial services industry. However, during the drafting of the legislation, a lot of people expressed concern over the sharing of information between different types of companies, such as insurers and bankers, who would have new opportunities to "cross-sell" under G-L-B that they did not have under Glass-Steagall.

The section of the law that most directly affects Web sites is titled "Disclosure of Nonpublic Personal Information." This section states that "Each financial institution has an affirmative and continuing obligation to respect the privacy of its customers.... A financial institution has an affirmative and continuing obligation to protect the security and confidentiality of its customers' nonpublic personal information." The basic implication for Web sites is the same as with COPPA: when the data handled by the site is of a type that is covered by the legislation, protection of the data is required by law. In fact, G-L-B has created security standards that financial institutions must meet (links to these can be found at http://eprivacygroup.com/sources).

Under G-L-B, a financial institution is prohibited from disclosing nonpublic personal information to a nonaffiliated third party (either directly or through an affiliate), unless the institution has

- Disclosed to the consumer, in a clear and conspicuous manner, that the information may be disclosed to such third party

- Given the consumer an opportunity to direct that the information not be disclosed

- Described the manner in which the consumer can exercise the nondisclosure option

A separate part of the legislation specifically outlaws obtaining nonpublic personal information through deception (a practice often referred to as *pretexting*, such as impersonating a customer to access personal information). Bear in mind that G-L-B does not just apply to banks and insurance companies. The law defines "Financial Institution" broadly, including any entity that engages in activities that are "financial in nature" and virtually any other financial activity that federal regulators may designate. This encompasses entities such as mortgage lenders and brokers, check cashing services, wire transfer services, travel agencies operated in connection with financial services, debt collectors, credit counselors, financial advisors, tax preparation firms, and more.

Any organization that comes under G-L-B is required to determine its policies and practices with respect to privacy—specifically in disclosures of nonpublic personal information to affiliates and nonaffiliated third parties; disclosures of nonpublic personal information of persons who have ceased to be customers of the institution; the categories of nonpublic personal information the institution collects; and the protections provided to assure the confidentiality and security of nonpublic personal information.

G-L-B mandates security practices, requiring implementation of a comprehensive written information security program that includes administrative, technical, and physical safeguards for customer records and information appropriate to the size and complexity of the organization and the nature and scope of its activities. The organization's board of directors, or an appropriate committee of the board, must approve and oversee the development, implementation, and maintenance of the information security program. Also the organization is required to exercise appropriate due diligence in selecting and monitoring service providers, who must implement appropriate security measures to meet the objectives of the guidelines. In other words, if you are responsible for any Web sites belonging to organizations in the financial field, or even to companies servicing such organizations, appropriate security for those sites may be required by law.

CHALLENGE

Management decides that the company's IIS Web site needs to be upgraded to allow customers to order products and pay by credit card. What are the privacy implications? Does the addition of credit card payment processing require that your site be G-L-B compliant? What other privacy laws may apply to your site if you add this feature?

First, you present these questions to corporate counsel so that you will have a formal and up-to-date opinion on file to document any privacy-related design decisions you make.

You will probably be informed that accepting credit card payments alone does not bring your company under G-L-B. However, if you were to offer phase payments, where a portion of the purchase price for an expensive item is billed to the customer's card in installments, there may be a G-L-B implication.

> ## CHALLENGE *(continued)*
>
> Regardless of G-L-B implications, you will want to update your Web site's privacy statement to reflect the collection of personal information, such as billing address and phone number, necessary to process credit card payments. You may wish to assure shoppers that such information will not be sold to third parties or used for marketing purposes without their explicit permission, which, if given, can be revoked at any time.
>
> Also of course, you will want to make sure the site's security measures are adequate to protect credit card information during transmission, processing, and storage.

Health Insurance Portability and Accountability Act

Do not be tempted to skip this section if your Web site has nothing to do with health insurance. The legislation commonly referred to as HIPAA covers a lot more data than the name suggests. If your Web site is even remotely related to healthcare, medicine, or pharmaceuticals, you should at least read enough about HIPAA to know whether or not it applies to your site.

For many consumers, HIPAA is better known as the Kennedy-Kassebaum Act, passed in 1996 to make it easier for people to keep health insurance coverage when they change jobs. The framers of the legislation, Senators Kennedy and Kassebaum, realized that it would increase the cost of health insurance—for example, by limiting the ability of insurers to deny claims or coverage due to pre-existing conditions. To offset this, the law attempted to encourage a trend toward computerization of medical records, notably in the area of billing and payment. Numerous studies had indicated that the standardization of billing codes could generate enormous financial benefits to insurers and healthcare providers, notably in terms of faster, more accurate payments with fewer clerical staff requirements. Unfortunately, early industry efforts had failed to agree upon such standards, so HIPAA imposed them in a section of the law referred to as "Administrative Simplification."

The reason your Web site might be affected by HIPAA is that within the "Administrative Simplification" section, lawmakers addressed the potential loss of privacy associated with computerizing medical data. Under the Privacy Rule, one of several rules that have been promulgated to enforce HIPAA, any organization or entity covered by the legislation is forbidden to use or disclose protected health information, except in the specific circumstances laid out in the rule. Furthermore, it states that "A covered entity must have in place appropriate administrative, technical, and physical safeguards to protect the privacy of protected health information."

These safeguards are spelled out in a separate Security Rule that "defines the security requirements to be fulfilled to preserve health information confidentiality and privacy as defined in the law." The Security Rule mandates safeguards for physical storage and maintenance, transmission, and access to individual health information. It applies not only to the transactions adopted under HIPAA, but to all individual health information that is electronically maintained or transmitted. Fortunately, the Security Rule does not require specific technologies to be used. It is assumed solutions will vary from business to business, depending on the needs and technologies in place.

Who and What Is Affected by HIPAA?

To a greater or lesser extent, HIPAA affects all healthcare organizations, including all healthcare providers, health plans, physician offices, employers, public health authorities, life insurers, clearinghouses, billing agencies, information systems vendors, service organizations, and universities. The Privacy Rule mandates protection for the privacy of information related to an individual's health, treatment, or healthcare payment. The Privacy Rule gives individuals the right to receive written notice of information practices and to access and amend their health information. Plans and providers also have to provide an audit trail of health information disclosures and get individuals' written authorization for use of their information for purposes other than treatment, payment, or healthcare operations. Organizations must also limit the information disclosed to the minimum amount necessary. As of this time, the compliance deadline for the Privacy Rule is April 2003, although some of the details are still being worked out. A compliance deadline for the Security Rule has not yet been set, although it is hard to see how any "covered entity" could comply with the Privacy Rule without implementing the kinds of measures outlined in the Security Rule.

For Web sites, the implications of HIPAA are much the same as those of the fair information practice principles. Notice will need to be provided whenever personal health information is supplied via the Web site, and that notice will need to be HIPAA complaint. Such information should be encrypted in transit (SSL should meet the requirements) and protected when stored (which typically means not storing it on the Web server itself). You may be called upon to provide, via the Web site, access by individuals to their information, but you should approach this with caution. Unless you can implement strong authentication, it will be difficult to guarantee that you are providing access to the appropriate person, which raises the prospect of unauthorized disclosures. It may well be that traditional methods, such as paper forms presented in person, will need to be used.

TIP If you are having trouble getting management to pay attention to HIPAA, you might point out that the law calls for severe civil and criminal penalties for noncompliance, including fines up to $25,000 for multiple violations of the same standard in a calendar year, even if they are not intentional. The knowing misuse of individually identifiable health information carries fines up to $250,000 and/or imprisonment up to 10 years.

Privacy Laws Worldwide

In recent years, many countries have passed new laws or updated old laws in the realm of privacy. Although your Web site is visible to the entire world, you do not necessarily need to know about all of these laws. However, depending on the purpose and scope of your

Web site, you should probably have some idea of the privacy laws outside your country. The preceding sections assume that your Web site is located in the U.S., and therefore potentially subject to those U.S. laws described herein; hopefully, some copies of this book will find their way beyond the United States. That does not mean that all of the world's privacy laws are covered here—instead, references to sites have been provided for those who need them. The following discussion examines one non-U.S. example, the European Union, or EU, to cover many countries at once; it also illustrates an important privacy and security issue known *transborder data flows*.

The EU Data Protection Directive

The EU is a geographic, economic, and political entity currently composed of 15 member countries: Austria, Belgium, Denmark, Finland, France, Germany, Greece, Ireland, Italy, Luxembourg, The Netherlands, Portugal, Spain, Sweden, and the United Kingdom. For those unfamiliar with the EU, or unclear as to why its privacy policies could be of importance, you should note that the total population of the EU is greater than all of North America and its membership encompasses 10 of the world's 15 richest nations.

As far back as the 1980s, some members of the EU were creating data privacy legislation modeled after the principles and guidelines described earlier in this chapter, establishing some fundamental protections for data subjects. For example, the UK passed the Data Protection Act in 1984, which addressed the Enforcement/Redress principle by establishing the office of Data Protection Commissioner, with whom all data controllers must register. A *data controller* is defined as anyone who determines the purposes for which and the manner in which any personal data are, or are to be, processed; in broad terms, anyone who has a database containing information about people. This publicly accessible registry lists the name and address of the data controller and a general description of the processing of personal data performed by the data controller. Individuals can consult the register to find out what processing of personal data is being carried out by a particular data controller. (The UK Data Protection Act was substantially updated in 1998, but it stuck to this database registration approach, which conveniently illustrates the extent to which the European and American approaches differ.)

While members of the EU are free to create their own laws, they also have an obligation to harmonize those laws within the Union. Hence the Data Protection Directive (DPD) was passed in 1995 to harmonize data protection laws. The DPD went into effect in 1998, not only setting common standards for protection of data but also establishing "the fundamental rights and freedoms of natural persons, and in particular their right to privacy, with respect to the processing of personal data." Under DPD personal data must be

- Processed fairly and lawfully
- Collected for specified, explicit, and legitimate purposes
- Adequate, relevant, and not excessive in relation to the purposes for which they are collected
- Accurate and, where necessary, kept up to date

- Kept in a form that permits identification of data subjects for no longer than is necessary for the purposes for which the data were collected or for which they are further processed

This is basically a restatement of well-established principles, but the DPD also stipulates that "the transfer to a third country of personal data which are undergoing processing or are intended for processing after transfer may take place only if...the country in question ensures an adequate level of protection." In other words, the DPD prohibits the transfer of data relating to individuals to non-EU countries considered "unsafe" destinations for protection of personal data. Based on what you have read so far in this chapter, it should not come as a surprise that the U.S. is considered "unsafe." Here is a diplomatic statement of the situation from the Web site of the U.S. Department of Commerce.

> While the United States and the European Union share the goal of enhancing privacy protection for their citizens, the United States takes a different approach to privacy from that taken by the European Union. The United States uses a sectoral approach that relies on a mix of legislation, regulation, and self regulation. The European Union, however, relies on comprehensive legislation that, for example, requires creation of government data protection agencies, registration of data bases with those agencies, and in some instances prior approval before personal data processing may begin. As a result of these different privacy approaches, the Directive could have significantly hampered the ability of U.S. companies to engage in many trans-Atlantic transactions.

U.S./EU Safe Harbor

Fortunately, the U.S. Department of Commerce was able to bridge these different privacy approaches by negotiating a streamlined means for U.S. organizations to comply with the DPD. In consultation with the European Commission, the Department of Commerce developed a Safe Harbor framework that was approved by the EU in July 2000. The department's Web site describes this as

> An important way for U.S. companies to avoid experiencing interruptions in their business dealings with the EU or facing prosecution by European authorities under European privacy laws. Certifying to the safe harbor will assure that EU organizations know that your company provides "adequate" privacy protection, as defined by the Directive.

TIP   Safe Harbor is not necessary in two situations: when the data subject consents to the transfer, or when the transferor commits to "adequate safeguards" for the treatment of the data in the receiving country through a contract between transferor and transferee. Both of these exceptions can be used to keep data flowing into the U.S. from the EU.

Any U.S. company certifying its privacy practices to the Safe Harbor can satisfy EU organizations that the company provides "adequate" privacy protection, as defined by the directive. To qualify, an American company agrees to seven Safe Harbor principles.

These read like yet another statement of basic privacy principles and can be found on the Safe Harbor section of Department of Commerce Web site (http://www.export.gov/safeharbor/). To date, more than 100 companies are listed as certified companies.

TIP The concept of Safe Harbor was mentioned earlier in the context of COPPA, and in fact, TRUSTe, one of the organizations approved by the FTC to offer Safe Harbor for COPPA, also offers an EU Safe Harbor program. Clearly, there is the potential to cover a lot of bases by signing up with TRUSTe, but you cannot simply buy protection by paying the licensing fee. You must do all that is necessary to comply with TRUSTe's requirements. These are discussed later in the chapter in "Web Privacy Seals."

TOOLS FOR BUILDING AND IMPLEMENTING PRIVACY POLICIES

Security professionals are accustomed to using tools to help get a job done, such as network scanners to find vulnerabilities on a network. Products and services are already emerging to help implement and audit privacy policies.

Web Privacy Products

Reference has already been made to privacy policy generators such as those from the Direct Marketing Association (DMA) and the Organization for Economic Cooperation and Development (OECD). While a privacy policy generator can get you started, the products in this section aim to go a step further and help you implement and enforce your privacy policies.

PrivacyRight

A company called PrivacyRight offers its TrustFilter system to simplify the management of sensitive customer information. It can integrate with an enterprise's existing customer-information management structures, and it helps to provide a single, secure point at which to access a consumer's collected information. The TrustFilter suite consists of a permissions engine and an audit server. The permissions engine is a Java-based enterprise middleware platform that enforces privacy regulations, policies, and preferences by evaluating requests for data and comparing them to dynamic-access-control rule sets. The permissions engine includes a suite of privacy rules tailored to comply with specific legislative requirements. Support for multiple rule sets facilitates compliance with conflicting privacy legislation (such as when state rules supersede federal rules).

The audit server is designed for IT administrators and consumers to help in managing the permissions and usage of consumer data. It records functions of the TrustFilter system, authentication details for disclosure requests, and whether requests were permitted or denied. An audit report can be delivered to authorized users through the Web or in hard copy, as required. Administrators can view reports detailing the status of policy change notifications and authorization requests, aiding in compliance initiatives.

IDcide

The PrivacyWall product family from IDcide is designed to help you make sure your Web sites do not violate users' privacy. PrivacyWall thoroughly analyzes even the most complex Web sites and reports about everything that is crucial for the person in charge of privacy to know. For example, a PrivacyWall system shows all the personal questions asked anywhere on the site, warns about Web constructs that cause leakage of sensitive personal information, discovers Web pages that accidentally publicize personal information, and detects Web sites that are operated without management's approval or knowledge.

Two products are in the PrivacyWall family. The PrivacyWall Site Analyzer can be used remotely to analyze Web sites, either by you or by a consultant who has licensed the product. With it you can quickly understand the site's handling of personal information and define appropriate privacy policy. The PrivacyWall Site Monitor addresses the needs of in-house privacy and security officers. It is easily installed as a passive part of the infrastructure and provides continuous oversight of privacy compliance.

IBM Tivoli Privacy Wizard

Available free from IBM's Web site, the Tivoli Privacy Wizard transforms written privacy policies into electronically expressed privacy rules that can be understood by enterprise privacy monitoring and enforcement software or exported to standards-based privacy rule sets, such as P3P. You can import existing privacy policies or use the tool's graphical user interface to create or refine privacy policies based on laws or organizational requirements. The tool provides a way to define who can use what data for what purpose and provides automatic links to enterprise privacy management software.

Other Privacy Services

If you don't want to invest in the licensing fee for a privacy tool, or if you are short on personnel to address Web site privacy, you can hire someone to do some of the work for you. For example, Privacy Council provides a service called Privacy Scan, a detailed examination of your Web site that provides the following information:

- An inventory of cookies on your Web site—including specific locations and life spans—plus P3P implications at a variety of settings and values

- A comparison of apparent cookie behavior relative to the stated privacy policy

- An interpretation of cookie conduits, combinations of cookies and forms, and the security implications of cookies

- Security implications and specific recommendations regarding privacy practices in general, P3P policies specifically, and compliance issues

Following the scan, experts at Privacy Council analyze the data, relative to industry laws and practices and the company's stated privacy policy. These experts then create a report that explains the findings, makes specific recommendations, and offers guidance on the next steps. Similar services are available from large consulting firms such as PricewaterhouseCoopers and IBM Global Services, or from smaller "boutique" firms such as ePrivacy Group.

Web Privacy Seals

This section provides additional information about privacy seal programs currently available. The basic idea of a Web privacy seal is simple enough: You license the seal from an organization, normally for a fee. You bring your site into compliance with the standards represented by the seal. You place the seal symbol on your Web pages. When a user clicks the seal, a message verifies that the site complies with the standards represented by the seal.

TRUSTe

A non-profit organization backed by contributions from many of the largest Internet companies, TRUSTe has developed what is so far the most widely recognized privacy seal. The TRUSTe seal program comprises three main elements:

- **Program principles** Address the privacy practices and procedures that will keep your Web site in step with fair information practices.

- **Oversight** The measures that TRUSTe takes to ensure that licensed Web sites adhere to posted privacy policies.

- **Resolution** The role TRUSTe plays in resolving privacy concerns or complaints raised by consumers or TRUSTe with respect to your site.

After you have completed a formal application to become a TRUSTe licensee, a TRUSTe representative will review your site for adherence to the program principles, privacy statement requirements, and trust mark usage. A representative will then periodically review your site to ensure compliance with posted privacy practices and program requirements, and to check for changes to your privacy statement.

TRUSTe regularly "seeds" Web sites, which is the process of tracking unique identifiers in the site's database. Without telling you, TRUSTe will submit unique user information to the site and monitor the results to ensure that your site is practicing information collection and use practices that are consistent with its stated policies. In addition, TRUSTe has established a convenient online watchdog reporting form that anyone can use to report suspected violations of trust mark misuse. A key element of the success of the TRUSTe program is the ability of the community at large to report violations of posted privacy policies, misuse of the TRUSTe trust seal, or specific privacy concerns pertaining to a licensee. For more information, see http://truste.org.

BBBOnLine

The BBBOnLine Privacy program awards a privacy seal to businesses that have proven to meet the high standards set in the program requirements, including posting of an online privacy notice meeting rigorous privacy principles, completion of a comprehensive privacy assessment, monitoring and review by a trusted organization, and participation in the programs consumer dispute resolution system. For more information see http://bbbonline.com.

Specialized Seals

Several privacy seal variations are available, including the Children's Privacy, EU Safe Harbor, and E-Health seals from TRUSTe. Other seals can be used to bolster your site's credibility, such as BBBOnLine's Reliability Seal that attests to an online merchant's customer service record. The Health On the Net Foundation (http://www.hon.ch/) for medical and health Web sites manages the HONcode seal in support of a code of conduct that addresses the reliability and credibility of healthcare information on Web sites.

Platform for Privacy Preferences Project

One Web site privacy tool that merits its own section is the Platform for Privacy Preferences Project, or P3P. This is not so much a product as a technology developed by the World Wide Web Consortium (W3C). The goal is defined as follows:

> To provide a standardized set of multiple-choice questions, covering all the major aspects of a Web site's privacy policies. Taken together, they present a clear snapshot of how a site handles personal information about its users. P3P-enabled Web sites make this information available in a standard, machine-readable format.

This means that when someone visits a P3P-enabled Web site using a P3P-enabled browser, the browser compares the site's privacy snapshot to the consumer's own set of privacy preferences. In this manner, P3P is said to enhance user control "by putting privacy policies where users can find them, in a form users can understand, and, most importantly, enables users to act on what they see."

Since W3C also describes P3P as, "a simple, automated way for users to gain more control over the use of personal information on Web sites they visit," there is something of a dichotomy between the implied automated comparison of site to user privacy preferences and the emphasis on users doing it for themselves. Indeed, this has led to criticism from privacy advocates who claim that P3P will not work because users will not want to read all of the different privacy policies they encounter; thus they will turn on automatic negotiation with broad settings so as not to slow down their surfing, much like users currently do with cookie settings and security settings.

Privacy advocates also feel that P3P sidesteps the question of what online privacy standards should be, and that could even be construed as facilitating the coexistence of a wide range of approaches to handling personal data, some of which may be invasive. Furthermore, P3P lacks support for the fifth of the five fair information practice principle: Enforcement/Redress. A site can claim to follow certain standards in principle while violating them in practice and still pass P3P inspection.

Thus it remains to be seen whether P3P will become a useful tool for Web site privacy management. Nevertheless, if you decide not to provide a P3P policy on your Web site you might still want to make sure that applications on the site that use cookies, such as adverts, will still function correctly when accessed via a default installation of

Internet Explorer 6 (explained in the next section). To see a number of tools that help you do this, go to http://eprivacygroup.com/sources.

P3P in Internet Explorer6

To give you a better idea of what P3P means in practice, consider how it appears to users of Internet Explorer 6 (IE6), the latest release (as of this writing) of Microsoft's free Web browser. IE6 implements a portion of the P3P standard and is being heavily promoted as supporting new privacy features and improved cookie filtering—that is, support for P3P. Users can configure IE6 privacy options on the Privacy, Content, and Advanced tabs in the Internet Options dialog box, giving users more control over cookies and more information on a Web site's privacy policy. These settings determine how IE6 acts when it encounters P3P-encoded privacy statements on a Web site.

When browsing a Web site, IE6 checks whether the site provides P3P privacy information. If it does not, the user does not receive any warning, but IE6 will still block any cookies according to the user's privacy settings. If the site does provide does P3P privacy information, IE6 compares the user's privacy preferences to the site's P3P policy and decides whether to allow the site to set cookies or restrict them. If any cookies are blocked because the user's privacy preference's don't match the site's policy, a warning message pops up the first time this occurs, explaining that a cookie has been blocked. The next time that a cookie is blocked, a status bar icon is displayed. Here is the warning message:

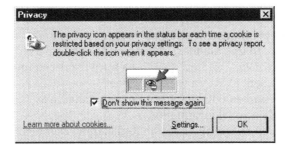

IE6 includes six preconfigured cookies settings, ranging from Accept All Cookies to Block All Cookies, with the default set to Medium. Custom privacy settings can also be imported, but it is expected that most users will use the default setting. The Medium setting automatically restricts cookies that use personal identifiable information for secondary purposes or transfers such information to recipients beyond the site being visited. This setting does, however, allow sites to use cookies to collect data that may be needed for product delivery services. The actual settings that constitute the Medium setting are as follows:

- Blocks third-party cookies that do not have a compact privacy policy
- Blocks third-party cookies that use personally identifiable information without your implicit consent
- Restricts first-party cookies that use personally identifiable information without implicit consent

Whenever cookies are blocked after the initial privacy warning, an icon appears in the browser's status bar indicating that IE6 has taken a privacy protection action because of a cookie. The user can click the icon to view a Privacy Report, as shown in Figure 12-2, which lists the content of the Web page.

The Privacy Report provides a link to the privacy summaries relating to the content of any item in the list, as shown in Figure 12-3. Users can also request a Privacy Report at any time via the View menu.

Because IE6 is likely to make users more aware of privacy issues—in particular the use of cookies—and because it makes it easier for users to block certain types of cookies, your company will probably want to make sure that its Web applications do not trigger unnecessary IE6 interference.

P3P in Practice

P3P aims to achieve "informed consent through user choice," whereby an individual can access sufficient information that he or she can make an informed decision on whether to permit further use of personal data or decline further use of their data, helping to establish trust on the part of the user that personal data will be provided only to Web sites whose personal data use and disclosure practices are in accordance with the user's expectations. Moreover, that decision can be delegated to a software agent acting on behalf of the individual by design or default. The P3P protocol is intended to support negotiations in a wide variety of contexts, including the following:

- Implicit data provision (in particular the click stream, or series of pages visited at a Web site)

- Explicit data provision (such as answers provided by Web users in Web forms)

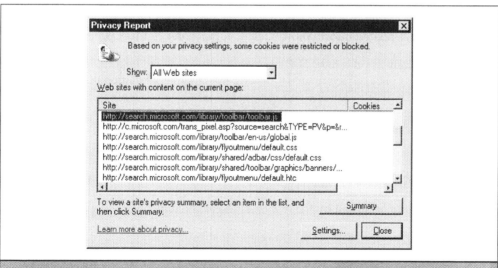

Figure 12-2.   This Privacy Report shows from where a Web page's content is coming, with a link to the privacy summaries relating to the content.

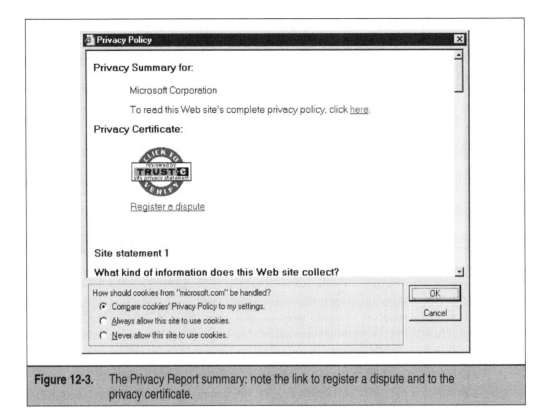

Figure 12-3. The Privacy Report summary; note the link to register a dispute and to the privacy certificate.

- Explicit data provision from an established Web user profile (such as a set of terms that reflect a person's interests and are commonly used in searching and consumer-related information, such as contact and product preferences)

If your company decides to be P3P compliant, it needs to create a P3P version of the Web site privacy policy, which means rounding up a lot of information and definitions that are required by P3P. Someone will need to be tasked with categorizing all data captured and classifying all cookies used by the site. It is important to make a note of all data collected, what happens to it, who has access to it, and for how long it is kept. This information will be fed into a P3P generator that will create a machine-readable version of the policy. If the site is complex and uses third-party services, this could take several person-days and require an understanding of the business processes involved. On the plus side, this process creates a valuable document for future reference and site support.

The information required by P3P includes the following:

- The organization that is collecting information
- The type of information that is being collected
- How the information will be used

- Whether the information will be shared with other organizations
- Whether users can access personal information and change how the organization can use it
- How disputes with the organization are resolved
- How the organization will retain the collected information
- Where the organization publicly maintains detailed information about its privacy policies

Fortunately, a P3P Policy Generator can be used to assist in creating a machine-readable P3P-compliant policy file. A generator prompts for all the necessary information so that the policy is correctly and fully formatted in XML. Several of these generators are currently available, and online links to these can be found at http://eprivacygroup.com/sources. Based on the current P3P Specification from the W3C P3P site, the following information is required by the policy generator:

- **Entity** Who you are and how a user can contact you
- **Disclosure** Where your written, human-readable policy is located on your site
- **Assurances** What third party or law insures that you are doing what you say you are
- **Data Collection and Purpose** What data elements are you collecting and how are you using them

Any collected data has four defined classifications under P3P:

- **Data Category** Fourteen data categories, plus "other," are predefined.
- **Specified Use** One or more of six specified purposes can be assigned.
- **Recipients** One or more of six possible recipient options can be assigned.
- **Retention** Five options cover how long the information is being retained, ranging from no retention to indefinite retention.

After the necessary information has been entered into the P3P generator, the generated file is saved as policy1.xml. If multiple P3P policies exist, they are numbered policy2.xml, policy3.xml, and so on. The generator also creates a policy reference file, called p3p.xml, which contains any includes and excludes, as well as any more specific task classifications that Web browsers will use to navigate the P3P policies and apply the correct policy to each page. Pages and whole directories can be included and excluded as long as all pages and directories are ultimately accounted for.

The P3P policy file(s) and the policy reference file are then uploaded to the server's root directory. The P3P Web site at http://www.w3.org/P3P/validator.html can be used to validate the site's compliance with P3P and report any errors. Once compliant, you can register your site as a P3P-compliant site with W3C P3P Initiatives.

P3P Action Plan

You first need to decide whether your site is going to be P3P compliant. If so, you should determine whether the current privacy policy complies with the P3P Guiding Principles Document; if not, you need to bring it into compliance. (If the site does not yet have a privacy policy, you can develop one that is compliant from the outset.) Bear in mind that the decision to comply with P3P is not without its risks, as outlined in the next section.

A privacy officer or similar person should be designated to organize the task of P3P data gathering and documentation. Be sure that this includes a review of the directory structure of the site to ensure easy management of P3P include/exclude instructions. Also, review the status of all third-party services with regard to P3P.

One optional aspect of P3P should probably be addressed before firing up the P3P Policy Generator—the ability to respond to disputes from users. P3P allows, but does not require, the designation of one or more resolution methods. This can be your existing customer service department, an independent organization such as a seal program like TRUSTe, or processes that might exist under an applicable law—for example, in the UK, that would be the Data Protection Act of 1998. Because there are solid business reasons for having a dispute-resolution process in place anyway, it makes sense to include it in your P3P compliance.

WEB PRIVACY AND LIABILITY

Web sites can be a huge asset to an organization, but they are not without risk. Earlier chapters described Web security risks. Unfortunately, even more risks are involved in doing the right thing—like posting a privacy statement. Just as a Web site's claims about security can create liability if they are not backed up, so, too, can privacy claims.

Privacy Statements and the FTC

The best known example of a company being held accountable for promises made in the privacy statement on its Web site is Eli Lilly, one of the world's largest pharmaceutical companies and maker of the extremely successful antidepressant Prozac, worldwide sales of which exceeded $2 billion every year from 1995 to 2000. Starting in 2000, several Lilly Web sites, including lilly.com and prozac.com, invited visitors to sign up for a service called "Medi-messenger" that would send e-mail messages reminding you to take or refill your medication. Between 600 and 700 people provided Lilly with their e-mail addresses and began receiving reminder messages.

In 2001, Lilly decided to discontinue the service and on June 27 it e-mailed participants to inform them of this decision. Unfortunately, this particular message was sent to the entire list at once, accidentally revealing the e-mail addresses of all the recipients to all other recipients in the "To" section of the message. The results were unpleasant, to say the least, beginning with a lot of bad publicity, followed by internal disruption and external legal action. Some recipients of the Medi-messenger termination message felt their right to privacy had been violated and they turned to the American Civil Liberties Union (ACLU), which took the matter to the FTC. The FTC filed a complaint against Lilly, noting that the privacy statement posted at the lilly.com and prozac.com Web sites said, in part: "Eli Lilly and Company respects the privacy of visitors to its Web sites, and we feel it is important to maintain our guests' privacy as they take advantage of this resource." The FTC alleged that "Lilly's claim of privacy and confidentiality was deceptive because Lilly failed to maintain or implement internal measures appropriate under the circumstances to protect sensitive consumer information, which led to the company's unintentional June 27th disclosure of Medi-messenger subscribers' personal information (i.e. e-mail addresses)."

Having to respond to the FTC added substantial legal and administrative costs to the initial impact of this privacy incident on Lilly. In an attempt to prevent a similar incident, the company imposed a ban on e-mail addressed to more than one person—you don't have to be an e-mail expert to know how burdensome that would be. Meanwhile, hundreds of pages of documents had to be assembled and reviewed before being turned over to the FTC, which used outside privacy experts to help with the analysis. (Disclaimer: my company, ePrivacy Group, provided advice to the FTC on this matter; all of the information disclosed here is a matter of public record, and is available at http://www.ftc.gov.)

Eventually, Lilly reached a settlement with the FTC that avoided any admission of legal violations but required the company to comply with a hefty list of conditions that include the following:

- Establish and maintain a four-stage information security program including reasonable and appropriate administrative, technical, and physical safeguards to protect consumers' personal information against any reasonably anticipated threats or hazards to its security, confidentiality, or integrity.

- Protect such information against unauthorized access, use, or disclosure.

- Designate appropriate personnel to coordinate and oversee the program.

- Identify reasonably foreseeable internal and external risks to the security, confidentiality, and integrity of personal information, including any such risks posed by lack of training.

- Address any identified risks in each relevant area of its operations, whether performed by employees or agents, including management and training of personnel; information systems for the processing, storage, transmission, or disposal of personal information; and prevention and response to attacks, intrusions, unauthorized access, or other information systems failures.

You might say that all of the above is something any responsible company should be doing anyway, but now Lilly has the added burden of having to document all of this to the government and execute it under close government scrutiny, with the threat of further sanctions if the government does not like how things are going. Given all this, you might be wondering how the problem arose in the first place. Surely Lilly had policies and procedures in place to protect sensitive consumer information? Indeed, the company did. What the FTC found to be lacking was adequate awareness of the sensitivity of certain information on the part of the employees who handled the e-mail program. Specifically, the program that sent out the offending message was not tested as well as it would have been if the people responsible had fully understood the implications of an error of the type that occurred.

 SECURITY ALERT   E-mail is not encrypted by default. Sending any sensitive information via unencrypted e-mail is risky. For example, even without the inadvertent disclosure that happened in the Lilly case, there was a risk of disclosure for everyone who received or read e-mail from the Prozac reminder service via their employer's network at work. A network administrator running a packet inspector or even someone backing up the mail server could have seen the content and source of the message and drawn embarrassing conclusions. Note that the proposed HIPAA Security Rule effectively outlaws the use of unencrypted e-mail for personally identifiable medical information.

If you read the public documents in this case, you may conclude that the FTC might have been more lenient if the company had been able to produce evidence that the relevant employees had been given privacy awareness training. The FTC repeatedly points to training as the best way to mitigate further incidents. Less obvious is what a company can do to avoid the liability inherent in promising customers that their privacy will be protected, other than making a good-faith effort to live up to that promise.

Privacy Statements and P3P

You get a different take on privacy policies and P3P if you listen to some privacy advocates. They object to the fact that no enforcement or redress is required in P3P. Indeed, it is entirely possible to craft your P3P policies so they look good, even if you have no intention of standing by them (of course, if you take this approach you risk the ire of the FTC and other possible legal actions). At the same time, the implementation of P3P in IE6 is construed by some privacy advocates to be a "forced adoption" of a flawed privacy standard. Some commentators have said that the P3P filters "punish administrators who fail to publish properly coded P3P privacy policies by blocking or impeding their cookies" (from Benjamin Wright, founding author of *The Law of Electronic Commerce* [Aspen Law & Business, 1990–2000]). According to Wright,

> The P3P coding language raises, for any corporation, government agency or other institution that uses it, a lawsuit danger. A privacy policy written in it exposes the organization to liability, with little or no escape. A privacy policy, even one written in computer codes, can be legally enforceable like a contract. In lawsuits filed in 1999, plaintiffs forced US Bancorp to pay $7.5 million for misstatements in a privacy policy posted on its Web site.

Wright sees Web site administrators facing a dilemma: how to satisfy IE6's technical requirement for P3P codes while sidestepping liability. As a remedy, he proposes a legal disclaimer, written as a new code in the P3P syntax. The new code is DSA, short for "disavow P3P and any liability it carries." Web administrators are free to use DSA in "compact" P3P privacy policies. Administrators are also free to reference or repeat the following statement:

> The DSA token in a compact P3P privacy policy means this: The P3P codes and so-called P3P privacy policies we publish have no meaning and carry no obligation or liability. They are fictitious. We disavow any significance to those codes and policies and reject all aspects of the P3P protocol. We employ P3P codes only as technical switches to enable our Web site to function properly. Some Web browsers require those codes to trigger the function of certain cookies. Our use of P3P is completely unrelated to any privacy or data policies that we may be bound to. For more information, see http://www.disavowp3p.com.

> Here you have one possible solution to liability issues arising from P3P, although you should run it by the legal department before implementing it. It remains to be seen whether P3P matures sufficiently to meet its designers' original objectives or is discarded as a failed attempt to automate something that is more effectively accomplished by companies adhering to high standards and people exercising good judgment.

WEB PRIVACY AND E-MAIL

The Lilly case highlights the relationship among e-mail, Web sites, and privacy. The person or department running the company Web site may not be the same person or department that sends out e-mail to customers, but the Web site is often the common link—the source of e-mail addresses, as well as the place where customer expectations are set, particularly with respect to privacy. This section should help you avoid many of the problems that this relationship can cause.

E-mail or Spam?

These days, many companies make extensive use of e-mail to communicate with existing and potential customers. We are not talking about the unsolicited bulk e-mail known in the vernacular as *spam*, but legitimate customer dialog conducted via e-mail and targeted marketing messages sent to people who have opted to receive such e-mail. Typical examples are the message I get every month from my credit card company telling me that my latest statement is available for my perusal at the company Web site or the weekly message I get from my favorite airline letting me know of special airfares currently available on the company's Web site. Like the e-mail reminder service operated by Lilly, these examples illustrate the complex relationship that often exists among Web sites, e-mail, and privacy.

Many Web sites ask visitors for their e-mail addresses. Earlier in the chapter, you learned how to bracket such requests with a suitable privacy notice, but it is also important that someone within the organization take responsibility for upholding the terms of such notice. For example, who will tell the marketing department that there are limits on the type and frequency of messages that can be sent to these addresses? Who will make sure management understands that, unless specifically stated in the Web site privacy statement, these e-mail addresses cannot be sold or traded to another company, even if your company is faced with bankruptcy and wants to consider these addresses a disposable asset?

These are important questions, because if there is one area of company activity that privacy advocates watch more closely than any other, it is e-mail. And nothing can tarnish a company's reputation faster than accusations of spamming. This is hardly surprising, given the way most people feel about spam. According to Fran Meier, executive director of TRUSTe, "Consumers consider spam an intrusion on their privacy." This section is intended to help you navigate the e-mail privacy minefield.

Responsible E-mail

If you want a starting point for your efforts to make sure your site is associated with responsible e-mail practices, you should become familiar with the "Six Resolutions for Responsible E-Mailers." These were created by the Council for Responsible E-mail (CRE), which was formed under the aegis of the Association for Interactive Marketing (AIM), a subsidiary of the Direct Market Association (DMA). Despite the excess of acronyms, these resolutions are useful guidelines for any organization's use of e-mail for marketing purposes, they are presented here:

- Marketers must not falsify the sender's domain name or use a nonresponsive IP address without implied permission from the recipient or transferred permission from the marketer.

- Marketers must not purposely falsify the content of the subject line or mislead readers from the content of the e-mail message.

- All bulk e-mail marketing messages must include an option for the recipient to unsubscribe (be removed from the list) from receiving future messages from that sender, list owner, or list manager.

- Marketers must inform the respondent at the time of online collection of the e-mail address for what marketing purpose the respondent's e-mail address will be used.

- Marketers must not harvest e-mail addresses with the intent to send bulk unsolicited commercial e-mail without consumers' knowledge or consent. (*Harvest* is defined as compiling or stealing e-mail addresses through anonymous collection procedures such as via a Web spider, through chat rooms, or other publicly displayed areas listing personal or business e-mail addresses.)

- The CRE opposes sending bulk unsolicited commercial e-mail to an e-mail address without a prior business or personal relationship. (*Business* or *personal relationship* is defined as any previous recipient-initiated correspondence, transaction activity, customer service activity, third-party permission use, or proven offline contact.)

CHALLENGE

The head of marketing asks you to send her a file of e-mail addresses that have been input on the technical support registration page of your company's Web site. What do you do?

Obviously, a detailed answer will depend upon the exact nature of your company's organizational structure, but since you have been reading this chapter you know enough to ask what use marketing intends to make of these addresses.

Suppose the answer is "include them in the mailing list for an e-mail marketing campaign." You would be well advised to suggest that the company review the form on which the addresses were submitted and the Web site's privacy statement. Marketing to addresses that were not supplied with a clear understanding that they would be used for such purposes is not advisable. Depending upon your privacy statement, it could be a violation of your company's privacy policy. Going ahead with such a violation could not only annoy customers, but it could draw the attention of industry regulators, such as the FTC.

Of course, you will have to decide for yourself if it is your job or responsibility to point this out to management.

Basic E-mail Precautions

Perhaps the most basic precaution is this: Never send a message unless you are sure you know what it will look like to the person who receives it. This covers the formatting, the language you use, and above all, the addressing. If you want to address the same message to more than one person at a time, you have four options, each of which should be handled carefully. If you place the e-mail addresses of all recipients in the "To" field, or place one or more in the "Cc" field, all the recipients will be able to see the addresses of the other people to whom you sent the message. This is sometimes appropriate for communications within a small group of people, but if the number of people in the group exceeds 20, or if you do *not* want everyone to know who is getting the message, move all but one of them to the "Bcc" field, as shown in Figure 12-4.

If the disclosure of recipients is likely to cause any embarrassment whatsoever, do a test mailing first. Send a copy of the message to yourself and at least one colleague outside the company, and then have them look at the message to make sure the "Bcc" additions are done correctly.

A close second among basic e-mail precautions is this: never send messages to anyone who might be offended by receiving it. In other words, know your audience. Get as much assurance as you can that the people on the list opted to be on the list. Always include a preemptive apology, such as "We apologize if you received this message in error."

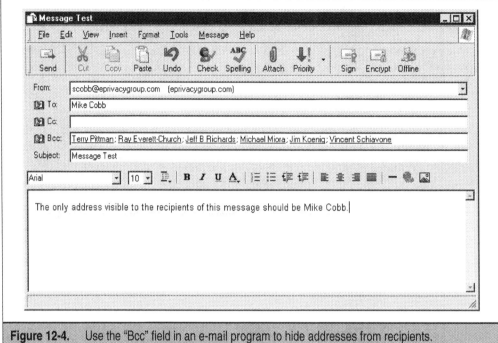

Figure 12-4. Use the "Bcc" field in an e-mail program to hide addresses from recipients.

And be sure to provide a simple way for recipients to opt out of any further mailings. (A link to a Web form is best for this. Avoid asking the recipient to reply to the message. If the e-mail address to which you mailed the message is no longer their primary address, they may have trouble opting out.)

Somewhere between a precaution and a recommendation is to use professional e-mail software for large mailings. These can send individual, customized messages to each person on the list, which avoids problems related to the use of the "Bcc" field. In Figure 12-5 you can see an example, Group Mail Pro, which stores e-mail addresses in a database and builds messages using a merge feature. The program also offers extensive testing and filtering of messages and the ability to set sending options, such as timed batch sending.

E-mail Privacy Technology

Privacy seals have helped Web sites demonstrate their commitment to privacy standards. The non-profit organization that created the most widely recognized Web privacy seal, TRUSTe, also puts its name on a privacy seal for e-mail through the Trusted Sender Program.

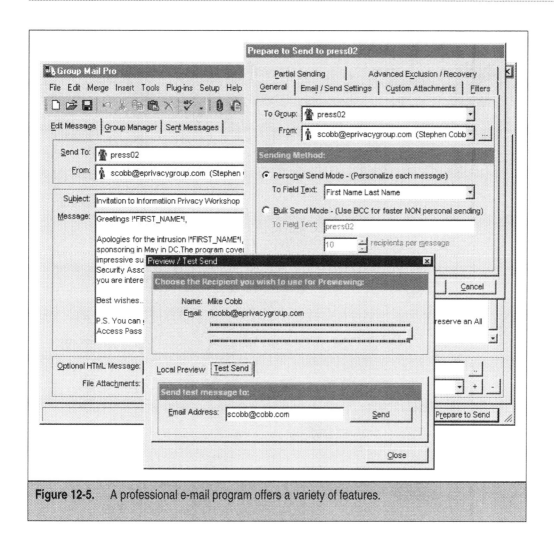

Figure 12-5. A professional e-mail program offers a variety of features.

Commercial e-mailers who participate in the program place a unique trust "stamp" at the top right of each e-mail they send out, as shown in Figure 12-6.

The stamp signifies to the consumer on the receiving end that the message is from a trustworthy company that respects consumer privacy. The TRUSTe logo appears prominently in the stamp, along with the date that the message was stamped and the e-mail address of both sender and intended recipient. This stamp is known as a *Postiva Trust Stamp* because it is created with ePrivacy Group's Postiva technology, which uses encryption to defeat would-be impostors and enables the message recipient to perform an interactive verification of the message at a special Web site, http://www.postiva.com— all without any need for plug-ins, downloads, or modifications to standard e-mail clients.

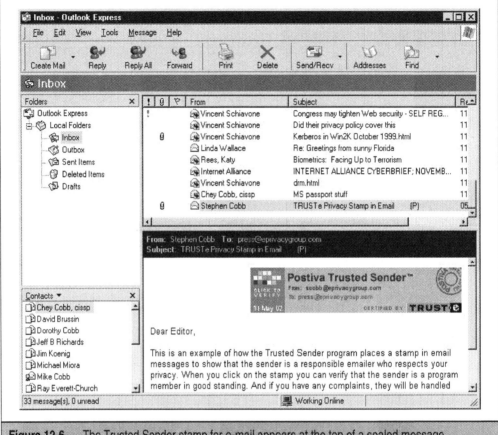

Figure 12-6.   The Trusted Sender stamp for e-mail appears at the top of a sealed message.

FINAL THOUGHTS

This chapter has surveyed all of the many ways in which privacy concerns can impact a Web site. With the tools, techniques and strategies presented here, you should be well equipped to make privacy a strong point, for both your Web site and your organization, rather than a potential source of embarrassment, bad publicity, or legal action. Remember, the two keys to delivering on the privacy promises your Web site makes to your customers are good security and full awareness on the part of all who handle personal information that it should be indeed be handled with care.

CHECKLIST

- ☐ Document all the personal data collected by your IIS Web site (include data that you log, such as IP addresses of visitors, information that you record for cookies, Web bugs, and so on).

- ☐ Find out who in your organization is responsible for privacy and establish a communication channel with them.

- ☐ Make sure a readily accessible privacy statement is posted on your Web site to tell visitors what private data you collect and why.

- ☐ Review the privacy principles and laws in this chapter to determine whether any of them need to be addressed specifically by your Web site's privacy statement and/or information collection and handling procedures.

- ☐ Review the procedures in place on your IIS Web site to protect any private data you collect, up to or beyond any of the applicable standards mandated in the relevant legislation.

- ☐ Offer visitors to your Web site a way to contact you regarding privacy concerns they may have about your site.

- ☐ If your IIS Web site sells goods or services, consider joining a privacy seal program to provide visitors with third-party proof that you have appropriate privacy policies in place.

- ☐ If your Web site collects e-mail addresses for further communication with visitors/clients, make sure appropriate policies are in place for using those addresses, such as documented opt-in permissions and accessible opt-out provisions.

- ☐ Conduct an internal privacy audit of your Web site to uncover anything you might have missed.

- ☐ Arrange for an external privacy audit of your Web site to uncover anything else you might have missed.

PART IV

Appendixes

APPENDIX A

Security Resources

I t is important that you keep informed about security information being offered by software vendors and other sources. When a new exploit is discovered or a virus makes its way around the network, software company Web sites are a good first place to look for help. Remember that when you are being attacked, they to are also being attacked. They should be working just as hard to bring you a secured product as you are at securing their product.

It can also be enlightening to visit some hacker Web sites and monitor the posting and information available on those sites. These sites often include downloads of tools that can be useful in your vulnerability testing.

SECURITY WEB SITES

Software company sites are a good place to pick up how-to information on securing their software. You should also read appropriate security bulletins available from the vendors, user groups, and security institutes on a regular basis. Subscribe to security bulletins from vendors and other organizations. Generally, at a vendor's site, you can get information on known security bugs for their systems and possible solutions. Sometimes software vendors can provide a wealth of information on a fix or help with a virus or security breach. They may also offer patches or software upgrades to close the holes found in their software.

It is also important that you keep informed about general security issues. A lot of good Web sites out on the Internet can help you stay abreast of the latest threats and vulnerabilities, and some also offer information about the latest knowledge and trends used by security professionals to help keep computing safe. Locate the sites that can supply the information you need and visit them frequently. A few that come to mind are SANS, Windows IT Security, Ntbugtraq, and CERT, a center of Internet security expertise. Many of these sites offer bulletins, news stories, and other related security information.

Subscribe to the security bulletins or newsletters, and join a discussion forum—the more knowledge you can gain is certainly a plus for you.

A few of the many useful Internet security sites are listed here:

Web Site	Address
Computer Emergency Response Team Coordination Center	http://www.CERT.org
SANS (System Administration, Networking, and Security) Institute	http://www.sans.org
Incidents.org, a SANS-maintained tracking site	http://www.incidents.org
CarnegieMellon Software Engineering Institute	http://www.sei.cmu.edu/
Computer Security Institute	http://www.gocsi.com
DShield.org	http://www.dshield.org
Cooperative Association for Internet Data Analysis	http://www.caida.org
SecurityFocus	http://www.securityfocus.com/
WebAttack.com	http://www.webattack.com/

Web Site	Address
NTBugtraq	http://www.ntbugtraq.com/
Windows IT Security	http://www.windowsitsecurity.com/
BUGTRAQ Hyperarchive	http://bugtraq.inet-one.com/
Help Net Security	http://www.net-security.org/
Cryptography and Security (by Ron Rivest)	http://theory.lcs.mit.edu/~rivest/crypto-security.html
W3C Security Information	http://www.w3.org/Security/
Global Information Assurance Certification	http://www.giac.org/
CIAC (Computer Incident Advisory Capability)	http://www.ciac.org/ciac
ISSA—Information Systems Security Association	http://www.issa.org
Computer Security News Daily	http://www.mountainwave.com
Infosec News	http://www.infosecnews.com

HACKER WEB SITES

Why not visit the same Web sites the people causing all these problems visit? You have probably heard about a hacker Web site or two, so go take a look, as this can be a real eye opener. A short listing of some well-known hacker sites is shown here:

Web Site	Address
Cult of the Dead Cow	http://www.cultdeadcow.com
Hackers.com	http://www.hackers.com/
Insecure.org	http://www.insecure.org
Antionline.com	http://www.antionline.com
2600 Hacker Quarterly	http://www.2600.com
DMOZ Open Directory Project	http://dmoz.org/Computers/Hacking/

Many hacking sites come and go frequently. One of the best ways to find them is to use a search engine like Yahoo! or Google and search on the topic *hacking sites* and various other derivatives of the words. Google even maintains a list with brief descriptions of the sites at http://directory.google.com/Top/Computers/Hacking/.

GLOSSARY

Alert A formatted message describing a circumstance relevant to network security. Alerts are often derived from critical audit events.

Anomaly detection A method of security management in which intrusions are detected by looking for activity that is different from the user's or system's normal behavior.

Application level gateway (firewall) A firewall system in which service is provided by processes that maintain complete TCP connection state and sequencing. Application level firewalls often re-address traffic so that outgoing traffic appears to have originated from the firewall, rather than from the internal host.

Attack An attempt to bypass security controls on a computer which results in an unauthorized state change that alters, releases, or denies data, such as the manipulation of files or the adding of unauthorized files. Whether an attack will succeed depends on the vulnerability of the computer system and the effectiveness of existing countermeasures.

Audit trail In computer security systems, a chronological record of system resource usage. This includes user log-in, file access, other various activities, and whether any actual or attempted security violations occurred, both legitimate and unauthorized.

Authentication (authenticate)	To positively verify the identity and validity of a claimed user, object, or other entity in a computer system, which often serves as a prerequisite to allowing access to resources in a system.
Authentication header (AH)	A field that immediately follows the IP header in an IP datagram and provides authentication and integrity checking for the datagram.
Automated security monitoring	All security features needed to provide an acceptable level of protection for hardware; software; and classified, sensitive, unclassified or critical data, material, or processes in the system.
Availability	Assuring that information and communications services will be ready for use when expected.
Back door	A hole in the security of a computer system deliberately left in place by designers or maintainers. Synonymous with a trap door, it is a hidden software or hardware mechanism used to circumvent security controls.
Breach	The successful defeat of security controls that could result in a penetration of the system. A violation of controls of a particular information system such that information assets or system components are unduly exposed.
Buffer overflow	Occurs when more data is added to a buffer or holding area than the buffer can handle. This is due to a mismatch in processing rates between the producing and consuming processes, and it can result in system crashes or the creation of a back door leading to system access.
Bug	An unwanted and unintended property of a program or piece of hardware, especially one that causes the program or hardware to malfunction or leave a system vulnerable to penetration.
C2 classification	A level with the U.S. Department of Defense standard 52000.28, the Trusted Computing System Evaluation Criteria (TCSEC) designating a system that is certified for Controlled Access Protection by implementing a security model with user IDs and variable permissions based on the IDs.
Center for Education and Research in Information Assurance and Security (CERIAS) (Formerly Computer Operations, Audit, and Security Technology, or COAST)	A multiple project, multiple investigator laboratory in computer security research in the Computer Sciences Department at Purdue University. It functions with close ties to researchers and engineers in major companies and government agencies. Its research is focused on real-world needs and limitations, with a special focus on security for legacy computing systems.

CGI scripts Allow for the creation of dynamic and interactive Web pages. They also tend to be the most vulnerable part of a Web server (in addition to the underlying host security).

Chernobyl packet Also called Kamikaze packet. A network packet that induces a broadcast storm and network meltdown. Typically an IP Ethernet datagram that passes through a gateway with both source and destination Ethernet and IP address set as the respective broadcast addresses for the subnetworks being gated.

Circuit-level gateway One form of a firewall that validates TCP and UDP sessions before opening a connection. Creates a handshake, and after that takes place, it passes everything through until the session is ended.

Commercial off-the-shelf software Software from a commercial vendor. This software is a standard product, not custom developed by a vendor for a particular organization or government project.

Common Gateway Interface (CGI) The method that Web servers use to allow interaction between servers and programs. It's generally used on UNIX-based Web systems, although CGI is also supported on early versions of Microsoft Web servers.

Compromise An intrusion into a computer system in which unauthorized disclosure, modification, or destruction of sensitive information may have occurred.

Computer fraud Computer-related crimes involving deliberate misrepresentation or alteration of data to obtain something of value.

Computer security Technological and managerial procedures applied to computer systems to ensure the availability, integrity, and confidentiality of information managed by the computer system.

Computer security incident Any attack, intrusion, or attempted intrusion into an automated information system. Incidents can include probes of multiple computer systems.

Confidentiality Assuring information will be kept secret, with access limited to appropriate persons.

Countermeasures Action, device, procedure, technique, or other measures that reduce the vulnerability of an automated information system. Countermeasures that are aimed at specific threats, and vulnerabilities involve more sophisticated techniques, as well as activities traditionally perceived as security.

Crack The name of a popular hacking tool used to decode encrypted passwords. System administrators also use Crack to assess weak passwords by novice users to enhance the security of the automated information system.

Cracker One who breaks security on an automated information system.

Cracking The act of breaking into a computer system.

Crash A sudden, usually drastic failure of a computer system.

Cryptanalysis 1) The analysis of a cryptographic system and/or its inputs and outputs to derive confidential variables and/or sensitive data including clear text. 2) Operations performed in converting encrypted messages to plain text without initial knowledge of the crypto-algorithm and/or key employed in the encryption.

Cryptography The art of science concerning the principles, means, and methods for rendering plain text unintelligible and for converting encrypted messages into intelligible form.

Cryptographic hash function A process that computes a value (referred to as a *hashword*) from a particular data unit in a manner that, when a hashword is protected, makes manipulation of the data detectable.

Cyberspace The world of connected computers and the society that gathers around them. Commonly known as the Internet.

Data-driven attack A form of attack that is encoded in innocuous seeming data that is executed by a user or a process to implement an attack. A data-driven attack is a concern for firewalls, because it may get through the firewall in data form and launch an attack against a system behind the firewall.

Data Encryption Standard (DES) 1) An unclassified cryptographic algorithm adopted by the National Bureau of Standards for public use. 2) A cryptographic algorithm used for the protection of unclassified data, published in Federal Information Processing Standard (FIPS) 46. The DES, which was approved by the National Institute of Standards and Technology (NIST), is intended for public and government use.

Defense A process that integrates and coordinates policies and procedures, operations, personnel, and technology to protect information and defend information systems. Defenses are conducted through information assurance, physical security, operations security, counter-deception, counter-psychological operations, counterintelligence, electronic protect, and special information operations. Defensive operations ensure timely, accurate, and relevant information access while denying adversaries the opportunity to exploit friendly information and information systems for their own purposes (pending approval in JP 1-02).

Denial of Service (DoS) Action(s) that prevents any part of an automated information system from functioning in accordance with its intended purpose.

Dialer A program that repeatedly dials the same telephone number. This is benign and legitimate for access to a bulletin board system (BBS) or malicious when used as a Denial of Service (DoS)attack.

DNS spoofing Assuming the DNS name of another system either by corrupting the name service cache of a victim system or by compromising a domain name server for a valid domain.

Encapsulating Security Payload (ESA) A mechanism to provide confidentiality and integrity protection to IP datagrams.

False negative Occurs when an actual intrusive action has occurred, but the system allows it to pass as nonintrusive behavior.

False positive Occurs when the system classifies an action as anomalous (a possible intrusion) when it is a legitimate action.

Fault tolerance The ability of a system or component to continue normal operation despite the presence of hardware or software faults.

Firewall A system or combination of systems that enforces a boundary between two or more networks. A gateway that limits access between networks in accordance with local security policy. The typical firewall is an inexpensive micro-based UNIX box kept clean of critical data that includes many modems and public network ports but just one carefully watched connection back to the rest of the cluster. Numerous types of firewalls exist that are based on different types of application models, such as a circuit-level gateways or application-level gateways, using different filtering models such as packet filtering or stateful inspection.

Fishbowl	To contain, isolate, and monitor an unauthorized user within a system to gain information about the user.
Fork bomb	Also known as logic bomb. Code that can spawn copies of itself. A fork bomb "explodes," eventually eating all the process table entries and effectively locks up the system.
Hacker	A person who enjoys exploring the details of computers and how to stretch their capabilities. A malicious or inquisitive meddler who tries to discover information by poking around. Where it used to be confined to person who enjoys learning the details of programming systems and how to stretch their capabilities, as opposed to most users who prefer to learn on the minimum necessary, the term has evolved to mean anyone who breaks into a computer system.
Hacking	Unauthorized use, or attempts to circumvent or bypass the security mechanisms of an information system or network.
Hacking run	A hack session extended long outside normal working times, especially one that lasts longer than 12 hours.
Host	A single computer or workstation that can be connected to a network.
Host-based	Information, such as audit data from a single host, that may be used to detect intrusions.
IDEA (International Data Encryption Algorithm)	A private key encryption-decryption algorithm that uses a key that is twice the length of a Data Encryption Standard (DES) key.
Information security	1) The result of any system of policies and/or procedures for identifying, controlling, and protecting from unauthorized disclosure. 2) Information whose protection is authorized by executive order or statute.
Information warfare	Actions taken to achieve information superiority by affecting adversary information, information-based processes, and information systems, while defending our own information, information based processes, and information systems. Any action to deny, exploit, corrupt, or destroy the enemy's information and its functions; protect themselves against those actions; and exploit their own military information functions.
Integrity	Assuring information will not be accidentally or maliciously altered or destroyed.

Internet worm A worm program (*see* Worm) unleashed on the Internet that invades an information system. Worms generally are spread from system to system through some kind of automated mechanism.

Intrusion Any event of unauthorized access or penetration to an automated information system (AIS) that attempt to compromise the integrity, confidentiality, or availability of a resource.

Intrusion detection Pertaining to techniques that attempt to detect intrusion into a computer or network by observation of actions, security logs, or audit data. Detection of break-ins or attempts either manually or via software expert systems that operate on logs or other information available on the network.

IP splicing/hijacking An action whereby an active, established session is intercepted and co-opted by the unauthorized user. IP splicing attacks may occur after an authentication has been made, permitting the attacker to assume the role of an already authorized user. Primary protections against IP splicing rely on encryption at the session or network layer.

IP spoofing An attack whereby a system attempts to impersonate another system illicitly by using the other systems IP network address.

Key A symbol or sequence of symbols (or electrical or mechanical correlates of symbols) applied to text to encrypt or decrypt

Key escrow The system of giving a piece of a key to each of a certain number of trustees such that the key can be recovered with the collaboration of all the trustees.

Keystroke monitoring A specialized form of audit trail software, or a specially designed device, that records every key pressed by a user and every character of the response that the automated information system (AIS) returns to the user.

Leapfrog attack Use of user ID and password information obtained illicitly from one host to compromise another host. The act of Telneting through one or more hosts to preclude a trace (a standard cracker procedure).

Letterbomb A piece of e-mail containing live data intended to do malicious harm to the recipient's machine or terminal. Under UNIX, a letterbomb can also try to get part of its contents interpreted as a shell command to the mailer. The results of this could range from silly to Denial of Service (DoS).

Local area network (LAN)	A computer communications system limited to no more than a few miles and using high-speed connections (2 to 100 Mbps). A short-haul communications system that connects ADP devices in a building or group of buildings within a few square kilometers, including workstations, front-end processors, controllers, switches, and gateways.
Logic bomb	Also known as a fork bomb. A resident computer program that, when executed, checks for a particular condition or particular state of the system that, when satisfied, triggers the perpetration of an unauthorized act.
Mailbomb	an e-mail sent to urge others to send massive amounts of e-mail to a single system or person with the intent to crash the recipient's system. Mailbombing is widely regarded as a serious offense.
Malicious code	Hardware, software, of firmware that is intentionally included in a system for an unauthorized purpose—for example, a Trojan Horse.
Metric	A random variable x representing a quantitative measure accumulated over a period of time.
Mimicking	Synonymous with impersonation, masquerading, or spoofing.
Mockingbird	A computer program or process that mimics the legitimate behavior of a normal system feature (or other apparently useful function) but performs malicious activities once invoked by the user.
Multihost-based auditing	Audit data from multiple hosts that is used to detect intrusions.
National Computer Security Center (NCSC)	Originally named the DOD Computer Security Center, the NCSC is responsible for encouraging the widespread availability of trusted computer systems throughout the United States federal government. With the signing of NSDD-145, the NCSC is responsible for encouraging the widespread availability of trusted computer systems throughout the Federal Government.
Negative Acknowledgment attack (Nak attack)	A penetration technique that capitalizes on a potential weakness in an operating system that does not handle asynchronous interrupts properly, thus leaving the system in an unprotected state during such interrupts.
Network	Two or more machines interconnected for communications.

Network-level firewall A firewall in which traffic is examined at the network protocol (IP) packet level.

Network security Protection of networks and their services from unauthorized modification, destruction, or disclosure; provision of assurance that the network performs its critical functions correctly and that no harmful side-effects occur. Network security includes providing for data integrity.

Network weaving Another name for leapfrogging.

Nonrepudiation Method by which the sender of data is provided with proof of delivery and the recipient is assured of the sender's identity, so that neither can later deny having processed the data.

Open Systems Interconnection (OSI) A set of internationally accepted and openly developed standards that meet the needs of network resource administration and integrated network utility.

Open systems security Provision of tools for the secure internetworking of open systems.

Packet A block of data sent over the network that transmits the identities of the sending and receiving stations, error-control information, and a message.

Packet filter Inspects each packet for user-defined content, such as an IP address, but does not track the state of sessions. This is one of the least secure types of firewall.

Packet filtering A feature incorporated into routers and bridges to limit the flow of information based on predetermined communications such as source, destination, or type of service being provided by the network. Packet filters let the administrator limit protocol-specific traffic to one network segment, isolate e-mail domains, and perform many other traffic control functions.

Packet sniffer A device or program that monitors the data traveling among computers on a network.

Passive attack Attack that does not result in an unauthorized state change, such as an attack that only monitors and/or records data.

Passive threat The threat of unauthorized disclosure of information without changing the state of the system. A type of threat that involves the interception, not the alteration, of information.

Penetration The successful unauthorized access to an automated system.

Penetration signature   The description of a situation or set of conditions in which a penetration could occur or of system events that in conjunction can indicate the occurrence of a penetration in progress.

Penetration testing   The portion of security testing in which the evaluators attempt to circumvent the security features of a system. The evaluators may be assumed to use all system design and implementation documentation—that may include listings of system source code, manuals, and circuit diagrams. The evaluators work under the same constraints applied to ordinary users.

Perimeter-based security   The technique of securing a network by controlling access to all entry and exit points of the network. Usually associated with firewalls and/or filters.

Perpetrator   The entity from the external environment that is taken to be the cause of a risk. An entity in the external environment that performs an attack—a hacker.

PGP (Pretty Good Privacy)   A freeware program used primarily for secure electronic mail.

Phage   A program that modifies other programs or databases in unauthorized ways—especially one that propagates a virus or Trojan Horse.

PHF   A phone book file demonstration program that hackers use to gain access to a computer system and potentially read and capture password files.

PHF hack   A well-known and vulnerable CGI script that does not filter out special characters (such as a newline) input by a user.

Phracker   An individual who combines phone phreaking with computer hacking.

Phreak(er)   An individual fascinated by the telephone system. Commonly, an individual who uses his or her knowledge of the telephone system to make calls at the expense of another.

Phreaking   The art and science of cracking the phone network.

Physical security   The measures used to provide physical protection of resources against deliberate and accidental threats.

Piggyback   The gaining of unauthorized access to a system via another user's legitimate connection.

Ping of Death   The use of Ping with a packet size higher than 65,507. This will cause a Denial of Service (DoS).

Plaintext Unencrypted data.

Private key cryptography An encryption methodology in which the encryptor and decryptor use the same key, which must be kept secret. This methodology is usually used by only a small group.

Probe Any effort to gather information about a machine or its users for the apparent purpose of gaining unauthorized access to the system at a later date.

Procedural security *See* Administrative security.

Profile Patterns of a user's activity that can detect changes in normal routines.

Promiscuous mode When the interface is in promiscuous mode, it reads all information (sniffer), regardless of its destination. Normally, an Ethernet interface reads all address information and accepts the data payload (the non-IP header information) only destined for itself.

Protocol Accepted methods of communications used by computers; a specification that describes the rules and procedures that products should follow to perform activities on a network, such as transmitting data. If they use the same protocols, products from different vendors should be able to communicate on the same network.

Prowler A program that is run periodically to seek out and erase core files, truncate administrative logfiles, "nuke" lost and found directories, and otherwise clean up.

Proxy A firewall mechanism that replaces the IP address of a host on the internal (protected) network with its own IP address for all traffic passing through it. A software agent that acts on behalf of a user, typical proxies accept a connection from a user, make a decision as to whether or not the user or client IP address is permitted to use the proxy, perhaps performs additional authentication, and then completes a connection on behalf of the user to a remote destination.

Public key cryptography Type of cryptography in which the encryption process is publicly available and unprotected, but in which a part of the decryption key is protected so that only a party with knowledge of both parts of the decryption process can decrypt the cipher text.

Replicator   Any program that acts to produce copies of itself. Examples include a program, worm, fork bomb, or virus. It is even claimed by some that UNIX and the C language are the symbiotic halves of an extremely successful replicator.

Retro-virus   A virus that waits until all possible backup media are infected, too, so that it is not possible to restore the system to an uninfected state.

Risk assessment   A study of vulnerabilities, threats, likelihood, loss or impact, and theoretical effectiveness of security measures on a system. The process of evaluating threats and vulnerabilities, known and postulated, to determine expected loss and establish the degree of acceptability to system operations.

Risk management   The total process used to identify, control, and minimize the impact of uncertain events. The objective of the risk management program is to reduce risk and obtain and maintain Designated Approving Authority (DAA) approval.

Root kit   A hacker security tool that captures passwords and message traffic to and from a computer. A collection of tools that allows a hacker to provide a back door into a system, collect information on other systems on the network, mask the fact that the system is compromised, and do much more damage. Root kit is a classic example of Trojan Horse software. It is available for a wide range of operating systems.

Router   An interconnection device that is similar to a bridge but serves packets or frames containing certain protocols. Routers link LANs at the network layer.

Routing control   The application of rules during the process of routing so as to choose or avoid specific networks, links, or relays.

RSA algorithm   RSA stands for Rivest-Shamir-Aldeman. A public-key cryptographic algorithm that hinges on the assumption that the factoring of the product of two large primes is difficult.

Rules-based detection   The intrusion detection system (IDS) detects intrusions by looking for activity that corresponds to known intrusion techniques (signatures) or system vulnerabilities. Also known as misuse detection.

Samurai   A hacker who hires out for legal cracking jobs, snooping for factions in corporate political fights, lawyers pursuing privacy-rights and First Amendment cases, and other parties with legitimate reasons to need an electronic locksmith.

Secure network server A device that acts as a gateway between a protected enclave and the outside world.

Security A condition that results from the establishment and maintenance of protective measures that attempt to ensure a state of inviolability from hostile acts or influences.

Security administration The management constraints and supplemental controls established to provide an acceptable level of protection for data from either accidental or unauthorized, intentional modification, destruction, or disclosure.

Security Administrator Tool for Analyzing Networks (SATAN) A tool for remotely probing and identifying the vulnerabilities of systems on IP networks. A powerful freeware program that helps to identify system security weaknesses.

Security architecture A detailed description of all aspects of the system that relate to security, along with a set of principles to guide the design. Describes how the system is put together to satisfy the security requirements.

Security assessment An analysis of the vulnerabilities of an automated information system (AIS). Information acquisition and review process designed to assist a customer to determine how best to use resources to protect information in systems.

Security assurance A level of confidence that the security features and architecture of an system accurately mediates and enforces the security policy.

Security audit 1) A search through a computer system for security problems and vulnerabilities 2) The detailed examination of configuration, records, and activities to ensure compliance with established controls, policy, and operational procedures. 3) To recommend any indicated changes in controls, policy, or procedures.

Security domains The sets of objects that a subject has the ability to access.

Security features The security-relevant functions, mechanisms, and characteristics of an automated information system's hardware and software.

Security incident Any act or circumstance that involves classified information that deviates from the requirements of governing security publications—such as compromise, possible compromise, inadvertent disclosure, and deviation.

Security kernel   The hardware, firmware, and software elements of a trusted computing base that implement the reference monitor concept. It must mediate all accesses, be protected from modification, and be verifiable as correct.

Security level   The combination of a hierarchical classification and a set of nonhierarchical categories that represents the sensitivity of information. For example, C2 is a security level with the Department of Defense Trusted Computing System Evaluation Criteria (TCSEC).

Security perimeter   The boundary where security controls are in effect to protect assets.

Security policies   The set of laws, rules, and practices that regulate how an organization manages, protects, and distributes sensitive information. A formal presentation of the security policy enforced by the system. It must identify the set of rules and practices that regulate how a system manages, protects, and distributes sensitive information.

Security requirements   Types and levels of protection necessary for equipment, data, information, applications, and facilities.

Security service   A service provided by a layer of operating system, application, or other communicating systems that ensures adequate security of the systems or of data transfers.

Security violation   An instance in which a user or other person circumvents or defeats the controls of a system to obtain unauthorized access to information contained therein or to system resources.

Server   1) A system that provides network service, such as disk storage and file transfer. 2) A program that provides such a service. 3) A kind of daemon that performs a service for the requester, which often runs on a computer other than the one that the server runs.

Simple Network Management Protocol (SNMP)   Software used to control network communications devices using TCP/IP.

Skipjack   An National Security Agency (NSA)-developed encryption algorithm for the Clipper chip. The details of the algorithm are unpublished.

Smurfing   A Denial of Service (DoS) attack in which an attacker spoofs the source address of an echo-request Internet Control Message Protocol (ICMP) (Ping) packet to the broadcast address for a network, causing the machines in the network to respond en masse to the victim, and thereby clogging its network.

Snarf   To grab a large document or file for the purpose of using it with or without the author's permission.

Sniffer   A program used to capture data across a computer network. Used by hackers to capture user ID names and passwords. Software tool that audits and identifies network traffic packets. A sniffer can also be used legitimately by network operations and maintenance personnel to troubleshoot network problems.

Sniffing   This is listening with software to the client network interface, server network interface or network wire for packets that interest the user. When the software sees a packet that fits certain criteria, it logs it to a file. The most common criteria for an interesting packet is one that contains words like *login* or *password*.

Spam   1) To crash a program by overrunning a fixed-site buffer with excessively large input data. 2) To cause a person or newsgroup to be flooded with irrelevant or inappropriate messages.

Spoofing   Pretending to be someone else to gain access to a system. The deliberate inducement of a user or a resource to take an incorrect action. Impersonating, masquerading, and mimicking are forms of spoofing.

SSL (Secure Sockets Layer)   A session layer protocol that provides authentication and confidentiality to applications.

Subversion   Occurs when an intruder modifies the operation of the intrusion detector to force false negatives to occur.

SYN flood   When the SYN queue is flooded, no new connection can be opened.

TCP/IP (Transmission Control Protocol/ Internetwork Protocol)   The suite of protocols the Internet is based on.

Tcpwrapper   A software tool for security that provides additional network logging and restricts service access to authorized hosts by service.

Terminal (TTY) watcher	A hacker tool that allows hackers with even a small amount of skill to hijack terminals. It has a graphical user interface (GUI).
Threat	The means through which the ability or intent of a threat agent to adversely affect an automated system, facility, or operation can be manifested. A potential violation of security.
Threat assessment	Process of formally evaluating the degree of threat to an information system and describing the nature of the threat.
Tiger	A software tool that scans for system weaknesses.
Tinkerbell program	A monitoring program used to scan incoming network connections and generate alerts when calls are received from particular sites or when log-ins are attempted using certain IDs.
Topology	The map or plan of the network. The physical topology describes how the wires or cables are laid out, and the logical or electrical topology describes how the information flows.
Trace packet	In a packet-switching network, a unique packet that causes a report of each stage of its progress to be sent to the network control center from each visited system element.
Traceroute	An operation of sending trace packets for determining information; traces the route of UDP packets for the local host to a remote host. Normally traceroute displays the time and location of the route taken to reach its destination computer.
Tranquillity	A security model rule stating that the security level of an active object cannot change during the period of activity.
Tripwire	A software tool used for security. Basically works with a database that maintains information about the byte count of files. If the byte count has changed, it will identify it to the system security manager.
Trojan Horse	An apparently useful and innocent program containing additional hidden code that allows the unauthorized collection, exploitation, falsification, or destruction of data.
Trusted Computer System Evaluation Criteria (TCSEC)	Department of Defense specifications that define security levels and requirements for a system that employs sufficient hardware and software assurance measures to allow its use for simultaneous processing of a range of sensitive or classified information.

Vaccines Programs that injects themselves into an executable program to perform a signature check and warn if any changes have been made.

Virus A program that can "infect" other programs by modifying them to include a possibly evolved copy of itself.

Vulnerability 1) Hardware, firmware, or software flow that leaves open an automated information system for potential exploitation. 2) A weakness in automated system security procedures, administrative controls, physical layout, internal controls, and so forth, that could be exploited by a threat to gain unauthorized access to information or disrupt critical processing.

War dialer A program that dials a given list or range of numbers and records those that answer with handshake tones, which might be entry points to computer or telecommunications systems.

Wide Area Information Service (WAIS) An Internet service that allows you to search a large number of specially indexed databases.

Wide area network (WAN) A physical or logical network that provides capabilities for a number of independent devices to communicate with each other over a common transmission-interconnected topology in geographic areas larger than those served by local area networks (LANs).

Worm An independent program that replicates from machine to machine across network connections, often clogging networks and information systems as it spreads.

APPENDIX C

Reference Tables

Two of the most important areas of configuration in Windows 2000 and IIS are also the most complicated; Directory Permissions and Local Security Policy. We made a number of recommendations for those settings that we feel are good choices for most secure Web sites, but if you wish to do your own research and make your own conclusions, the following tables from the Microsoft Windows 2000 Operations Guides will help to explain the choices and options.

We have also included a table of protocol numbers if you are using the Windows 2000 TCP/IP stacks filtering feature and you want to write your own rules.

SUGGESTED DIRECTORY PERMISSIONS FOR WINDOWS 2000 AND IIS

Directory or file	Suggested Max Permissions
C:\	Installers: Change Authenticated Users: Read Server Operators: Change
files	Installers: Change Authenticated Users: Read Server Operators: Change
IO.SYS, MSDOS.SYS	(none)
BOOT.INI, NTDETECT.COM, NTLDR	(none)
AUTOEXEC.BAT, CONFIG.SYS	(none)
C:\TEMP	Authenticated Users: (RWXD)*(NotSpec)
C:\WINNT\	Installers: Change Authenticated Users: Read Server Operators: Change
files	Authenticated Users: Read Server Operators: Change
Netlogon.chg	(none)
\WINNT\config\	Installers: Change Authenticated Users: Read Server Operators: Change
\WINNT\help\	Installers: Change Authenticated Users: Add & Read Server Operators: Change
*.GID, *.FTG, *.FTS	Authenticated Users: Change
\WINNT\inf\	Installers: Change Authenticated Users: Read
*.ADM files	Authenticated Users: Read

Table C-1. Windows 2000 And IIS Suggested Directory Permissions

Directory or file	Suggested Max Permissions
*.PNF	Installers: Change Authenticated Users: Read Server Operators: Change
\WINNT\media\	Installers: Change Authenticated Users: Read Server Operators: Change
*.RMI	Authenticated Users: Change
\WINNT\profiles\	Installers: Add&Read Authenticated Users: (RWX)*(NotSpec)
..\All users	Installers: Change Authenticated Users: Read
..\Default	Authenticated Users: Read
\WINNT\repair\	(none)
\WINNT\system\	Installers: Change Authenticated Users: Read Server Operators: Change
\WINNT\System32\	Installers: Change Authenticated Users: Read Server Operators: Change
files	Authenticated Users: Read Server Operators: Change
$winnt$.inf	Installers: Change Authenticated Users: Read Server Operators: Change
AUTOEXEC.NT, CONFIG.NT	Installers: Change Authenticated Users: Read Server Operators: Change
cmos.ram, midimap.cfg	Authenticated Users: Change
localmon.dll, decpsmon.*, hpmon.*	Installers: Change Authenticated Users: Read Server Operators: Change
\WINNT\System32\config\	Authenticated Users: List
\WINNT\System32\drivers\ (including \etc)	Authenticated Users: Read
\WINNT\System32\viewers	Authenticated Users: Read Server Operators: Change
C:\...*.EXE, *.BAT, *.COM, *.CMD, *.DLL	Authenticated Users: X
IIS Home Directory	Site Content Administrators: Read and Write Authenticated Users: Read

Table C-1.   Windows 2000 And IIS Suggested Directory Permissions *(continued)*

LOCAL SECURITY POLICY SETTINGS

User Right	Description
Access this Computer from the Network	Determines which users and groups are allowed to connect to the computer over the network.
	This user right is defined in the Default Domain Controller Group Policy object and in the local security policy of workstations and servers. The default groups that have this right on each platform follow:
	Workstations and Servers
	Administrators
	Backup Operators
	Power Users
	Users
	Everyone
	Domain Controllers
	Authenticated Users
Act as Part of the Operating System	This policy allows a process to authenticate as any user, and therefore gain access to the same resources as any user. Only low-level authentication services should require this privilege.
	The potential access is not limited to what is associated with the user by default, because the calling process may request that arbitrary additional accesses be put in the access token. Of even more concern is that the calling process can build an anonymous token that can provide any and all accesses. Additionally, the anonymous token does not provide a primary identity for tracking events in the audit log.
	Processes that require this privilege should use the *LocalSystem* account, which already includes this privilege, rather than using a separate user account with this privilege specially assigned. By default, only the *LocalSystem* account has the privilege to act as part of the operating system.

Table C-2.　Local Security Policy Settings

User Right	Description
Backup Files and Directories	Determines which users can circumvent file and directory permissions for the purposes of backing up the system. Specifically, the privilege is similar to granting the following permissions to the user or group in question on all files and folders on the system: Traverse Folder/Execute File List Folder/Read Data Read Attributes Read Extended Attributes Read Permissions This user right is defined in the Default Domain Controller Group Policy object and in the local security policy of workstations and servers. The default groups that have this right on each platform are Workstations and Servers Administrators Backup Operators Domain Controllers
Bypass Traverse Checking	Determines which users can traverse directory trees, even though the user may not have permissions on the traversed directory. This privilege does not allow the user to list the contents of a directory, only to traverse directories. This user right is defined in the Default Domain Controller Group Policy object and in the local security policy of workstations and servers. The default groups that have this right on each platform are Workstations and Servers Administrators Backup Operators Power Users Users Everyone Domain Controllers Authenticated Users

Table C-2. Local Security Policy Settings *(continued)*

User Right	Description
Change the System Time	Determines which users and groups can change the time and date on the internal clock of the computer. This user right is defined in the Default Domain Controller Group Policy object and in the local security policy of workstations and servers. The default groups that have this right on each platform are Workstations and Servers Administrators Power Users Domain Controllers Server Operators
Create a Pagefile	Determines which users and groups can create and change the size of a pagefile. Creating a pagefile is accomplished by specifying a paging file size for a given drive in the System Properties Performance Options. This user right is defined in the Default Domain Controller Group Policy object and in the local security policy of workstations and servers. The default is to allow administrators the ability to create a pagefile.
Create a Token	Determines which accounts can be used by processes to create a token which can then be used to get access to any local resources when the process uses NtCreateToken() or other token-creation APIs. This user right is defined in the Default Domain Controller Group Policy object and in the local security policy of workstations and servers. It is recommended that processes requiring this privilege use the *LocalSystem* account, which already includes this privilege, rather than using a separate user account with this privilege specially assigned.
Debug Programs	Determines which users can attach a debugger to any process. This privilege provides powerful access to sensitive and critical operating system components. This user right is defined in the Default Domain Controller Group Policy object and in the local security policy of workstations and servers. By default, only administrators and *LocalSystem* accounts have the privileges to debug programs.

Table C-2. Local Security Policy Settings *(continued)*

User Right	Description
Deny Access to this Computer from the Network	Determines which users are prevented from accessing a computer over the network. This policy setting supercedes the Access This Computer From The Network policy setting if a user account is subject to both policies. This user right is defined in the Default Domain Controller Group Policy object and in the local security policy of workstations and servers. By default, only the *LocalSystem* account has the privilege to be used by processes to generate security audits.
Deny Logon as a Batch Job	Determines which accounts are prevented from being able to log on as a batch job. This policy setting supercedes the Log On As A Batch Job policy setting if a user account is subject to both policies. This user right is defined in the Default Domain Controller Group Policy object and in the local security policy of workstations and servers. By default, there are no users denied logon as a batch job.
Deny Logon as a Service	Determines which service accounts are prevented from registering a process as a service. This policy setting supercedes the Log On As A Service policy setting if an account is subject to both policies. This user right is defined in the Default Domain Controller Group Policy object and in the local security policy of workstations and servers. By default, there are no accounts denied logon as a service.
Deny Logon Locally	Determines which users are prevented from logging on at the computer. This policy setting supercedes the Log On Locally policy setting if an account is subject to both policies. This user right is defined in the Default Domain Controller Group Policy object and in the local security policy of workstations and servers. By default, there are no accounts denied the ability to log on locally.

Table C-2.   Local Security Policy Settings *(continued)*

User Right	Description
Enable Computer and User Accounts to be Trusted	Determines which users can set the *Trusted for Delegation* setting on a user or computer object. The user or object that is granted this privilege must have write access to the account control flags on the user or computer object. A server process running on a computer (or under a user context) that is trusted for delegation can access resources on another computer using a client's delegated credentials, as long as the client's account does not have the Account cannot be delegated account control flag set. This user right is defined in the Default Domain Controller Group Policy object and in the local security policy of workstations and servers. The default groups that have this right on each platform are Workstations and Servers (none) Domain Controllers Administrators Misuse of this privilege or of the Trusted For Delegation setting could make the network vulnerable to sophisticated attacks using Trojan horse programs that impersonate incoming clients and use their credentials to gain access to network resources.
Force Shutdown from a Remote System	Determines which users are allowed to shut down a computer from a remote location on the network. This user right is defined in the Default Domain Controller Group Policy object and in the local security policy of workstations and servers. The default groups that have this right on each platform are Workstations and Servers Administrators Domain Controllers Server Operators
Generate Security Audits	Determines which accounts can be used by a process to add entries to the security log. The security log is used to trace unauthorized system access. This user right is defined in the Default Domain Controller Group Policy object and in the local security policy of workstations and servers. By default, only the *LocalSystem* account has the privilege to be used by processes to generate security audits.

Table C-2.   Local Security Policy Settings *(continued)*

User Right	Description
Increase Quotas	Determines which accounts can use a process with *write property* access to another process to increase the processor quota assigned to the other process. This user right is defined in the Default Domain Controller Group Policy object and in the local security policy of workstations and servers. The default groups that have this right on each platform are Workstations and Servers Administrators Domain Controllers This privilege is useful for system tuning, but can be abused as in a denial-of-service attack.
Increase Scheduling Priority	Determines which accounts can use a process with write property access to another process to increase the execution priority assigned to the other process. A user with this privilege can change the scheduling priority of a process through the Task Manager user interface. This user right is defined in the Default Domain Controller Group Policy object and in the local security policy of workstations and servers. The default groups that have this right on each platform are: Workstations and Servers Administrators Domain Controllers Administrators
Load and Unload Device Drivers	Determines which users can dynamically load and unload device drivers. This privilege is necessary for installing drivers for Plug and Play devices. This user right is defined in the Default Domain Controller Group Policy object and in the local security policy of workstations and servers. The default groups that have this right on each platform are: Workstations and Servers Administrators Domain Controllers Administrators
Lock pages in Memory	*This privilege is obsolete and, therefore, is never checked.* This policy determines which accounts can use a process to keep data in physical memory, preventing the system from paging the data to virtual memory on disk. Exercising this privilege could significantly affect system performance.

Table C-2. Local Security Policy Settings *(continued)*

User Right	Description
Logon as a Batch Job	Allows a user to be logged on by means of a batch-queue facility. For example, when a user submits a job by means of the task scheduler, the task scheduler logs that user on as a batch user, rather than as an interactive user. This user right is defined in the Default Domain Controller Group Policy object and in the local security policy of workstations and servers. By default, only the *LocalSystem* account has the privilege to be logged on as a batch job. See also the Deny Logon As A Batch Job policy. In the initial release of Windows 2000, the task scheduler automatically grants this right as necessary.
Logon as a Service	Determines which service accounts can register a process as a service. This user right is defined in the Default Domain Controller Group Policy object and in the local security policy of workstations and servers. By default, no accounts have the privilege to log on as a service.
Logon Locally	Determines which users can log on at the computer. This user right is defined in the Default Domain Controller Group Policy object and in the local security policy of workstations and servers. The default groups that have this right on each platform are Workstations and Servers Administrators Backup Operators Power Users Users Guest Domain Controllers Account Operators Print Operators To allow a user to log on locally to a domain controller, you have to grant this right by means of the Default Domain Controller Group Policy object.

Table C-2. Local Security Policy Settings *(continued)*

User Right	Description
Manage Auditing and Security Log	Determines which users can specify object access auditing options for individual resources such as files, Active Directory objects, and Registry keys. A user with this right can use the Security tab in the security permission set editor's Properties dialog box to specify auditing options for the selected object. This user right is defined in the Default Domain Controller Group Policy object and in the local security policy of workstations and servers. By default, only administrators have the privilege to manage auditing and the security log. This policy does not allow a user to specify that file and object access auditing be enabled in general. In order for such auditing to take place, the Audit object access setting under **Audit Policies** must be configured.
Profile Single Process	Determines which users can use Windows NT and Windows 2000 performance monitoring tools to monitor the performance of nonsystem processes. This user right is defined in the Default Domain Controller Group Policy object and in the local security policy of workstations and servers. By default, only administrators and *LocalSystem* accounts have the privilege to profile a single nonsystem process.
Profile System Performance	Determines which users can use Windows NT and Windows 2000 performance monitoring tools to monitor the performance of system processes. This user right is defined in the Default Domain Controller Group Policy object and in the local security policy of workstations and servers. By default, only administrators and *LocalSystem* accounts have the privilege to profile a single nonsystem process.

Table C-2.   Local Security Policy Settings *(continued)*

User Right	Description
Remove Computer from Docking Station	Determines which users can undock a laptop computer from its docking station. This user right is defined in the Default Domain Controller Group Policy object and in the local security policy of workstations and servers. On servers and workstations, Administrators, Power Users, and Users have the right to remove a laptop computer from its docking station on computers that contain "clean installations" of Windows 2000 (that is, they weren't upgraded from a previous version of Windows). If you have upgraded the computer's operating system from Windows NT to Windows 2000, this right to remove the laptop computer from its docking station must be explicitly granted to the appropriate group or user.
Replace a Process Level Token	Determines which user accounts can initiate a process to replace the default token associated with a launched subprocess. This user right is defined in the Default Domain Controller Group Policy object and in the local security policy of workstations and servers. By default, only *LocalSystem* accounts have this privilege.
Restore Files and Directories	Determines which users can circumvent file and directory permissions when restoring backed up files and directories, and which users can set any valid security principal as the owner of an object. This user right is defined in the Default Domain Controller Group Policy object and in the local security policy of workstations and servers. The default groups that have this right on each platform are Workstations and Servers Administrators Backup Operators Domain Controllers Server Operators

Table C-2.   Local Security Policy Settings *(continued)*

User Right	Description
Shut Down the System	Determines which users logged on locally to the computer can shut down the operating system using the Shut Down command. This user right is defined in the Default Domain Controller Group Policy object and in the local security policy of workstations and servers. The default groups that have this right on each platform are Workstations and Servers Administrators Backup Operators Power Users Users Domain Controllers Account Operators Server Operators Print Operators
Synchronize Directory Service Data	This policy setting is not used in the initial release of Windows 2000.
Take Ownership of Files and other Directories	Determines which users can take ownership of any securable object in the system including Active Directory objects, files and folders, printers, registry keys, processes, and threads. This user right is defined in the Default Domain Controller Group Policy object and in the local security policy of workstations and servers. By default, only administrators have the privilege to take ownership of files or other objects

Table C-2.   Local Security Policy Settings *(continued)*

PACKET FILTERING PROTOCOL NUMBERS

Windows 2000 includes a limited ability to filter packets, on a per-adapter basis, using the port number, the protocol type, or a combination of the two. You configure this feature under Network and Dial-up Connections | TCP/IP Properties | Advanced | Options | TCP/IP filtering for the adapter on which you want to filter.

One use for this feature would be as a poor man's firewall, where the Windows 2000 system is acting as a router between two intranet subnets. Beyond the well known TCP and UDP protocols, there are a wide range of other Internet Protocols you can filter on as documented in Table C-3. These assigned Internet protocol numbers— shown here in decimal notation—are from IETF IPv4, Request for Comments (RFC) 791I.

Decimal	Keyword	Protocol
0	HOPOPT	IPv6 Hop-by-Hop Option
1	ICMP	Internet Control Message
2	IGMP	Internet Group Management
3	GGP	Gateway-to-Gateway
4	IP	IP in IP (encapsulation)
5	ST	Stream
6	TCP	Transmission Control
7	CBT	CBT
8	EGP	Exterior Gateway Protocol
9	IGP	Any private interior gateway (used by Cisco for their IGRP)
10	BBN-RCC-MON	BBN RCC Monitoring
11	NVP-II	Network Voice Protocol
12	PUP	PUP
13	ARGUS	ARGUS
14	EMCON	EMCON
15	XNET	Cross Net Debugger
16	CHAOS	Chaos
17	UDP	User Datagram
18	MUX	Multiplexing
19	DCN-MEAS	DCN Measurement Subsystems
20	HMP	Host Monitoring
21	PRM	Packet Radio Measurement
22	XNS-IDP	XEROX NS IDP
23	TRUNK-1	Trunk-1
24	TRUNK-2	Trunk-2
25	LEAF-1	Leaf-1

Table C-3. Assigned Internet Protocol Numbers

Decimal	Keyword	Protocol
26	LEAF-2	Leaf-2
27	RDP	Reliable Data Protocol
28	IRTP	Internet Reliable Transaction
29	ISO-TP4	ISO Transport Protocol Class 4
30	NETBLT	Bulk Data Transfer Protocol
31	MFE-NSP	MFE Network Services Protocol
32	MERIT-INP	MERIT Internodal Protocol
33	SEP	Sequential Exchange Protocol
34	3PC	Third-Party Connect Protocol
35	IDPR	Inter-Domain Policy Routing Protocol
36	XTP	XTP
37	DDP	Datagram Delivery Protocol
38	IDPR-CMTP	IDPR Control Message Transport Proto
39	TP++	TP++ Transport Protocol
40	IL	IL Transport Protocol
41	IPv6	Ipv6
42	SDRP	Source Demand Routing Protocol
43	IPv6-Route	Routing Header for IPv6
44	IPv6-Frag	Fragment Header for IPv6
45	IDRP	Inter-Domain Routing Protocol
46	RSVP	Reservation Protocol
47	GRE	General Routing Encapsulation
48	MHRP	Mobile Host Routing Protocol
49	BNA	BNA
50	ESP	Encap Security Payload for IPv6
51	AH	Authentication Header for IPv6
52	I-NLSP	Integrated Net Layer Security TUBA
53	SWIPE	IP with Encryption
54	NARP	NBMA Address Resolution Protocol
55	MOBILE	IP Mobility
56	TLSP	Transport Layer Security Protocol (using Kryptonet key management)
57	SKIP	SKIP
58	IPv6-ICMP	ICMP for IPv6

Table C-3.   Assigned Internet Protocol Numbers *(continued)*

Decimal	Keyword	Protocol
59	IPv6-NoNxt	No Next Header for IPv6
60	IPv6-Opts	Destination Options for IPv6
61		Any host internal protocol
62	CFTP	CFTP
63		Any local network
64	SAT-EXPAK	SATNET and Backroom EXPAK
65	KRYPTOLAN	Kryptolan
66	RVD	MIT Remote Virtual Disk Protocol
67	IPPC	Internet Pluribus Packet Core
68		Any distributed file system
69	SAT-MON	SATNET Monitoring
70	VISA	VISA Protocol
71	IPCV	Internet Packet Core Utility
72	CPNX	Computer Protocol Network Executive
73	CPHB	Computer Protocol Heart Beat
74	WSN	Wang Span Network
75	PVP	Packet Video Protocol
76	BR-SAT-MON	Backroom SATNET Monitoring
77	SUN-ND	SUN ND PROTOCOL-Temporary
78	WB-MON	WIDEBAND Monitoring
79	WB-EXPAK	WIDEBAND EXPAK
80	ISO-IP	ISO Internet Protocol
81	VMTP	VMTP
82	SECURE-VMTP	SECURE-VMTP
83	VINES	VINES
84	TTP	TTP
85	NSFNET-IGP	NSFNET-IGP
86	DGP	Dissimilar Gateway Protocol
87	TCF	TCF
88	EIGRP	EIGRP
89	OSPFIGP	OSPFIGP
90	Sprite-RPC	Sprite RPC Protocol
91	LARP	Locus Address Resolution Protocol
92	MTP	Multicast Transport Protocol

Table C-3.   Assigned Internet Protocol Numbers *(continued)*

Decimal	Keyword	Protocol
93	AX.25	AX.25 Frames
94	IPIP	IP-within-IP Encapsulation Protocol
95	MICP	Mobile Internetworking Control Pro
96	SCC-SP	Semaphore Communications Sec. Pro.
97	ETHERIP	Ethernet-within-IP Encapsulation
98	ENCAP	Encapsulation Header
99		Any private encryption scheme
100	GMTP	GMTP
101	IFMP	Ipsilon Flow Management Protocol
102	PNNI	PNNI over IP
103	PIM	Protocol Independent Multicast
104	ARIS	ARIS
105	SCPS	SCPS
106	QNX	QNX
107	A/N	Active Networks
108	IPComp	IP Payload Compression Protocol
109	SNP	Sitara Networks Protocol
110	Compaq-Peer Compaq Peer Protocol	
111	IPX-in-IP	IPX in IP
112	VRRP	Virtual Router Redundancy Protocol
113	PGM	PGM Reliable Transport Protocol
114		any 0-hop protocol
115	L2TP	Layer Two Tunneling Protocol
116	DDX	D-II Data Exchange (DDX)
117	IATP	Interactive Agent Transfer Protocol
118	STP	Schedule Transfer Protocol
119	SRP	SpectraLink Radio Protocol
120	UTI	UTI
121	SMP	Simple Message Protocol
122	SM	SM
123	PTP	Performance Transparency Protocol
124	ISIS over IPv4	
125	FIRE	

Table C-3. Assigned Internet Protocol Numbers *(continued)*

Decimal	Keyword	Protocol
126	CRT	Combat Radio Transport Protocol
127	CRUDP	Combat Radio User Datagram
128	SSCOPMCE	
129	IPLT	
130	SPS	Secure Packet Shield
131	PIPE	Private IP Encapsulation within IP
132	SCTP	Stream Control Transmission Protocol
133	FC	Fibre Channel
134-254	Unassigned	
255		Reserved

Table C-3. Assigned Internet Protocol Numbers *(continued)*

APPENDIX D

Microsoft IIS Authentication Methods

IS has several authentication options that you can enable in the Internet Services Manager. This appendix will help you understand the choices and point out the advantages and disadvantages.

ANONYMOUS AUTHENTICATION

Anonymous Authentication gives users access to the public areas of your Web site without prompting them for a user name or password. When a user attempts to connect to your public Web site, your Web server assigns the user to the Windows user account called IUSR_*<computername>*, where *<computername>* is the name of the server on which IIS is running.

If Anonymous Authentication is enabled, IIS will always try to authenticate using it first, even if other methods are enabled. In some cases, the browser will prompt the user for a user name and password.

When you use Anonymous Authentication in IIS, you have the option to Allow IIS To Control Password. When you allow IIS to control the password, the user is no longer logged on to the server locally. The user is logged on using a network logon. Network logons have a few notable problems when dealing with IIS. For example, accessing a remote resource on another server (even a Windows 2000 server that is trusted for delegation) may be impossible. If you find you are having problems of this manner, turn off the Allow IIS To Control Password option in the Internet Service Manager. Be sure that you reset the password in User Manager to ensure that it is correct for this user account.

BASIC AUTHENTICATION

The Basic Authentication method is a widely used, industry-standard method for collecting user name and password information. With Basic Authentication, the Web browser on the client computer displays a dialog box into which users can enter their previously assigned Windows 2000 account user names and passwords. When your IIS server verifies that the user name and password correspond to a valid Windows user account, a connection is established.

The advantage of Basic Authentication is that it is part of the HTTP specification and is supported by most browsers. The disadvantage is that Web browsers using Basic Authentication transmit passwords in an unencrypted form. By monitoring communications on your network, someone could easily intercept and decipher these passwords by using publicly available tools. Therefore, Basic Authentication is not recommended unless you are confident that the connection between the user and your Web server is secure, such as a direct cable connection or a dedicated line.

INTEGRATED WINDOWS AUTHENTICATION

Integrated Windows Authentication is a secure form of authentication involving a cryptographic technique called *hashing*. The result of this process is a secure exchange between client and server that is not feasible to decrypt.

Unlike Basic Authentication, Windows Integrated Authentication does not initially prompt users for a user name and password. The current Windows user information from the current session on the client computer is used for the integrated Windows Authentication. However, if the authentication exchange initially fails to identify the user, the browser will prompt the user for a Windows user account user name and password, which it will process by using integrated Windows Authentication.

Integrated Windows Authentication can use both the Kerberos v5 authentication protocol and its own challenge/response authentication protocol. If Directory Services is installed on the server, both the Kerberos v5 protocol and a Windows challenge/response protocol are used; otherwise, only the challenge/response protocol is used.

Unfortunately, only Microsoft Internet Explorer, supports the Windows Integrated Authentication Method. Therefore, Integrated Windows Authentication is best suited for an intranet environment, in which both user and Web server computers are in the same domain, and administrators can ensure that every user has Microsoft Internet Explorer.

CLIENT CERTIFICATE MAPPING

You can associate, or map, client certificates to Windows user accounts on your Web server. After you create and enable a certificate map, each time a user logs on with a client certificate, your Web server automatically associates that user to the appropriate Windows user account. This way, you can automatically authenticate users who log on with client certificates without requiring the use of either Basic Authentication or Integrated Windows Authentication. You can either map one client certificate to one Windows user account or many client certificates to one account. For example, if you had several different departments or businesses on your server, each with its own Web site, you could use many-to-one mapping to map all of the client certificates of each department or company to its own Web site. This way each site would provide access only to its own clients.

INDEX

D

UDP (User Datagram Protocol),
22, 37
intranet
    attacks to, 6–7
    domains, 95–97
    employees as threat to, 4–5
    encryption of data on, 346
    filtering on, 187–190
    firewalls and routers, 195
IP addresses
    Content-Location header, 82–83
    filtering, 28, 190–194
    FTP access based on, 291–293
    logging and auditing, 164
    SMTP service restrictions
      based on, 309
ISA Server 2000, 254
ISAPI filters, 340–343

❖ J

JavaScript. *See* active content.

❖ K

Kennedy-Kassenbaum Act, 384–385

❖ L

local security management
    ACL (Active Control List).
      See rights and permissions.
    anonymous log-ins, 76, 97,
      121–127, 128–130

    auditing. *See* audits.
    checklist for, 135
    Internet Guest Account,
      126–127
    intranet vs. Internet sites, 97
    log files. *See* log files.
    MMC (Microsoft Management
      Console), 69–70, 96–107
    templates, 101–107
    tools for, 99–101
log files
    archiving, 157–159
    ASP errors written to, 348,
      350–353
    checklist for, 170–171
    configuring, 144–152
    crashes, 217
    Event Log, 152
    event message categories,
      140–141
    exporting or converting to
      text files, 210–211
    extended properties, 149–151,
      168–169
    FTP activity, 286
    IIS log files, 144, 147–152,
      164–169
    intrusion detection. *See* IDS
      (intrusion detection system).
    lack of, 27
    management of, 144–159
    maximum size, 144, 145
    monitoring, 209–211
    moving location of, 153–154
    NNTP service, 295
    overview of, 138–142
    overwrite behavior, 144, 145
    privacy issues, 377

Z

INTERNATIONAL CONTACT INFORMATION

AUSTRALIA
McGraw-Hill Book Company Australia Pty. Ltd.
TEL +61-2-9415-9899
FAX +61-2-9415-5687
http://www.mcgraw-hill.com.au
books-it_sydney@mcgraw-hill.com

CANADA
McGraw-Hill Ryerson Ltd.
TEL +905-430-5000
FAX +905-430-5020
http://www.mcgrawhill.ca

**GREECE, MIDDLE EAST,
NORTHERN AFRICA**
McGraw-Hill Hellas
TEL +30-1-656-0990-3-4
FAX +30-1-654-5525

MEXICO (Also serving Latin America)
McGraw-Hill Interamericana Editores S.A. de C.V.
TEL +525-117-1583
FAX +525-117-1589
http://www.mcgraw-hill.com.mx
fernando_castellanos@mcgraw-hill.com

SINGAPORE (Serving Asia)
McGraw-Hill Book Company
TEL +65-863-1580
FAX +65-862-3354
http://www.mcgraw-hill.com.sg
mghasia@mcgraw-hill.com

SOUTH AFRICA
McGraw-Hill South Africa
TEL +27-11-622-7512
FAX +27-11-622-9045
robyn_swanepoel@mcgraw-hill.com

**UNITED KINGDOM & EUROPE
(Excluding Southern Europe)**
McGraw-Hill Education Europe
TEL +44-1-628-502500
FAX +44-1-628-770224
http://www.mcgraw-hill.co.uk
computing_neurope@mcgraw-hill.com

ALL OTHER INQUIRIES Contact:
Osborne/McGraw-Hill
TEL +1-510-549-6600
FAX +1-510-883-7600
http://www.osborne.com
omg_international@mcgraw-hill.com